The Politics of Rural Russia,

1905–1914

Studies of the Russian Institute, Columbia University

THE
Politics
of Rural Russia

1905–1914

EDITED BY

LEOPOLD H. HAIMSON

Indiana University Press   Bloomington and London

THIS BOOK HAS BEEN PUBLISHED WITH THE ASSISTANCE
OF A GRANT FROM THE MELLON FOUNDATION.

Manufactured in the United States of America

Library of Congress Cataloging in Publication Data
Main entry under title:
The Politics of rural Russia, 1905–1914.
(Studies of the Russian Institute, Columbia University)
Includes index.
1. Russia—Politics and government—1904–1914—Addresses, essays, lectures.
2. Peasantry—Russia—Addresses, essays, lectures.
I. Haimson, Leopold H.
II. Series: Columbia University. Russian Institute. Studies.
DK262.P55   320.9'47'08   78–62420
ISBN 0–253–11345–8   1 2 3 4 5 83 82 81 80 79

CONTENTS

To the beloved memory of Mildred O'Brien, who
contributed so much to the completion of this volume.

PREFACE

Most of the contributions to this volume were originally conceived, over a decade ago, in the setting of a Columbia University graduate seminar that was devoted to an examination of various aspects of Russian politics between the revolutions of 1905 and 1917. Even at this early stage of their work, the participants were animated by a common concern: to relate the evolution of "high politics" in the capital—within the government, at the Court, in the State Duma and State Council, as well as the interaction between the state power and the spokesmen for various political parties and factions represented in Russia's national representative institutions—to the movement of political attitudes among the various constituencies in the Russian body politic that these spokesmen of "opinion" represented or purported to represent. As our work progressed, we became increasingly aware of two common sets of problems and themes that confronted us in our study of various aspects of Russian political life during these years.

The first and most evident of these was the extent and tenaciousness of the grip that a remarkably small and homogeneous group of Russian society—the thirty-odd thousand families of the landowning nobility, whose rule of the Russian countryside had been restored after the Revolution of 1905—held over the political process right up to the Revolution of 1917, and especially during the years leading up to the outbreak of the First World War. Wherever we looked in our explorations of Russian politics during these years—at the heated debates of the various projects of local reforms submitted to the review of the Council of Local Economy of the Ministry of Internal Affairs during Stolypin's tenure; at the stresses and strains of the politics of the State Duma and State Council, and their periodic and increasingly frequent surfacing in such celebrated affairs as the Western Zemstvo crisis; at the submerged conflicts and, eventually, the open splits, which by the eve of the war divided all the liberal and moderate parties and parliamentary groups, including those of the moderate right, as an atmosphere of almost total paralysis descended on Russia's legislative chambers—we ultimately found, in the shaping and unfolding of these crises, the decisive imprint and ultimate constraint imposed by the political attitudes and behavior of the thirty thousand families that dominated the Russian countryside, and through it Russian political life as a whole.

But the second and perhaps more novel common theme that our explorations suggested stemmed from the sense that underlying the rigidity of political life under the political system redefined after the coup d'état of June 1907 was the growing psychological distance—indeed the growing chasm—between the political cultures that were still prevalent in the Russian countryside, among the many millions of the communal peasantry but also among the *pomeshchiki* who lorded over them, and the more modern political cultures that were now so rapidly emerging among the lower as well as the upper strata of urban, commercial, industrial Russia. It was in these differences in political cultures, and the differences in perception for which they made—not only of political parties and their programs but ultimately of the very nature of political representation and of the political process—that we finally sought the explanation for the political obliviousness of the Russian countryside to the growing clamor for change that was heard in urban Russia. By the same token, it was also in these contrasts of political cultures, and not merely in the mechanics of political power, as redefined under the System of Third of June, that we sought the key to an understanding of the torturous character of the prewar political crisis and of the dynamics of the second Russian pre-Revolution as a whole.

The papers originally contributed in this 1968 seminar eventually matured into doctoral dissertations, some of which are shortly to appear in print as individual monographs. But because of the common problems and issues that our work continued to address, we found it useful to reconvene, following the completion of these studies—this time in the setting of one of the Russian Institute's Advanced Seminars—to seek to integrate in one volume some of the major findings that we had reached.

It will be obvious to the reader that, because of the nature of the individual studies that most of us had pursued over the last decade, the volume we were eventually able to put together is necessarily unbalanced. Most of our contributors, including Dr. Geoffrey Hosking of the University of Essex, who agreed to join our collective effort, have been mainly concerned with the politics of the landed nobility, whose domination of Russian politics was considerably enhanced, throughout the period under our purview, by the political passivity and seeming malleability of the peasants over whom they ruled and managed to control. The factors that made for the political passivity of most Russian peasants during these years (in contrast, at least at first sight, to the assertiveness that these peasants displayed in 1905–1907 and in 1917) are discussed in Eugene Vinogradoff's essay, as well as in my own concluding observations. But we are the first to recognize that this phenomenon and, more generally, the immensely difficult subject of the evolution of the Russian peasantry's political culture in the early twentieth century, deserve far closer and more systematic attention than we have been able to devote to them in this volume. It is our hope that notwithstanding the formidable methodological and substantive problems involved, we, as well as other scholars, may be able to study this subject in greater depth in the years to come, but we also hope that even our stab at its exploration in this volume may prove of some interest.

The acknowledgments that we need to make for what we have managed to achieve are far more than *pro forma*. One of the early readers of this volume noted that whatever merits he distinguished in its contributions were in part a tribute to the International Research and Exchanges Board (IREX), and to the value of the archival research in the Soviet Union by young, as well as older, American scholars, which IREX has done so much to encourage under the terms of our cultural exchange agreements. I heartily concur with this sentiment, but also wish to express our profound gratitude to those *sotrudniki* in Soviet historical archives (especially at TsGAOR and TsGIA) who were helpful to us in the exploration of the archival sources on which almost all the contributions to this volume partly or largely rest. At TsGIA, I particularly wish to thank Serafima Grigoreva Sakharova for her consistent and devoted attention over the last decade, and at the Chief Archival Administration and TsGAOR, Mikhail Iakoblevich Kapran, Boris Ivanovich Kaptelev, and their respective staffs. I also want to thank those of our Soviet colleagues who, in one way or another, guided our initial steps through the labyrinth of the archives we examined, and indeed often directed our attention to some of the major problems that we explored in these sources. Most particularly, I wish to thank Professor E. D. Chermenskii of the Historical Faculty of the University of Moscow and Dr. V. S. Diakin of the Institute of History of the Academy of Sciences of the USSR in Leningrad, both of whom pioneered in their own right in the study of Russian political and social developments between 1905 and 1917, for their generous help and counsel during the years of our work in the Soviet Union. Neither of them is likely to concur with all of our interpretations and conclusions, but I hope that the angle of vision that we have brought to bear—from a different cultural and historical perspective—on some of the very sources that they have studied with such care in their own work may prove of more than passing interest to them.

In the United States, we wish to thank the staff of the Russian Institute at Columbia, and in particular Mr. John Hanselman, who did so much to keep our Advanced Seminar going through the two years of discussions and repeated revisions of manuscript, which eventuated in the completion of this book. I personally owe more than passing thanks to Eugene Vinogradoff and Roberta Manning, who kept track of some of this editorial work during the periods I had to spend away from the United States. Roberta Manning's large imprint on this volume is suggested by the number of papers that she contributed individually as well as in collaboration with other contributors. But I also wish to thank her, Joann Haimson, and my colleagues and friends Terence Emmons, Alexander Erlich, Andrzej Kaminski, Marc Raeff, and Reginald Zelnik for their helpful substantive criticisms and editorial suggestions about my own contributions to this volume. My debt to them is all the greater for their willingness to read unwieldy and almost indigestible first drafts and to suggest ways to achieve in the final copy greater economy and intelligibility. I also wish to thank the Indiana University Press and look forward to further association with them in the publication, through the Russian Institute Series, of studies of other aspects of Russian political and social history in the nineteenth and early twentieth centuries. Finally, I want to express my appreciation to my dear friends Alexander and Helene Bennigsen, and the whole Bennigsen clan —including Sibelle and Vatan—for so graciously putting up with me during the completion of my work on this volume.

LEOPOLD H. HAIMSON
New York—Les Codouls, 1978

Introduction: The Russian Landed Nobility and the System of the Third of June

LEOPOLD H. HAIMSON

The chief object of the contributions to this volume will be to describe the political role that the Russian countryside—and particularly the remarkably small group of landed nobles who ruled it, with the assistance of the provincial officials of the tsarist bureaucracy—played under the regime that became known, after the coup d'état of June 1907, as the System of the Third of June.

The politics of the Russian countryside have traditionally been assigned a large place in historical accounts of 1905 and its background: after all, it is difficult to ignore the fact that "zemstvo" liberalism and the social and political disaffection among the landed nobility on which it bred, along with the peasants' agrarian disorders of 1905–1907, were significant factors in Russia's First Revolution. The politics of rural Russia have also figured, though less prominently, in analyses of the Revolution of 1917 and its Civil War aftermath. But ours may well be the first volume to attempt to consider systematically the weight that the rulers of rural Russia carried in the Russian body politic during the period between these two major revolutions, even though in the absence of such studies it is impossible to determine on what social basis the political system of Imperial Russia actually rested in the critical decade between 1907 and 1917: to establish the sources of its short-term political resilience, as well as of its eventual dramatic collapse.

The lack of attention to this subject, at least until recent years, is partially explainable by the fact that the events of Russia's Second Revolution—from March to October 1917—were largely shaped in urban, commercial, industrial Russia, with the countryside appearing,

1

at least in the short run, to fall rather rapidly into line. And it is even true that in the years that followed—as civil war spread to the whole Russian land—it was urban Russia that largely contributed the ideologies and the political and military cadres of the various camps that then fought over the future of the Russian body politic.

It is not, therefore, altogether surprising that since 1917 the attention of most Western as well as Soviet historians has been riveted on the politics of urban Russia, as they have sought to unravel the antecedents and the eventual unfolding of the Russian Revolution. This emphasis is all the more understandable when we consider that most of the analyses that these historians inherited from prerevolutionary political observers were themselves characterized by the same narrow focus of attention. It is in this connection that we come to the heart of our concern: the historiographical problem posed by the assumptions—and more broadly the perceptual set—that we have inherited, by and large unconsciously, from the descriptions of the politics of pre-1917 Russia that were drawn for us by contemporaries. Most of these contemporary descriptions, as well as memoiristic accounts, were recorded by men who, whatever the shades of their politics, were predominantly members of Russia's urban intelligentsia, or at least representative of its urban culture. Even when they sought to take account of the political facts of rural life, most of these men almost inevitably projected onto it values, perceptions—and a sense of the ultimate significance of phenomena and events—that had been shaped, and continued to the end to be fed, by the dynamics of urban life. Above all, it was almost impossible for these urbanized men not to believe that the politics in which *they* were involved—the parties of which *they* were members, the platforms that *they* supported, and the issues over which *they* so fervently fought—were not necessarily the politics of *all* of Russia. And during the long stretch of time in which the countryside appeared dormant, and irresponsive to their pleas, it was even more difficult for them to conceive that its politics, or more precisely what appeared in their eyes to be its *lack of politics,* could really weigh decisively on Russia's immediate political destiny, *or even provide a significant explanation for its contemporary situation.*

Thus it was, for example, that when, after the coup d'état of June 1907, the realization of their political defeat descended on the councils of the Kadet party, it was difficult for many of its leaders, and more generally for the urban intelligentsia from which the party drew most of its members, to believe that they had suffered a truly enduring setback. To be sure, some Kadet observers were quick to attribute their party's defeat to errors of political judgment on the part of their own leaders as well as of their would-be allies to the left. But by the same token, these critics assumed that since the errors of their own party had been largely responsible for its defeat, this outcome was within their own power to redress: a more moderate, rigorously constitutional stance, a responsible posture of "organic opposition"—the advocacy within and outside the Duma's walls of tangible, if more limited, reforms and the systematic pursuit of equally moderate, "responsible" political tactics to achieve them—would eventually regain for them the support of a parliamentary majority in the Duma, even under the onerous terms of the new electoral system.

By 1912, buoyed by the signs of mounting opposition in urban Russia, the leaders of the Kadet party believed that their time had come, and they entered the electoral campaign to the Fourth Duma with high hopes, as well as with the firm conviction that the condition for their fulfillment was to maintain throughout the campaign the moderate and responsible political stance that they had assumed since the opening of the Third Duma. And most of the members of the Kadet Central Committee found it hard to believe their ears when the chief author of the strategy, P. N. Miliukov, finally told them, in light of the election returns, that the hopes and the strategy had proven bankrupt. Indeed, it was only on the very eve of the war that most Kadet leaders finally came to realize that within the existing political framework, the path of reform, of peaceful political change—and indeed, the formation of the opposition majority in the Duma without which it could not even be pursued—appeared beyond reach.

In retrospect, the Kadets' earlier optimism, especially on the eve of the Fourth Duma elections, may well appear astonishing. After all, the leaders of the Kadet party were politically far more sophisticated than they have sometimes been represented (or indeed represented themselves); and they were far from oblivious of the administrative pressures and restrictions under which the elections were to be held, not to speak of the sheer mechanics of an electoral system of which their party had been one of the chief victims in the elections, held five years earlier, to the Third Duma.

The optimism becomes more understandable when we ask ourselves what were the sources of information available by 1912 to Kadet leaders about the politics of rural Russia. As the reports to the Kadet Central Committee indicate, local party organization had by this time withered away even in most provincial towns (so, for that matter, had the local organizations of all other parties, including the Octobrists).

Under the circumstances, aside from their readings of a largely urban press, Kadet leaders now gathered their impressions of rural Russia primarily from their periodic lecture tours of provincial cities (especially provincial capitals). It was from their talks with the party activists and sympathizers who attended these lectures that Kadet leaders drew their sense of the mood of provincial society and of the countryside.

Little did the Kadet leaders realize in the course of these conversations that they were really talking to themselves, or more precisely to representatives of a liberal provincial intelligentsia who had become as estranged as they were from the mood of rural Russia. For by 1912, not to speak of the time of the Beilis case, the members of this provincial intelligentsia—journalists, lawyers, doctors, and even many officials (including ones of noble origin)—and those noble landowners who resided at least on a part-time basis in the same provincial cities and towns, moved in almost entirely different worlds, with no genuine points of contact. As one commentator put it,[1] the inhabitants of these two worlds still met—more or less peacefully—at the theater, on the boulevard, in the public park. But they now belonged to different clubs, attended different public lectures, and were no longer welcome at each others' soirées. It is hardly surprising, therefore, that it took the returns of the Fourth Duma elections to make Kadet leaders realize that the mood of the voters of the urban curiae was not necessarily that of rural Russia, and even then they did not admit the full political implications of this fact—so grim were the political alternatives that they raised.

Marxist commentators were quicker to recognize after the Stolypin coup d'état the resiliency, at least in the short run, of the political system it had created. Given their rejection of the path of reform and continued advocacy of revolution, it was easier for them to do so. Most readers will be familiar with the explanatory scheme that Lenin drew to account for this resiliency of the System of the Third of June: the conception of a "Bonapartist" regime, or more precisely of a political and social system seeking to adapt to the requirements of capitalist development—and to the pressures of the social formations that this development fostered—even while continuing to maintain its earlier sources of support among the more traditionally oriented elements of its service class, and among the *pomeshchiki*, the more traditionally minded noble landowners of the countryside.

Actually, this formulation is but an approximation of Lenin's thought, for his most characteristic and basic assumption was that *all* the political, social, and economic dimensions of the System of the Third of June were profoundly distorted by the various remnants of the peculiar historical heritage that it had preserved. The *whole* body politic—and *all* the social formations represented in it—constituted, in varying combinations and degrees, amalgams of precapitalist and capitalist elements, reflecting Russia's current general condition of *polukrepost-nichestvo*, semiserfdom. Even the groups in national life most closely identified with the dynamics of the new capitalist age—the commercial industrial class of the cities and towns, but also their increasingly "bourgeois" intelligentsia; those landowners of the countryside who were now engaged in the modernization of their estates, but also the kulaks, the class of rich peasants now growing even more rapidly at the expense of the middle and poor peasants under the spur of the Stolypin land reforms—were but grotesque, caricaturized versions of Western capitalist development, profoundly marked in their political psychology and behavior, just as in their socioeconomic situation, by Russia's cursed heritage of autocracy, arbitrariness, and serfdom.

As Lenin saw it, the political expression of this curious amalgam of past and present in national politics was a regime balancing itself, depending on the nature of the specific policies it sought to pursue, between alternative right-center (i.e., right *cum* Octobrist) and left-center (i.e., Kadet *cum* Octobrist) majorities in the Duma—a precarious balancing act, to be sure, but one that accounted for the political resiliency now being displayed by the tsarist regime, as well as for its ultimate fragility.

Even this scheme (from which Lenin partially deviated in practice by the eve of the First World War) involved a considerable over-estimation of the political support for the Regime of the Third of June among the social groups represented in urban, commercial, industrial Russia, an overestimation that was understandable, to be sure, within the peculiar perspective of Lenin's own revolutionary goals. Besides, we should note that most of Lenin's Menshevik opponents (their earlier enthusiasm about a "bourgeois" revolution notwithstanding) also wrestled with some variant of this conception, especially during the depressing years of political quiescence in urban Russia up to the eve of the First World War. In fact, it was even more psychologically imperative for the Mensheviks—more unqualifiedly persuaded, as they were, of the backwardness, the "political idiocy," of the countryside—to believe that, if the tsarist regime now seemed to have regained a measure of political stability, it was because it had managed, at least temporarily, to win some political base in urban capitalist Russia, especially among its "big" commercial-industrial class. Notwithstanding the hackles that he occasionally raised, the most heterodox of the Menshevik commentators on this subject, Ermansky, was not alone among Menshevik observers in wondering whether, under these circumstances, another "bourgeois" revolution was really in the cards for Russia—or whether, if another revolution did come, it would not from its very outset see the Russian bourgeoisie firmly encamped on the side of reaction.[2]

What all these various contemporary views of Russia's political situation and of her likely immediate future basically shared, of course, was the assumption that the Regime of the Third of June could not possibly have won, or maintained, however brief a measure of political stability without staking out some kind of political base in urban as well as rural Russia, without adapting to some degree to the political and social values, and the economic needs and aspirations, of at least *some* of the constituent groups of this newer, more vital part of the Russian body politic.

It may well be argued that this assumption was negatively confirmed, in the long run, by the dramatic collapse of the tsarist regime. But what is more significant for our purposes is that it profoundly affected and distorted all judgments of *immediate* realities, and these distortions were passed on, largely unexamined, to later generations of historians. In most contemporary as well as subsequent political analyses of the Regime of the Third of June, this bias was reflected, for example, in a tendency to overestimate the political weight that the "big bourgeoisie," the commercial-industrial class, carried in the councils of the Union of 17 October, the more moderate of the political formations, which, for a time, provided the Regime of the Third of June with a major share of its political support in "society."[3] It also induced many contemporary as well as subsequent commentators to minimize the degree to which members of the commercial-industrial class, and more generally voters of the more prosperous first curiae of the cities and towns, had in fact moved to the left by the outbreak of the First World War. Finally, and perhaps most important, it caused many observers to minimize the gravity of the political dilemmas that already confronted the councils of Russian liberalism by the eve of the war, and, more broadly, to perceive inadequately the character of the political crisis that was already besetting urban Russia—in its confrontation of the political cultures of rural Russia—even before the guns sounded to open the last chapter in the history of the tsarist regime.

One of the chief purposes of this volume will be to bring out, at least implicitly, the nature of this confrontation by examining at close hand the political attitudes and behavior of the constituent groups of rural Russia, as well as the role that their political cultures actually played in the System of the Third of June. Most of our attention will be focused on a remarkably small and cohesive social group, the Russian landed nobility—or more precisely, those of its male members over twenty-five years of age who possessed and maintained estates large enough to qualify them for full census in elections to the zemstvos, the State Council, and the State Duma.

Historians have readily recognized the significance of the role that this group—essentially, the adult male members of approximately thirty thousand families of the landowning nobility—exercised in the governance and politics of Imperial Russia before 1905: that it was they who effectively ruled over rural Russia by virtue of their preponderant position in local organs of self-government, as well as through the political, social, and economic controls that they maintained, under normal circumstances, over the peasants who leased or worked part of their land. Historians have recognized equally readily that it was these landed nobles who effectively dominated (chiefly through their provincial and county marshals of nobility) the actual workings of a provincial bureaucratic machinery, which, in any event, did not extend its tentacles much beyond the various provincial capitals, and which continued to depend, *de facto* if not *de jure*, on representatives of the landed nobility to implement their directives.

This is not to deny the seriousness of the rift that had been exposed by the turn of the century between the government's central bureaucracy and much of the rank and file of this provincial landed nobility. The crisis of Russian agriculture, which had caused many of these landed nobles to return to their estates in the 1880s and seek, as best they could, to administer them more profitably; a return to the land, which had also caused them to immerse themselves with a new zest and intensity of purpose in the activities of their corporate organizations and of local organs of self-government; the government's own policies of forced-draft industrialization of the 1890s, to which many of these noble landowners were quick to attribute much of the blame for their current economic difficulties; the administrative tutelage that the government sought to maintain and tighten over organs of local self-government precisely as these nobles' "involvement" in these organs grew in intensity—all contributed to a genuine disaffection

among these provincial nobles, which the liberal movement successfully tapped after the turn of the century for its sources of initial
support. One may even explore and test the view, recently expounded
by some Soviet as well as Western historians, that as the tsarist bureaucracy grew in importance—drawing into its ranks in steadily
larger numbers men from other estates as well as nobles who did not
originate from the hereditary landed nobility—a dimension of social
and cultural conflict (which had never been entirely absent) between
the bureaucracy and the landed nobility was aggravated, and contributed to the severity of the political crisis.[4]

In her contribution to this volume, Roberta Manning has sought to
explore these social dimensions of the political conflict between the
state power and the landed nobility after the turn of the century. Her
essay substantially adds to our sense of the breadth and the depth of
the political disaffection that the landed nobility underwent by the
summer of 1905. Even more importantly, she has successfully drawn
for us a picture of the psychological dynamics that underlay the new
image of their potential role in national life to which many of these
provincial nobles were genuinely, if temporarily, converted during this
period of disaffection; as well as the process of reaction that caused
most of them, already by the time of the elections to the First Duma,
largely to give up this new self-image, although not entirely to revert
to their earlier conception of their relationship to state and society.

Indeed, it bears emphasizing that neither psychologically nor from
an institutional point of view did the Regime of the Third of June
simply restore a *status quo ante*. During the premiership of P. A.
Stolypin, this regime saw, however briefly, the unleashing of the reforming instincts of part of the state bureaucracy. But precisely in
response to these pressures for reforms—and in particular for the
"democratization" of the institutions of local self-government, which
the nobility had so exclusively dominated since the late eighteenth
century, as well as for the extension and rationalization of bureaucratic
rule in the countryside—the Stolypin era also witnessed the effective
political mobilization of the provincial landowning nobility. No longer
willing to entrust its fate to the state power and its officials, this nobility was now also more firmly in a position in the new political framework that had emerged by June 1907 to resist whatever innovative
tendencies the bureaucracy was inclined to display whenever such
innovations were seen by noble landlords to impinge on their ruling
position in the Russian land.

Indeed, here lay a crying contradiction, which the eventual fate of Stolypin's sweeping projects of local reforms would fully unveil. Even as it sought to reshape the institutional system as well as the agricultural organization of Russia's countryside in a spirit more in accord with its conception of modernity, the Stolypin regime found itself compelled to concede, willy-nilly, a greater share of political power to the one group in society whose social and economic decline these institutional changes were designed to reflect, if not to accelerate.

In my view, the most significant, if perhaps the most controversial, of the implications of the contributions to this volume will be to suggest that precisely as a result of Russia's post-1905 political constitution —of the emergence of the reorganized State Council, but also of the State Duma (once the elections to it were revamped by the legislation of June 1907), as well as of that often ignored proto-Duma, the Council of Local Economy of the Ministry of Internal Affairs (which was revived, partially under the pressure of the landed nobility, after the government's original projects of local reforms were submitted to the Second Duma)—a minute group of Russian society, amounting to little more than thirty thousand nobles of the countryside, found itself in a better position to resist the government's administrative and legislative initiatives in the last decade of the tsarist regime than it had been since the late eighteenth century.

One dimension of this domination of the political system by the landed nobility needs to be elaborated here. It is the mechanics of the system that governed elections to the State Duma, and the modifications introduced in it at the time of the Stolypin coup d'état. With some major modifications, the Law of June 3, 1907, left intact the basic structure of the electoral system, which had been drawn up in the summer of 1905 and modified in December 1905 to govern Duma elections. This legislation had divided those males over twenty-five years of age to whom it had given the suffrage into a series of curiae. With the exception of the voters of twenty-five major cities who were granted direct suffrage, the voters of the various curiae into which the body politic was divided were to select separately and by stages (varying in numbers for different curiae) provincial electors (*vyborshchiki*), who were eventually to gather at their respective provincial electoral assemblies to select the quota of curial and at-large deputies allocated to their particular provinces.

By the time it was issued, the legislation under which the elections to the First Duma were held bore a compromise character reflecting the various conflicting considerations that had been raised during long conferences, in summer and fall of 1905, at which the legislation had been discussed.[5] In these discussions the argument prevailed that an electoral system resting on the principle of representation by *sosloviia* (hereditary estates), under which noblemen, peasants, and townsmen would elect separately representatives to the Duma (a principle feebly advocated by a few diehards of the bureaucracy and the landed nobility) would not be politically viable: it would not be acceptable to the masses of the population, especially in Russia's urban centers; nor, for that matter, did it appear justified by the current political behavior of the landed nobility. So did the argument prevail that no significant segment of the population could be disfranchised, if political tranquility was to be restored (the tsar was particularly insistent on this point). Yet, even while realizing this, the majority of those who participated in these debates ultimately recoiled from the adoption, at least for the moment, of the principle of direct and equal suffrage advocated by liberal spokesmen, for fear of allowing the *nizi*, the lower strata of Russian society, to overwhelm its more "cultured" and propertied elements.

The solution adopted was to retain the compromise between the property and *soslovie* criteria of the curial system originally worked out in the summer of 1905 (for the so-called Bulygin Duma), but to broaden the suffrage to allow for some representation of all major groups of the population. As it ultimately emerged on December 11, 1905, the legislation thus reflected an amalgam of long-term as well as short-term considerations about the Russian body politic: about what public opinion would, and would not, stand for at this moment; but also about where the constituent groups of Russian society might be headed politically in Russia's painful evolution from a society of *sosloviia* into a society of classes.

The heaviest legacy of the past was reflected in the decision to establish a separate curia for the seventy-odd million members of the communal peasantry. This decision to provide a separate curia for communal peasants could be theoretically justified in a curial system otherwise resting on property criteria on the ground that the land allotments (*nadely*) that qualified the peasants who held them to vote in this curia could not be freely bought or sold, and thus did not constitute *private property*, under the complex regulations of the Emancipation and post-Emancipation legislation. (As we shall see, this rationale was given additional conviction under the Law of December 11 by the provision that communal peasants who *had* acquired land in private title *were* allowed to vote in the curia that was assigned to landed proprietors.)

In any event, qualified voters of the communal peasantry, or more precisely of these peasants' *selskie obshchestva* (the bodies that selected the village communes' elected officials and helped administer their affairs), were, under the terms of the 1905 legislation, to elect anew, in the first stage of the Duma elections in their curia, their representatives on the *volost'nye s"ezdy*, these peasants' organs of self-administration at the district level. The members of these district assemblies were then to select from their own midst representatives (*upol'nomochennye*) to county assemblies (*uezdnye s"ezdy*). And these county assemblies, in turn, were to elect, once again from among their own members, the quota of provincial electors (*vyborshchiki*) allocated to the curia of the communal peasantry in their respective counties. It was these provincial electors who were eventually to represent the communal peasantry in the transactions of the various provincial electoral assemblies at which deputies to the State Duma were to be selected. (See figure 1.)

In the minds of its authors, this complicated and cumbersome system of separate and indirect elections was clearly intended to segregate as much as possible communal peasants from other categories of voters. But as the records of the conferences at which the system was designed clearly indicate, this decision, *as originally conceived*, reflected a variety of motives. One of them admittedly was not to allow Duma elections to be swept entirely by a sea of peasant votes. But another equally compelling consideration—which had influenced the character of peasant legislation since Emancipation—was a genuine desire to *protect* communal peasants from other groups in society as well as from themselves: to safeguard these purportedly politically unsophisticated, if not illiterate, peasants from the wiles of outside political agitators, and indeed from the political pressures of other groups in the countryside, including nobles; to ensure that at every stage in the elections peasants would select representatives known to them, and capable of effectively representing their interests, so that in this fashion the Duma to be convened would include a large body of deputies truly representative of the peasant estate.

Underlying all these arguments, it must be remembered, was the conviction, still widely held in government circles when the Law of December 11 was issued, that, *if left to themselves*, the masses of the

FIGURE 1

Elections to the First State Duma

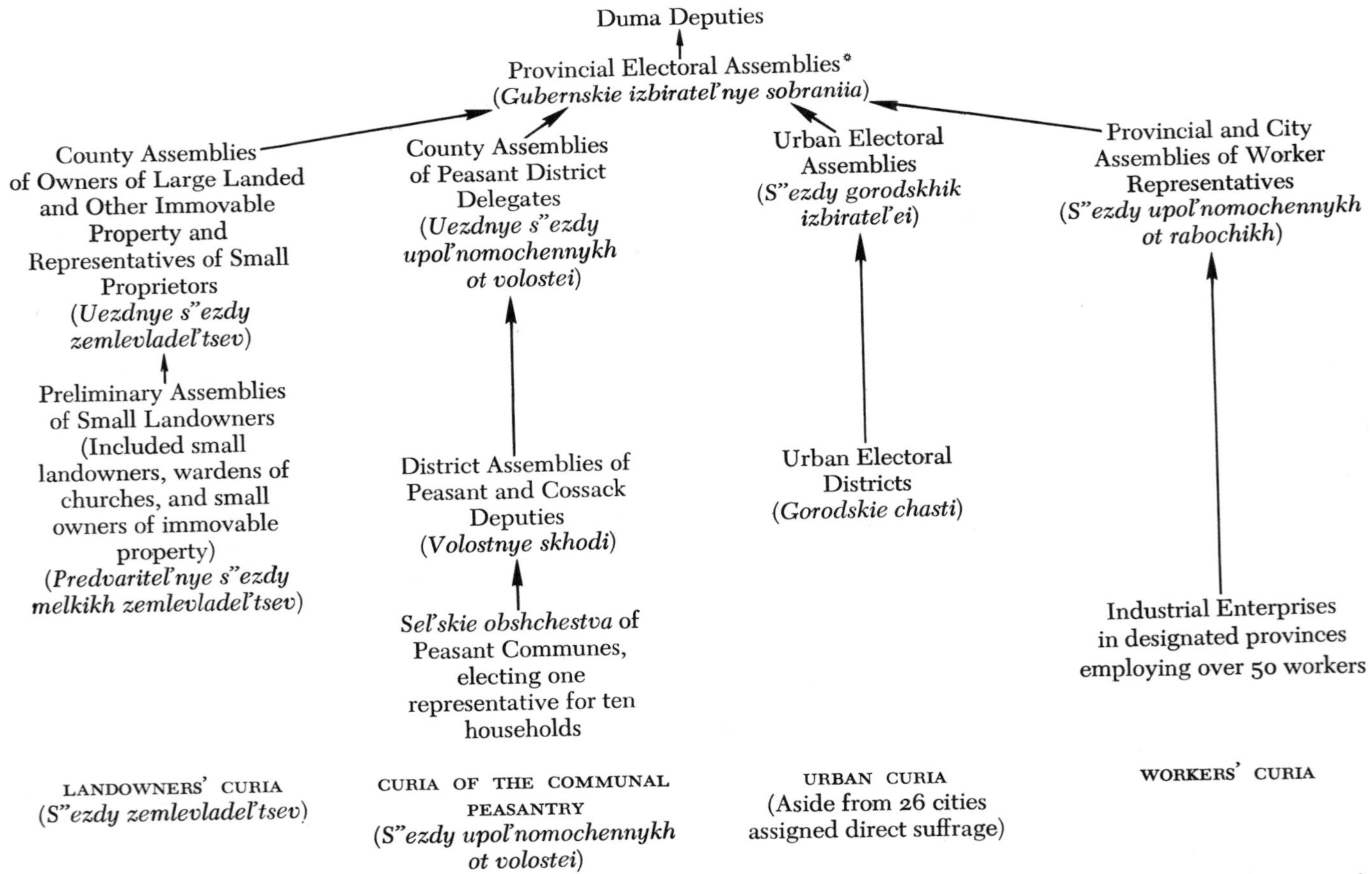

Duma Deputies

Provincial Electoral Assemblies*
(*Gubernskie izbiratel'nye sobraniia*)

Urban Electoral
Assemblies
(*S"ezdy gorodskikh
izbiratel'ei*)

Provincial and City
Assemblies of Worker
Representatives
(*S"ezdy upol'nomochennykh
ot rabochikh*)

County Assemblies
of Peasant District
Delegates
(*Uezdnye s"ezdy
upol'nomochennykh
ot volostei*)

Urban Electoral
Districts
(*Gorodskie chasti*)

Industrial Enterprises
in designated provinces
employing over 50 workers

WORKERS' CURIA

County Assemblies
of Owners of Large Landed
and Other Immovable
Property and
Representatives of Small
Proprietors
(*Uezdnye s"ezdy
zemlevladel'tsev*)

District Assemblies of
Peasant and Cossack
Deputies
(*Volostnye skhodi*)

URBAN CURIA
(Aside from 26 cities
assigned direct suffrage)

Preliminary Assemblies
of Small Landowners
(Included small
landowners, wardens of
churches, and small
owners of immovable
property)
(*Predvaritel'nye s"ezdy
melkikh zemlevladel'tsev*)

Sel'skie obshchestva of
Peasant Communes,
electing one
representative for ten
households

CURIA OF THE COMMUNAL
PEASANTRY
(*S"ezdy upol'nomochennykh
ot volostei*)

LANDOWNERS' CURIA
(*S"ezdy zemlevladel'tsev*)

* One curial deputy at each provincial electoral assembly was elected by the peasant curia alone; all others were elected on an at-large basis.

Russian peasantry would elect to the Duma representatives who would prove faithful to their tsar and to the motherland. Indeed, the sincerity of this conviction, and more generally of the desire to ensure a genuine and significant representation of the peasant estate in the Duma to be elected was tangibly reflected in several provisions of the electoral law.

In the first place, the county assemblies of the peasant curia (*s"ezdy upol'nomochennykh ot volostei*) were assigned 43 percent of the total number of electors allocated to the fifty-one provincial electoral assemblies of European Russia—far from proportional representation, to be sure, but still a greater number than that assigned to any other curia. Another provision specified that the first order of business of each provincial electoral assembly was to be the selection of one peasant curial deputy from among the electors representing the peasant curia. In the legislation of December 1905 the peasant curia was the only one so singled out; all the other deputies allocated to each province, having to be elected *at large*, by majorities or pluralities of the electors from *all* curiae attending the provincial electoral assemblies. And the statute as originally drawn further specified that *only* the electors from the communal peasantry in attendance at the provincial electoral assemblies were to participate in the selection of their curial deputies.

Finally, we should remind the reader of the political role that the 1905 legislation enabled the peasantry to play in the elections of the landowners' curia by allowing *all* peasants owning land in private title to vote in this curia. Indeed, the electoral law provided that the landowners' curia—the second major curia in which voters of the countryside were segregated—was to include all qualified voters owning land in private title, or other immovable property, regardless of their *soslovnost'*, their hereditary estate affiliation.

To be sure, even under the terms of the 1905 legislation, in the landowners' curia a special weight was assigned in the electoral process to large proprietors (most of whom were in fact nobles), on the grounds of the "exceptional" cultural as well as economic role that they were alleged to play in the countryside. Specifically, all proprietors who qualified for full census in their respective provinces were entitled to participate *directly* in the county assemblies that selected the quota of provincial electors allocated to the landowners' curia in their respective counties. But the electoral law also provided that *all other* land proprietors, however small their holdings, as well as eligible owners of small immovable property in the countryside, were entitled to attend preliminary assemblies (*predvaritel'nye s"ezdy*) to select representatives (*upol'nomochennye*), who in turn were allowed to participate, side-by-side with proprietors qualifying for full census, in the transactions of the county assemblies of the landowners' curia. (See figure 1.)

This is not to deny the ultimate inequity of the legislation, even in its original formulation. The Law of December 1905 allocated some 32 percent of the total number of provincial electors in the fifty-one provinces of European Russia to the landowners' curia. Of these, a major portion would actually consist of large proprietors with full census, of whom no more than thirty thousand were probably on the rolls of the various county assemblies of this curia, and a much smaller number actually voted. But the fact remains that in the First and even the Second Duma elections (when the electoral rules were already substantially modified), peasant smallholders participating in the county assemblies of the landowners' curia also managed to elect a good many of their own numbers to the various provincial electoral assemblies. (According to the governors' reports to the Council of Ministers, 26 percent of the provincial electors of the landowners' curia selected in the elections to the First Duma were in fact peasant smallholders, and only 46 percent large noble landowners.)[6]

The last major curia defined by the electoral law of December 1905 was established for urban voters outside of the twenty-five major cities that were allowed direct suffrage. Notwithstanding the opposition sentiments that the authors of the legislation undoubtedly expected of them, the county assemblies of these urban voters were assigned a rather generous quota of some 23.5 percent of the total number of provincial electors in the fifty-one provinces of European Russia. It has been estimated that altogether, in these fifty-one provinces, the quota of provincial electors allocated to the landowners' curia (1,955) amounted to one elector per two thousand landowners; that of the urban curia (1,352) to one per four thousand city-dwellers; that of the curia of the communal peasantry (2,532) to one per thirty thousand peasants; and that of the curia for qualified industrial workers outside the twenty-five major cities to one per ninety thousand.[7]

Thus, even in its 1905 version, this electoral system was a far cry from the one-man-one-vote demanded by the spokesmen of liberal and radical opinion. It discriminated heavily against voters in the peasant curia and very sharply in favor of the thirty thousand large proprietors with full census who were entitled to vote directly in the county assemblies of the landowners' curia. Yet even under these provisions, the provincial electors of the curia of the communal peasantry were able to elect a near majority of peasant deputies in the elections to the First Duma: partly by combining forces at the provincial electoral assemblies with peasant smallholders elected from the landowners' curia; partly, when necessary, by engaging in coalition politics with the electors from the urban curia, as well as with the admittedly small number of large landowners who still held on to their liberal and "people-loving" sentiments of the past. The political cohesion displayed by the peasant smallholders of the landowners' curia and the electors of the curia of the communal peasantry was especially remarkable. Through their alliance, peasant electors managed to gain an absolute majority in twelve provincial electoral assemblies, in addition to the thirteen where they had been assured such a majority by the electoral law, and they used these majorities to elect to the First Duma 210 deputies from their own estate (out of a total of 524).

At first, the government was by no means displeased with the result, as a great many of these peasant deputies of the First Duma (in contrast to the Second Duma's peasant deputies, who would be largely drawn from the politically suspect peasant intelligentsia) were in fact "*serye*," "grey" peasants, truly representative in their social economic profiles of the masses of the Russian peasantry. But the hopes that these rank-and-file peasants would prove politically conservative were quickly dispelled. Because of their burning desire for a radical solution of the land question at the expense of the now sobered-up landowning nobility, the "grey" peasant deputies of the First Duma were irresistibly drawn into the camp of the opposition. The peasants' clamor for the expropriation of gentry land could not be stilled even after the dissolution of the First Duma and the issuance by decree of the new Stolypin land legislation. And this, more than any other single issue, was the chief catalyst for the Stolypin coup d'état of June 1907—for the forcible dissolution of the Second Duma and the arbitrary imposition of a new law to govern Duma elections.

The new electoral law bluntly and sweepingly sought to achieve its purpose—of returning, at long last, a safe and conservative Duma majority—in a number of ways: by introducing a variety of devices to make the electoral process more susceptible to administrative manipulation; by redefining the criteria of eligibility to the various curiae; and, above all, by drastically reducing the number of electors and deputies that had been allocated to all the groups of the population that had been drawn into the political opposition in the first two Duma elections, while increasing just as drastically the electoral weight of those segments of the electorate that could now be expected to return safe progovernmental majorities.

Many of these new provisions have been adequately discussed elsewhere, and need not detain us unduly.[8] They included a drastically reduced representation for Russia's borderlands (by over 50 percent), as well as an increased guaranteed representation for the politically more loyal Russian minorities of their populations. The number of major cities allowed direct suffrage was drastically reduced (from twenty-five to seven), and the remaining urban voters were divided into two curiae (see figure 2): a first urban curia for well-to-do urban voters, who were now expected to vote for conservative or at least moderate candidates; and a second urban curia, which was assigned a smaller quota than the first, for the far more numerous but politically suspect urban voters who did not meet the census requirements for the first curia. (This proved to be one of the few incorrect calculations of the authors of the new electoral law, for in the Third, and especially in the Fourth Duma elections, even the more prosperous voters of the first urban curia voted predominantly for the opposition.)

But the most drastic, and also the most effective, changes in the new electoral law were those that affected the politics of the countryside. The changes imposed on the curia of the communal peasantry included the restriction of the suffrage in it to heads of households permanently residing in their *sel'skoe obshchestvo* and regularly engaged in the cultivation of their land allotments. (This modification had already been introduced by a "clarification" of the Governing Senate on the eve of the Second Duma elections but had only been applied haphazardly in these elections, and with little political effect.) The new law also eliminated the provision for the reelection of the membership of the peasants' district assemblies in the first stage of Duma elections in the peasant curia, as well as the requirement that the curial deputies of the peasant curia be selected by the peasant electors alone. (Like the curial deputies who were also assigned by the new electoral law to the landowners' and urban curiae, they were now to be elected by majorities or pluralities of the electors from *all* curiae attending the provincial electoral assemblies.)

The political impact of these various changes in the electoral procedures of the peasant curia will be scrutinized later in this volume (see Eugene Vinogradoff's essay, pp.222–25, and my concluding section, pp.286–88). Suffice it to say at this point that, in my view, they would not have been fully effective in achieving their purpose of ensuring a docile peasant electorate without the drastic alterations that were also imposed in the character and functioning of the landowners' curia, and especially in the proportion of provincial electors who were

FIGURE 2

Elections to the Third and Fourth State Dumas

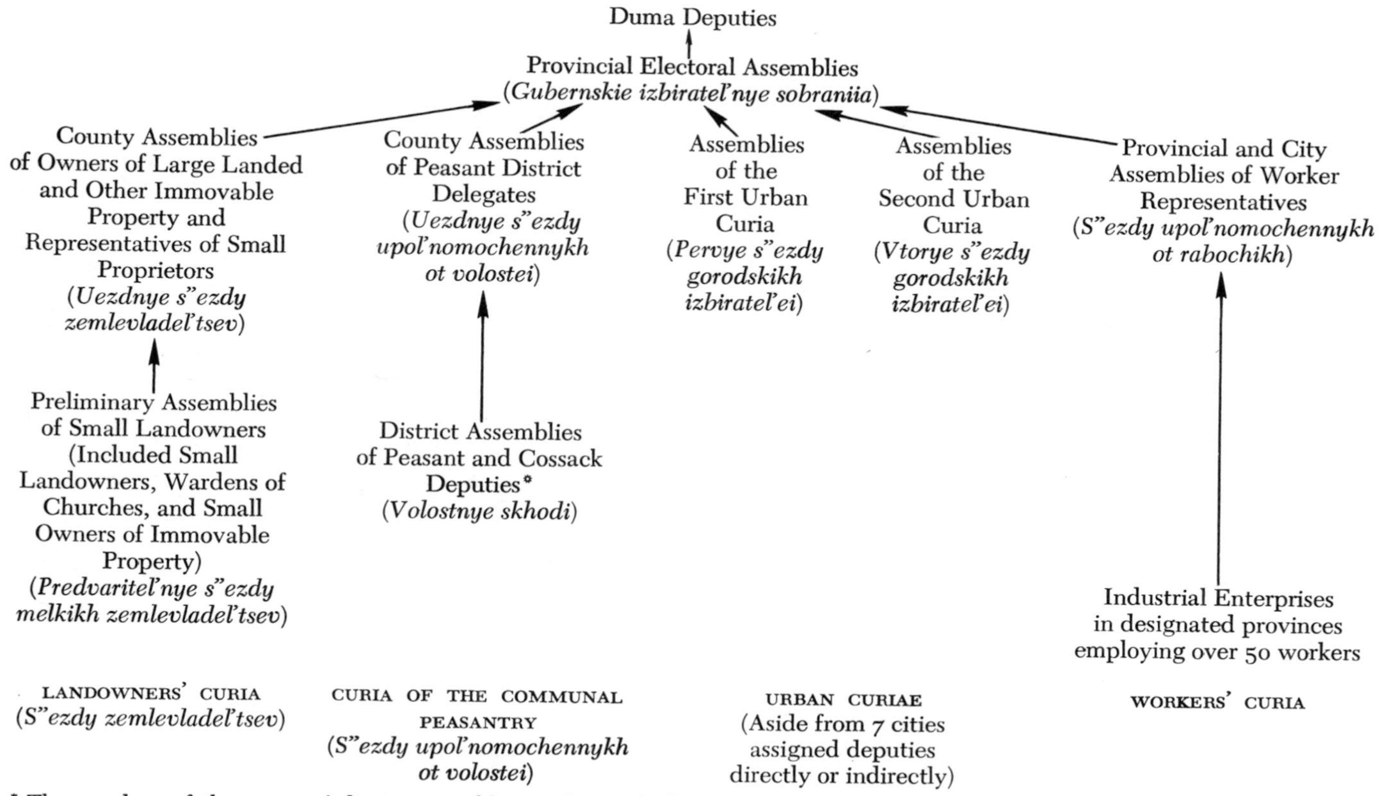

Duma Deputies

Provincial Electoral Assemblies
(*Gubernskie izbiratel'nye sobraniia*)

Assemblies of the First Urban Curia
(*Pervye s"ezdy gorodskikh izbiratelei*)

Assemblies of the Second Urban Curia
(*Vtorye s"ezdy gorodskikh izbiratelei*)

Provincial and City Assemblies of Worker Representatives
(*S"ezdy upol'nomochennykh ot rabochikh*)

County Assemblies of Peasant District Delegates
(*Uezdnye s"ezdy upol'nomochennykh ot volostei*)

County Assemblies of Owners of Large Landed and Other Immovable Property and Representatives of Small Proprietors
(*Uezdnye s"ezdy zemlevladel'tsev*)

Preliminary Assemblies of Small Landowners
(Included Small Landowners, Wardens of Churches, and Small Owners of Immovable Property)
(*Predvaritel'nye s"ezdy melkikh zemlevladel'tsev*)

District Assemblies of Peasant and Cossack Deputies *
(*Volostnye skhodi*)

Industrial Enterprises in designated provinces employing over 50 workers

LANDOWNERS' CURIA
(*S"ezdy zemlevladel'tsev*)

CURIA OF THE COMMUNAL PEASANTRY
(*S"ezdy upol'nomochennykh ot volostei*)

URBAN CURIAE
(Aside from 7 cities assigned deputies directly or indirectly)

WORKERS' CURIA

* The members of the peasants' district assemblies no longer had to be elected anew by the *sel'skie obshchestva* in the first stage of the Duma elections in this curia.

now assigned to this curia relative to the peasant curia. It was these alterations that made it apparent to the vast majority of Russian peasants that the new Duma to be elected would be a *"barskaia"* Duma, one so dominated by large noble landowners that it was hardly likely to be considerate of the aspirations of the peasant estate, *and above all* of the peasants' dream of a new Black Partition. The various modifications imposed by the new law did in fact ensure the domination of the electoral process by the large landowners of the countryside.

In the first place, the law drastically restricted the access to the landowners' curia of the peasant smallholders of private land, who in the First Duma elections, it will be recalled, had managed to gather some 22 percent of the provincial electors in this curia. Clarifications issued by the Governing Senate on the eve of the elections to the Second Duma had already prohibited members of the peasant *soslovie* holding land in private title from voting in the landowners' curia if they also held allotment land qualifying them to vote in the curia of the communal peasantry (or even if the land the peasants held in private title had been purchased with the help of mortgages issued by the Peasant Bank). The Law of June 3 now prohibited peasants from voting in the landowners' curia even if they had bought out their allotment land—simply by virtue of the fact of their still being technically members of a *sel'skoe obshchestvo*, the administrative unit in which all members of a village commune had to be legally enrolled.[9] As a result, the only peasant smallholders left on the rolls of the landowners' curia were small proprietors who had long been completely isolated, socially as well as economically, from other members of the peasant estate, and who, because of this isolation, could be expected not to play any significant part in the political process.

In addition, a number of administrative devices were legalized and widely used by the Ministry of Internal Affairs in the Third and Fourth Duma elections to minimize further the political role that these isolated peasant proprietors might play in these elections. Preliminary assemblies of small proprietors could themselves be subdivided according to the relative size of the landholdings of the voters on their rolls. Depending upon what opportunity dictated, members of the clergy who qualified as small proprietors by virtue of being wardens of church property could be assigned to separate subcuriae or combined with other small proprietors. Preliminary assemblies were held with little or no advance warning and only in county towns, often far removed from the residences of peasant voters.[10] In substance, everything was done to discourage small peasant proprietors who still qualified from voting in the landowners' curia, and because of these obstacles as well as political indifference or disillusionment, they no longer bothered to do so. Only some 10 percent of the 275,000 small proprietors still on the rolls actually voted in the elections to the Third Duma, and the percentage was probably even lower in the Fourth Duma elections (by far the lowest rate of participation of any curia or subcuria).[11] And the overwhelming majority of these 10 percent were wardens of Orthodox churches and other qualified members of the Orthodox clergy who, pursuant to the government's instructions, had been mobilized by their church hierarchy to ensure the election of safe conservative majorities.

Despite the noises sounded by the opposition, these representatives of the clergy did not usually exploit the frequent numerical superiority and discipline of their ranks to select provincial electors, and eventually Duma deputies, chiefly from their own midst. Heeding the instructions of their superiors to select whenever possible majorities of conservative noble landowners, they were largely content, both at the county assemblies of landowners and at the provincial electoral assemblies, to elect but a relatively modest proportion of members of the clergy, and to blackball noble proprietors only in those rare instances when they still espoused opposition sentiments.[12] (By the Fourth Duma elections, however, representatives of the Orthodox clergy also sought to blackball with some frequency those noble candidates who had displeased them by their excessive zeal in the promotion of legislation in support of religious toleration and of state control of parish elementary schools.) The net result of the new measures and practices I have described was to ensure, in almost all provinces of the empire, the total domination of the landowners' curia by the thirty-thousand-odd large proprietors who qualified for full census, and of whom little over ten thousand actually voted in the Third and Fourth Duma elections.[13]

Under the circumstances, only one further measure was required to ensure the domination by large landowners of the whole electoral process, and thereby the return of safe progovernmental majorities to the Duma: to increase drastically the proportion of electors allocated to the landowners' curia at the various provincial assemblies. This step was unashamedly taken by the authors of the Law of June 3, largely at the expense of voters of the peasant curia. The new law raised the aggregate proportion of electors of the landowners' curia from 31 percent to 50.4 percent of the total number of electors in the fifty-one provincial electoral assemblies of European Russia, and it reduced the proportion of electors from the curia of the communal peasantry from 43 percent to 22 percent. To be sure, this relative percentage of electors from the landowners' and peasant curiae was unevenly distributed among the various provincial electoral assemblies. Even so, electors of the landowners' curia were ensured an absolute majority in thirty-one of the fifty-one provinces of European Russia. And in an effort to eradicate all traces of peasant radicalism from the electoral process, this redistribution was particularly dramatic in those provinces with vast peasant majorities (especially in the Central Agricultural and Volga regions) that had been most heavily beset by agrarian disorders in 1905–1907 and had elected to the first two Dumas especially radically minded deputies, at least on the land question.[14]

The sum total of these changes proved, in actual practice, to be a considerable overinsurance. Indeed, as these measures were mechanically applied by lower officials, with little regard for the specific conditions prevalent in each province, the consequent results were often absurd. In many cases, because of the scarcity of large landowners, fewer voters actually appeared at county assemblies of the landowners' curia than the quota of electors allocated to them, with the result that these assemblies were unable to elect their full complement of electors.[15] To be sure, such absurd cases were the exception rather than the rule (although as a result of the gradual disappearance of large landowners from the countryside, their number, in both zemstvo and Duma elections, steadily increased as the war approached). In the elections to the Third Duma, for example, enough qualified voters *did* attend the various county assemblies of the landowners' curia to elect a complement of 2,542 provincial electors (out of the aggregate of 5,150 assigned to all curiae in fifty-one provinces of European Russia). The statistics compiled by the Electoral Commission of the Ministry of Internal Affairs give us rather precise data on who these 2,542 electors, who now controlled the electoral process, were.[16]

By hereditary estate characteristics (*soslovnost'*), 1,542 were nobles (60.7 percent), and 553 priests (21.8 percent); in combination with the representatives of the clergy, generally subservient to official direction, noble landlords now controlled 82.5 percent of the provincial electors of the landowners' curia. The figures about the estate characteristics of other electors in this curia are not without interest, however: 117 (4 percent) were Honorary Citizens (*pochetnye grazhdane*, an honorific title that was bestowed only upon non-nobles); 121 (5 percent) were *kuptsy* (by estate classification, merchants); 47 (2 percent) were *meshchane* (in rough translation, petty bourgeoisie, the term traditionally applied in Russia's society of *sosloviia* to the artisans and shopkeepers of Russia's cities and towns); and finally, 43 (1.7 percent) were of the peasant estate. In and of themselves, these figures clearly suggest the extremely minor political role that, with the exception of the clergy, non-nobles (whether owners of large or small property) now played in the landowners' curia, and especially how drastically members of the peasant estate had now been eliminated from effective political participation in this curia.

Other data of the Electoral Commission provide us with a more rounded picture of the profiles of these Third Duma provincial electors of the landowners' curia. The figures on their age distribution and educational backgrounds are noted below,[17] but let us take note here of some other, politically most crucial, indices.

By nationality (*natsional'nost'*, defined by the electors' attributed native language): 70 percent were classified as Great Russians; 10 percent as Little Russians (i.e. Ukrainians); 4 percent as White Russians; 7 percent as Germans; 1 percent as Tartars; and two single electors (0.1 percent) as Latvians. By religion: 85 percent were described as Orthodox or Old Believers; 6 percent as Protestants; 7 percent as Catholics; 1 percent as Moslems; and a single lonely elector as Jewish! This exceptionally high percentage of Russian Orthodox electors partly reflected, of course, the effectiveness of the device of subdividing the landowners' curia by nationality, and in fact religion, whenever indicated, to increase the weight of Russian Orthodox voters in the electoral process.

By occupation (*zaniatie*), an especially illuminating category when viewed in conjunction with hereditary estate definition: 17 percent were listed, or listed themselves, as engaged in government service; and 16 percent in public service. 37 percent were listed as landowners, and 21 percent as priests. This made up the vast bulk of the occupations of the electors of the landowners' curia. Of the remaining electors, only 2 percent were listed as engaged in a free profession; 3 percent in some commercial-industrial activity; 3 percent as agriculturalists (*zemledel'tsy*, in most cases presumably members of the peasant estate); and but two electors (0.08 percent) as engaged in handicrafts or industrial labor.

And finally, by political tendency: 62 percent were classified as "rights"; 23 percent as "moderates"; 8 percent as "lefts"; and 7 percent as "unidentified." (The political meaning of these terms will be scrutinized later in this volume.)

There are, it seems to me, two striking general features in the occupational statistics I have listed above, especially when we consider them in conjunction with those in other categories. The first is the extraordinarily low percentage not only of private peasant agriculturalists (elected from the preliminary assemblies), but also of members of the free professions (doctors, lawyers, and the like), as well as of electors described as engaged in some form of commercial-industrial activity. In substance, under the new electoral system, the landowners' curia—and given its majority of provincial electors, the electoral process as a whole—was now altogether dominated by Russian Orthodox noble landowners, with the assist of the Orthodox clergy.

The other notable feature is the persistent display, even in the abstract language of statistics, of the dual collective persona—the dual socioeconomic identity and role—affirmed by these elected spokesmen of the Russian landowning nobility: that of landowners, to be sure, but also that of members of a service class. As we have seen, to qualify in this curia *all* these noble electors had to be landowners; yet, half of them characterized themselves "by occupation" as engaged in some form of state or public service. To be sure, these nobles now usually exercised this state or public service in their local provinces, if not their local counties; as we shall see, an immensely important political fact. Many, if not most, of them were county or provincial marshals of nobility, chairmen, or at least members, of county and provincial zemstvo boards and the like. Almost all of them were now fully enmeshed in the public activities, and more broadly, in the various dimensions of the collective social, cultural, economic, and political life of the provincial nobility. But the fact remains that it was from this dual, Janus-like self-image—and the reality of present as well as past service (usually in the military)—as much as from their positions as landowners administering their estates that these Russian provincial nobles still drew their system of values, their sense of identity and purpose: their *claim* to rule, as well as the reality of their power.

Our percentage of electors from the noble estate would be substantially swelled if we took account of other curiae, especially of the two urban curiae. Of the 754 electors representing the 150,000-odd voters on the rolls of the first urban curia in the elections to the Third Duma, 19 percent were listed as nobles (the majority of the electors in this curia being classified by *soslovnost'* as Honorary Citizens [18 percent] and merchants [32.5 percent], although by no means all of these electors were actually engaged in commercial-industrial activities). And of the 550 electors selected by the 800,000 urban voters segregated in the second urban curia, an even greater proportion (33.6 percent) were listed as nobles, by far the largest *soslovie* category among electors in this curia!

However, it would be highly deceptive to draw any political conclusions from the data I have just cited. In the Third Duma elections, for example, the voters of the second urban curia elected a majority of 58 percent of provincial electors who were officially classified as "lefts" (only 15 percent being listed as "rights," 17 percent as "moderates," and 10 percent as "unidentified"). While the prosperous voters of the urban first curia, contrary to the government's expectations, returned in these elections a "leftist" plurality of 34 percent (33 percent being listed as "rights," 24 percent as "moderates," and 9 percent as "politically unidentified").[18] These were completely different returns, as we have seen, from those of the now overwhelmingly conservative landowners' curia (62 percent "rights," 23 percent "moderates," 8 percent "lefts," and 7 percent "unidentified").

To be sure, all these statistics are about provincial electors. Even so, they are indicative, at least to some degree, of the social profiles and political inclinations of the voters who actually selected them. What the figures suggest—and the suggestion is confirmed by the less comprehensive data in our possession on the voters themselves—is that in the elections to the Third Duma, and even more so to the Fourth Duma, a nobleman living in a city, educated at a university, engaged in teaching or in a free profession (or by this time, even in government service) was far more likely than not to hold and articulate the same political and social attitudes as a non-noble who otherwise shared the same background and life experience.

It bears repeating that at this point in the painful evolution of Russia's traditional society of estates, the group of provincial noblemen with which this volume will be largely concerned could be identified not by any single one but rather by a combination—a syndrome—of objective characteristics. Like the provincial electors whom they selected from their midst to their county assemblies, the members of this group were nobles, in most cases hereditary nobles, qualifying for full census in the landowners' (or noble) curia in elections to the State Duma, the State Council, and the county and provincial zemstvo assemblies. Our data, however impressionistic, allow us to be even more precise than this.[19] Most of them were owners of substantial estates, although smaller on the average than those of the provincial electors whom they selected. By and large, neither the poorest nor the wealthiest noble landowners were really full-fledged members of this tightly knit provincial society: the poorest, even if they barely qualified for full census, because they could not economically afford to partake fully in this society's corporate life; the richest, the owners of great *latifundii* (of ten thousand *desiatiny* or more), because they did not choose to do so, usually preferring to entrust to stewards the administration of their estates in order to participate on a full-time basis in the far more glittering (and politically and economically profitable) life of the Court and the capitals.

Even in their earlier existence, most of the noble "middle" landowners on whom we shall focus our attention had usually followed remarkably similar paths: most of them had graduated from secondary schools, often ones reserved in practice, if not in theory, for nobles; some had also graduated from higher educational establishments, usually of a military or technical character. Only a very few, an even lesser percentage than that of the provincial electors whom they selected (let alone of the deputies who eventually represented them in the Duma), were graduates of universities, institutions that almost invariably stamped those who had attended them with sharper and more articulate political and social attitudes than these rank-and-file voters of the provincial landowning nobility usually displayed.

Just as their provincial electors, most of the rank-and-file members of this provincial landowning nobility had at one time served the state, if, again, in less glamorous and prominent posts than their representatives: most often in the military, but also occasionally in the civil bureaucracy, especially its technical arm. Now retired majors, captains, or even lieutenants, or retired civil servants, they had returned, often by their late thirties or early forties, to manage their estates as best they could, and to partake in the life, the responsibilities, and the honors of their provincial society. Many of them now held residences, at least on a part-time basis, in their county towns, or on occasion in their provincial capitals, but most did spend considerable stretches of their existence on the estate, "administering" the work and life of their peasants, visiting one another, and sharing through their own corporate organizations as well as through the county and provincial zemstvos a common political as well as social life.

In substance, in the picture that we piece together from the various official and unofficial reports available to us about them, this rank and file of the Russian provincial landowning nobility emerges as perhaps duller, greyer, less prosperous, less prominent, and especially less articulate than those whom they selected to represent them at their provincial electoral assemblies. But together with them, they did constitute a tight, almost hermetic, culture, which now, just as before the great peasant disorders of 1905–1907, effectively ruled rural Russia.

By the fall of 1907 the countryside was quiet, and at least on the surface it might well have appeared to a visitor that nothing had ever happened to mar this tranquility. Indeed, as we shall see, in the elections to both the Third and Fourth Dumas, the still qualified voters of the curia of the communal peasantry, heeding the injunctions of their landlords, their land captains, and their priests, duly elected for the most part safe, seemingly conservative, obedient representatives, who by and large contributed to the swelling of the conservative majorities in the various provincial electoral assemblies. We shall later consider how and why they did so. But suffice it to say at this point that this political fact added a further increment to the enormous weight that the representatives of the noble landowners of provincial Russia were now able to exercise in the State Duma, just as in the State Council and the zemstvos.

In the various contributions to this volume, we shall examine how these men actually exercised their political power: the political and social attitudes that they and their representatives displayed, and the various ways in which they made these attitudes felt. And in an effort to understand them more fully, we shall review the tortuous political path that they had followed to reach this point in their political development—including their tumultuous journey through the maelstrom of Russia's First Revolution—before calm was restored, for however brief a period, in their own ranks as well as among the other inhabitants of the Russian countryside.

Our survey of gentry politics under the Regime of the Third of June will take us to the center of the political stage—to consider the role that the various parties and factions that represented, or purported to represent, the Russian landed nobility during these years played in Russia's national representative institutions, as well as to examine the influence that some of these noble organizations—most notably the United Nobility—sought to exercise *directly* over various circles in the government bureaucracy and at the Court, in an effort to influence policies even before they were finally formulated, and/or submitted for legislative approval. But the most notable feature of many of these investigations is that they will seek to relate the movement of national politics to the politics of the countryside, and especially to the attitudes and political culture of the thirty-thousand-odd families of the landed nobility that stubbornly continued to rule it throughout the period on which we shall focus attention.

NOTES

1. S. Elpatevskii, "Zhizn' idet," *Russkoe Bogatstvo*, no. 1 (January), 1914.
2. A candid expression of the doubts of Menshevik leaders on this subject,

and more generally of their response to the views expounded by Ermansky, is to be found in the still unpublished correspondence between A. N. Potresov and Iu. O. Martov during this period. This correspondence, consisting of some two hundred letters exchanged between 1908 and 1913, is preserved in the Nikolaevsky Archives at the Hoover Institution.

3. A recent example of this overestimation in Soviet historiography is the work of Ia. Avrekh. See, *inter alia*, his *Tsarizm i tret'eiiunskaia sistema*, Moscow, 1966.

4. Recent Soviet works that, at least implicitly, express this point of view include A. P. Korelin, "Dvorianstvo v poreformennoi Rossii (1861–1904 gg.)," *Istoricheskie zapiski*, vol. 87, pp.91–173; A. P. Korelin, "Rossiiskoe dvorian-stvo i ego soslovnaia organizatsiia (1861–1904 gg.)," *Istoriia SSSR*, 1971, no. 5, pp.56–81; P. A. Zaionchkovskii, *Rossiiskoe samoderzhavie v kontse XIX stoletiia*, Moscow, 1970; and particularly Iu. B. Solov'ev, *Samoderzhavie i dvorianstvo v kontse XIX veka*, Leningrad, 1973.

5. The most important and revealing of these conferences were those held at Peterhof from July 19 to July 26, 1905 (prior to the issuance of the Law of August 6 for the so-called Bulygin Duma), as well as at Tsarskoe Selo on December 5 and 7, 1905, prior to the issuance of the Law of December 11, 1905, under which the elections to the First Duma were held. A full transcript of the Peterhof Conference was smuggled out and published by Os-vobozhdenie in the fall of 1905 (*Petergofskoe soveshchanie o proekte Gosu-darstvennoi Dumy*, Berlin, n.d.), and reproduced (*Petergovskiia soveshchaniia o proekte Gosudarstvenno Dumy. Kakuiu Dumu khoteli dat' narodu Nikolai II i ego ministry*, Gos. Tip., 1917). A less complete transcript of the December 1905 Conference at Tsarskoe Selo is to be found in *Byloe*, no. 3, September 1917.

For analyses of these and other discussions and projects leading to the institution of the State Duma and the eventual formulation of the electoral law of December 11, 1905, as well as of the specific provisions of this law, see M. Sidel'nikov, *Obrazovanie i deiatel'nost' Pervoi Gosudarstvennoi Dumy*, Izdatel'stvo Moskovskogo Universiteta, 1962; Howard D. Mehlinger and John M. Thompson, *Count Witte and the Tsarist Government in the 1905 Revolution*, Indiana University Press, 1972; and especially Gilbert S. Doctorow, "The Introduction of Parliamentary Institutions in Russia During the Revolution of 1905–1907" (Ph.D. diss., Columbia University, 1974).

6. See Tsgia (Central State Historical Archive, Leningrad), fond 1276, opis 2, delo 9a; and Sidel'nikov, table 2, p.136.

7. N. E. Lositskii, *Izbiratel'naia sistema Gos. Dumy*, St. Petersburg, 1912, quoted in Sidel'nikov, pp.76–77.

8. Western studies include Samuel Harper, *The New Electoral Law for the Russian Duma*, Chicago, 1908; Marc Szeftel, "The Reform of the Elec-toral Law to the State Duma on June 3, 1907," *Studies Presented to the International Commission For the History of Representative and Parliamen-tary Institutions*, vol. XXXIII, London, 1968; Alfred Levin, "June 1907: Action and Reaction," in A. D. Ferguson and A. Levin, eds., *Essays in Rus-sian History: A Collection Dedicated to George Vernadsky*, Hamden, Con-necticut, 1965; and Alfred Levin, *The Third Duma, Elections and Profile*,

Archon Books, Hamden, Connecticut, 1973. Useful contemporary Russian analyses include V. Vodovozov, *Kak proizvodiatsia vybory v gos. dumu po zakonu 3 iiunia 1907 goda*, St. Petersburg, 1907; and F. Dan, *Novyi izbiratel'nyi zakon*, Metropol', 1907.

9. The relevant articles of the electoral law of June 3, 1907, were:

> Article 62.   Persons belonging to village and district [volost'] *obshchestva* of a county are not to be included in the rolls of landowning and urban voters of that county, even if they otherwise meet the requisite census requirements.
> Article 63.   Possession of peasant or [cossak] station allotment lands, as well as of land subject to restrictions applying to the peasantry [*krest'ianskoi povinnostnoi zemli*] in Lifliand province and on Oesel Island, as well as of peasant household plots [*uchastki*] in Kurliand province, does not give their owners the right to be enrolled on the electoral rolls of land proprietors, even when these lands have been purchased in private title [*vykupleny v sobstvennost'*].

The full text of the new electoral law is printed in Ministerstvo vnutrennykh del, *Izvestiia zemskogo otdela*, no. 6 (June 1907). The text of the relevant articles is on p.211.

10. Third Duma electoral procedures are discussed at some length in Alfred Levin, *The Third Duma, Election and Profile*, especially chapters 1, 7, and 8. For my own impressions of the conduct of the Third, as well as Fourth, Duma elections, I have largely drawn on the various official reports preserved in TsGIA, fond 1327 (*Deloproizvodstvo po vyboram v Gosudarstvennuiu Dumu*), particularly opis 2.

11. See statistical data recorded in M. V. D. (Ministerstvo vnutrennykh del), *Vybory v Gosudarstvennuiu Dumu Tret'ego Sozyva. Statisticheskii otchet Osobogo Deloproizvodstva*, St. Petersburg, 1911.

12. This is the general impression one draws from the official reports from various provinces in TsGIA, fond 1327, opis 2. This impression is confirmed by the statistics on the provincial electors selected by the various county assemblies of the landowners' curia.

13. Some thirty-one thousand large landowners were on the rolls on the eve of the Third Duma elections. We do not have precise figures on how many of them actually voted. What we do know is that out of the total of thirty-eight thousand who qualified to vote at the county assemblies of the landowners' curia, including *both* large landowners with full census and the representatives elected by the preliminary assemblies of small proprietors (overwhelmingly priests, as we have seen) only some sixteen thousand, or 42 percent, actually appeared on election day. Given the fact that the rate of participation at these county assemblies by representatives of the clergy was generally very high (in response to the injunctions of the church hierarchy), that of the large noble landowners was obviously considerably lower than the overall average of 42 percent, but we do not know precisely how low.

See the aggregate data on voting patterns in the various curiae in M. V. D., op. cit., pp.100–101.

14. In Kursk province, for example, the number of electors of the peasant curia was reduced from seventy-eight to thirty-one, and that of the land-

owners' curia raised from fifty-one to sixty-eight. In Saratov and Samara, the numbers of peasant electors were reduced respectively from sixty-four to twenty-seven, and ninety-seven to thirty-three; while those of the electors of the landowners' curia were raised from fifty-one to sixty-eight, and fifty-two to seventy-six. In Tambov, one of the most troubled provinces of the C.A.R. in 1905–1907, the peasants' representation was cut from ninety-two to twenty-six, and that of the landowners' raised from sixty-two to seventy! See Harper, op. cit., p.43, Table I.

15. In his contemporary study of the Third Duma elections, Samuel Harper has described for us a particular case in point, which I single out from many other such cases to be found in the reports of the electoral commissions on the Third and Fourth Duma returns, only because of its especially graphic character. The example involves Viatka province, a province of the Urals that consisted overwhelmingly of peasants, who, according to the 1905 census, constituted 2,945,000 out of 3,365,000 of the population. Only 10,000 members of the landowning nobility (including women and children) were recorded by the census in this province, and most of these noble landowners were in fact absentee owners (of timberland which did not require them to be in place to administer their estates). Notwithstanding these demographic characteristics, the Law of June 3, 1907, increased the number of electors assigned to the landowners' curia in Viatka province from thirty-three to fifty, while reducing that of the curia of the communal peasantry from ninety-eight to twenty-three. But to perceive the full impact of this reallocation, let us consider a particular county in this province, Sloboda. Already under the terms of the old electoral law, under which the landowners' curia of Sloboda county had been assigned four electors, only six voters had in fact appeared at the county assembly of landowners in both the First and Second Duma elections to select the four electors allocated to them. Harper describes these voters as follows: a Mr. Slaiev, a landowner; a Mr. Bogaevsky, the steward of the owner of a local estate deputized by his employer to vote for him; two priests, elected to the county assembly by the Preliminary Assembly of Small Proprietors, and two additional large landowners, the brothers Vakhrushev.

Under the new electoral law of June 1907, the landowners' curia of Sloboda county was allocated eight instead of four electors. At the same time, the new law disqualified three of the six voters who had attended its county assembly in the first two Duma elections: the two brothers Vakhrushev, because although they owned enough land in private title to qualify them for full census under the old law, they were now technically disqualified as members of a *sel'skoe obshchestvo* of the communal peasantry; and Mr. Bogaevsky, because the law no longer allowed the steward of an estate to represent his employer. Thus, only Mr. Slaiev and the two priests remained qualified to vote in a county assembly of the landowners' curia, which was now supposed to select from its own ranks eight electors to the Provincial Electoral Assembly! This, in a county in which the number of electors assigned to the curia of the communal peasantry had now been reduced from seven to two, and that of urban electors from three to two. See Harper, op. cit., pp.44–47.

16. See statistical table in M. V. D., op. cit., pp.272–73.

17. 3 percent of the electors of the landowners' curia were classified as being between twenty-five (the minimum legal age) and thirty; 12 percent as between thirty and thirty-five; 35.2 percent as between thirty-five and forty-five; 28.5 percent as between forty-five and fifty-five; and 21 percent as over fifty-five. This was a notably older age distribution than that of the electors of the second urban curia, and especially of the workers' curia (43 percent of whom were between twenty-five and thirty years of age!); but younger than that of the electors, selected under the Law of June 3 by the peasant curia, and especially by the well-to-do voters of the newly established first urban curia.

By education: 37 percent of the electors of the landowners' curia were classified as having received some form of higher education (i.e., in theological academies, in the case of the electors from the clergy; usually in some military or technical establishment, in the case of noble landlords). 47 percent were described as having received secondary education; and 16 percent, only elementary or home education. (See M. V. D., ibid.)

18. See M. V. D., ibid.

19. These impressions are partially drawn from the descriptions of, and statistical data on, nobles voting in the landowners' curia, contained in the official reports from various provinces about the elections to the Third and Fourth Dumas in TsGIA, fond 1327, opis 2.

Zemstvo and Revolution: The Onset of the Gentry Reaction, 1905–1907

ROBERTA THOMPSON MANNING

Gentry* liberalism was one of the more distinctive attributes of the political life of pre-Revolutionary Russia. Throughout the nineteenth century, from the generation of the Decembrists to the Revolution of 1905, the voices of liberal noblemen were repeatedly raised in defense of political liberty and the rights of "society" at large. Nowhere was this apparent anomaly more evident than in the local elective institutions of self-government, the zemstvos, for these so-called classless assemblies were in reality the political preserve of the landowning gentry.[1] With the foundation of the zemstvos, gentry liberalism found an institutionalized political base. The new assemblies rapidly attracted the more liberal and public-spirited of the landed nobility, offering these formerly superfluous men of Russian society a practical outlet for their energies and commitment, a legal counterpart of the contemporary populist movement. While the liberals were never more than a small minority within the zemstvos, they played a highly prominent and respected role far out of proportion to their numbers by virtue of their dedication to the zemstvo cause and their capacity for hard work.

Providing much of the manpower for the "small deeds" of daily zemstvo life, the liberals also contributed substantially to the gradual politicization of these institutions. Around the turn of the century, as the landed gentry was increasingly estranged from the Russian government by the mounting bureaucratic assault on zemstvo autonomy and

* The term gentry is used here to refer to that segment of the landed nobility involved with agriculture and public affairs in the localities.

30

Witte's deliberate policy of industrializing the country at the expense of the agricultural sector, the liberals within the zemstvos scored striking success in convincing the more conservative and passive rank-and-file deputies that the local institutions of self-government could serve as a potent weapon in the gentry's political struggle with the central authorities. At the same time, the zemstvos as never before or since attempted to strengthen their hand in this conflict by speaking out in the name of Russian "society" and actively seeking political allies among their own third element intelligentsia employees and the local peasant masses. These developments, of course, culminated in 1904–1905, when a rising tide of liberal sentiments within the zemstvos spilled over into the well-known series of congresses, which, in short order, presented the state with an escalating sequence of political demands—for a national legislative assembly in November 1904,[2] for "four-tail" suffrage (universal, equal, secret, and direct manhood franchise) in April 1905,[3] and for a broad range of social reforms by the following autumn, including the compulsory expropriation of private landholdings in favor of the land-hungry peasantry.[4]

When a national assembly did finally convene, however, in the form of the first two State Dumas, support for the new institution was not forthcoming from the zemstvos. Confronted with the conflict between the First Duma and the government over the prerogatives of the national assembly, the zemstvos maintained a pointed silence, although they had previously favored legislative powers for the new representative body.[5] Meanwhile quite a few zemstvo deputies were involved as individuals in the organization of the United Nobility,[6] an association that was conceived from the very first by its founders as a conservative counterweight to the Duma.[7] In the end, not a single provincial zemstvo assembly and very few county (*uezd*) bodies bothered to protest against the dissolution of the Duma whose calling they had formerly so fervently desired.[8]

During the brief existence of the Second State Duma, the zemstvos, abetted by the United Nobility, devoted considerable time and energy to the organization of the last, now largely forgotten 1907 Zemstvo Congress.[9] Putting forth the slogan, "Is not the opinion of five hundred zemstvos worth more than that of five hundred Duma deputies?" the organizers of this congress publicly challenged the authority of the Duma to reform local government, including the zemstvos;[10] and some of them privately hoped that the congress would spark a constitutional crisis and thereby hasten the dismissal of the Duma.[11] Meeting at last on June 10, the morrow of the Stolypin coup d'état, the participants in the 1907 Zemstvo Congress readily sanctioned that event by their tribute to its authors—Nicholas II and Stolypin[12]—and by their advocacy of an electoral system for the zemstvos strikingly similar to the new June 3 Duma Election Law, a far cry from the four tails of 1905.[13]

The prevailing interpretation of the liberal outburst of these years, advanced among others by the right Kadet Vasilii Maklakov,[14] seems at first glance to account for this political about-face on the part of the zemstvos. Seeking to explain the relative radicalism of Russian liberals in 1905, Maklakov maintained that the leadership of the liberal movement had recently been captured by dogmatic, doctrinaire "intellectuals," who ousted the moderate gentry zemstvo men of yesteryear. Hence, the 1905 congresses were not at all indicative of the opinions of the gentry rank and file of the zemstvos. But the Maklakov thesis taken at face value rapidly breaks down when applied to the zemstvo movement of 1905. In the first place, the participants in the zemstvo congresses were not newcomers or outsiders. Rather, with few exceptions, the delegates from the very first were noble landowners of considerable property, and all of them were current zemstvo deputies with long histories of public service in local elective offices.[15] Roughly a third of the more than one hundred men attending the initial *ad hoc* gathering of November 1904 held the important post of chairman of a provincial zemstvo board (*uprava*), an elective position that required administrative confirmation and, hence, was generally restricted to the more moderate of the leading activists. Subsequently, almost all the zemstvo delegates attending the congresses were actually elected for this purpose in the provinces. Because of strong administrative pressures, zemstvo representatives were usually selected in private conferences of deputies, not official zemstvo sessions; but the electoral procedures utilized went unchallenged until the very end of the year, when the mood in the localities had changed substantially.[16]

Also, initially, persons outside the zemstvo movement were not welcome at the congresses even as observers. The highly influential Union of Liberation leader, the historian P. N. Miliukov, for all his close personal and political ties with the leaders of the congresses, had to watch the proceedings of the April 1905 meeting from an adjoining room through a half-closed door so that he could not possibly influence the deliberations of the zemstvo men.[17] It is true that in the second half of the year such precautions were abandoned when, in preparation for the coming Duma elections, representatives of first the city dumas and then the nonzemstvo provinces were added to the congresses, and Miliukov himself came to play a rather active role. But until the end the leadership remained in the hands of zemstvo men of long standing, who continued to dominate the debates and proceedings of these meetings and to control the influential organizing bureau of the congresses. Besides, long before that time, the basic political program of the congress had already been adopted.

Yet Maklakov's allegations are not entirely without foundation, for the 1905 congresses cannot be considered truly representative of the zemstvos as a whole. Composed exclusively of the members of zemstvo executive boards and the more active and committed deputies, these national conclaves consisted from their very inception of men who were generally better educated, more public-spirited, more politically conscious—and far more inclined to liberal, even democratic views—than the zemstvo rank and file, not to mention the general gentry electorate of these institutions. For the routine conduct of daily zemstvo business rendered the national zemstvo leaders acutely aware of the poverty and sufferings of the local peasant population, while exposing them directly to the influences and democratic aspirations of the third element intelligentsia employees—the doctors, school teachers, agronomists, etc., who staffed the many, expanding enterprises of the local zemstvo assemblies and who tended to sympathize quite openly with the revolutionary parties of the left, the Socialist-Revolutionaries and, to a lesser extent, the Social Democrats. At the same time, the zemstvo leaders, by virtue of their very activism, were far more likely to have experienced directly the arbitrariness and obscurantism of the local bureaucracy. The bureaucratic offensive against zemstvo autonomy in these years was all too often directed against the projects and persons of the more active and committed deputies, increasing substantially the oppositional propensities of many formerly moderate, even somewhat conservative men.

The resulting disparity between the political outlook of the national zemstvo leaders and that of their political base in the localities was enhanced by the existence of deep-seated social differences between the two groups. These differencs were most striking in the case of the militant constitutionalists, who dominated the 1904–1905 congresses and their organizing counsels, and who were to join the Kadet party in large numbers at the end of the year.[18] By and large the men of the zemstvo right and center, who subsequently filled the ranks of the "progressive," Octobrist, or right-wing parties had received an upbringing and education, fairly typical of the landed gentry at large, i.e., they had tended to conclude their formal schooling with graduation from one of the military Cadet Corps that were established in the

eighteenth century to prepare the offspring of the noble estate for traditional careers in the armed forces. Those among them who had gone
on to the university had majored overwhelmingly in law, the traditional academic major of the contemporary European elite, including
the upper strata of the Russian service nobility. Members of the zemstvo left, on the other hand, were far more likely to have received at
least some higher education and to have majored in "nongentry" fields,
especially those related to the natural sciences—the science-mathe-
matics faculty, engineering, agronomy, and medicine (see table 1), all
fields that the Imperial Russian government tended to regard as potentially "subversive."

Not surprisingly, the most common occupation among the national
zemstvo leaders, irrespective of political tendency, was agriculture,
since almost all the delegates to the zemstvo congresses owned rather
substantial amounts of land (between 1100 and 1700 *desiatiny* on the

TABLE 1

*Educational backgrounds of the participants in the 1905 and
1907 zemstvo congresses. (Data was available for 142 of the
267 participants in the 1905 and 1907 congresses.)*

Future political affiliation	No higher edu- cation	Military edu- cation	Corps of Pages	Higher education			Total
				Law	Science ori- ented	Other	
Kadets	4	8		19*	23	3	57
Progressives		4		5	1		10
Octobrists	2	7	2	17	5	4	37
Right of Octobrists	3	10	3	10	8	4	38
Total	9	29	5	51	37	11	142

* Four of the Kadets who majored in law went on to become professors of law,
while only one Octobrist, one progressive, and no members of the right did.

SOURCES: TsGAOR fond 102, opis 5, delo 1000/1905, pp.43–46; *Zhurnaly i
postanovleniia vserossiiskago s"ezda zemskikh deiatelei v Moskve s 10 po 15 iiunia
1907 goda* (Moscow, 1907) pp.107–112; *Gosudarstvennaia duma v portretakh
27/4 1906 8/vii* (St. Petersburg, 1906). N. Pruzhanskii, *Pervaia Rossiskaia gosudarstvennaia duma* (St. Petersburg, 1906); Rossiia. Gosudarstvennaia Duma.
Ukazatel k stenograficheskim otchetam vtoroi sozyv gosudarstvennoi dumy (St.
Petersburg, 1907); *Chleny vtoroi gosudarstvennoi dumy* (St. Petersburg, 1907);
Tretei sozyv gosudarstvennoi dumy. Portrety, biografii i avtobiografii (St. Petersburg, 1919); and *Chetvertyi sozyv gosudarstvennoi dumy khodozhestvennyi al'bom
s portretami i biografiiami* (St. Petersburg, 1913); and *Entsiklopedicheskii slovar'*
(published by Granat and Co.), vol. 23.

TABLE 2

Occupations of the participants in the 1905 and 1907 zemstvo
congresses (insofar as possible as stated by the delegates
themselves; data was available for 97 out of 267 participants).

Future political affiliation	Agriculture	Public activist	Free professions	Total
Kadets	16	2	20	38
Progressives	3	2	3	8
Octobrists	13	15	4	32
Right of Octobrists	12	7		19
Total	44	26	27	97

Derived from the same sources as table 1.

average).[19] The future Kadets, however, despite their often extensive landholdings, were more prone than either moderate or conservative elements to practice one of the free professions at some point of their careers and to be somewhat less concerned with the management of their family estates,[20] while the latter were inclined to bow to parental pressures or family traditions and to enter state service for a brief period before settling down to a life of agriculture and public service in the localities (see tables 2 and 3). In this way, the career patterns—and life styles—of the dominant element in the 1904–1905 zemstvo congresses resembled not so much those of their own gentry constitu-

TABLE 3

Involvement of participants in the 1905 and 1907 zemstvo
congress in state service, either military or civilian, for
terms of five years or more. (Data was available*
for 142 of the 267 participants.)

Future political affiliation	Military service over five years	Civil service over five years	Total
Kadets	2	1	3
Progressives		1	1
Octobrists	2	9	11
Right of Octobrists	3	9	12
Total	8	20	28

* This table has been limited to service of five years or longer to exclude those who served merely to fulfill their universal military service requirement. Most participants served less than five years.

Derived from the same sources as tables 1 and 2.

ents as those of the radical intelligentsia, that broad, amorphous social grouping that cut across all classes and estates of pre-Revolutionary Russian society to include all professionally trained men and women estranged from the existing political order and concerned with the sufferings of "the people."[21]

In fact, the zemstvo left was largely composed of what can only be called a "gentry intelligentsia," an intermediate social grouping that combined many of the key attributes and attitudes of *both* the gentry and the intelligentsia at large. Of course, such a social category had existed in some form since the very inception of the intelligentsia in Russia. It is common knowledge that the overwhelming bulk of the first generations of the intelligentsia, from Radichev through Herzen, were men of noble origins. Throughout the first half of the nineteenth century, however, such noble *intelligenty* were estranged from their social milieu no less than from the existing political order. Only with the abolition of serfdom and the creation of the zemstvo institutions did educated noblemen of an oppositional bent choose to direct their political efforts toward the landed gentry of the provinces, who proved increasingly receptive to the political appeals of the liberals. For the half century separating the abolition of serfdom from the outbreak of the Revolution of 1905 had witnessed the transformation of the landed nobility from the favored child of the Russian autocracy into a social group engulfed in crisis, both economic and political.

Traditionally a social category based on a combination of land-ownership and state service, the hereditary landed nobility now found *both* its time-honored functions in the Russian social-political order undermined by the forces of modernization and change. The unprecedented loss of noble landholdings in the second half of the nineteenth century is common knowledge, as are the causes of this development—the inability of many noble proprietors to adjust to the post-Emancipation order, the long depression in the price of grain at the end of the nineteenth century, and the industrialization policies of the Russian government.[22] Less well known, however, is the fact that increasing numbers of noble landowners did not passively accept the loss of the last cherry orchard but actively struggled against their economic fate by turning to the land and involving themselves as never before in the daily management and direction of their family estates. By the outbreak of the 1905 Revolution, such efforts managed to slow considerably the previously precipitous economic decline of the landed nobility as a whole.[23] But the economic position of most surviving landowners remained extremely precarious, and life on the land was almost always a harsh, continuous, rather ungentlemanly struggle for existence, which engendered many social tensions contributing to the rise of the Liberation Movement among the landed gentry in 1905.[24]

At the same time that the hereditary landed nobility was suddenly confronted with an economic crisis of major proportions, its traditional political, i.e., service, role was being ever more rapidly assumed by an increasingly well-educated and professionalized bureaucracy, composed largely of landless men of non-noble origins.[25] By 1897, only 51 percent of the military officer corps and 30 percent of all civilian officials were noblemen by birth; and overwhelmingly these new officials, even the most highly placed among them, failed to establish any but the most casual contact with the land.[26]

Under these conditions it is not surprising that record numbers of gentry landowners in 1904 and 1905 were swept into the opposition to the old political order, which was organized and led in large part by the liberal Union of Liberation and its allies among the zemstvo constitutionalists. Consequently the basic political platform of the national zemstvo congresses was reflected, although somewhat belatedly and not always completely, in the addresses and resolutions of the local zemstvos and noble corporations. For example, in the winter of 1904–1905, notwithstanding the immediate, overwhelming swell of sentiment in favor of the establishment of some form of representative government,[27] less than half of the provincial zemstvos (fourteen of the thirty-four assemblies) endorsed in full the constitutionalist program of the November Congress majority for the foundation of a national assembly with *legislative* powers, i.e., a body that would limit the authority of the autocratic tsar.[28] But by the summer over three-fifths of all provincial assemblies (twenty-one zemstvos) had embraced such views,[29] and by the opening months of 1906 clearly constitutionalist revolutions had been adopted by almost three-quarters of the provincial zemstvos (twenty-five assemblies),[30] including at least four of the half-dozen-odd assemblies that had originally explicitly insisted on the preservation of the autocracy in the course of 1905 (see table 4).[31]

A similar evolution occurred in regard to the electoral system. Less than a third of all provincial zemstvos (ten assemblies) ever accepted four-tail suffrage at any one time,[32] since many zemstvo men honestly believed that direct elections could not be rapidly organized in a country with a largely illiterate population (see table 5). But at least three of the "tails" (universal, equal, and secret franchise) were favored by half of the provincial zemstvos meeting in the summer of 1905,[33] and by two-thirds of them (twenty-four assemblies) by the winter of

TABLE 4

The political evolution of the provincial zemstvo assemblies
on the question of the powers of the national assembly.

Political program	Winter 1904–1905		Summer 1905		Winter 1905–1906	
	No.	%	No.	%	No.	%
Legislative powers for the national assembly	14	44.1%	21	61.7%	25	73.5%
National assembly with powers equal to those of the tsar	—	—	5	14.7%	4	11.8%
Consultative assembly	12	35.3%	5	14.7%	3	8.9%
Preservation of the autocracy	6	17.6%	3	8.9%	0	0%
Undecided	2	5.9%	0	0%	2	5.9%
Total	34	100%	34	100%	34	100%

Derived from the sources listed in notes 28–30.

1906.[34] Only eleven assemblies at most explicitly rejected direct elections,[35] and these were clearly offset by the zemstvos favoring the fourth "tail." The remaining zemstvos were simply unable to reach a conclusion on the subject of direct elections, although they were well aware that four-tail suffrage was a key plank in the political platform of the national zemstvo congresses.

TABLE 5

The political evolution of the provincial zemstvo assemblies
in regard to the electoral system for the national assembly.

Political program	Winter 1904–1905		Summer 1905		Winter 1905–1906	
	No.	%	No.	%	No.	%
Three or more "tails"	2	5.9%	14*	53.8%	23*	67.8%
Elections through the zemstvos (elected by the 1864 law)	3	8.9%	6	23.1%	5	14.7%
Elections by estates	1	3%	0	0%	0	0%
Undecided	28	82.3%	6	23.1%	6	23.1%
Total	34	100%	28	100%	34	100%

* Ten of these assemblies favored four-tail suffrage. Derived from the sources listed in notes 33–34.

The leftward revision of the political program of the local zemstvos was accompanied by an escalation in tactics as well. After the demands of a June 6 deputation of zemstvo leaders to the tsar for the immediate convocation of a national assembly elected by universal suffrage failed to obtain any tangible political results, the provincial zemstvos began to promote the political mobilization of the peasant masses in hopes of forcing reforms on the recalcitrant autocracy. With this goal, zemstvo assemblies and their executive organs openly engaged in political propaganda, distributing leaflets and brochures and sponsoring public meetings and discussions. Many of them expanded the zemstvo economic councils, the organs responsible for the formulation of zemstvo agricultural policies, to include representatives of the peasantry, who immediately utilized this new forum to voice far-reaching demands for the expropriation of gentry lands. The Saratov provincial zemstvo and the Petrovskii uezd assembly, as well as individual zemstvo deputies throughout the country, actually went so far as to encourage the organization of local chapters of the Peasants Union to enable the neighboring peasantry to defend their own group interests.[36]

The political initiatives of the zemstvo men, despite their increasingly radical nature, were apparently not at all unwelcome to the rank-and-file gentry landowners of the provinces, for the traditionally conservative provincial noble assemblies and their elective officials, the marshals of the nobility, soon joined the zemstvos in the opposition movement. This, indeed, was an unexpected development. Throughout the nineteenth and early twentieth centuries, the zemstvos by and large tended to represent only the more civic-minded and involved of the local gentry, men willing to forego some personal sacrifices of both time and money for the public weal, since even minimal participation in zemstvo elections and meetings, not to speak of committee work, required periodic visits to the county or provincial capitals, journeys financed entirely at the expense of the voters or deputies themselves.[37] In contrast, the provincial noble societies embraced much—if not all—of the potential electorate of the zemstvos. Under law, all noble landowners possessing the minimum property requirement for voting in the first (nobles') curia of the zemstvos were able to participate directly in the assemblies of the nobility so that these conclaves, which rarely convened more frequently than at three-year intervals, and which were marked by a flurry of provincial social activity, attracted many of the more politically indifferent—and generally conservative—of the gentry rank and file as well as some absentee magnates and high officials who usually did not deign to participate in zemstvo affairs.[38]

Yet in the winter of 1904–1905, the regular triannual assemblies of the nobility overcame the innate conservative bias of their member-ship and openly defied an 1865 regulation prohibiting them from dis-cussing affairs of state,[39] thereby engaging in political activity for the first time since the emancipation of the serfs. At that time, the noble assemblies of over half of the zemstvo provinces convened with a record turnout of local nobles and embarked on a campaign of political ad-dresses and petitions similar to that previously launched by the zem-stvo men.[40] Over two-thirds of these assemblies—a proportion not much inferior to that of the concurrent winter sessions of the provincial zem-stvos—called for the establishment of some sort of national representa-tive assembly.[41] Although most of the noble societies, unlike the zem-stvos, continued to insist on the preservation of the autocratic powers of the tsar,[42] a good third of them followed the precedent set by the zemstvo men and eliminated even the traditional salutation "Autocrat" from their addresses and appeals to the monarch,[43] while a majority of these assemblies specifically stipulated that the new elective assembly should represent the entire nation, not just the nobility.[44] Hence, it is not at all surprising that the political program of the noble cor-porations, like the zemstvos before them, evolved steadily to the left throughout the year (see table 6). By the following winter (1905–1906) all but one of the noble assemblies that managed to meet and discuss politics omitted all references to the autocracy from their political addresses and endorsed the new order established by the October Manifesto, urging only the speedy convocation of the new national assembly—the State Duma.[45]

Meanwhile the chief elective officials of these assemblies—the pro-vincial marshals of the nobility—also emerged to echo, although faintly at first, the political program of the zemstvo men. To be sure, the first in a series of national conferences of marshals of the nobility, which convened at the end of 1904, repudiated the political program of the recent November 1904 Zemstvo Congress by explicitly endorsing the preservation of the autocracy, while timidly limiting its call for popular representation to a demand for the addition of elected representatives from the zemstvos, city dumas, and corporate organizations of the various estates (the nobility, merchantry, and peasantry) to the State Council, an organ of the higher bureaucracy that, by the middle of the nineteenth century, had come to draft the final version of all legislative proposals.[46] But by the early summer of 1905, under the pressure of the persistent Russian defeats in the war with Japan and repeated bu-reaucratic delays in the implementation of basic reforms which were

TABLE 6

The political evolution of the provincial noble assemblies in 1905.

Political program	Winter 1904–1905		Spring 1905		Summer 1905	
National assembly with legislative powers	0	(0%)	0	(0%)	3[f]	(50%)
National assembly, powers equal to tsar (program of the Coalition Zemstvo Congress)	0	(0%)	0	(0%)	1[g]	(16.7%)
Representative assembly, no mention of the autocracy or its powers	6[a]	(35.3%)	2	(10%)	0	(0%)
Autocracy and a representative assembly	5[b]	(29.4%)	16	(80%)	2[h]	(33.3%)
Autocracy and "reforms"	5[c]	(29.4%)	2	(10%)	0	(0%)
Abstaining	1[d]	(5.9%)	0	(0%)	—	
Total	17	(100%)	20[e]	(100%)	6	(100%)

[a] The assemblies concerned were the Kazan, St. Petersburg, Tver, Novgorod, and Ufa noble corporations.

[b] The assemblies concerned were the Bessarabia, Kaluga, Kostroma, Nizhnii Novgorod, Pskov, and Iaroslavl noble corporations.

[c] The assemblies concerned were the Moscow, Orel, Riazan, Kursk, and Samara noble corporations.

[d] The assembly concerned was the Ekaterinoslav nobility.

[e] Precisely what noble corporations were involved cannot be determined, although their numbers included the Smolensk, Tambov, Kazan, Kursk, Riazan, Tver, and Kostroma nobilities.

[f] The assemblies concerned were the Ufa, Iaroslavl, and Don noble corporations.

[g] The assembly concerned was the Chernigov noble corporation. (In addition, the Kovrov county noble assembly of Vladimir province adhered to this position.)

[h] The assemblies concerned were the Kursk nobility and the noble corporations of Ozel Island. In addition the Bogodukhovskii county noble assembly of Kharkov province also adhered to this position.

Derived from the sources listed in notes 40–44 and *Novoe vremia*, no. 10476, May 4/17, 1905, p.2; no. 10437, Mar. 26/April 8, 1905, p.3; no. 10468, April 26/ May 9, 1905, p.4; no. 10466, April 24/May 7, 1905, p.2; no. 10527, Jun. 24 Jul. 7, 1905, p.1; no. 10512, Jun. 9/22, 1905, p.2; *Russkiia vedomosti* XLII, no. 168, Jun. 24, 1905, pp.1–2; no. 159, Jun. 15, 1905, p.3; no. 178, Jul. 4, 1905, p.2; no. 160, Jun. 16, 1905, p.2; and TsGIA fond 1283, opis 1, delo 19 (1905), pp.135, 142, 166, 130–34, 157–59.

now demanded by the entire nation, the marshals made an abrupt political about-face and sent an official delegation to the tsar in support of the most recent zemstvo congress, which had demanded a broad-powered national assembly elected by universal and equal suffrage. By then, the habitually cautious and highly loyal marshals, themselves influential officials who occupied responsible positions in local administration, had become so estranged from the existing political order that they openly declared that "the government has come to represent something alien, hostile, and unbearable."[47] In an unprecedented move, they pointedly dropped the autocratic title from their political petitions to the tsar, and their national leader, the usually mild-mannered and proper Prince P. N. Trubetskoi of Moscow, forgot all vestiges of court etiquette in his political fervor, taking advantage of his reception by the monarch to remind Nicholas II rather curtly of his personal shortcomings as a national leader: "Here today you have the mercy to receive us and to agree with us, but tomorrow you will receive Count Dorrer [the marshal of Kursk province, currently politically isolated on the extreme right wing of the provincial gentry] and you will agree with him."[48]

Trubetskoi's breach of manners was no personal aberration but yet another dramatic sign of the political agitation gripping the most moderate and traditionally minded gentry political activists by midyear. For we must remember that the marshals of the nobility, by virtue of their key administrative role in the localities and the fact that this office was generally considered a good starting point for a career in the Ministry of the Interior, were far more closely bound to state service than most other prominent gentry activists of the time, occupying some shady ground between official servants of the central government and genuinely independent representatives of local landed interests.[49] In addition to the marshals, the far right of the gentry political spectrum—the Patriotic Union, the Union of Russian Men (*soiuz russkikh liudei*), and the June 24 Deputation, elements from which the basic leadership cadre of the future United Nobility was to emerge—responded to the oppositional upsurge among the landed gentry in the summer of 1905 by adding their voice to the clamor for popular representation in national affairs. Only they sought vainly to limit the scope of the coming reforms by calling for autocracy *and* a "*zemskii sobor*," a representative institution of vague authority and duration, elected by the basic estates of the Russian Empire.[50]

Of course, the emergence of a united oppositional front among the landed gentry was not a spontaneous development but the result of considerable organizational work on the part of the liberals. Everywhere the prime impetus to political action in the local zemstvos and noble societies came from the zemstvo congress delegates, aided by *ad hoc* constitutionalist caucuses that had arisen among gentry activists in recent years and were loosely affiliated with the Union of Liberation, the leading liberal organization in 1905, through a national organization of zemstvo constitutionalists. As a result, the more militant and liberal deputies usually arrived at the 1905 meetings of the zemstvo and noble societies with completed draft projects of political addresses already in hand, while the more conservative elements were quite often taken by surprise, unorganized and unprepared. Yet one cannot simply dismiss the oppositional upsurge among the landed gentry in 1904 and 1905 as a largely artificial phenomenon conjured out of thin air by the machinations of the liberals. For the political addresses and resolutions of this period were almost always adopted unanimously or by crushing majorities after thorough discussion in assemblies that were marked by record attendance on the part of official delegates as well as the general public. Moreover, in order to engage in political activity at all, many of these assemblies had first to abandon past practices and to defy openly the orders and regulations of the local administration, which attempted to stifle all manifestations of the Liberation Movement. In the process the 1905 sessions of the local zemstvos became the most turbulent and rebellious in the entire history of these institutions.[51]

Nonetheless, the leftward drift of gentry politics halted abruptly by the years' end, as an all-pervasive, rapidly spreading rank-and-file revolt against the old liberal leadership of the zemstvo movement swept through the local assemblies in the course of the regular winter sessions of the provincial zemstvos. Almost overnight large numbers of zemstvos repudiated the leadership of the 1905 congresses, denying the authority of these assemblies to speak out in the name of the zemstvos of all Russia.[52] Simultaneously, hastily organized coalitions of moderate and conservative elements, led by men who had previously supported the Liberation Movement, arose to challenge the authority of the most enthusiastic supporters of the zemstvo congress in the localities—the more liberal members of the provincial zemstvo executive boards, who had provided both a disproportionately large share of congress delegates and the nuclei of the constitutionalist caucuses that had operated so successfully in the local assemblies throughout 1905. In January and February 1906, 40 percent of the provincial zemstvos currently meeting administered official reproofs to their executive boards; and significantly all but one of the men thus censured were closely connected with the new liberal Constitutional Democratic (Kadet) party, the direct political heir of the Union of Liberation and the 1905 zemstvo congresses.[53]

The turnabout in zemstvo politics was in many ways a product of the times, for by the end of 1905 several important developments had intervened to temper the oppositional fervor of the zemstvos' gentry constituency and to turn them against the leadership of the Liberation Movement. First, the government at long last moved to remedy the most pressing grievances of the gentry by putting an end to the disastrous war with Japan and accepting substantial political reforms in the form of the Bulygin Ukaz of August 6, 1905, and then the October Manifesto. The government's concessions were soon followed by the outbreak of major peasant disorders on the estates of the gentry rivaling in scope and intensity the great Pugachev Rebellion of the eighteenth century. Throughout much of the Black Soil Center in a wide belt stretching from Kursk and Chernigov to the Volga, the agrarian movement not infrequently approached full-scale countywide revolts, characterized by vast property damage as the enraged peasants attempted to "burn out" gentry landowners and prevent their return to the soil.[54] However, the 1905 peasant disorders, unlike the previous serf rebellions or the agrarian movement of 1917, was directed primarily against the *property*, not the person, of the landowner. Consequently few noblemen, if any, perished at the hands of the peasants in 1905, and a large proportion of the disorders reported were confined to meadow and forest lands, most of which had remained in gentry hands after Emancipation, leaving the peasants without adequate amounts of firewood or pasture lands. Nevertheless, the disorders set off a "Great Fear," a wave of mass hysteria among the landed gentry of the provinces, reminiscent of the opening days of the French Revolution of 1789, as large numbers of noble proprietors fled the Russian countryside[55] and attempted to divest themselves of their estates by engaging in mass panic land sales that ultimately resulted in the loss of 10 percent of all remaining noble landholdings during a brief two-year period, 1906–1908.[56]

The impact of the agrarian disorders on zemstvo politics was felt almost immediately, particularly in the Central Agricultural Region and along the Volga, where the disorders were largely concentrated.[57] To be sure, gentry activists did not waver in their support of representative government. On the contrary, ever large numbers of local zemstvos, convinced that only the immediate convocation of a broadly based national assembly could curb popular discontent, went on to embrace legislative powers and the three tails at this time (see tables 6 and 7). Yet the landed gentry's newfound concern for the security of their property was already beginning to overshadow many of their previous political commitments, as demonstrated by the sudden waning of zemstvo concern for the civil liberties of citizens, which had figured prominently in all the addresses and resolutions of 1905. In the winter of 1905–1906, the zemstvos generally remained silent in the face of widespread administrative arrests and other violations of individual rights by the government in an attempt to curb the spreading revolution, prompting the governor of Smolensk province to report with some satisfaction that "those measures undertaken by the government to pacify the country and restore the necessary order, which a year ago would have called forth mass protests in the zemstvo, are presently approved by a majority of the assembly as inevitable and sad necessities."[58] Meanwhile over a third of all provincial zemstvos (twelve assemblies) actively endorsed such measures, petitioning the government to delay the introduction of the "freedoms" promised by the October Manifesto and to continue to rule by martial law until "law and order" had been restored in Russia.[59]

Simultaneously, many assemblies contributed directly to the repressive atmosphere of the times by launching their own political purges of left-wing zemstvo employees, who were held personally responsible for the outbreak of the agrarian revolution. Charging that zemstvo employees had neglected zemstvo business to engage in "revolutionary agitation," the provincial zemstvos began to dismiss dozens of old-time zemstvo employees and to shut down entire areas of vital zemstvo activities. Although the current budgetary problems of the zemstvos were often cited as the reason for this move, the services and personnel eliminated and the geographic incidence of the cutbacks belie these claims.[60] For example, in Saratov, Tula, and Voronezh, the schools closed down in the name of "economy" were precisely the ones that had recently experienced student strikes,[61] while mass firings of zemstvo employees—as opposed to individual dismissals—were inevitably confined to the provinces reporting the highest concentration of peasant disorders at the end of 1905 (Kursk, Saratov, Voronezh, Chernigov, Poltava, Ekaterinoslav, and Simbirsk).[62] At the same time, in spite of the universal concern for "thrift," funding for apolitical services like roads and bridges was not affected by the cutbacks, while money could always be found for conservative or patriotic causes dear to the hearts of the zemstvo men. In Tula, where basic zemstvo services were among the most drastically reduced in all Russia, the provincial zemstvo assembly allocated 25,000 roubles for armed Cossack guards to protect the estates of local landowners.[63] Likewise, the Kharkov zemstvo, which was "forced" to eliminate eight of the eleven zemstvo doctors in the province right after a major cholera scare, still found 10,000 roubles in surplus funds to erect a monument to the defenders of Port Arthur, the site of a major Russian defeat in the Japanese War.[64]

Finally, the agrarian disorders also sparked the rank-and-file revolt against the zemstvo leadership of 1905 by bringing the latent social differences within the zemstvo movement to the surface of zemstvo politics. In general the zemstvo leaders, particularly those associated with the new Kadet party, did not respond to the peasant disorders in the same way as their provincial following. Instead the Kadets, who tended to be the most professionally oriented of the zemstvo leaders— and the least involved with agriculture—attempted to utilize the peasant unrest in order to strengthen their hand in their ongoing conflict with the government, insisting that the sacrifice of part of the gentry's remaining lands was "a small price to pay" for political liberty. As a result, the last two of the 1905 zemstvo congresses—September and November—barely tempered their opposition to the now seemingly conciliatory state, beset on all sides by the expanding revolution; and in hopes of attracting the peasant vote in the coming Duma elections and capturing a majority of seats in the national assembly, they went on to espouse the compulsory expropriation of private landholdings[65] at a time when local gentry activists were beginning to stress the sanctity of private property and to call for more police protection in the countryside.[66] Consequently it is not surprising that a small group of moderate zemstvo men, who subsequently provided the organizing nucleus of the Octobrist Party, withdrew from the national zemstvo congress of November 1905 in protest against recent policies, taking their case to the provinces with striking success.[67] For, in the eyes of their fellow noblemen, the agrarian uprisings had transformed the Kadets from outspoken critics of the bureaucratic state into outright traitors to the noble estate, who were collaborating with the local intelligentsia to politicize the peasant masses and turn them against the landed gentry. Everywhere the most damning charge leveled against the censured Kadet-dominated executive boards was the liberals' close, often personal relationships with the "revolutionary" third element intelligentsia employees of the zemstvos.[68]

Although the position of the Kadets within the zemstvo movement was severely shaken by the outbreak of peasant disorders at the end of 1905, the fate of zemstvo liberalism was not sealed until the experiences of the first two State Dumas had been fully assimilated by the local gentry. For when the long-awaited national assembly finally convened, it was clear that the peasants, aided by the vagaries of the election law and an unexpected display of estate solidarity, had managed to elect a peasant-dominated chamber, in which even the deputies of noble origins, whose ranks included many former leading lights of the zemstvo movement, were committed to the far-reaching —and possibly unlimited—compulsory expropriation of private lands.[69] At the same time, the convocation of a national assembly, contrary to the expectations of gentry political circles, did not pacify the rebellious population. Rather, the agrarian debates in the Duma merely set off a new round of peasant disorders.[70] The gentry's political travails did not end with the untimely dissolution of the First Duma. Quite the opposite, the elections to the Second Duma essentially repeated the experiences of the first elections in spite of greater efforts on the part of moderate and conservative parties and a minor rightward revision of the election law.[71] The new and even more radical Duma seemed likely to enact compulsory expropriation into law *and* to reform local government, including the zemstvos, in a manner that would radically undermine the political hegemony of the gentry in the provinces.

The unexpected peasant victories in the Duma elections not only threatened the livelihood, way of life, and very existence of the gentry constituency of the zemstvos. It fundamentally challenged *both* aspects of their new and rather precarious personal and social identities. By the outbreak of the Revolution of 1905, the basic cadre of zemstvo activists tended to come from that growing stratum of the noble estate that had responded to the economic dislocations of Emancipation and the worldwide depression in grain prices by becoming more and more personally involved with agriculture and the daily management of their family estates. Yet prompted by a lingering "service psychology,"[72] instilled in noble landowners by centuries of gentry education and upbringing and by the legal training received by many of them in the universities, the public service performed by these men was no less important to them and their new social identities than their agricultural concerns. As late as the Third and Fourth State Dumas—1908 and 1912—approximately half of the deputies of noble origins, whose career patterns showed a similar dual involvement with agriculture and provincial affairs, listed "agriculture" as their profession, while an identical proportion considered their occupation to be that of "public activist" (*obshchestvennyi deiatel'*), a broad, almost untranslatable term that was generally applied to all those active in elective offices or philanthropic work outside the confines of the ruling bureaucracy.[73]

The political activity of the local zemstvos and noble societies was deeply rooted in this dual identity of their landowning constituency

in the provinces. The new national assembly that was universally demanded by gentry spokesmen in 1905 was intended to provide the
landed nobility with both an institutionalized voice in the affairs of
state, which were increasingly dominated by a largely landless bureaucracy that did not hesitate to intervene in purely local zemstvo
matters, *and* a political base from which they could fight the current
Witte economic system, which greatly hindered, if not actually
harmed, their agricultural pursuits. Even though the bulk of gentry
activists throughout the course of 1905 had carefully couched their
public political appeals in the name of Russian "society" at large, few
of them privately doubted that the landed gentry, as the most educated
and politically experienced social group in the country, would play a
highly prominent, if not dominant, role in the new national assembly
even under a three- or four-tail franchise. Indeed, this was also the
opinion of the government, which took special pains in preparing the
Duma electoral law to secure the representation of the peasantry from
the probable political incursions of the gentry.[74]

These assumptions were reinforced in the minds of many zemstvo
activists by the paternalistic, often patronizing, attitude toward the
peasant masses that had permeated the Liberation Movement among
the landed gentry from its very inception. Gentry activists of all political complexions failed to regard peasants as an autonomous group.
Consequently, the zemstvo leadership made no attempt to involve the
peasantry in the opposition movement until the summer of 1905, when
all hopes for reforms from above had obviously floundered on the intransigence of Nicholas II, and the lower classes had already moved
into political action on their own, engaging in increasingly widespread
agrarian uprisings and urban rebellions. Even then the prime aim of
the liberal gentry in this regard was to harness the energies of the
Russian people to their own political ends and to direct the mass movement into more pacific channels.[75]

The appearance of large-scale agrarian disorders at the end of 1905
obviously failed to change the landed gentry's general view of the
peasant masses and their future political role. From the first the gentry
rank and file tended to regard the 1905–1906 agrarian disorders as a
natural disaster like a flood or an earthquake. The peasant participants
were regarded not as conscious human beings acting in their own self-
interest but as a wild, unconscious mob, a physical force no more
responsible for its actions than a winter's blizzard or a summer thun-
derstorm. In this way, many of the more conservative gentry activists
readily exonerated the peasantry and increasingly tended to discount

economic factors like peasant poverty or legitimate land hunger as the cause of the peasant unrest, preferring to seek a scapegoat for the agrarian revolution in the third element employees of the zemstvos and their liberal, usually Kadet, patrons on the zemstvo executive boards. Other gentry activists, especially those in the liberal camp— not only Kadets but initially many Octobrists as well—championed a limited form of expropriation, hoping to barter a part of the gentry's remaining landholdings for continued gentry "political hegemony over the peasant masses."[76]

Hence, the peasant sweep of the first two Duma elections came as an enormous surprise to gentry activists of all political camps, striking a direct blow at gentry political pretensions from which the noble landowners of the provinces never fully recovered. Instead of the much desired national assembly that would watch over the economic interests of the landed gentry, the new State Duma threatened the property of private landowners much more drastically than the Witte System at its very worst. Moreover, the unusual group solidarity that the peasants displayed in both the Duma elections and the 1906–1907 zemstvo elections that soon followed[77] threatened to exclude gentry landowners from a meaningful political role not only in the national assembly but also in the localities, as soon as the government's far-reaching projects of zemstvo reform would be adopted by the Duma. As a result, the sudden, totally unexpected advent of the peasantry on the Russian political scene prompted a major relignment of zemstvo politics, transforming institutions that had traditionally served as a liberal, liberalizing force within the Russian social-political order into a highly conservative force, one of the bastions of a widespread and rapidly growing gentry reaction.

The gentry reaction took several forms. Perhaps the most dramatic was the zemstvos' total repudiation of their former liberal leaders, including many men whose names previously had been virtually synonymous with the zemstvo movement. The nationwide campaign against the old left-wing leadership of the zemstvo movement did not subside at the end of the 1905–1906 winter sessions but continued unabated, contributing to the disastrous liberal rout in the zemstvo elections of 1906–1907, when liberalism of the Kadet variety lost once and for all its political base in the zemstvos.[78] The Kadets were cast out of the zemstvo movement at this time because their actions in the first two Dumas in support of compulsory expropriation of private lands revealed once again that they were willing to subordinate the legitimate concerns of the landed gentry to their own political ambitions to emerge the leading political force in these peasant-dominated chambers.

Yet the gentry reaction did not stop with the expulsion of the Kadets from the zemstvos. The zemstvo elections of 1906–1907 marked a decisive and fateful watershed in the history of these institutions. Despite considerable efforts expended by the old "zemstvo majority" of 1905 in alliance with other "progressive" zemstvo men, the liberals were never to regain their previous influence in the zemstvos.[79] On the contrary, subsequent elections resulted in an even greater political setback for the progressive cause, which was irreversibly identified with the immediate results of the Liberation Movement—the peasant disorders and the gentry's minority status in the first two State Dumas. In 1909 and again in 1912 a number of left Octobrists, including D. N. Shipov, the leader of the moderate zemstvo minority at the 1905 congresses and once the most highly venerated zemstvo man in all Russia, suffered the same fate as the 1905 majority before them, going down to a decisive defeat at the hands of a new generation of self-professed "apolitical" zemstvo men who did not deign to affiliate themselves with any of the new national political parties.[80] As a result of these developments, when the right Kadet and future head of the Provisional Government of 1917, Prince G. E. L'vov, the Tula board chairman of 1905 and the national director of zemstvo war relief work during the Russo-Japanese War, was advanced at the beginning of the First World War through a complicated political maneuver on the part of the Kadets to head the All-Russian Union of Zemstvos, he had not served as a zemstvo deputy, even on the county level, for well over four years.[81]

The gentry reaction also entailed a major revision of the political program of the zemstvos. Now realizing that even the limited franchise of the October Manifesto, much less a political order based on full human equality, would entail the loss of their property and political position, the large majority of gentry activists in the localities began to opt for exclusory measures to preserve artificially the political preponderance of the numerically insignificant landed nobility. The change in zemstvo opinion in this regard first appeared in the winter sessions of 1905–1906, when the specter of peasant land hunger prompted a few assemblies to revise their notions of precisely who should constitute the political nation. At that time, the Riazan and Tula zemstvos, both of which had advocated "a broad suffrage" in the summer of 1905,[82] rejected universal and equal elections, accepting the arguments of the Octobrist leader Prince N. S. Volkonskii that "such a system is feasible, but it is scarcely possible to count on positive results from it in view of the present misunderstandings over the land. We would risk that all landowners would be thrown overboard from the state administration; the interests of the minority would not be guaranteed."[83]

In the spring of 1907, after the elections to the first two Dumas had amply borne out Volkonskii's dire predictions, such considerations were made even more explicit by spokesmen for the zemstvo congress, like the Octobrist State Council representative from the Tula zemstvo, M. D. Ershov, a leading member of the United Nobility and of the Organizing Bureau of the 1907 Zemstvo Congress. In 1905 Ershov, as a member of the moderate Shipov minority within the zemstvo congresses, had supported a form of three-tail suffrage—the election of representatives to the national assembly by the local zemstvos, which would first have been reformed according to "democratic principles."[84] By the eve of the 1907 Congress, however, he had substantially amended his earlier views. While Ershov still insisted on the selection of Duma deputies by zemstvos reformed along nonestate lines, he wanted these bodies to be restructured in such a manner as to leave them in the hands of "the present zemstvo men," who would provide the "unconscious" electorate with "an existing cadre of leaders."[85] Ershov's more conservative associate on the congress bureau, the future Nationalist leader P. V. Krupenskii of Bessarabia, stated the issue even more bluntly, declaring that "One hundred thirty million peasants should not lead us; rather we should lead them."[86]

The turnabout in zemstvo opinion on the electorate system was not as drastic as it might seem. Zemstvo commitment to universal and equal suffrage had never been as unambiguous as the many resolutions in favor of such measures might suggest. In fact, the zemstvo gentry had always subordinated the principle of universal suffrage to their own political ambitions. Even in 1904–1905 most zemstvos openly opposed the application of universal suffrage to local self-government, espousing instead a return to the 1864 zemstvo election law, a system weighted in favor of large landed property,[87] while the far more liberal zemstvo congress did not go much beyond a denunciation of the estate-based 1890 electoral law, calling for a type of zemstvo reform that would involve in zemstvo work "the best forces of the local population," a euphemism for the more educated segments of provincial society.[88] Even the reluctance of many local zemstvo assemblies to accept all four of the "tails" demanded by the national zemstvo congress for Duma elections apparently stemmed from a deep-seated, although not entirely conscious fear on the part of many gentry activists that such a franchise might very well deprive noble landowners of their "rightful" share of political influence in national affairs. After all, the argument most frequently advanced by the advocates of three-tail suffrage, which was overwhelmingly preferred by the local zemstvos, was that direct elections (the fourth tail) could not produce "conscious results" since the large electoral districts required by Russian geography would prevent the participants in the political process from being acquainted with one another. What many of these men actually meant by this was that the peasant masses, unlike their elective leaders (the village and volost elders and peasant zemstvo men, who were likely to emerge as electors under any sort of indirect system), would not necessarily recognize or accept as local representatives gentry leaders of the zemstvo of whom they might not even have heard. Instead the peasant masses, in contrast to their leaders who quite often were little more than clients of prominent local noblemen or high administrative figures, might very well respond to the radical programmatic appeals of the revolutionary parties.[89]

The most important manifestation of the gentry reaction, however, was the political organization of the gentry right. The newly mobilized conservative elements among the landed gentry did not stop with revising the political program of the zemstvo movement and effectively eliminating the liberals from provincial politics. They soon adapted the tactics of the Liberation Movement to their own ends, creating a series of political pressure groups and countervailing authorities in the form of the United Nobility and the 1907 Zemstvo Congresses, which emulated the 1905 congresses and attempted quite successfully to mobilize the local zemstvos and noble societies behind a common political program. These organizations contributed to the coming of the June 3, 1907, coup d'état by encouraging the government to dissolve the first two peasant-dominated Dumas and by agitating for a curtailment of the franchise.[90] They also played *the* major role in blocking the attempts of the reformist Prime Minister P. A. Stolypin to expand the role of propertied elements other than the nobility in local self-government, thus achieving a necessary political counterpart to his well-known agrarian reforms.[91] The result of these activities was the Third of June System, an extremely inflexible—and hence potentially unstable—political order in which virtually all elective institutions, on both the national and local levels, were dominated by the numerically small and once more rapidly declining gentry.[92]

The defeat of the First Russian Revolution—and the role played by gentry landowners in this process—gives rise to a perplexing question: why did the liberals expend so much time and energy in mobilizing the landed gentry, a social group inherently inimical to the liberal cause? For the collapse of the liberal gentry opposition of 1905 and the emergence of the gentry reaction were probably foregone conclusions. The gentry opposition of the early twentieth century was never a unitary political movement but rather a strange, Janus-faced amalgam of progressive and retrogressive elements. While the gentry left, particularly the Kadets among them, were motivated by a desire to transform the superannuated autocracy into a modern political society, based on popular sovereignty and the equality of all citizens before the law, the typical provincial landowner was attracted to the Liberation Movement by a desire to regain his lost political influence in the counsels of state.

Nevertheless the future Kadets directed a considerable part of their organizational efforts toward the landed gentry in the early part of the twentieth century because the political—and social—differences within the gentry were not clearly perceived before 1905 and because the landed gentry offered the liberals definite organizational advantages over all other social groupings. Not only was the liberals' approach to the gentry greatly facilitated by the fact that many liberal leaders came from—and continued to operate politically in—this social milieu. But before 1905 the landed gentry alone of all existing social groups possessed an institutionalized political base in the form of the corporations of the nobility and the far more important zemstvo assemblies, the only elective bodies currently purporting at least in theory to represent all the traditional estates of the Russian population. Thus the liberals could simply direct much of their political energies toward these existing institutions without having first to establish an elaborate organizational framework in which to operate. This situation facilitated political work at a time when all independent political associations were strictly prohibited by law, since the so-called classless zemstvos, by virtue of their elective character and all-class composition, could if necessary speak out in the name of Russian society as a whole.

However, the facility of the liberals' approach to the gentry does not provide us with the full answer to our question. A complete explanation of the liberals' concern with the political mobilization of the gentry must take into account fundamental characteristics of the Kadet party and Russian society in general. Because of the enormous social, cultural, and economic chasm that separated the privileged from the people under the Old Regime, the liberals, who overwhelmingly came from the upper strata of Russian society, simply felt more comfortable in directing their political appeals to their own kind. All too many gentry liberals, like their conservative counterparts, tended to regard the worker and peasant masses as little more than childlike creatures, moved mainly by irrational passions and desires.[93] This patronizing attitude toward the masses of the Russian people, which after 1905 would often be tinged with fear and distrust, was the prime reason why Russian liberalism failed to fulfill "the historic task" that many have rightly or wrongly attributed to it, and why the Kadet party did not long outlast the old political order that it so fervently opposed.

NOTES

1. Under the original 1864 Zemstvo Law, the landed nobility provided 42.4 percent of all zemstvo deputies on the uezd level and 81.6 percent on the provincial level. The estate-based 1890 Election Law merely incorporated *de facto* gentry hegemony within the zemstvo institutions into law, giving noble landowners 89.5 percent of all seats in the provincial zemstvos and 55.2 percent in the uezd assemblies. The proportion of noble deputies would, no doubt, be even greater had the Viatka, Vologda, Olonets, and Perm zemstvos been excluded from these estimates, since almost no noble landowners lived in these provinces. B. B. Veselovskii, *Istoriia zemstva za sorok let'* (St. Petersburg, 1909–1911), vol. III, pp.680–82.

2. *Listok osvobozhdenie*, no. 18, pp.1–2.

3. For the full text of the April resolution, see *Postanovleniia kostromskago chrezvychainago zemskago sobraniia s 30 maia po 11-ii iiunia 1905 g.* (Kostroma, 1905), pp.16–30.

4. *Russkiia vedomosti*, no. 251, Sept. 15, 1905, p.3.

5. Only the "peasant zemstvos" of Viatka and Olonets sent greetings to the First State Duma. *Novoe vremia*, no. 10901, Jul. 20/Aug. 2, 1906, p.4; Russia. Gosudarstvennaia duma. *Stenograficheskie otchety 1906 god sessiia pervaia* (St. Petersburg, 1906), vol. I, pp.6–7, 33, 37–8, 253, 587; and Veselovskii, *Istoriia*, IV, pp.38–39.

6. Virtually all the delegates to the First Congress of the United Nobility for whom detailed biographical data are available participated in zemstvo affairs. Among the 133 elected representatives to the First Congress were fifty-eight zemstvo deputies, forty-one uezd marshals of the nobility and twenty-two provincial marshals (the marshals of the nobility chaired the local zemstvo assemblies *ex officio*). For a list of congress participants see TsGAOR fond 434, opis 1, delo 5/4, 1906, pp.278–82. Biographical information on gentry political activists has been derived largely from the sources listed in table 1 below.

7. See TsGAOR fond 434, opis 1, delo 1/2, 1906, pp.121–31, 10–12, and *Kruzhok dvorian vernykh prisiago otchet s"ezda 22–25 aprelia 1906 goda* (Moscow, 1906), esp. pp.14–15.

8. At most only a half dozen of the 359 uezd zemstvos in the country objected to the dismissal of the Duma. Veselovskii, *Istoriia,* IV, pp.38–39.

9. For the relationship of the United Nobility to the June 1907 Zemstvo Congress, see TsGAOR fond 434, opis 1, delo 75, 1906/07, pp.76–124, delo 10/38, 1906/07, p.169, and delo 77/307, 1907, pp.1–3.

10. See the statements of the prime organizers of the congress, Counts A. A. Uvarov and D. A. Olsuf'ev of the Saratov zemstvo, in *Zhurnal chrez-vychainago vologodskago gubernskago zemskago sobraniia 29 maia 1907 goda* (Vologda, 1907), pp.7–9 and Count D. A. Olsuf'ev, *Ob uchastii zemtsy o obsuzhenii zemskoi reformy* (St. Petersburg, 1907), esp. pp.14–15.

11. TsGAOR fond 434, opis 1, delo 76, 1906/07, p.96, and *Zhurnal zasedanii chernigovskago gubernskago zemskago sobraniia chrezvychainoi sessii 1907 goda* (Chernigov, 1907), p.8.

12. *Novoe vremia,* no. 11224, Jun. 13/26, 1907, p.2, and *Golos Moskovy* no. 135, Jun. 12, 1907, p.2.

13. *Stenograficheskie otchety 1-go vserossiskago s"ezda zemskikh deiatelei v Moskve zasedanii 10–15 iiunia 1907 g.* (Moscow, 1907) and *Zhurnaly i postanovleniia vserossiiskago s"ezda zemskikh deiatelei v Moskve s 10 po 15 iiunia 1907 goda* (Moscow, 1907).

14. Vasilii Maklakov, *Vlast' i obshchestvennost' na zakate staroi Rossii* (Paris, 1936), and *The First State Duma* (Bloomington, Indiana, 1964). For western adaptations of the Maklakov thesis, see Viktor Leontowitsch, *Geschichte des Liberalismus in Russland* (Frankfurt am Main, 1957); George Fischer, *Russian Liberalism: from Gentry to Intelligentsia* (Cambridge, 1958); and Shmuel Galai, *The Liberation Movement in Russia 1900–1905* (Cambridge, 1973). In a recent article Gregory Freeze has questioned the applicability of the Maklakov thesis to the period immediately preceding the Revolution of 1905, maintaining that the radicalization of the liberal program was prompted not by a change in the social composition of the liberal movement but by the need to create an all-class coalition against the autocracy. See Gregory Freeze, "A National Liberation Movement and the Shift in Russian Liberalism, 1901–03," *Slavic Review,* vol. XXVIII, no. 1 (Mar. 1969).

15. For a list of the men attending the November 1904 Zemstvo Congress, see *Listok osvobozhdenie,* no. 18, pp.1–2. The elected delegates to the subsequent congresses are listed in TsGAOR fond 102, opis 5, delo 1000/1905, pp.43–46. Biographical information for the congress participants has been derived in the main from the proceedings of the provincial zemstvo assemblies, the *Ukazateli* to all four State Dumas (contained in the stenographic proceedings), and *Vsia Rossiia* (St. Petersburg, 1903, 1912). The only delegates of non-noble origins at the November 1904 Congress—besides the representatives of the so-called peasant provinces who played a very minor role in the national congresses—were V. M. Khizniakov of Chernigov and P. A. Safonov of Kostroma. The noble delegates for whom biographical data was available—over half the total number—owned approximately 1500 *desiatiny* of land on the average, with a median holding of around 1000 *desiatiny.*

16. Even the Kursk zemstvo, the most conservative assembly in the country, did not venture to criticize the way in which zemstvo representatives to the congresses were selected until the end of the year, although the subject

was discussed in the assembly in the summer of 1905. At that time. however, M. Ia. Govorukho-Otrok, soon to be a leading activist in the United Nobility and a successful right wing candidate for board chairman, attacked the government for refusing to allow the Kursk zemstvo to elect their representatives to the congress in an official session. *Zhurnaly zasedanii ekstrennago kurskago gubernskago zemskago sobraniia 10–11 iiunia 1905 goda* (Kursk, 1905), p.18.

17. Paul Miliukov, *Political Memoirs, 1905–1917* (Ann Arbor, 1967), p.19.

18. The constitutionalists held a two-to-one majority at the November 1904 Congress. Of the congress participants whose future political affiliation can be determined with any precision, thirty-seven subsequently joined the Constitutional Democratic (Kadet) party; fifteen the Octobrists; and one the far right, while eleven more adhered to the miniscule "progressive parties" that were to sit between the Kadets and the Octobrists in the State Dumas. In addition, the future Kadets occupied all but one of the seats on the original Organizing Bureau of the Zemstvo Congress. These proportions were to hold for future congresses as well. *Listok osvobozhdenie* no. 18 (Nov. 20/Dec. 3, 1905), pp.1–2 and TSGAOR fond 102, opis 5, delo 1000/1905, pp.43–46 and the sources listed in table 1.

19. Roberta Thompson Manning, "The Russian Provincial Gentry in Revolution and Counterrevolution, 1905–07," (Ph.D. diss., Columbia University, 1975), p.95.

20. For example, the Tver "estate" of Ivan I. Petrunkevich was a bog, purchased in order to acquire the minimum property requirement to participate in the first curia of the zemstvo elections. Prince D. I. Shakhovskoi of Iaroslavl sold the considerable holdings that he had inherited from his parents in order to "spare" his children of the noxious influences of growing up in "a pomeshchik's milieu," while F. I. Rodichev was considered little more than "a gentleman farmer." The *relative* indifference of the Kadets to agriculture should not be unduly exaggerated, for a number of prominent Kadets—D. D. Protopopov of Samara, Prince Pavel Dolgorukov of Moscow, and Prince G. E. L'vov of Tula—were actively involved with the management of their family estates in the years before the Revolution of 1905. However, L'vov and Protopopov both turned away from agricultural concerns after 1905 (L'vov, to sell scrap metal in the city) while Dolgorukov appears to have been more a timber merchant engaged in a large-scale lumber business rather than an ordinary gentry farmer. I. I. Petrunkevich, "Iz zapisok obshchestvennago deiatelia vospominaniia," *Arkhiv russkoi revoliutsii*, vol. XXI (Berlin, 1934); A. Tyrkova-Vil'iams, *Na putakh k svobode* (New York, 1952), pp.110–11; Peter B. Struve, "My Contacts with Rodichev," *Slavonic and East European Review* XII (1933/4), pp.360–61; T. I. Polner, *Zhizhennyi put Kniazia Georgiia Evgenievicha L'vova* (Paris, 1932), esp. pp. 24–33; Prince P. D. Dolgorukov, *Velikaia razrukha* (Madrid, 1964), pp.321–22; and D. D. Protopopov, "Iz nedavniago proshlago (Samara v 1904–05 gg)," *Russkaia Mysl* XXVIII no. 11 (November, 1907), pp.16–35.

21. This, indeed, was how their fellow noblemen tended to perceive them. For example the marshal of the nobility of Tambov province, V. M. Andreevskii, described the Kadets in his memoirs as a group of "lawyers, professors, doctors, etc." V. M. Andreevskii, "Vospominaniia i dr. materialy Vladimir

Mikhailovich Andreevskago v chlena Gos. soveta" (Mss. in the Columbia University Russian Archive), p.55.

22. See Terence Emmons, "The Russian Landed Gentry and Politics," *The Russian Review*, vol. XXXIII, no. 3 (July 1974); Geroid T. Robinson, *Rural Russia Under the Old Regime* (New York, 1932), pp.129–37; and Theodore H. Von Laue, *Sergei Witte and the Industrialization of Russia* (New York, 1963), pp.28, 109–10, 168–69.

23. For a discussion of this development, see Manning, "The Provincial Gentry," pp.19–56.

24. The influential marshal of the nobility of Moscow province, Prince P. N. Trubetskoi, estimated that as many as four-fifths of all noble land-owners were unable by the turn of the century to support their families adequately on their earnings from agriculture alone. TsGIA fond 1283, opis 1–1902, delo 87, pp.11–12. For a good description of the difficulties confronting an individual noble proprietor, see N. A. Pavlov, *Zapiska zemlevladel'tsa* (Petrograd, 1915).

25. Although this process was well under way in the civil service by the early nineteenth century, it seems to have proceeded particularly rapidly in the wake of the abolition of serfdom as the economic conditions of the post-Emancipation era forced many noble proprietors to direct their energies away from the central government toward their estates in the provinces. Marc Raeff, *The Origins of the Intelligentsia: the Eighteenth Century Nobility* (Englewood Cliffs, New Jersey, 1966), pp.107–10; Walter M. Pintner, "The Social Characteristics of the Early Nineteenth Century Bureaucracy," *Slavic Review*, vol. 29 (September 1970), pp.435–38; Walter M. Pintner, "The Russian Higher Civil Service on the Eve of the 'Great Reforms,'" *Journal of Social History*, Spring 1975, pp.55–68; A. P. Korelin, "Dvorianstvo v poreformennoi Rossii (1861–1904 gg.)," *Istoricheskie zapiski*, vol. 87, pp. 91–173; P. A. Zaionchkovskii, "Soslovnyi sostav ofitserskogo korpusa na rubezhe XIX-XX vekov," *Istoriia SSSR*, 1973, no. 1 (January–February), pp. 148–54; and N. Rubakin, *Rossiia v tsifrakh opyt statisticheskoi kharateristiki soslovno-klassovago sostava naselenie russkago gosudarstva* (St. Petersburg, 1912), esp. pp.60–66.

26. By 1905, half of all noble families owned no land at all (compared to 15 percent in 1861), while over two-thirds of the highest officials in the land—the occupants of the first four grades of the state service—held less than 100 *desiatiny* apiece, enough for a sizable summer retreat or even several of them but scarcely a sufficient quantity of land for any serious economic undertaking given the current low level of intensity of Russian agriculture. The remaining third of these high officials clearly belonged to the landed aristocracy, owning on the average more than 14,000 *desiatiny* of land. Thus little room was left at the top of the state service for the average noble landowner who currently held 495 *desiatiny* of land. A. P. Korelin, "Rossisskoe dvorianstvo i ego soslovnaia organizatsia (1861–1904 gg.)," *Istoriia SSSR*, 1971, no. 5, pp.59–60.

27. During the regular winter sessions of 1904–1905, four-fifths of all provincial zemstvos (twenty-eight assemblies) demanded the establishment of a national representative assembly in the face of immense administrative pressures to prevent any political discussions in the zemstvos.

28. The zemstvos concerned were the assemblies of Bessarabia, Viatka, Voronezh, Kostroma, Moscow, Poltava, Samara, Saratov, Smolensk, Tauride, Ufa, Kharkov and Vladimir. *Doklady bessarabskoi gubernskoi zemskoi upravy gubernskomu zemskomu sobraniiu XXXVI ocherednoi sessii v 1904 godu i zhurnaly zasedanii sobraniia* (Bessarabia, 1905), part ii, pp.25–27; *Zhurnaly viatskago gubernskago zemskago sobraniia XXXVIII-i ocherednoi sessii (zasedanii 1–16 dekabria 1904 goda)* (Viatka, 1905), pp.123–27, 143–45, 230; *Zhurnal voronezhskago gubernskago zemskago sobraniia ocherednoi sessii 2–15 ianvaria 1905 g.* (Voronezh, 1905), pp.6–7; *Postanovleniia ekaterinoslavskago gubernskago zemskago sobraniia XXXIX ocherednoi 1904 goda sessii* (Ekaterinoslav, 1905), pp.157–60; *Postanovleniia kostromskago ocherednogo gubernskago zemskago sobraniia sessii 1904 goda* (Kostroma, 1905), pp.27–29, 49; *Postanovleniia moskovskago gubernskago sobraniia ocherednoi sessii 1904 goda* (Moscow, 1905), p.5; *Zhurnaly poltavskago gubernskago zemskago sobraniia 40 ocherednogo sozyva 1904 goda* (Poltava, 1905), pp.7–8; A. N. Naumov, *Iz utselevshikh vospominaniia 1868–1917* (New York, 1954), vol. I, pp.359–62; D. D. Protopopov, "Iz nedavniago proshlago (Samara v 1904–1905 gg.)," *Russkaia mysl'* XXVIII (November 1907), part ii, pp.26–29; *Zemstvo i politicheskaia svoboda: zhurnal kommissii-sobraniia saratovskago gubernskago zemstva* (Paris, 1905), pp.9–30, 57; *Zhurnaly XXXIX ocherednogo saratovskago zemskago sobraniia 9–19 ianvaria 1905 goda* (Saratov, 1905), pp.7–9, 14; "Adresa i zaiavleniia zemskikh sobranii," *Osvobozhdenie*, no. 63, January 20 (7), 1905, pp.11–12, and no. 65, February 9 (January 27), 1905, p.255; *Zhurnaly zasedanii tavricheskago gubernskago zemskago sobraniia XXXIX ocherednoi sessii s 9 po 18 ianvaria 1905 goda* (Tauride, 1905), pp.11–12; *Zhurnaly tverskago ocherednogo gubernskago zemskago sobraniia sessii 1904 goda zasedanii 30 ianvaria–12 fevralia 1905 g.* (Tver, 1905), pp.8–9; *Sbornik postanovlenii ufimskago gubernskago zemskago sobraniia s prilozheniiami XXX ocherednoe sobranie i XXVI chrezvychainoe sobranie 1905 goda* (Ufa, 1905), pp.2–4; *Zhurnaly XL ocherednogo khar'kovskago gubernskago zemskago sobraniia 1905 goda* (Kharkov, 1905), p.6; *Zhurnaly ekstrennykh vladimirskikh gubernskikh zemskikh sobranii 11-go maia i 11-go avgusta 1905 goda* (Vladimir, 1905), p.42.

29. In addition to the zemstvos listed in note 28, the Vologda, Novgorod, Riazan, Simbirsk, Chernigov, and St. Petersburg zemstvos had come to endorse legislative powers. *Zhurnaly vologdskago gubernskago zemskago sobraniia sessii s 19 maia po 5 iiunia 1905 goda* (Vologda, 1905), p.71; *Sbornik postanovlenii zemskikh sobranii novgorodskoi gubernii za 1905 goda* (Novgorod, 1906), pp.30–40; *XXXV chrezvychainoe riazanskoe gubernskoe zemskoe sobranie 1905 goda 27, 28 iiunia* (Riazan, 1905), prilozheniia 21; *Ruskiia vedomosti* No. 209 August 4, 1905, p.2; *Zhurnaly zasedanii chernigovskago gubernskago zemskago sobraniia ekstrennoi sessii 15–23 maia 1905 goda* (Chernigov, 1905), pp.73–74 and prilozheniia 355; and *Zhurnaly zasedanii chrezvychainago S-Petersburgskago gubernskago zemskago sobraniia 16, 18, i 19 maia 1905 goda* (St. Petersburg, 1905), pp.28–29 and prilozheniia p.141.

30. At this time, the Kaluga, Olonets, Orel, and Pskov zemstvos joined those listed in notes 28 and 29 by adhering in full to the political program of the November 1905 Zemstvo Congress minority, which essentially re-

garded the October manifesto as a constitution that established a legislative assembly limiting the autocratic powers of the tsar. *Zhurnaly XLII ochered-nogo kaluzhskago gubernskago zemskago sobraniia s 1 dekabria 1905 g.* (Kaluga, 1906), pp.43–45; *Zhurnaly olonetskago gubernskago zemskago so-braniia sessii XXXIX-i ocherednoi 19 noiabria-17 dekabria 1905 g. i chrez-vychainykh 21–23 marta i 16–17 maia 1906 goda* (Petrozavodsk, 1905); TsGIA fond 1288, opis 2, delo 76–1906, pp.98, 26–27, 83–84, 97; and "Tele-gramy," *Novoe vremia*, no. 10678, December 6/19, 1905, p.2.

31. At the beginning of 1905, the Kazan, Perm, Riazan, Simbirsk, Olonets, and Kursk zemstvos insisted on the preservation of the autocratic powers of the tsar. But by the summer none of the above-mentioned zemstvos that met were using the autocratic title, although the Orel zemstvo, which had fa-vored a consultative assembly the previous winter, now called for the preser-vation of the autocracy. Before the year was out, however, three of these assemblies—the Riazan, Simbirsk, and Orel zemstvos—had rallied to the cause of legislative powers for the national assembly. *Postanovleniia ka-zanskago gubernskago zemskago sobraniia 40 ocherednoi sessii* (Kazan, 1905), part i, p.33; *Zhurnaly permskago gubernskago zemskago sobraniia XXXV ocherednoi sessii i doklady kommissii semu sobraniiu* (Perm, 1905), p.187; *XL ocherednoe riazanskoe gubernskago zemskago sobranie 1904 g. noiabria-dekabria* (Riazan, 1905), p.125; *Zhurnaly simbirskago gubernskago zem-skago sobraniia ocherednoi sessii 1904 g.* (Simbirsk, 1905), p.xiii; *Zhurnaly zasedanii XL ocherednoi kurskago gubernskago zemskago sobraniia 1905 g.* (Kursk, 1905), p. 102; and *Zhurnaly chrezvychainago orlovskago gubern-skago zemskago sobraniia zasedanii 24, 25 iiunia i 20 avgusta 1905 goda* (Orel, 1905), pp.3–16.

32. In the summer of 1905, four-tail suffrage was advocated by the Vo-logda, Novgorod, Saratov, Simbirsk, Tver, Ufa, Chernigov, Kostroma, Mos-cow, and Iaroslavl zemstvos. In the autumn they were joined by the Vladimir assembly but by then the Vologda zemstvo had repudiated the fourth tail—direct suffrage.

33. Of the assemblies concerned, the Vologda, Novgorod, Saratov, Sim-birsk, Tver, Ufa, Chernigov, Kostroma, and Moscow zemstvos favored a four-tail electoral system, while the Orel and Tauride assemblies sup-ported three tails and the Voronezh, Smolensk, and Kharkov zemstvos rec-ognized four tails as "ideal" but recommended three-tail suffrage for the first elections. *Zhurnaly vologodskago gubernskago zemskago sobraniia sessii s 19 maia po 5 iiunia 1905 goda* (Vologda, 1905), pp.71–72; and prilozheniia pp.787–88; *Sbornik postanovlenii zemskikh sobranii novgorod-skoi gubernii za 1905 goda*, vol. I, pp.30–40; *Zhurnaly tverskago ochered-nogo gubernskago zemskago sobraniia sessii 1904 goda zasedanii 10 ian-varia–12 fevralia 1905 g. i chrezvychainago sobraniia 7–9 iiunia 1905 g.*, p.1107; *Sbornik postanovleniia ufimskago gubernskago zemskago sobraniia s prilozheniiam XXX ocherednoe sobranie i XXXVI chrezvychainoe sobranie 1905 goda*, p.1096; *Zhurnaly zasedanii chernigovskago gubernskago zem-skago sobraniia ekstrennoi sessii 15–23 maia 1905 goda*, pp.227–28; *Posta-novleniia kostromskago chrezvychainago gubernskago zemskago sobraniia s 30 maia po 1 iiunia 1905 g. i ocherednogo gubernskago zemskago sobraniia sessii 1905 g.*, pp.35–41; *Zhurnaly voronezhskago gubernskago zemskago so-*

braniia chrezvychainoi sessii 1–3 iiulia 1905 goda (Voronezh, 1905), pp.13–22; *Zhurnaly chrezvychainago khar'kovskago gubernskago zemskago sobraniia 12 iiunia 1905 goda* (Khar'kov, 1905), p.84; *Zhurnaly chrezvychainago orlovskago gubernskago zemskago sobraniia 24–25 iiunia i 20 avgusta 1905 goda*, pp.20–35; *Zhurnaly zasedanii tavricheskago gubernskago zemskago sobraniia chrezvychainoi sessii s 7 po 8 iiunia 1905 goda* (Tauride, 1905), p.11; and *Russkiia vedomosti*, no. 163, June 19, 1905; no. 194, July 20, 1905; and no. 209, August 4, 1905.

34. In addition to the zemstvos listed in note 33, the Kaluga, Olonets, Poltava, Pskov, Vladimir, Iaroslavl, Perm, Orel, and St. Petersburg zemstvos had come to support three-tail suffrage while the Nizhnii Novgorod zemstvo now supported universal suffrage. *Zhurnaly XLII ocherednogo kaluzhskago gubernskago zemskago sobraniia s 1 dekabria po 11 dekabria 1905 g.*, pp.43–45; *Zhurnaly ochered. vladimirskago gub. zem. sobraniia ochered. ses. 1905 g.* (Iaroslavl, 1906), p.199; *Zhurnaly permskago gub. zem. sobraniia XXXVI ochered. ses.* (Perm, 1906), p.78; *Zhurnaly olonetskago gub. zem. sobraniia ses. XXXIX-i ochered. 19 noiabria–17 dekabria 1905 g.*, p.122; TsGIA fond 1288, opis 1, delo 76–1906, p.98; *Zhurnaly poltavskago gubernskago zemskago sobraniia 41 ochered. sozyva 1905 goda* (Poltava, 1906), p.15; *Zhurnaly zasedanii S-Petersburgskago gub. zem. sobraniia sorokovoi ochered. ses. 1–21 dekabria 1905 goda* (St. Petersburg, 1905), p.27; and *Novoe vremia*, no. 10678, December 6/19, 1905, p.2.

35. The assemblies concerned were the Vologda, Ekaterinoslav, Kazan, Kaluga, Olonets, Orel, Penza, Poltava, Pskov, St. Petersburg, and Tauride zemstvos.

36. *Russkiia vedomosti*, no. 199, July 25, 1905, p.2, and P. P. Maslov, *Agrarnyi vopros* (St. Petersburg, 1908), vol. II, pp.198–201.

37. It is true that the chairmen and members of the zemstvo executive boards did receive a salary for their efforts. See Terence Emmons, "The Beseda Circle, 1899–1905," *Slavic Review*, September 1973, p.468. Emmons has estimated that the salary of a provincial board chairman compared favorably with those of state officials, university professors and physicians; however, it is not clear whether the much lower salaries paid to the members of zemstvo boards and to uezd board chairmen were as generous. V. F. Shlippe, the chairman of the Vereisk uezd zemstvo board (Moscow province) maintained in his memoirs that his salary as chairman did not cover the extensive amount of travelling that the post required. V. F. Shlippe, untitled memoirs (Mss. in the Columbia University Russian Archive), pp. 86–87.

38. For a perceptive discussion of the differences in the social composition of the zemstvos and noble societies, see V. F. Gurko, *Features and Figures of the Past* (Stanford, 1939), pp.204–205.

39. A. P. Korelin, "Rossiskoe dvorianstvo i ego soslovnaia organizatsiia (1861–1904 gg.)," *Istoriia S.S.S.R.*, 1971, no. 5, pp.75–76.

40. At that time, the noble assemblies of seventeen of the thirty-four zemstvo provinces with elected marshals (the societies of Bessarabia, Ekaterinoslav, Kazan, Kaluga, Kostroma, Kursk, Moscow, Nizhnii Novgorod, Novgorod, Orel, Pskov, Riazan, Samara, St. Petersburg, Tver, Ufa, and Iaroslavl) met and only a single one of them—Ekaterinoslav—neglected to adopt

a political resolution. For summaries of these meetings and the addresses adopted by them, see TsGIA fond 1283, opis 1, delo 19 (1905), pp.1–2, 8–9, 15–16, 63–64, 119; *Novoe vremia*, no. 10346, December 18/31, 1904, p.2; no. 10348, December 20, 1904/January 2, 1905, p.2; no. 10371, January 19/ February 1, 1905, p.13; no. 10375, January 23/February 5, 1905, p.3; no. 10378, January 26/February 8, 1905, p.14; no. 10382, January 30/February 12, 1905, p.6; no. 10384, February 1/14, 1905, p.5; no. 10387, February 4/17, 1905, p.5; no. 10414, March 3/16, 1905, p.1; *Russkiia vedomosti*, no. 340, December 7, 1904, p.3; no. 20, January 22, 1905, p.3; no. 22, January 24, 1905, p.1; no. 25, January 27, 1905, p.2; no. 50, February 21, 1905, p.3; *Grazhdanin*, XXXIX, no. 8, January 27, 1905, p.20; *Khoziainin*, no. 6, February 10, 1905, pp.226–27; and *Pravital'stvennyi vestnik*, December 15, 1904, p.3.

41. The noble societies concerned were Bessarabia, Kazan, Kaluga, Kostroma, Kursk, Nizhnii Novgorod, Novgorod, Pskov, St. Petersburg, Samara, Tver, Ufa, and Iaroslavl.

42. 58.5 percent of the noble societies meeting in the winter of 1904–1905 (ten assemblies) called for the retention of the autocracy. The assemblies concerned were the Kazan, Kursk, Moscow, Novgorod, Orel, Riazan, Samara, St. Petersburg, Tver and Ufa nobilities.

43. In the winter of 1904–1905 the omission of the title "Autocrat" from many of these addresses and petitions should be regarded more as the result of a political compromise between various factions within a given noble assembly rather than as a conscious desire on the part of the majority of the assembly to limit the powers of the tsar. However, the neglect of this title was no trivial matter. As late as the mid-nineties, when the Tver zemstvo presented Nicholas II with an address that did not contain this salutation, the monarch was so outraged that the political rights of its author, F. I. Rodichev, were abrogated for over a decade.

44. Only the nobilities of Samara and Kursk wished to limit the national representative body to delegates of the nobility.

45. At that time, little more than nine noble assemblies located in zemstvo provinces were able to meet because of the revolutionary conditions prevailing in many provinces. The assemblies concerned were the Vladimir, Ekaterinoslav, Kazan, Kursk, Nizhnii Novgorod, Orel, Tambov, Tula, and Iaroslavl nobilities. Of these only the Vladimir assembly used the autocratic title and only Kursk neglected to endorse the October Manifesto. The latter, however, for the first time that year made no reference to the autocracy. See TsGIA fond 1283, opis 1–1906, delo 15, pp.2, 8–9, delo 12 (1906), pp.14–15, and delo 11 (1905), p.48; TsGAOR fond 434, opis 1, delo 3/3, pp.32–33; *Novoe vremia*, no. 10728, Jan. 25/Feb. 7, 1906, p.1; no. 10757, Feb. 24/ Mar. 9, 1906, p.5; and no. 10769, Mar. 8/21, 1906, p.2; *Russkiia vedomosti*, no. 33, Feb. 3, 1906, and no. 65, Mar. 8, 1906, p.3; and *Rossiia*, no. 16, Jan. 19, 1906, p.1.

46. TsGIA fond 1283, opis 1, delo 19 (1905), pp.23–27; *Osvobozhdenie*, no. 63, Jan. 20/7, 1905, pp.222–23; and Princess Olga Trubetskaia, *Kniaz S.N. Trubetskoi (Vospominaniia sestry)* (New York, 1953), pp.90–91.

47. TsGIA fond 1283, opis 1, delo 19 (1905), pp.149–54, and *Osvobozhdenie*, no. 75, Aug. 16/3, 1905, pp.431–32.

48. Trubetskaia, p.149.

49. For a discussion of the role and duties of the marshals of the nobility, see M. A. Katkov, *Rol' uezdnykh predvoditelei dvorianstva v gosudarstvennom upravlenie Rossii K voprosu o reforme uezdnogo upravlenie* (Moscow, 1914), and Count Constantine Benckendorff, *Half a Life: Reminiscences of a Russian Gentleman* (London, 1954), p.124.

50. *Novoe vremia*, no. 10529, Jun. 26/Jul. 9, 1905, p.1, and *Russkiia vedomosti*, no. 170, Jun. 26, 1905, p.2.

51. A number of assemblies at this time undertook "zemstvo strikes," the interruption or termination of a zemstvo meeting as a form of political protest. See Manning, "The Russian Provincial Gentry," pp.120–26.

52. At this time only one provincial zemstvo assembly—that of Kostroma—gave the November 1905 congress majority its unqualified support, and it did so by a very narrow margin, while fifteen of the thirty-four provincial zemstvo assemblies explicitly denied the authority or the representative nature of the congress. TsGIA fond 1288, opis 2, delo 76–1906.

53. Five of the nine board chairmen censured by their assemblies at this time were actual members of the Kadet Party (Prince G. E. L'vov of Tula, V. P. Obninskii of Kaluga, F. A. Golovin of Moscow, A. D. Iumatov of Saratov and S. M. Barataev of Simbirsk), and a sixth (A. K. Paramonov of Kherson) later supported the Kadets in the First Duma. Two others (Baron A. F. Stuart of Bessarabia and N. V. Raevskii) were considered "progressives," but they were closely associated with the zemstvo majority throughout 1905. Only in Poltava was the chairman of a censured board affiliated with the Octobrist Party. Yet the case of Poltava appears to be the exception that proves the rule since the object of the assembly's attacks was not so much the Octobrist chairman, F. A. Lizogub, as the board member V. Ia. Golovnia, the editor of a local Kadet-oriented newspaper, *Poltovshchina*. For after the board resigned under the pressure of the assembly, all members except Golovnia were immediately reelected by large majorities. TsGIA fond 1288, opis 2, delo 76–1906, pp.252, 157; *Novoe vremia*, no. 10731, Jan. 28/Feb. 10, 1906, p.4; *Chrezvychainoe gubernskoe zemskoe sobranie 28 iiunia 1905 goda. Doklady Bessarabskoi gubernskoi zemskoi upravy gubernskomu zemskomu XXXVIII ocherednoi sessii v 1905 goda i zhurnaly zasedaniia sobranii chrezvychainoe gubernskoe zemskoe sobranie 25 marta 1906 goda* (Kishnev, 1906), vol. II, pp.180–98, 68–79, 91–113, 174–75, 239; *Zhurnaly poltavskago gubernskago zemskago sobraniia 41 ocherednogo sozyva 1905 goda* (Poltava, 1906), pp.9–10; *Zhurnaly ocherednogo saratovskago gubernskago zemskago sobraniia sessii 1905 goda* (Saratov, 1906), pp.383–534; *Zhurnaly zasedanii XLII ocherednogo kaluzhskago gubernskago zemskago sobraniia s 1 dek. po 11 dek. 1905 g.* (Kaluga, 1906), pp.52–62; *Postanovleniia moskovskago gubernskago zemskago sobraniia chrezvychainoi sessii 1906 goda 17–28 fevralia i 10 aprelia 1906 goda* (Moscow, 1906), pp.50–86; *Zhurnaly chrezvychainago tul'skago gubernskago zemskago sostoiashagosia 20–28 fevralia 1906 goda vmesto ne razreshennago g. ministrom vnutrennikh del XLI ocherednogo* (Tula, 1906), pp.40–44, 122; *Zhurnaly simbirskago gubernskago zemskago sobraniia ocherednoi sessii 1905 goda* (Simbirsk, 1906), pp.cviii–cii, 180; *Khersonskoe gubernskoe zemskoe sobranie chrezvychainoi*

sessii 21–23 fevralia 1906 goda i doklady komissii (Kherson, 1906), pp. 125–30.

54. See S. M. Dubrovskii, *Krest'ianskoe dvizhenie v revoliutsii 1905–07 g.g.* (Moscow, 1956); "Agrarnoe dvizhenie v Rossii v 1905–06 g.g.," *Trudy vol'nogo ekonomicheskago obshchestva* 1908, nos. 3–5, and *Novoe vremia* for October, November, and December, 1905.

55. See, for example, *Novoe vremia*, no. 10673, Dec. 1/14, 1905, p.6 and no. 10676, Dec. 4/17, 1905, p.6.

56. I. G. Drozhdov, *Sud'by dvorianskago zemlevladeniia v Rossii i tendentsii k ego mobilizatsii* (Petrograd, 1917), pp.25–29, 64–68.

57. Most of the zemstvos cited by the Ministry of the Interior as persisting in their "radicalism" were located in regions that did *not* experience major peasant disturbances. See TsGIA fond 1288, opis 2, delo 76–1906, p.245.

58. TsGIA fond 1288, opis 2, delo 76–1906, p.197. At this time only the Vladimir and Khárkov provincial zemstvos objected to the mass arrests of local public activists. *Zhurnaly ocherednogo vladimirskago gubernskago zemskago sobraniia 1905 goda*, pp.46–47, and *Zhurnaly khar'kovskago gubernskago zemskago sobraniia chrezvychainykh sessii 18 marta i 18 aprelia 1906 goda* (Kharkov, 1906), pp.37–40.

59. The assemblies concerned were the Vologda, Kaluga, Olonets, Orel, Poltava, Pskov, St. Petersburg, Voronezh, Moscow, Ekaterinoslav, Perm, and Smolensk zemstvos. Only two provincial zemstvos—Ufa and Kazan—demanded the immediate introduction of the civil freedoms promised by the October Manifesto.

60. See V. Golubev, "Zemskaia reaktsiia," *Bez zaglaviia* 1906, no. 4, pp. 137–38, for the most concise analysis of the financial problems of the zemstvos at this time. See also TsGIA fond 1288, opis 2, delo 76–1906, pp.251–52, 11–12, 21–29, 79–90, 166–68, 180–84, 197–216, 226, 238, 244–50; *Russkaia mysl*, Mar. 1906, p.224; "Zemskoe obozrenii," *Samoupravlenie*, no. 1 and no. 2 (Nov. 10, 1906, and Dec. 15, 1906); and B. B. Veselovskii, "Koe shto o nastroeniakh zemlevladel'tsev," *Obrazovanie*, April 1906.

61. *Bez zaglaviia*, 1906, no. 4, p.138 and TsGIA fond 1288, opis 2, delo 76-1906, pp.11–12.

62. *Bez zaglaviiai*, 1906, no. 4, p.138; TsGIA fond 1288, opis 2, delo 76-1906, pp.252, 28; *Novoe vremia*, no. 10726, Jan. 23/Feb. 5, 1906, p.5 and no. 10710, Jan. 7/20, 1906, p.5.

63. *Zhurnaly chrezvychainago tul'skago gubernskago zemskago sobraniia sostaishagosia 20–28 fevralia 1906 goda* (Tula, 1906), pp.21–26, 68, 73, 39–40.

64. *Russkiia vedomosti*, no. 21, Jan. 22, 1906, p.2.

65. Ibid., no. 251, Sept. 15, 1905, p.3; no. 254, Sept. 18, 1905, pp.3–4; and *Novoe vremia*, no. 10609, Sept. 14/27, 1905, p.2; no. 10051, Nov. 9/22, 1905, p.5.

66. See Manning, "The Russian Provincial Gentry," pp.314–36.

67. To be sure, the Octobrist leaders also initially endorsed a limited form of compulsory expropriation, breaking with the Kadets over their attitude toward the government. However, the men who flocked to support the Octobrists in their campaign against the old zemstvo leadership did not ac-

cept this part of the Octobrist program. Consequently provincial pressure forced the party to revise its agrarian program drastically at the Second Octobrist Party Congress in February 1906. *Novoe vremia*, no. 10730, Jan. 27/Feb. 9, 1906, p.2, and D. N. Shipov, *Vospominaniia i dumy o perezhitom* (Moscow, 1918), pp.421–22.

68. *Novoe vremia*, no. 10755, Feb. 22/Mar. 7, 1906, p.4.

69. Approximately half of the deputies to the first two State Dumas were members of the peasant estate, while only a third of the deputies came from the nobility. Warren B. Walsh, "The Composition of the Dumas," *The Russian Review*, vol. 8, no. 2 (1949), pp.111–16. See Manning, "The Russian Provincial Gentry," pp.362–63, 514–15.

70. Dubrovskii, pp.42–57.

71. Aleksei Smirnov, *Kak proshli vybory vo 2-ii gosudarstvennuiu dumy* (St. Petersburg, 1907).

72. The phrase is that of the Saratov landowner and gentry activist N. A. Pavlov. Pavlov, p.79.

73. Of the 216 persons of noble origins in the Third State Duma, approximately one-quarter (fifty-four persons) described their occupation as that of "agriculture," while forty-four described their vocation as "public activists." The proportions remained roughly the same for the Fourth Duma. Of the 210 nobles in that assembly, fifty-three cited agriculture as their profession, while thirty-five called themselves public activists. It is indicative of the confused social consciousness of the times that yet another quarter of the noble deputies who possessed virtually identical career patterns did not apply either of these terms to themselves and failed to list a profession. See Russia. Gosudarstvennaia duma. *Tretei sozyv gosudarstvennoi dumy. Portrety, biografii i avtobiografii* (St. Petersburg, 1910), and *Chetvertyi sozyv gosudarstvennoi dumy. Khodozhestvennyi fototipicheskii al'bom s portretami i biografiiami* (St. Petersburg, 1913).

74. Petrunkevich, pp.386–87 and *Petergofskoe soveshchanie o proekte gosudarstvennoi dumy* (Berlin, no date), cited in Gilbert S. Doctorow, "Institutional Reform, 1905–07" (Columbia University seminar paper, 1970), p.26.

75. For the leading zemstvo activists' attitudes toward the peasantry, see the debates on the July 1905 Zemstvo Congress's Appeal to the People in *Osvobozhdenie*, no. 76, and TsGAOR fond 102, opis 5, delo 1000/1905.

76. See, for example, the article by Prince D. I. Shakovskoi in Prince P. D. Dolgorukov and I. I. Petrunkevich (eds.), *Agrarnyi vopros* (Moscow, 1905), vol. I.

77. TsGIA fond 1288, opis 2–1907, pp.19–20, 26, 31–32, 38; *Samouprav-lenie*, no. 27, Jul. 14, 1907, p.17; and B. B. Veselovskii, "Zemskoe nastroeniia (po povodu sessii uezdnykh sobranii)," *Obrazovanie*, XV, no. 11 (Nov. 1906), part ii, pp.52–53.

78. TsGIA fond 1288, opis 2, delo 2–1907, pp.2–52, and Veselovskii, *Istoriia zemstva*, IV, p.58.

79. For examples of such attempts, see TsGAOR fond 102, opis 9, delo 35/108, pp.4–6, 24–27, 261–66, and Shipov, pp.519–31.

80. Ruth Delia MacNaughton, "The Provincial Nobility and Political Trends in the Zemstvo, 1906–1910" (Columbia University M.A. essay, 1972), p.114.

81. Like Shipov, L'vov was defeated in the 1909–10 elections in his home uezd of Aleksinsk (Tula), seat of his family estate. However, he had not served in the provincial zemstvo since 1907, when he was ousted as board chairman and provincial deputy. Shlippe, pp.154–59 and T. I. Polner, *Zhiznennyi put Kniazia Georgiia Evgenievicha L'vova* (Paris, 1932), pp.175–77, 127.

82. *XXXV chrezvychainoe riazanskoe gubernskoe zemskoe sobranie 1905 goda 27, 28 iiunia* (Riazan, 1905), pp.21–22; *Zhurnaly chrezvychainago tul'skago gubernskago zemskago sobraniia 16–17 iiulia 1905 goda; Zhurnal chrezvychainago tul'skago gubernskago zemskago zasedaniia 5 noiabria 1905* (Tula, 1905), pp.3–4.

83. *41 ocherednoe riazanskoe gubernskoe zemskoe sobranie 1905 g.*, pp. 125–28, and *Russkiia vedomosti* no. 309, Nov. 23, 1905, p.1.

84. Shipov, pp.312–13.

85. M. D. Ershov, *Zemskaia reforma v sviaze s gosudarstvennym izbiratel'nym zakonom* (St. Petersburg, 1907).

86. *Stenograficheskie otchety 1-go vserossiiskago s"ezda zemskikh deiatelei v Moskve zasedanii 10–15 iiunia 1907 g.* (Moscow, 1907), p.32. The reader must not assume, however, that gentry activists in 1907 agreed on the *means* by which they could assure their political preponderance over those "one hundred thirty million peasants." The Octobrist leadership, including Ershov, tended to favor an electoral system based on the amount of zemstvo taxes paid, weighted toward the wealthier taxpayers, while the gentry right preferred elections by estates. Most moderates—including many rank-and-file Octobrists—wanted the electoral system to be based on *landownership*, maintaining that the tax system favored by the Octobrist leaders would unduly favor the owners of commercial and industrial property over the gentry. The 1907 Zemstvo Congress adhered to the moderate position, while the more conservative United Nobility opted for a compromise between elections by estates and a system based on landownership. Nevertheless, the main concern of *all* the gentry activists involved was to insure the position of the landed nobility within the new political order. Ibid., pp.12–54, 66–143, 155–213. *Zhurnal i postanovleniia vserossiiskago s"ezda zemskikh deiatelei v Moskve s 10 po 15 iiunia 1907 goda* (Moscow, 1907), pp.52–59, and *6-i material po voprosu o mestnoi reforme postanovleniia chrezvychainykh i ocherednykh gubernskikh dvorianskikh sobranii po voprosu o mestnoi reforme* (St. Petersburg, 1908).

87. In the course of 1904–1905 virtually all the provincial zemstvos demanded the repeal of the 1890 estate-based election law; but only the Vladimir zemstvo assembly wished to replace it with four-tail suffrage. Most of the others espoused a return to the 1864 franchise, based on landed property, or a system founded on the amount of zemstvo taxes paid. For examples of these resolutions, see *Pravo*, nos. 26 and 27 (June, 1904), and the sources listed in notes 27–30.

88. *Listok osvobozhdenie* no. 18, p.1.

89. However, the elections to the first two Dumas demonstrated that the gentry moderates' wager on indirect elections alone was rather misplaced.

90. For a detailed discussion of these events, see Manning, "The Russian Provincial Gentry," pp.514–609.

91. V. S. Diakin, "Stolypin i dvorianstvo (proval mestnoi reformy)," *Problemy krest'ianskogo zemlevladenie i vnutrennoi politiki Rossii Dookiabr'-skoi period* (Leningrad, 1972), pp.231–74.

92. The only elective institutions in the Third of June System that remained outside the domination of the landed gentry were the city dumas. See the paper by MacNaughton and Manning, this volume, p.185.

93. The best examples of such attitudes can be found in the proceedings of the July, September, and November 1905 Zemstvo Congresses as well as the more conservative 1907 Zemstvo Congresses. See *Osvobozhdenie*, no. 76, Sept. 1612, 1905; TsGAOR fond 102, opis 1, delo 1000/1905, Ch. I to 4; *Novoe Vremia*, no. 10651, Nov. 9/12, 1905; *Russkiia vedomosti*, XLII, nos. 295–96, Nov. 9–10, 1905, and no. 302, Nov. 16, 1905; N. Stroev *Istoricheskii moment I. Moskovskii s"ezd zemskii i gorodskikh deiatelia* (St. Petersburg, 1906), and *Stenografichskie otchety 1-go vserossiskago s"ezda zemskikh deiatelei v Moskve zasedanii 10–15 iiunia 1907 g. passim.*

The Octobrists and
the Gentry, 1905-1907:
Leaders and Followers?

MICHAEL C. BRAINERD

The crisis of 1905 created a new political environment in Russia. The social upheaval and governmental collapse did not quite add up to a revolution. Yet the endemic and mounting tensions under the old regime had now burst out into the open. Precariously balanced relationships and conventional patterns of deference were irrevocably destroyed. Social, economic, and ethnic cleavages were exacerbated, and the vital concerns of Russian subjects of all classes became suddenly politicized. Moreover, new institutions were created: a limited monarchy, a unified cabinet headed by a premier, a broadly representative legislature, and political parties. Thus, Russia was propelled, without benefit of a gradual transition, from absolutism into the age of mass politics, from the eighteenth century into the twentieth.

If the landowning gentry did not wish to have reforms forced upon them, if they wished to defend as much as possible of their economic, political, and social advantages, they would have to play an active role in the period of recovery. As the state emerged from the crisis of 1905, the gentry[1] was presented with several alternatives. One possible response to the new circumstances was to absorb and develop the tradition of zemstvo liberalism—traditions that encompassed the political idealism of the 1870s as well as the humanitarian and economic "small deeds" of the eighties, and that had been renewed in the national congress movement after 1896. It was the legacy of the finest spirits the provincial nobility had produced, imbued with a sense of responsibility for the rural community, profoundly moral and antibureaucratic. Here perhaps was a political tradition that the gentry could call its own, and through which it could serve the nation. But zemstvo liberalism had unmistakable shortcomings: it was parochial, essentially rural, and too patiently meliorist for a time of crisis. It was founded on the assumption that landowners and villagers could work together peacefully to resolve common problems—a premise that was being challenged by vivid evidence of class conflict in the countryside. The "illuminations" of 1905 (burning of manor houses and outbuildings) might be regarded as a passing phase of excess, but the first Duma elections in early 1906, in which peasant majorities blackballed gentry candidates and demanded massive expropriation of estate lands as the legislature's first priority, showed that cooperation was most probably a fantasy.

A second alternative was to reinvigorate the noble *soslovie,* to exploit the privileges of the first estate. The gentry dominated the zemstvos and could turn these bodies to the defense of the landowners against the intelligentsia and the peasants. Moreover, the *dvorianstvo* possessed its own representative institutions, the assemblies of the nobility, which had the right to petition the ruler directly. The events of 1905 and the victory of radicals in the zemstvo congresses revitalized the corporate nobility. In 1906 its representatives met in a national congress and a permanent organization, the United Nobility, was created to act as an extraparliamentary pressure group on behalf of the legal and economic privileges of the nobility. But *soslovnost'* was a concept manifestly outdated in the twentieth century, and its advocates were backward-looking at a time when, as even conservatives admitted, modernization was unavoidable. It bore little relation to economic and social reality—and indeed ran contrary to it, for the exercise of their privileges isolated the nobility, unnecessarily antagonized other social groups, and exposed the weakness of the landowners. The government, threatened by intelligentsia constitutionalism on one side and massive peasant rebellion on the other, might simply decide that the gentry were superfluous.[2] The gentry must appear to act not for themselves alone but for the welfare of the state and the whole nation.

There was still another alternative: the Russian gentry could adapt to the parliamentary form of politics and organize a political party. This alternative was represented by the Union of October 17, one of the two principal parties that grew out of the zemstvo congresses. At the congress of zemstvo and city representatives that met in November 1905, the minority, led by the founders of the Union, held that the majority, dominated by the Constitutional Democrats, had lost its mandate.[3] This was so not only because the congresses had adopted a radical political and social program but especially because the majority had refused to acclaim the Imperial Manifesto of October 17, creating a representative legislature and promising civil liberties. The moderate minority declared:

> The congress, insofar as it speaks for provincial Russia, should have assisted in calming society and rendered its support to the government, instead of dictating the conditions of its exacting program. . . . We think that the zemstvo assemblies and city dumas which sent us would have adopted different resolutions in a political crisis of such severity. They would have considered it their duty to assist the government. . . .[4]

Thus the Octobrists took their stand in the mainstream of pre-1905, loyal zemstvo liberalism.

While this might seem a step backward, it offered a possibility of something quite new. Octobrism's dual base in the two "solid" classes of local self-government, the landowners and urban property owners, contained a potential for leadership more consistent with the program of general modernization and with a representative legislature. The Octobrists were not a party of the gentry alone and could thus give a more "national" color to their activities. At the same time, the Union never had any serious appeal for workers and peasants; thus, it was tacitly but solidly grounded in the interests of private property. Realization of Octobrism's potential depended in part, however, on whether, after the immediate revolutionary threat subsided, the gentry could transcend the boundaries of *soslovie*, particularly the traditional values and interests separating them from urban property owners.

The Union of October 17 combined two very different strains of political thought and two diverse futures lay before it. It could follow the program of moderate gentry liberalism, the harmonious vision of a reconciliation of social conflict and removal of the bureaucratic obstacle between tsar and people. Or it could develop along the lines of a partisan political party, drawing its support mainly but not exclusively from Russia's propertied classes. From 1905 to 1907 the Union's leaders wrestled with this choice (which was not, of course, as clear to them as we see it historically). During that time support for their position was tested several times in Duma elections. Finally, in October 1907, when the Third Duma convened, the Octobrists formed the largest party group (*fraktsiia*) in it, though they lacked a majority. Whom did this fraction represent? What were the implications of the Union's difficult first years for the success or failure of the Third Duma?

These are questions that must be answered before Russia's constitutional period can properly be understood.

At its founding, the Union was headed by a man who personified moderate gentry liberalism and whose national reputation and influence were the Octobrists' greatest asset. President of the Moscow zemstvo board for a decade, D. N. Shipov (1851–1920) had been, at the turn of the century, the zemstvos' principal spokesman in their resistance to the policies of the Witte government. As the initiator of the clandestine zemstvo congress of 1902, Shipov had fathered the zemstvo "movement" but came to dissent from the constitutionalist majority after November 1904.

Shipov's political philosophy was rooted in Slavophile monarchism rather than western liberalism, and it was thoroughly moral and religious.[5] Reform in Russia, he believed, should be consonant with Russian cultural traditions, and its goal should be to restore the lost spiritual bond between tsar and people. Constitutional separation of powers, as practiced in the West, he found repugnant, because it implied a conflict of interests and was, therefore, alien to the Russian understanding of life.[6] By the same logic, "politics," as the word is generally understood, was equally alien to Shipov's intellectual tradition.[7] He bitterly resented at first the tsar's decision in August 1905 to take the constitutional path. Nevertheless, once the constitutional principle had received official endorsement, Shipov first resigned himself to the fact and then consistently advocated a faithful adherence to the chosen course in order to restore respect for the government and the monarchy.

The other major figure at the inception of the Union of October 17 was A. I. Guchkov (1862–1936). Guchkov had emerged at the congress of zemstvos and cities in September 1905 as a catalytic figure in the liberal movement: "The appearance of A. I. Guchkov introduced a clear schism. It made possible a new and more precise expression of political ideas and separated the participants of the congress into political parties."[8] The issue that Guchkov grasped was Polish autonomy. He demanded that the liberals deny political autonomy for any of the nationalities subject to the Russian crown (except Finland). "If we diverge on this question alone," he said, "we are political enemies; and if we agree, we are allies."[9] Of course, the delegates were hopelessly divided on other issues, especially the land question. But it had been difficult to defend the minority's position against a suspicion of self-interest. By challenging the patriotism of his adversaries, Guchkov placed the minority on less vulnerable grounds and dealt a decisive blow to the unity of Russian liberalism.

Guchkov threw himself into political combat with the same zest he had once shown fighting for the Boers in South Africa. His adventurous character has often been cited as a partial explanation of Guchkov's political success. But daring alone could not have won him the respect of the veterans of the zemstvo movement. He was able to move into leadership of the minority chiefly because of his political acumen, a quality that many of the older generation of gentry liberals lacked. Guchkov had a good sense of timing and fearlessly exploited controversial issues for the sake of publicity. It was Guchkov, according to Shipov, who first proposed the idea of a party to replace the congresses as the national organ of the zemstvos and city dumas.

Guchkov was chosen a delegate from the Moscow city duma to the July and September congresses. But it would be a mistake to see him then, or at any time in his career, simply as a representative of Moscow industrial or commercial interests. Although his family occupied a middling status in the Moscow merchantry,[10] he spent hardly any time in business activities. His political role was more that of an *intelligent* than of a leader and spokesman of the business community.[11] Indeed, in the fall of 1905 he rejected the concept of political parties representing only business and committed himself instead to the Octobrist Union with its potentially broader social base.

If Shipov was a neo-Slavophile, Guchkov was an unapologetic Westernizer. He saw Russia's future prosperity dependent on her ability to compete with the other powers militarily and economically. In the age of imperialism, competition urgently demanded modernization of the state, the military, the economy, and society. It made sense to adopt the patterns that had proven their worth in the West, especially in Britain and Germany. Consequently, Guchkov had no hesitation in affirming the suitability of constitutional government for Russia. It was a pragmatic necessity:

> For a long time I have viewed constitutional monarchy as the political form necessary to insure the complete and fundamental reconstruction of our way of life. Doubtless, at one time another outcome was possible, and the autocratic system which created our great nation and solved many internal problems still had a brilliant future ahead. If the autocracy had been conscious of its historic mission to use its great powers to serve the interests of the mass of the people, if it had become demo-

cratic, it would have earned the right to a glorious existence. But it was diverted and became linked to the narrow interest of one estate [*soslovie*]. Thus it became responsible for the evil done in its name by the self-seeking and was brought to ruin.[12]

Guchkov's liberalism perhaps most closely resembled that of the mid-nineteenth-century European nationalists. On one hand, it incorporated constitutionalism and the bourgeois rejection of aristocratic privilege. On the other, it was characterized by rhetoric about national destiny and a special reverence for the state. For Guchkov the concept of a "democratic autocracy" presented no paradox, and he claimed for the Octobrists, in contrast to the Kadets, the virtue of *gosudarstvennost'*.

What united Shipov and Guchkov, despite their many philosophical differences, was agreement about the bureaucratic autocracy's dangerous neglect of the nation's needs and the consequent necessity of a constitution to revitalize the state. They further agreed on the importance of the institutions of local self-government—the zemstvos and city dumas—as a source of legitimate, experienced, and moderate representatives for the nation in the new parliamentary system.

The Octobrist central committee was fully as complex a partnership as that of Shipov and Guchkov. There were two separate and equal divisions of the committee: one in Moscow, the other in St. Petersburg. Both central committees included gentry and nongentry, but the Petersburg committee was entirely composed of leading public figures and businessmen of the capital. All representatives of the provincial gentry were members of the Moscow central committee, even when their homes were closer to St. Petersburg. Nongentry men had a slight numerical predominance in both committees. The original membership of the Moscow central committee in December 1905 included five gentry *zemtsy* (Shipov, P. A. Heyden, M. A. Stakhovich, N. S. Khomiakov, and N. S. Volkonskii),[13] six representatives of commerce and industry (A. I. Guchkov, V. P. and P. P. Riabushinskii, S. I. Chetverikov, N. M. Perepelkin, and A. I. Gennert), and a prominent attorney (F. N. Plevako). The Petersburg group included three noble landowners (P. L. Korf, M. V. Krasovskii, and V. V. Gudovich) as well as seven members who were not (F. E. Enakiev, P. A. Tarasov, A. N. Nikitin, N. N. Pertsov, A. Ia. Brafman, G. G. Lerkhe, and Iu. N. Miliutin).[14] But numerical preponderance and the fact that they provided most of the Octobrists' funds[15] did not automatically give the nongentry members a dominant role. The nobles more than made up for lack of numbers by their prominence and wide contacts in the provinces. They were all gentry "notables," leaders in the zemstvos and the corporate organizations of the nobility. Respected by their peers as temperate, cultured, and socially responsible figures, their opinions and their patronage were important forces in local affairs, where old ways persisted notwithstanding the ostensible beginning of the constitutional era.

The Octobrist program, despite this assembly of talent, was not a very significant contribution to political discourse. Although it borrowed much from the liberal platform that had taken shape since 1903, it was evasive, ambiguous, and incomplete. It endorsed the basic civil rights and advocated the rule of law. It called for immediate convocation of a State Duma (not a constituent assembly) elected by "general" (*obshchii* not *vseobshchii*—universal) suffrage but did not mention how the elections should be conducted. This was transparently disingenuous, since the Octobrist leaders were known to oppose direct elections in the countryside, and the November zemstvo congress minority resolution had rejected them. The proposed legislative program—improvements of agriculture, minimal concessions to labor, expansion of local self-government, universal secular elementary education, and judicial independence—offered nothing surprising and avoided controversy even at the cost of coherence. In the matter of land reform, the Octobrists accepted the principle of compulsory redistribution of some estate land, but only as a last resort, with fair compensation, in cases where the need was of national importance.[16] This formula was crucial in the Union's appeal to the gentry, for it denied the peasants' claim to all the land (the radical thesis) and asserted instead the inviolability of private property (subject to the state's right of eminent domain). Thus, the dangers of representative government, from the landowners' point of view, might be reduced.

The program's first article stressed the patriotic slogan for which the Octobrists were most noted: the integrity of the empire. Otherwise, even the Union's founders never gave the document great significance. It was one of the necessary trappings of a political organization, but not a platform to which anyone could be held. The ambiguities and omissions testify to the haste with which the founders covered up, instead of reconciling, their differences. In place of the program, Octobrist propaganda focused on the even more ambiguous October Manifesto. Specific issues of reform were submerged under patriotic rhetoric, though the "principles" of October 17 remained unrealized.

A binding program would, indeed, have been a hindrance, since the goal was to create a large, rather than a disciplined, organization. The Union (or "league") of October 17 grew as a loose alliance of individuals and groups opposed to revolution but in favor of constitutional monarchy. The negligible significance of the Octobrist program was emphasized in an appeal composed by Shipov:

> Entry into the Union of October 17 cannot in any way violate or conflict with the autonomy of the individual parties which join it; and their different convictions on various political, social, and economic questions can be no obstacle to the organized cooperation of parties and persons pursuing at present one common principal goal.[17]

Only revolutionaries and partisans of the old regime were specifically excluded. In short, the Union of October 17, because of the urgency of the crisis and the dominance of the Shipovian line in its creation, was not conceived as a political party at all, but as a broad coalition for the attainment of a single, common short-term goal: to arrest the revolution at the stage marked by the October Manifesto.

Inescapably, therefore, the Octobrists faced enormous problems in entering the parliamentary era. There was an acute need for leadership, and in the areas of organization and doctrine the Octobrists had not made a good beginning. The "league," heterogeneous, loosely guided, and professedly nonpartisan, was by nature unsuited to a parliamentary party. The ideology needed for a sense of common purpose was largely unformulated. The collaboration of gentry and bourgeoisie rested principally on a mutual antagonism to popular revolution. The crucial question for the Octobrists was whether—as the revolutionary crisis gave way to more normal parliamentary politics—they could create a coherent organization with distinct goals and a dependable constituency.

The first attempt to come to grips with these problems was made at a joint session of the central committees in St. Petersburg on January 8–9, 1906. On the agenda were the convocation of the first congress of the Union, scheduled for early February, and plans for the electoral campaign. The first question was whether to invite only members of the Union of October 17 (including the "union" parties) to the congress or to open it to all "moderate progressive elements." Shipov favored a broadly defined center, but Guchkov bluntly insisted on the futility of a nonpartisan strategy. The immediate task, he declared, should be to build up the Union's organization and "define its physiognomy." He warned that the discord and complications inevitable in an open congress would paralyze the Octobrists and distort the outcome. It was essential not to lose the opportunity to refine and publicize the specifically Octobrist position on constitutional issues and reforms. Guchkov proposed to invite Octobrists only—in effect, a first step in converting the "league" into a more homogeneous political party.

Shipov, defending the idea of a nonpartisan coalition, demurred. "Theoretical" questions and articles of the program were subject to diverse interpretations even among Octobrists, he said, but there would be no disunity among moderates regarding the "practical, vital" matters, namely, convening the Duma without delay and electing as many moderate deputies as possible. Only Stakhovich and Korf supported Shipov. Twelve speakers agreed with Guchkov, citing various reasons: half of them raised organizational considerations and others felt that the objectives named by Shipov were not sufficient reason for a congress. The majority voted to hold a congress of Octobrists only.

Having won his first round, Guchkov outlined an agenda for the congress. There would be discussion of current events and government policies first. Then, most of the congress's time would be devoted to amplifying certain points of the program. Shipov, joined by Heyden, objected again to submitting the program to discussion, but Guchkov's view was adopted by a majority.

To be sure, Guchkov did not intend to discuss the whole program. He selected certain points that, he said, would serve to clarify the Union's position and improve its standing at the polls. An affirmation of constitutional monarchy would differentiate the Octobrists from the right. For the other flank Guchkov chose the Polish question.

This neatly balanced agenda could not long survive a discussion. Stakhovich suggested reinforcing the offensive against the left by adding a condemnation of political strikes. Other committee members proposed that the congress consider the questions of religious toleration and of minority (landowners') rights under the electoral law. Most important, of course, was the problem of land reform: Heyden insisted on including it, and Shipov maintained that if other specific issues were to be raised, it could not very well be avoided. Opposed were Korf, who found the significance attached to the problem exaggerated, and Miliutin, who asserted that the peasants' needs were not so much material as spiritual.[18] With good reason, therefore, Guchkov warned that it would be difficult to come out of such a discussion with honor; and Stakhovich predicted that any resolution that the congress might adopt on the agrarian question would be damaging and embarrassing. Nevertheless, the conferees voted seven to six for including it in the agenda.

Taking advantage of the unsatisfactory turn, Shipov and Korf moved to reconsider whether the congress should debate the program. A majority of nine against four were now opposed, apparently agreeing with Khomiakov that the result would be the opposite of the intended unity. Heyden and Stakhovich dissented, but Guchkov reversed himself, since, with the inclusion of the agrarian question, debate on the program would not serve his purposes. One part of his plan he salvaged by stipulating that local committees be urged to submit reports for use by the central committee on the nationalities question and the harm caused by strikes. The agenda of the congress, it was decided, would include reports on organization, government policies, and tactics.

The inadequacy of this outcome must have bothered both Shipov and Guchkov. The nationalities question would, in fact, be reinstated in the congress's agenda by the delegates themselves, as would the agrarian problem, the religious question, and labor reform. The central committee's decision in January deprived the congress of any possible significance either for consolidating the Octobrists as a party or for creating a nonparty, moderate electoral coalition. The announcement of the congress, signed by Shipov and Korf, was an attempt to recoup. All those who "sincerely desire peaceful reconstruction and the triumph of order, legality, and true freedom in Russia, all who equally reject both stagnation and revolutionary upheaval" were urged to become Octobrists in order to participate in the congress. This phraseology as well as the following declaration of goals suggest Shipov's authorship:

> [The immediate aims of the Octobrists are to elect] the best people, true supporters of the rights and freedoms proclaimed by the Imperial Manifesto of October 17, who are imbued with the consciousness that the popular representative assembly must strive to bring about a reconciliation in the country by means of creative legislative work and consolidation of the state power.[19]

The conference of January 8–9, 1906, revealed how far the founders of the Union of October 17 were from sharing a common understanding of objectives, tactics, and the meaning of Octobrism itself.

Shipov distrusted the Union from the outset and was aware of the dangers in its heterogeneity, though he himself was largely responsible for that. He preferred to continue with an ambiguous program, limited, short-term goals and an informal organization, which would make possible a continuation of the moral leadership of the veteran *zemtsy*. Recognizing the panicky mood of the Octobrists' constituencies, Shipov also feared a detailed discussion of sensitive issues. Finally, he wished to postpone narrowing the Octobrists' position until after the elections, in the hope that a new moderate party might be formed in the Duma to reunite the "best people" of the liberal zemstvo movement and exclude those whose principles were less than liberal.

Guchkov, on the contrary, recognized instinctively that the era of congresses, when a handful of *obshchestvennye deiateli* could claim to speak for the nation, was irretrievably closed. To participate in the new constitutional system, which assumed a competitive, parliamentary style of politics, he felt the need for a party with its own program and a definable constituency. He cautiously selected political, not socioeconomic, issues with which to identify the Octobrists; but he feared no essential contradictions between their constituency and his own goals. He had no loyalty to the zemstvo movement, and as early as September 1905 he had ruled out collaboration with the Kadets.

Significantly, Guchkov's proposal to give priority to organizational goals was upheld by most of the nongentry members of the central committee. Having no attachment to the tradition of congresses, which was an expression of gentry liberalism, nongentry Octobrists moved more easily into the era of political parties—it was probably not a coincidence that that was a context in which the preeminence of the nobility in political and social life might wane. The conditions that permitted Shipov to lead the Union with no regard for the opinion of its constituents made them uncomfortable. Hence their support for "defining the physiognomy" of the Octobrists, thus limiting the Union's identification with the personal views of Shipov and Heyden.

What were the Union's organization and membership like in 1905–1906? According to claims made at the first congress in early February, there were seventy-eight Octobrist organizations in thirty-six provinces. Twenty-three of them were in Moscow and St. Petersburg. A fragmentary picture of forty-one branches in twenty-one provinces, with a total enrollment of 24,348 members, can be assembled from various sources, especially from two series of reports submitted by provincial governors in response to Police Department inquiries in the fall of 1906 and again in late 1907.[20] Nominal membership in single units ranged from fifteen to several thousand, although between one hundred and four hundred was typical. Active membership in all cases was considerably lower.

Octobrist committees were usually located in the capital, and possibly one or two of the larger towns, of a province. As a rule the organization did not extend to the villages, which, as far as conservatives were concerned, were the purlieu of the extreme right, which benefitted from the efforts of village priests and officials. Subordinate to provincial and city committees were "sections" (*otdeleniia*), formed in the city wards and district (uezd) towns.

At the core of the Octobrists' active membership—drawn usually from the district and provincial zemstvos and the municipal dumas— were "solid" citizens, propertied or professional men. As in the central committees the initiative, but not numerical superiority, typically belonged to the landowners. In the early months of the Union's existence merchants, manufacturers, managers, and owners of city real estate deferred to the gentry, who took their inspiration from the zemstvo congress minority. Moreover, under the electoral law of December 11, 1905, the landowners were a far more important constituency than the bourgeoisie. The role of the Octobrist *zemtsy* was, therefore, crucial.

We have, fortunately, a detailed account of the local campaign of one gentry member of the Central Committee. There was no open political activity in P. A. Heyden's Opochka district of Pskov province until he himself arrived from Moscow on December 29.[21] With customary energy he at once formed a provincial Octobrist committee: among its twelve members were government officials, merchants, landowners, doctors, and one priest. When Heyden departed shortly after the New Year, however, the committee was beset by troubles. The provincial governor ruled that officials could not participate, and public organizational meetings were not permitted. The remaining members then had second thoughts about committing themselves openly and the committee disintegrated. Heyden returned for the election, but failed in a new attempt to create an Octobrist organization. A public meeting on February 17 attracted mostly radicals and went completely astray from its purpose—to name an Octobrist slate of candidates.

Heyden, to the distress of local authorities, made considerable efforts to expound the October Manifesto and preach constitutionalism to the peasants in their villages. He seemed oblivious to the villagers' lack of interest in lawmaking and their alarming resentment of what they considered his evasiveness on the only important question: when would they get more land? He did not attempt to recruit them for the Octobrists, and party labels in the end had no significance in the elections. Heyden triumphed over more liberal opponents first in Opochka, then in the provincial elections, not as an Octobrist but as a well-known and respected local figure. The peasants, who controlled the provincial assembly, chose him to head their delegation simply because he was the candidate they knew best and trusted most of all the "lords" to explain the mysteries of the Duma.

The basic reason for Octobrism's failure to strike roots in Opochka was probably the unimportance of the landed gentry, who were outnumbered by peasants even in the landowners' electoral curia. On the other hand, insofar as Octobrism had any influence, it took a characteristic form. The closest thing to an Octobrist organization was an informal, private group of "Heydenists," probably mostly zemstvo activists. There was little or no effort to reach a mass constituency, and no interest in political activity between elections.

This story suggests certain conclusions about the nature of the Octobrists' political activities. First, the Union's prospects were closely related to the activities of moderate zemstvo *deiateli* and depended on their ability to exploit personal constituencies. M. A. Stakhovich's role in Orel was much like Heyden's in Pskov. M. V. Rodzianko led his considerable following of moderates in Ekaterinoslav zemstvo affairs into the Union, although not on the basis of any clear program.[22] N. A. Khomiakov seemed to have little contact with the Union's organization in the city of Smolensk. But though he resembled Shipov in his disdain for partisan politics, he exercised the same moderating influence in the Smolensk Duma elections as he did in zemstvo affairs. The Volkonskii family's influence in Riazan similarly benefitted the Octobrists, even though a committee of the Union was not organized there until January 1906—and the purpose then was not to compete with the local monarchist party, but only to choose delegates to the Union's first congress.[23] A second conclusion suggests itself: a specifically Octobrist program, a campaign platform, and party organization seem not to have had much importance. And a third observation, which follows from the foregoing, is that the Octobrists' strongest potential constituency outside Moscow and St. Petersburg lay in the zemstvo gentry. Among these moderates, active in local affairs, the prestige of the Octobrist "notables" was the Union's greatest asset.

The elections to the First Duma were disastrous for the Octobrists' pretensions to be a major political force. Out of more than five hundred deputies, a preliminary estimate gave thirty Octobrists, but by official count at the opening of the session there were thirteen. Apparent Octobrist victories in Perm, Orel, and Olonets provinces evaporated in defections to the Kadets, the liberal Democratic Reform group, and the Trudoviki. Octobrist successes in Moscow province (three deputies), Riazan (three), and Tula (two) were hailed as important. But the significance of these few cases should not be exaggerated. The three "Octobrists" from Moscow province, for example, were in reality two candidates of the Trade and Industrial Party and one monarchist. The industrialists had bolted their electoral bloc with the Octobrists and joined the right in the provincial electoral assembly. This combination had succeeded in filling all four Duma seats, defeating the Octobrist candidates, Shipov and S. I. Chetverikov.[24]

In the twenty European Russian cities with direct elections the Kadets won overwhelmingly with 83 percent of the vote. The Octobrists' principal combination, the United Committee of Constitutional Monarchist Parties, was defeated on home ground in St. Petersburg. The sole Octobrist elected from the cities was from Ekaterinoslav, the only city where the majority of electors was to the right of the Kadets. In Tula city and in Taurus province local Octobrists joined with the Kadets against the far right, and moderate Kadets were elected (Prince G. E. Lvov in Tula), but these instances of cooperation with the Kadets were exceptional.

How did the Octobrists fare among the provincial landowning gentry? Only fragmentary information is available on the results of the first-stage elections in the land-proprietors' curia.[25] These partial results give the Octobrists 14 percent but show a surprisingly large proportion of the electors to the Octobrists' left (34 percent) and a significant proportion to their right (24 percent) with 26 percent independent or unknown. Obviously, among the land-proprietors' electors the Union of October 17 had not met a strongly sympathetic response.

This failure may be partially explained by the deceptive nature of the land-proprietors' curia. Under the electoral law of December 11, 1905, the votes of gentry landowners were much diluted by those of small and nongentry proprietors. One study identified less than 46 percent of land-proprietors' electors in forty-five provinces of European Russia as nobles, and far from all of them were large landowners. The rest of the electors were peasants (26 percent), bourgeois, clergy, and professional men.[26] This dilution is more than sufficient to account for the apparent extent of radicalism in the land-proprietors' curia. It is unlikely that there were many leftists among the more substantial gentry proprietors and still more unlikely that their peers would have voted for them. Much evidence points to such a conclusion: the extraordinary winter zemstvo sessions held in many provinces and the elections to the State Council from the nobility and from the zemstvos in March and April revealed a strong rightist trend. Inescapably, the gentry's political center of gravity was to the right of the Octobrists. The moderate center in Russian politics was, in fact, quite small, and the Union of October 17 found itself on the left wing of the provincial gentry.

All this testified eloquently to the failure of Shipov's ideal of a center union, a patriotic league excluding only the radical left and the reactionary right. The ambiguities of Octobrism did not appeal to an electorate polarized by the revolutionary crisis. Such successes as Octobrist candidates enjoyed in the First Duma elections were, we must conclude, largely personal.

Before the elections to the Second Duma the leadership of the Union had split. In the summer of 1906 a new party, Peaceful Renewal (*Mirnoe obnovlenie*), was created by P. A. Heyden and M. A. Stakhovich. Its program was significantly closer to the liberal mainstream. The most radical concession was in the area of land reform: the *Mirnoobnovlentsy* recognized the peasants' right to such land as they habitually rented and to land in excess of a maximum norm to be established for private estates. Heyden's avowed purpose was to create a party that could unite the moderate gentry with the peasants—the traditional rural "all-class" ideal of zemstvo liberals, now adapted to electoral politics under the law of December 11, 1905. Morally unable to accept the reality of the gentry reaction and disapproving of the policies of the new premier, P. A. Stolypin, Shipov at the end of July threw his support behind *Mirnoobnovlentsy*. Guchkov's instincts prompted him otherwise. At the first opportunity he put the question directly to the test. In response to the explosion of a bomb at Stolypin's summer residence, the government proclaimed harsh new measures against terrorism, including courts-martial. Liberals were outraged, but Guchkov declared his full support of Stolypin, at the same time expressing confidence that the government, while determined to restore order, was irrevocably committed to modernization. Response from the provinces favored Guchkov's stand for law and order as a precondition for reform without revolution, and the majority of the central committee did not follow Shipov, who quit the Union early in September.

Approaching the Second Duma elections, Guchkov affected a patriotic fervor and was hailed in the conservative press as the father of "national liberalism" in Russia. He revitalized the provincial organization, won a large contribution from the "greatest capitalists in Moscow," and began to publish a daily newspaper, *Golos Moskvy*. In the elections (held at the beginning of February 1907) the Octobrists appeared to fare a little better than before. The Second Duma had a right wing of about ninety deputies, among whom an early count identified twenty-six Octobrists.[27] An Octobrist fraction was soon formed with twenty members and nineteen "adherents," a form of affiliation that did not require even nominal agreement with the Union's program. Nevertheless, in the first-stage elections the Octobrists' popularity had not substantially improved.[28] After administrative manipulations that greatly reduced the influence of nongentry in the land-proprietors' curia, 24 percent of its electors were to the Octobrists' left, 18 percent were Octobrists, 5 percent were unknown or independent, and more than 50 percent stood to the Octobrists' right.

Despite Guchkov's efforts to publicize the Union's turn to the right, party programs and official candidacies hardly played a greater role in the second elections than in the first. In the interval, it is true, political consciousness on the right had increased in response to the First Duma's expropriatory land program, terrorism, and the recovery of government initiative under Stolypin. During 1906 a significant degree of differentiation among conservatives occurred.[29] The Union of the Russian People (SRN), the United Nobility, and various nationalist organizations presented vigorous alternatives to Octobrism. But the gentry voters, many of them newly politicized and in a reactionary mood, did not declare decisively for these alternatives, nor did they respond to the Octobrist appeal.

In local politics, in the first stage of the Duma elections and in the provincial electoral assemblies, a majority of the gentry identified themselves simply as *pravye* (rightists). This designation implied no precise program and it encompassed a broad spectrum of opinions, which opened a way for the Octobrists to improve their position somewhat. Moderately conservative landowners (*umerenno-pravye*) had reservations about the liberal and constitutional aspects of the Octobrist program, but they had not discarded the kinship and respect they felt for individual local notables who happened to be Octobrists. Thus many of the "rightists" supported Octobrist candidates in the provincial assemblies. At the outset of the Second Duma the Octobrists in turn took a friendly and cooperative attitude toward the deputies on their right. When the Octobrist fraction was organized, its moderate-rightist "adherents" were almost as numerous as the declared Octobrists.[30]

On legislative issues, however, the alliance of the Octobrists and moderate-rightists was put to a severe test because the leadership of the Octobrist group was relatively liberal. These "left" Octobrists joined with the Kadets in a demonstration of protest against the courts-martial, and they offered a compromise on the land question that conceded the compulsory transfer of some private estate land to the peasants.[31] These gestures left much of the fraction far behind, and they were made without the concurrence of the central committee, which certainly would not have consented. Thus, the Union was in disarray when its second congress met in May 1907.

Even more emphatically than the central committee had intended, the congress repudiated the "liberalism" of the Left Octobrists. The delegates showed a degree of hostility to the Second Duma and a preference for administrative repression that came close to a rejection of constitutional government. Guchkov and the committee barely contained the congress's movement to the right within the bounds of Octobrism. Further, many delegates were strongly sympathetic to extreme Russian nationalism. Patriotism had always served the Octobrists as an opening to the right, but Russian ethnocentrism was an embarrassment to the central committee. Some of the Union's most reliable support, financial and electoral, came from German elements in Moscow, St. Petersburg, the Baltic provinces, and New Russia. Also, the Octobrist leaders were on the whole too genteel to profess overt anti-Semitic or anti-Polish views. Consequently, nationalism could carry the Octobrists only so far.

Declining to espouse outright either the reaction that dominated the zemstvos and city dumas or the extreme nationalism promoted by representatives of the western provinces, and yet unable to take a firm constitutionalist stand, the Union verged on political extinction. The progovernment newspaper *Novoe vremia* withdrew its support, declaring, "This is a bore, not a party!"[32] The survival of the Octobrists seemed even more doubtful when they failed at the new zemstvo congress (meeting less than a fortnight after the coup d'état of June 3) to lead the gentry delegates to approval of the government's project for reform of local self-government. If the congress was, as *Golos Moskvy* called it, a "rehearsal for the Third Duma,"[33] it seemed certain that the Octobrists would be submerged by the right in the elections.

Instead, the Octobrists appeared in the Third Duma as the largest fraction, with 155 members and adherents, and were by common agreement considered to be the dominant party in the first three sessions. The new electoral law of June 3 had, of course, tipped the balance in favor of the landowners; but this fact, as the first two Duma elections had showed, was not necessarily an advantage for the Octobrists. Indeed, the data for the Third Duma elections—which are quite detailed—show the same weakness of the center in comparison with the right in the first stages.[34] As before, we have little information on the voters themselves, but there is much more for the provincial electors. Those of the land-proprietors' curia, who now composed 51 percent of the total number of provincial electors (more in most districts of the agricultural provinces), distributed by "political orientation," were 62 percent rightists, 23 percent moderates, 8 percent leftists and 7 percent unknown. The vague political terminology of this official tabulation underscores the government's resistance to the idea of a party system, and it is unclear what criteria were applied to distinguish moderates from rightists. Most probably, however, Octobrists were classified as moderates and amounted to about a fifth of the electors. In order to explain how the Octobrists overcame their weakness between the first elections and the opening of the Duma, it is necessary to examine the electoral process and the formation of fractions in detail.

Voting in the land-proprietors' curia were 10,191 large property owners, or only 35 percent of those eligible.[35] Also voting for the electors from the land-proprietors' curia were 5857 mandatories of small proprietors (mostly landowners), elected in preliminary assemblies. No basis exists in the statistics for determining the *soslovie* or political preference of the voters in the land-proprietors' curia. The electors they chose, however, besides having the general political complexion cited above were composed mostly of hereditary and personal nobles (61 percent) and clergy (22 percent). Eighty-seven percent were of the Russian nationality. Solely occupied in agriculture were 37 percent. Twenty-one percent were Orthodox clergy, 17 percent were in government service, and 16 percent were in private occupations.[36] Clearly, even under the law of June 3 the land-proprietors' curia was more diverse than is usually supposed. Large landowners accounted for slightly under two-thirds of the voters, and the role of the clergy—guided by the Ministry of the Interior and the Holy Synod—was important in assuring rightist majorities. Unfortunately, the data do not permit further investigation of the political preferences of any specific occupational or age groups or any *soslovie*. Interpretations of the Octobrists' success must be impressionistic, relying on inference, memoirs, and newspaper accounts.

When the deputies arrived in St. Petersburg, about one hundred had indicated a preference for the Octobrist fraction; of these about sixty were landowners and twenty-five bourgeois.[37] In all probability, a relatively small number of Octobrists had been elected as such to the Third Duma. Platforms and party candidacies, as before, played little part. On the other hand, local "parties" and personal followings, groupings among the gentry that often antedated 1905, were extremely important. That these combinations were sometimes called "Octobrist" should not obscure their essentially traditional, local, and personal character. In the first stages of the Third Duma elections, as in the Second, Octobrists were elected by the votes of "rightists." This effect was magnified by the advantages given the large proprietors under the June 3 electoral law. Furthermore, in view of the low rate of the land proprietors' participation in the Duma elections, it is likely that among the gentry voters there was a relatively high proportion of zemstvo activists. Such a hypothesis is supported by the fact that the Octobrist fraction in the Third Duma included thirty-two of the delegates to the June 1907 zemstvo congress. One participant recalled it as a "congress of the future Octobrist fraction."[38]

Among the *zemtsy* were many prominent Octobrists. These men did not usually attempt to give the elections a partisan character but collaborated with other conservatives to manage the Duma elections as smoothly as they traditionally had zemstvo affairs.[39] The elections in the provinces were very unlike those in the six large cities with separate representation, where deputies were elected directly, by party slates, in two curiae. Many of the provincial deputies were simply "moderates" (that is, moderate-rightists), chosen on the basis of local popularity and known antipathy for radical solutions.[40] As soon as the elections were over, Octobrist notables began vigorously to recruit for their fraction: this was the second stage in the process by which the Octobrists snatched victory from the jaws of defeat. Eight out of eleven of the Kharkov deputies were led by A. D. Golitsyn, V. A. Bantysh, and N. V. Savich to join the Octobrists. The entire Chernigov delegation of ten, guided by Iu. N. Glebov and M. A. Iskritskii (nominally a member of Peaceful Renewal but already in the Second Duma an adherent of the Octobrists), enrolled in the Octobrist fraction. N. A. Khomiakov also carried the entire Smolensk contingent into the fraction. In each of these cases the apparent preference of the provincial electors, according to the government survey, was rightist—overwhelmingly so in Kharkov and Smolensk and by a strong plurality in Chernigov. In a third stage, recruitment continued and even intensified in the capital, as the Octobrists competed with fractions on both their flanks for the still unaligned deputies. One right-wing source alleges that Guchkov, who had been elected from the city of Moscow, attempted in a social call at the club organized by extreme rightist deputies to induce defections to the Octobrist fraction.[41]

Thus, in contrast to their patent weakness before the elections and despite their flirtation with liberalism in the first two Dumas, the Octobrists enlarged their fraction, from 100 to 155 deputies, mostly at the expense of the right. What made such a coup possible? One factor, evident from the foregoing, was the prestige of local Octobrist notables. This influence transcended political differences to a remarkable degree: N. A. Melnikov of Kazan listed both liberals and extreme conservatives among the gentry Octobrists to whom he felt drawn.[42] A. D. Golitsyn wrote that the Kharkov deputies were impressed with the prestige of the Octobrist leaders, with Guchkov, and with the potential strength of the Octobrist fraction.[43] To uncommitted deputies who were not sufficiently impressed by these intangibles the Octobrists may have promised desirable committee assignments.[44]

In short, the Octobrists' power in the Third Duma was not based, in the usual sense, on a constituency among the voters. Their assets lay in the social affinities binding the zemstvo gentry, in the deference shown to the veteran *obshchestvennye deiateli,* and in the experience several of these figures had acquired in the Second Duma. The Octobrists could also capitalize on the personal leadership of Guchkov and on his presumed collaboration with Stolypin. Finally, though they lacked a majority, the Octobrists' center position seemed to give them the leverage to control the Duma. Against these strengths, however, must be weighed the lack of an agreed political platform or program of legislation. S. I. Shidlovskii accused Guchkov of a careless attitude toward the fraction's political unity[45]—an accusation that has frequently been cited. In fact, Guchkov did propose a minimum program of legislation at the first general assembly of the fraction, in order, he said, to give it a degree of homogeneity (*odnorodnost'*).[46] Right and Left Octobrists alike opposed him, and thus the Octobrist fraction had from the outset a fragile unity and an illusory strength.

The organization of so diverse a group was a problem to which, evidently, little serious thought was given. As chairman of the central committee, Guchkov headed the fraction. Supporting him was an executive bureau made up of deputies who were members of the Central Committee, or who had sat in the first two Dumas, and a few other prominent provincial Octobrists. Left Octobrists dominated the bureau —several of them were members of the Central Committee as well as veterans of the Second Duma whose experience was now very useful. Still, since their "liberalism" had been rebuked but not recanted, their dominant position in the party's bureau needs some explanation. Paradoxically, their liberalism was something the Octobrists could not do without. Though they sometimes embarrassed him, Guchkov maintained a close alliance with the Left Octobrists, for they were the bearers of the standards that distinguished Octobrism from the right: constitutional monarchy, legality, equality of *sosloviia* and nationalities, and modernization. Nationalism, another potentially vital force in the Octobrist fraction, tended to push its members toward the right. As the Octobrist deputies leaned to the right they slipped from Guchkov's control. While he needed the votes of the conservative majority of his fraction, Guchkov was bound to the Left Octobrists by their common commitment to a separate fraction and program. Thus, although the Left Octobrists were the Union's weaker faction, Guchkov's tactical reliance on them artificially enhanced their position in the Third Duma.

There was no effective caucus of the Octobrist fraction. Attendance at general meetings was low—the highest recorded was eighty-nine in 1909, when a revolt by the fraction's right wing threatened to tear the Octobrists apart. Discipline was a perennial problem, and there were several revisions of the fraction's charter, none of which overcame the fact that any serious attempt to enforce unanimity would have caused it to split.[47] From the first session the fraction divided into three identifiable factions: left (twenty to twenty-five members), right (about the same), and center. In the Fourth Duma the center took the name "Zemstvo-Octobrists," which might as well have been applied in the Third. This group was much smaller than one hundred deputies, if non-Octobrist adherents and those whose membership was only nominal are excluded. On the basis of very little evidence a reasonable estimate would be that there were fifty to sixty Zemstvo-Octobrists. It was here, if anywhere, that the moderate, responsible representatives of the nation, experienced in local self-government, in whose name the Union of October 17 had been founded, might be discovered.

The leading figures among the Zemstvo-Octobrists were such men as M. V. Rodzianko (Ekaterinoslav), E. P. Bennigsen (Novgorod), K. N. Grimm (Saratov), Prince I. A. Kurakin (Iaroslavl), professor M. M. Alekseenko of Kharkov University, and F. N. Plevako, doyen of the Moscow legal profession. The zemstvo style and attitudes that prevailed in the moderate center of the Octobrist fraction are clearly reflected in the memoirs of one deputy, N. A. Melnikov.[48] An active Union member who carried the burdens of organizing, campaigns, and the party newspaper in Kazan, Melnikov was warmly welcomed to the Duma by Guchkov and immediately became involved in the work of the executive bureau, to which he was later elected.

Melnikov was a young man (thirty-three years old in 1907), but already an experienced *zemets*. His estate was small, and at the university he had begun to study medicine, then turned to agriculture and a career in the zemstvo. Subsequently president of the Kazan provincial zemstvo for many years, Melnikov promoted extensive humanitarian and economic programs. Yet he was not a liberal in the programmatic sense. At the June 1907 zemstvo congress he opposed democracy on principle and proclaimed the benefits of gentry paternalism. Melnikov had identified with the Octobrists in 1905 because of their leadership in the attack on the Kadets at the zemstvo congresses and in the provinces. Although he did not sympathize with the "retrograde" faction in the zemstvos, he regarded radicalism as the greater danger.

Melnikov had joined the Union with reservations. His activism did not make him a partisan:

> Personally, I joined the Octobrists not because I agreed unconditionally with their program. The party framework often seemed confining. But when one has decided not to be only a spectator in politics, it is necessary to have some kind of a political passport. I preferred to get it where there were many representatives of the zemstvo world and people whose way of thinking was like mine.[49]

The world of partisan politics was not a comfortable environment for the typical Zemstvo-Octobrist. He retreated from political combat, and party discipline was a concept alien to his sense of individual dignity. Moreover, he was afflicted with a nagging sense of inferiority in relation to the intellectuals of the opposition. His impulse was not to debate or negotiate with the Kadets but to shun them and suppress them. The leading spokesmen of his fraction had an obligation to respond to Miliukov and Rodichev, but the rank-and-file Zemstvo-Octobrist was unprepared by his education and style of life for the intense partisanship, quick wit, and ultimate compromise required by parliamentary politics. He buried himself in committee work or, like Melnikov and K. N. Grimm, eventually resigned from the Duma.

The political habits that had induced the Kazan zemstvo and others to repudiate not just the zemstvo congress of November 1905 but even the one a year earlier were still alive for Octobrists like Melnikov. Despite their *de facto* acceptance of the Duma's legislative powers, the zemstvo Octobrists did not conceive of taking the initiative away from the government. The Third Duma was to realize the ancient ideal of cooperation between the central administration and gentry-dominated self-government. More than any of its predecessors, the Stolypin government had their confidence; the Duma's powers of review were held sufficient to control the long-resented bureaucracy; budgetary sanctions or direct legislative conflict would never become necessary.

To maintain the precarious unity of the fraction, Guchkov deliberately isolated it from outside influences that might upset the equilibrium and interfere with his tactical freedom. Leadership of the Union was transferred completely to the fraction's bureau. The central committee, left in the care of its pedantic secretary, K. E. Lindeman, was eliminated from decision-making. In contrast to the Kadet central committee, which met regularly in St. Petersburg and had authority over the fraction, the Moscow Octobrists heard only occasional reports from the Duma. The St. Petersburg central committee members, who had worked actively with the fraction in the Second Duma, were wholly ignored from the opening of the session.

The suppression of the central committee was accompanied by a deliberate neglect of the provincial organization. Whereas Guchkov had once looked to provincial Octobrists for support against Shipov, he now took pains to insulate himself and the fraction from them. Guchkov had fewer illusions than in 1906 about the Octobrists' ability to lead the provincial gentry. Ironically, though he had once seen the zemstvos as a base for turning the Octobrist league into a party with real force *vis-à-vis* the government, his ability to collaborate with and to influence Stolypin now depended on suppressing the party's organization and obscuring its "physiognomy." Allowed to follow their instincts, the Zemstvo-Octobrists would have blended with the right, as they did in local politics, and ceased to appear as a force for constitutional government and modernization.

Isolated from its constituencies, the fraction was more stable and, especially, more manipulable. Shidlovskii correctly observed that it became "like a tool in the hands of Guchkov," serving not a definite program but the tactical needs of its chief. But though Guchkov may have been politically ambitious and over-impressed with Stolypin, as Shidlovskii and others have charged, his goals could not be separated from real legislative accomplishments. The rebirth of the Union of October 17 in time for the Fourth Duma elections and the political survival of Guchkov himself depended absolutely on a creative and productive record in the Third Duma. The succeeding five years showed the futility of this calculation. Each test of strength between Guchkov and Stolypin (who was increasingly severely pressed from the right) resulted in defeat for the Octobrist leader—from the Naval General Staff Bill to the Western Zemstvo crisis. Guchkov could not rely on the fraction, which lacked will and discipline to resist the government or the court, and the Third Duma was unable to rise above the level of "legislative vermicelli." By 1912 the Octobrists were too weak to fight government interference in the elections on behalf of the right and too demoralized to overcome voter apathy.

The final act was played in the winter of 1913–14. At a conference of the fraction in November Guchkov declared that Russia was confronting a new revolutionary crisis because of the short-sightedness and incompetence of the government. He called upon the fraction—now from outside it, for he had not been returned to the Duma—to take an actively critical stance, to speak for the nation against the government:

> The evident danger of the present moment lies not in the parties of revolution, not in antimonarchist propaganda, not in antireligious teachings, not in propaganda for the ideas of socialism and antimilitarism, not in anarchist agitation against the State. Our historical drama is that we are forced to defend the monarchy against those who are the natural defenders of the monarchical principle, the Church against the ecclesiastical hierarchy, the army against its commanders, and the authority of the executive power against those who exercise it.[50]

A minority of the fraction, twenty-two Left Octobrists, responded favorably, but the majority resisted any change in tactics. First the Left Octobrists, then the Zemstvo-Octobrists resigned from the fraction, bringing to a natural death a body that could only exist in a state of paralysis. This final rejection of Guchkov by the Zemstvo-Octobrists clearly pointed out the weakness of the Union of October 17 as a political party. As long as it courted the zemstvo gentry and followed them to the right, it appeared strong. But whenever in the Third and Fourth Dumas it attempted to lead, to engage the government in combat with the political weapons provided by the constitution, the gentry refused to follow.

NOTES

1. The term "gentry," it seems to me, is useful as a designation for the provincial Russian noble landowner, especially toward the end of the nineteenth century, when the provincial nobility became reasonably distinct from the aristocracy of the court and upper bureaucracy. As a translation of the Russian "pomeshchik" it appropriately suggests a certain economic and social status and an intense involvement in rural affairs. A full comparison with the English gentry or of Russian provincial institutions with the English is not intended.

2. See the discussion at the Third Congress of the United Nobility, in March 1907. *Trudy tret'iago s"ezda upolnomochennykh dvorianskikh obshchestv* (St. Petersburg, 1907), p.255 and *passim*.

3. The Constitutional Democrats (Kadets) were the first to organize their party, meeting in Moscow on October 12–18. The Octobrist program was drafted at the end of October, but the formation of the Union was not announced until the close of the zemstvo congress.

4. From the papers of D. N. Shipov, ORBIL, f. 440, kn. 4, d., 4.

5. "My understanding of life is grounded in the religious consciousness which was inculcated in me since childhood, but it took shape finally under

the moral influence of two Russian thinkers—F. M. Dostoevskii and L. N. Tolstoi" (D. N. Shipov, *Vospominaniia i dumy* [Moscow: 1918], "Predislovie," n.p.).

6. *Vospominaniia i dumy,* p.329.

7. "The Slavophiles were animated by a bitter hostility to the very idea of the party system. They viewed political parties as organizations of factional interests, feverishly seeking by servile maneuvers or by intimidation the favors which the state itself was not legitimately entitled to bestow upon them." Leopold H. Haimson, "The Parties and the State," in Cyril E. Black, ed., *The Transformation of Russian Society* (Cambridge: Harvard University Press, 1960), p.115.

8. N. I. Astrov, *Vospominaniia* (Paris: YMCA Press, 1941), I, 314.

9. *Pravo,* 1905, no. 38, p.3172.

10. P. A. Buryshkin, *Moskva kupecheskaia* (New York: Chekhov, 1954), p.111.

11. Buryshkin, a peer (*Moskva kupecheskaia,* p.314), and P. N. Miliukov, an adversary (*God bor'by* [St. Petersburg, 1907], p.163), agree on this point. The intention here is not to deny Guchkov's role as a spokesman for capitalism in general but rather to stress that he acted as an individual and as a politician.

12. A. I. Guchkov, *Rech', proiznesennaia 5-go noiabria 1906 goda Predsedatelem Tsentral'nogo Komiteta Soiuza 17-go Oktiabria A.I. Guchkovym na obshchem sobranii v S.-Peterburge v zale Dvorianskogo Sobraniia* (Moscow, 1906), p.7.

13. The *zemtsy* were from Moscow, Pskov, Orel, Smolensk, and Riazan provinces respectively.

14. Korf was formerly and Gudovich actually marshal of the Petersburg nobility; Krasovskii was a senator with estates in Chernigov. Enakiev was an officer of several international oil and metal combines. Tarasov and Nikitin were industrialists. Pertsov, Brafman, and Lerkhe were professional men, and Miliutin (son of the mid-century bureaucrat-reformer, N. A. Miliutin) a wealthy and well-connected dilettante.

15. This is especially true for Moscow. None of the *zemtsy* were wealthy men, but the Guchkovs and Riabushinskiis and their friends among the industrialists and in the stock exchange had ample resources. In St. Petersburg not only Enakiev and Tarasov but also Gudovich, Korf, Lerkhe, and Miliutin probably tapped important sources of funds.

16. Even among Octobrists there was disagreement over whether "fair" compensation should be based on the inflated rental value of the land or on its actual productivity. Evading this issue, the program held that the Duma should decide.

17. TsGIA, f. 869, op. 1, d. 1289, l. 38.

18. "Nuzhda krest'ianskaia ne stol'ko zemel'naia, skol'ko dukhovnaia" (*Krasnyi arkhiv,* XXXV [1929], 170).

19. TsGAOR, f. 115, op. 1, d. 46a, l. 14.

20. See TsGAOR, f. 102, O.O. (1906), d. 9 and d. 828; f. 102, op. 7 (1906), d. 9 and d. 828; and f. 102, IV (1907), op. 99, d. 164.

21. V. B., "Opochetskiia vospominaniia o gr. P.A. Geidene," *Russkaia*

mysl', November and December 1907. The author's point of view is liberal but not partisan.

22. B. B. Veselovskii, *Istoriia zemstva za sorok let,* 4 vols. (St. Petersburg, 1909–11), IV:278–79.

23. *Russkoe slovo,* February 2, 1906. In emphasizing the Octobrist program in Tambov, V. M. Petrovo-Solovovo was a significant exception among the central committee *zemtsy.* His speech inaugurating the Union's Tambov committee was reprinted by the Octobrist central committee: *Soiuz 17 oktiabria, ego zadachi i tseli, ego polozhenie sredi drugikh politicheskikh partii* (Moscow, 1906). According to the provincial governor, Petrovo-Solovovo's agitation garnered the support of the "progressives" among the Tambov gentry, about one-third, for the Union. TsGAOR, f. 102, O.O. (1906), d. 828, ch. 14, ll. 1–2.

24. Shipov gave an account of these maneuvers in *Vospominaniia i dumy,* pp.427–29.

25. *Rech',* April 10, 1906. The term "land-proprietors" is used here, despite its awkwardness, to emphasize the social diversity of the curia (discussed below).

26. S. M. Sidel'nikov, *Obrazovanie i deiatel'nost' pervoi Gosudarstvennoi Dumy* (Moscow: Izdatel'stvo Moskovskogo Universiteta, 1962), p.136.

27. *Novoe vremia,* February 17, 1907.

28. The observations that follow are based on data for 90 percent of the provincial electors, compiled by Aleksei Smirnov, *Kak proshli vybory vo Vtoruiu Gosudarstvennuiu Dumu* (St. Petersburg, 1907), pp.234–39.

29. This differentiation is reflected in the governor's reports on changes in party strength between 1906 and 1907, for example, TsGAOR, f. 102, op. 99, d. 164.

30. A fraction of *Pravye* (Extreme Rightists) was also formed in the Second Duma, and several presumed Octobrists chose to join it. At the local level, however, and in the Third Duma elections the term *pravye* retained its broad sense.

31. M. Ia. Kapustin, in a speech on April 9, proposed giving the peasants unutilized estate land and land habitually rented to them by the landowners, who were to be compensated with state bonds.

32. May 10, 1907.

33. June 10, 1907.

34. Ministerstvo vnutrennykh del, *Vybory v Gosudarstvennuiu Dumu Tret'iago Sozyva* (St. Petersburg, 1911).

35. Of the voters eligible on the basis of a full *tsenz,* 95 percent qualified by the area of their landholdings. Also eligible were owners of mines and noncommercial property—most of the latter represented *dachi* and *usadby* in Moscow and St. Petersburg provinces.

36. It is unfortunate that the statistics do not differentiate hereditary and personal nobles, which would be an aid in distinguishing between gentry and civil servants. Note that only those with no other occupation were listed as *zemlevladel'tsy.*

37. Vladimir Gorn, "Spasiteli Rossii," *Russkaia mysl',* no. 1, 1908, p.64–65.

38. N. A. Melnikov, "19 let na zemskoi sluzhbe," p.128, in the Columbia Russian Archive. Forty-eight of the 158 delegates became members of the Third Duma; besides Octobrists there were 11 rightists and 5 opposition deputies.

39. S. I. Shidlovskii, *Vospominaniia*, 2 vols. (Berlin, 1923), I:109.

40. This was the thesis of a memorandum on tactics in organizing the fraction, submitted to the central committee by P. Kutler of Tambov. TsGIA, f. 869, op. 1, d. 1290, ll. 78–86.

41. A. S. Viazigin, *Gololobovskii intsident* (Kharkov, 1909), p.5.

42. "19 let na zemskoi sluzhbe," p.134.

43. A. D. Golitsyn, *Vospominaniia (obshchestvenno-politicheskii period)*, p.224, in the Columbia Russian Archive.

44. Viazigin, *Gololobovskii intsident*, p.5.

45. *Vospominaniia*, I: 202.

46. TsGAOR, f. 115, op. 1, d. 19, l. 138ff.

47. This was recognized already when the Octobrists yielded to the demand of the Right to exclude the opposition from the Duma's presidium in exchange for electing N. A. Khomiakov president.

48. "19 let na zemskoi sluzhbe," particularly pp.126–51, in the Columbia Russian Archives.

49. Ibid., p.130.

50. *Golos Moskvy*, November 10, 1913.

The Elections to the Third Duma: The Roots of the Nationalist Party

ROBERT EDELMAN

By the summer of 1907 noble landowners in the provinces had moved in a sharply conservative direction. As shown above, liberals were thrown out of the zemstvos in the elections of 1906–1907, and a considerable mass of noble landowners, galvanized by the events of the revolutionary years, began to speak out in sharp defense of their historic privileges and interests. The new electoral law issued after the coup d'état of June 1907 would assure these elements of the Russian nobility a preeminent position in the Duma. However, in neither the Third nor the Fourth Duma periods did a political formation emerge to organize them into a coherent political force. The group that came closest, in a structural sense, was the Russian Nationalist party.

Formed late in 1909, the Nationalists were unrepentant defenders of noble privilege and property. But although they were conservative, the Nationalists developed an approach to the organization and use of political power that resembled that of modern, Western, parliamentary parties. The organizational structure of their party differed from that of the more moderate Octobrists, and it contrasted even more sharply with the still more conservative extreme right fraction (*pravye*),* who sat between the Nationalists and the Duma's right wall. Despite their clear differences of program and organizational form, all three groups drew support primarily from the landed nobility. It is my intention here to explain these differences by analyzing the elections to the Third Duma in order to determine the ways, beyond ideology, in

* I shall use the Russian *pravye* (rights) to refer to the extreme right Duma fraction. Right, used in English, will simply serve as shorthand for right-wing.

which the Nationalists were unlike their closest political rivals. As a result of this examination, it will then become possible to identify those characteristics of the Nationalists' own social base which most strongly influenced their later development.

The primary purpose of the new electoral law was to reduce the political weight of the popular elements that had proven unreliable in the first two Dumas. The peasantry, which the government had hoped would be a conservative force, paid for having disappointed the state's hopes by losing 56 percent of its *vyborshchiki* (electors). Industrial workers lost just under a half of their electors. In contrast, the number of electors of the landowners' curia was increased by slightly less than a third.[1] Thus, the Third Duma gave little expression to the aspirations of the broad Russian public. Yet it accurately reflected the interests and political development of the large property owners who were assigned a dominant position by the new electoral law.

The decree of June third has been explained elsewhere.[2] Accordingly, I shall restrict myself to mentioning several structural and historical factors that permitted large landowners to control the electoral process beyond their already inflated share of the *vyborshchiki* (49 percent).[3] Of immense importance for the future development of the Nationalists were the discretionary powers granted to the Minister of the Interior, the most significant of which was the option to create curiae based on nationality in those regions in which Russian interests might be especially threatened. The June third decree had specifically stated that the new Duma should be "Russian in spirit," and the number of seats allotted to national minorities was sharply reduced.[4]

An extremely important segment of the landowners' electoral assembly was composed of clergy who served as the delegates of churches owning land in each district. In areas in which the Russian landowning element was either weak or suffered from absenteeism, the clergy played a crucial role as protectors of privilege.[5] Nevertheless, priests were by no means monolithic in their support of the forces of order. Nor did they always assume this task with enthusiasm. A reward of Duma seats was the usual compensation for services rendered.

The control of gubernia electoral meetings by a conservative, wealthy majority affected the composition of the Third Duma's peasant delegation.[6] As in the old law the electoral assembly of each gubernia was to elect at least one deputy from among the electors of the peasant curia. Previously, the peasants had chosen their own deputy; now this was to be done by the entire assembly. The assembly's majority sought to choose reliable men who fitted readily conservative stereotypes of the properly loyal peasants. This did not result in the selection of a chorus of toadies—on issues directly affecting the peasantry, the peasant deputies could be very militant. But most of them sat with the center and right factions, at least formally supporting those who had put them there.[7] It should therefore be stressed that neither the clergy nor the peasants in the Third Duma represented an independent stratum. Notwithstanding important individual exceptions, these groups went along with those nobles who dominated the Octobrist, Nationalist, and *pravye* fractions. Any analysis that might view them as diluting the basic class nature of the various conservative parties would ignore both social structure and historical experience.[8]

Analyzing the elections to the Third Duma is a difficult task. The evidence available does not afford a complete picture of all levels of the process. Archival materials on the conduct of the 1907 elections are sparse, and newspapers tend to be incomplete, contradictory, and episodic. Statistics have presented a problem. The only universally accepted figures have been those on the Duma members themselves. Information on the *vyborshchiki* has been more suspect, but the appearance of previously unused statistical material, prepared by the government, gives a more precise picture of this level of the process.[9] Below this level, one cannot venture with any degree of precision, although broad descriptions of social and economic structure are, of course, possible and necessary.

Serious difficulties also arise because of the imprecision of nomenclature. The political terms used to describe the *vyborshchiki* who attended the provincial electoral assemblies were especially vague. The broad descriptions "right," "moderate," and "left" were most commonly used. But these terms held different meanings for different people, and newspapers introduced their own variations. A generally accepted terminology never did emerge. On a more profound level, it should be remembered that choices of descriptive words and terms of reference were fundamental to the way in which various groups comprehended and perceived events. Thus, while the terminological confusion makes the electoral process less susceptible to the use of modern analytical techniques, the categories chosen by particular historical actors become, in and of themselves, extremely important for an understanding of the politics of the Regime of the Third of June.

In this sketch of the political landscape of the Duma, I shall first devote attention to the center and right-wing fractions that emerged there, broadly characterizing their programs and drawing social portraits of their Duma deputies. From this should emerge clues that will suggest in what direction to proceed in delineating the Nationalists' social base and future political development.

On the eve of the Duma's convocation, the Octobrist newspaper *Golos Moskvy*, drawing on its own earlier reports, broke down the center and right groups in the following manner:[10]

Octobrists	110
Moderates	29
Right nonparty	95
Bessarabian center party	8
Monarchist	33
Union of Russian People	32

This covered most of the terms used during the campaign. "Right nonparty" is perhaps the best description of that large bloc of deputies who did not define themselves in any way beyond the broad term "right." This breakdown shortly gave way to a more simplified division of Duma fractions as deputies picked to formal affiliations. The most commonly cited figures are those given by the leading Soviet specialist on the Third Duma, A. Ia. Avrekh:[11]

pravye	50
moderate right and National Group	97
Octobrists and their adherents	154
Progressisty	28
Kadets	54
Muslim group	8
Polish kolo	18
Trudoviki	13
Social Democrats	20

Before their merger in 1909, the Nationalists were divided into the moderate right fraction of seventy-six and the National Group numbering twenty-one. Flanked on the left by the center and majority fraction of the Octobrists, the future Nationalists quickly broke off from the *pravye* with whom they had been lumped at the opening of the Duma.

The *pravye* were a disparate collection of reactionaries, displaying little ideological unity or parliamentary discipline.[12] Their most publicized figures, all landlords, were the archreactionaries V. M. Purishkevich and N. E. Markov II, the Vilna deputy G. G. Zamyslovsky, and the Kiev sugar baron and landlord Count A. A. Bobrinsky. The attitudes of the *pravye* toward popular representation ranged from overt hostility to reluctant acceptance. Any further attempt to define their views quickly comes down to the overly familiar stereotype of Autocracy, Orthodoxy, and Nationality. Anti-Semitism and an obsession with repression of revolutionary activity were also common among them.[13] Beyond this rather vague characterization, one hesitates to venture. Mistrustful of political parties and Duma fractions, which were said to represent special interests, the *pravye* affirmed their loyalty to the autocracy, which in their view spoke for all Russia. They also rejected any political causes that might in any way undermine the indivisibility of the Empire. Few *pravye* deputies ever developed a close relationship with their constituents; indeed they sought to avoid the charge of representing specific local interests. For them, political parties were dangerous alien organizations that could only fragment the empire.

The anachronistic attitudes of the *pravye* fraction made its relationship with the popularly oriented Union of Russian People uncomfortable. The URP has been referred to as the social base of the *pravye*, even during the elections of 1907.[14] In point of fact, respectable rightists were not pleased with the Union. The mass agitation of a "new right," often associated with the Union, distressed respectable but reactionary nobles with its demagoguery.

Because of this fact, the electoral law of June Third sounded the death knell of the Union of Russian People. The URP became superfluous with the restriction of the franchise: the need to attract lower class votes had passed. Counterrevolution with all its *déclassé* connotations fell by the wayside, an ugly reminder of the turbulence of the revolutionary period.[15] The Union's mass membership, always exaggerated, began to evaporate even before the 1907 election campaign. Usually reliable governors' reports on the size of the Union vary widely. On June 7, 1907, the Kiev governor reported that the URP numbered 15,000 throughout the gubernia but that the group was not particularly active.[16] He also noted that 680 people belonged to the *Soiuz russkikh liudei,* and 400 were in the Union of Archangel Michael.[17] In Minsk, the URP was credited with only 450 members, while a group called the Russian Borderland Union was said to number 12,716.[18] National figures based on a compilation of all the governors' reports give some picture of the size of right-wing groups during 1907. The Union of Russian People was said to have 356,738 members, but numerous governors were quick to point out that their figures were based on reports for 1906, a time when the Union had been more active. 47,792 people were associated with various other right-wing groups, and 14,035 members were ascribed to the Octobrists. The URP and the Octobrists were the only two parties that appeared with any regularity in the reports, but the governors noted that many local branches of both parties were either inactive or had ceased to function.[19] Thus there remained a large group of uncommitted conservative voters even within the limitations imposed by the new electoral law. The grip of the URP on this group was slipping fast, and its relationship with the Duma *pravye*, for whom it might have provided support, was eroding quickly, since the latter had ceased to play a crucial role in the newly modified political arena.

Despite the sharp status distinction between the Duma *pravye* and the cadres of the URP, a social breakdown of the deputies themselves reveals them as something less than the pinnacle of Russian high society. Of all the center and right-wing factions, the *pravye* had the lowest percentage of noble members (twenty-three of fifty). They had more priests (eighteen), and these priests were more independent than the priests of any other faction. Peasants and two professional men made up the rest of the *pravye* deputies.[20] Altogether, theirs was an atypical social profile: in all other conservative factions the nobility played a more clearly dominant role.

Unsurprisingly, extreme rightists were strong in areas where the local landed nobility felt particularly threatened by the peasantry. Kursk, which had suffered severe damage from peasant disturbances during 1905 and 1906, had elected ten *pravye*. Elsewhere, the fraction was successful in gubernias where Russians were threatened by other nationalities. The presence of a large number of Jews usually gave rise to strong countersupport for the far right. Kherson gubernia, which included Odessa, with a population one-third Jewish, had sent four *pravye*. The western provinces were a stronghold: Volynia had elected ten *pravye*: the *pravye* had also won two of Vilna's three Russian seats.[21] The future Nationalists also drew support from the western provinces, and it should be remembered that both they and the extreme right had labelled themselves simply as "right" during the election campaign. Such Nationalist leaders as P. N. Balashev, D. N. Chikhachev, A. S. Gizhitsky, N. N. Ladomirsky, F. N. Bezak, and N. K. Von Gubbenet, to name just a few, had all used this general term.[22] In the west, far right groups usually represented an extreme and often distorted variety of the nationalism and anti-Semitism of their more numerous moderate neighbors. The *pravye* differed sharply with the future Nationalists on questions of political form. They mistrusted the kind of political party the Nationalists came to build, and did not share the Nationalists' positive feelings for Stolypin, with whom the new party was to work in close harmony after 1910.

Just to the left of the deputies of the moderate right sat the Octobrists and their adherents. Attempts to correlate the Octobrists' program with their social base are difficult. Most often characterized as a party of the nobility and the big bourgeoisie, the Octobrists, normally defenders of private property, haphazardly followed a mildly constitutionalist program that led them *on occasion* to assume positions contrary to the immediate interests of those propertied classes they were supposed to represent. Avrekh characterizes the Octobrists as "bourgeois in program but landlord in social base."[23] Elsewhere, he calls them the party of "the big bourgeoisie and the capitalizing landlords."[24] He seeks to distinguish the party's left wing as the bourgeois section; the right wing as landlord—a distinction that fails to hold up under the simplest empirical scrutiny.[25] Avrekh does recognize, however, that the role in the party of the bourgeoisie has been overstressed. Only 15 of the 124 Octobrist deputies in the Third Duma (third session) can be characterized as bourgeois.[26] Avrekh goes on to note that Octobrist deputies had roughly the same social background as the moderate rights.[27] To argue that the Octobrists' positions reflect in some *direct* way the peculiarities of their class composition does not explain their true nature, nor is it a useful guide to understanding the behavior of individual party members.

The multiclass base and broad appeal of the Union of October is revealed by a breakdown of its deputies according to *soslovie:*[28]

80 nobles
11 peasants
8 priests
15 bourgeois
8 professional men
2 cossacks

These men characterized themselves as: ". . . A constitutionalist center not striving toward the seizure of government power but at the same time steadfastly maintaining the rights of popular representation within the boundaries specified for it by the Fundamental Laws."[29] It was this ambiguous constitutionalism that attracted noble landlords schooled in the pre-1905 traditions of zemstvo liberalism. From the Duma statistics, the Octobrists emerge most sharply as a party of the landowning nobility. Of all the center and right fractions, it is the Octobrists who had the highest proportion of nobles (64.7 percent). The peasant and clergy elements in the faction were small, making it possible to characterize the Duma Octobrists as primarily nobles, representing that segment of the *dvorianstvo* which had received its political education in the zemstvos of central Russia with their quasi-liberal traditions. All zemstvo members were by no means liberal. Yet, those who were touched by the phenomenon of "zemstvo liberalism" were motivated by a concern for legality and social justice that led them to adopt positions, particularly concerning the peasantry and traditional privileges, that were often in opposition to their immediate interests as landlords. This did not mean that they rejected private property; merely that they were not always consistent in its defense.

Given these ideological ambiguities, described above by Michael Brainerd, Octobrist unity was always exceedingly frail. Largely derived from the ideas and hopes of its more progressive leadership, the Union's program inspired neither the entire Duma fraction nor most of the provincial Octobrists. So sympathetic an observer as the British diplomat, Neville Henderson, was to note in 1907: "They consist . . . of leaders without followers. . . . The views of their leaders are personal and do not represent those of the party as a whole. This statement perhaps explains the lack of public support for the Octobrists. . . ."[30] After an interview in 1908 with Khomiakov, Richard Seymour reported to London: "A split in the Octobrist party had already been foreshadowed and would not be a regrettable eventuality as that party had hitherto only been held together by force of circumstances and its membership were not inspired by any real unity of aims."[31] While these statements may be overdrawn, they do make clear that the Octobrists were by no means ideally suited to the task of organizing the gentry into a modern political party.

Having discussed their neighbors to the right and left, we are brought to the center of our concerns—those deputies who later became the Nationalist fraction. Once the forces on the right had coalesced, this group would consist of some seventy-four moderate rights and twenty-three members of the National Group, the number varying slightly from session to session. As we have seen, the party's deputies had been elected largely under the broad label "right," and we can say strikingly little about them at this early stage of their development. If we ignore the bourgeois wing of the Octobrists, the moderate rights and National Group present substantially the same social picture as the Octobrist fraction, making allowances for a somewhat larger number of peasants and members of the clergy. The Nationalist faction in the Third Duma (third session) consisted of:[32]

52 nobles
14 priests
16 peasants
 2 bourgeois (both *kuptsy*)
 3 cossacks

Of all the political factions in the Duma the Nationalists had the most
harmonious relationship with the members of the clergy in their ranks,
and the Nationalist peasants were an equally carefully selected group.
Thus, the nobles maintained complete control of the faction while
comprising a smaller percentage of their Duma delegation (57 percent)
than the Octobrist nobles made up of theirs. What is striking about
the men who eventually joined the Nationalist faction is the minimum
of preconceptions they brought to the Duma. Not tied to any party,
they were representative of that large element of noble sentiment that
felt the Duma *pravye* to be immoderate and the Octobrists to be too
enamored of dangerous constitutional notions and too eager to cooperate with the left. Although believers in autocracy, the moderate rights
nevertheless supported representative institutions and prudent reforms.
After 1905 the need for noble political organization, independent of
the autocracy, had become clear to them. These noblemen were evolving out of their traditional state service roles and groping for new
ways in the context of the Third of June Regime to manifest their
political independence. At the time of the 1907 election campaign none
of the existing political factions really appealed to them. Thus there
existed a large bloc of independent, uncommitted gentry sentiment that
the moderate rights in the Duma could be said to represent. In this
sense, the future Nationalist deputies bore a certain resemblance to the
newly elected English country gentlemen of the late eighteenth century described by Namier: "The distinguishing mark of the country
gentlemen was disinterested independence: he should not be bound
either to administration or to any faction in the House, nor to a mag-
nate in his constituency . . . he should owe his election to the free
choice of the gentlemen of the county. . . ."[33] In a report prepared for
the British Foreign Office Bernard Pares noted: "These [the moderate
rights] are country gentlemen who, having [had] no such class unity
as the English gentry, took no particular interest in parties until the
Reform movement. . . . The more apathetic of the country gentry now
woke to life and expelled the Cadets . . . from the zemstvo all over the
country."[34]

As we have seen, the representatives of these country gentlemen
in the Duma did not differ markedly from the Octobrists in their social
origins (*soslovie*). However, the use of several other criteria—landownership, education, geography, and occupation—enables us to distinguish
them from their neighbors to the left.

The two groups differed quite sharply in terms of educational background. Excluding those with military educations (because this cate-

gory implies a specific type of education), fifty-four of one hundred twenty-four Octobrists in the third session (45 percent) had received higher education, while only twenty-two of the eighty-nine future Nationalists (25 percent) had completed the university. This may account for the Octobrists' greater receptivity to a politics of ideas. In addition, thirty of those fifty-four Octobrists had attended the elite universities of Moscow and St. Petersburg, making them part of an educated aristocracy that had been at least touched by the major intellectual currents of the time. In contrast, only six of the university-trained Nationalists had been schooled in the capitals. The largest single group (6) had studied in Kiev at St. Vladimir.[35]

The sharpest difference, however, was geographical. The two parties drew their support from different regions rather than dividing the vote in each gubernia. A few provinces had elected deputies from both parties, but, as noted above, the pattern was for one of the conservative groups to dominate a gubernia's delegation; strong consensual traditions among the landed nobles who dominated most final electoral assemblies had much to do with this phenomenon. Nationalist deputies came primarily from the western borderlands. Thirty-three originated from the nine western gubernias originally included in Stolypin's controversial proposal to introduce zemstvos in the borderland. Of these, twenty-seven were from the six southwestern and Bielorussian provinces covered by the final bill—Kiev, Podol'e, Volynia, Minsk, Vitebsk and Mogilev. Kiev, with eight Duma members, and Minsk and Podol'e, with six each, had the largest Nationalist delegations. The three Northwest gubernias, Kovno, Vilno, and Grodno—later eliminated from the western zemstvo bill—had elected altogether only five future Nationalists. In other border areas the party had thirteen members. Bessarabia, under the influence of the enormously wealthy Krupensky family, had sent seven deputies, and Kherson four. In the left-bank Ukraine and in other gubernias near the western borders the future Nationalists had thirteen Duma members. Only eleven deputies came from the capitals or Central Russian gubernias, and five of these were from Tula, where the families of such leading Nationalists as V. A. Bobrinsky and Prince A. P. Urusov exercised a great influence on the local nobility. It is important to note that most of the eventual leadership of the Nationalist Party, which emerged from the moderate rights —P. N. Balashev, F. N. Bezak, S. M. Bogdanov, and D. N. Chikachev— came from the strongholds of Kiev and Podol'e. P. N. Krupensky and V. A. Bobrinsky were to play leading roles in Duma politics, but in internal party life they carried less weight than did the men from the west. The National Group of twenty-three deputies, which sat between the moderate rights and the *pravye* until the formation of the Nationalist faction, came from roughly the same areas as the moderate rights, but none of its members were from Kiev, Podol'e, or Minsk, the areas of the greatest strength of the moderate right. Grodno, Mogilev, Volynia, and Kursk had sent three deputies each. Other Nationalist Group members came from Kherson, Pskov, and Poltava. The leader of the group, Prince Urusov, came from Tula, just south of Moscow.[36]

The fundamental institutional distinction between the western gubernias and central Russia—the absence of zemstvos—affected the types of occupations the Duma members had previously pursued. The breakdown by party and occupation was:

	Octobrists	Future Nationalists
agriculture	22	12
military service	17	15
zemstvo service	66	27
state service	22	18

As there is a considerable overlap, these figures are not entirely convincing: many deputies had been engaged in different occupations at different times. But one basic distinction is clear: the Octobrists had grown out of the zemstvo movement with its peculiar approach to politics, while the future Nationalists, evolving from a once-strong service tradition, were not committed to any single field of endeavor.[37]

Landholding was more extensive among Octobrist deputies. Eighty-three of them owned tracts larger than 200 *desiatiny*, (*desiatin* = 2.7 acres). Forty-two of the Nationalists owned such tracts, the average being 1,686 *desiatiny*. The Octobrists who owned land averaged 2,349 *desiatiny*. These figures give some credence to the view that more economically secure landlords were more willing to forego class interest on occasion, while threatened elements would be concerned less with legality and more with survival. While it may be absurd to characterize as threatened any group whose average holding is over 1,500 *desiatiny*, we shall see below that the Nationalists did represent a segment of the nobility that was severely challenged on the most concrete day-to-day level.[38]

The Western Borderland

The Nationalists drew their greatest numbers as well as their leadership from the western borderland. The party received scattered support elsewhere, drawing in part on the bloc of uncommitted *dvorian-stvo* opinion mentioned above, but the peculiarities of the west had a crucial impact on Nationalist ideology, program, and organizational form. Since the middle ages this region had been dominated by the Poles. It had become, in 1794, part of the Russian Empire, but the area remained dominated by Polish noble landlords. After the Polish rebellion of 1830, still more Polish nobles moved into the area.[39] After the rebellion of 1863, however, Russian landowning in the area began to increase with state support: by 1907 Russians of all *soslovia* held more land than their Polish neighbors. Most of this land had originally been held by recently rewarded bureaucrats. These first Russian *pomeshchiki* had been especially prone to absenteeism, and they were deeply imbued with the service mentality. By 1907, however, second- and third-generation descendants, both female and male, held title to these estates, and many chose to remain on the land and farm.[40]

For all their recent gains, Russian noble landlords of the west still lived a precarious existence, challenged on the land by Poles and in the commercial life of the towns by Jews. Despite their control of resources, both Jews and Poles were only small minorities of the total population of the western provinces. The percentages for the nine western gubernias were:[41]

	Total Russians	Poles and Lithuanians	Jews	Germans
Vilna	61.05	25.99	12.71	
Vitebsk	84.93	3.38	11.69	
Volynia	73.73	6.16	13.20	5.73
Grodno	71.20	10.08	17.30	.10
Kiev	85.25	1.93	12.09	
Kovno	7.27	77.31	13.72	
Minsk	80.93	3.00	16.00	
Mogilev	85.93	1.03	12.06	
Podole	84.54	2.30	12.20	

The "Russian" category includes Great Russians, Bielorussians, and Ukrainians. Great Russians numbered only three or four percent of that total. The peasantry was primarily Ukrainian or Bielorussian. Thus, the Russian landlord was cut off from the peasantry by clearly perceived class divisions and separated from the Polish nobility by equally sharp national and religious barriers. Faced with this situation, Russian *pomeshchiki* came to fasten on to any means that might strengthen their position on the land and give them political power.

By invoking Russian nationalism, the west Russian gentry appealed to outside authorities for support in the struggle with Polish landowners. Not surprisingly then, the ethnic composition of the west provided the basis for the local Russians' special obsession with nationalism.[42]

This particular distribution of nationalities also serves to explain a fundamental institutional peculiarity of the western borderland. The zemstvo reform of 1864 had not been extended to the western provinces: to do so would have given control of local government to Polish nobles who, after the revolt of 1863, were considered politically untrustworthy. A law of April 2, 1903, created *appointed* zemstvos in Kiev, Podol'e, Volynia, Minsk, Vitebsk, and Mogilev. The members of these assemblies were chosen by the Ministry of Interior, and these peculiar institutions were deemed entirely inadequate by local Russian landlords.[43] To be sure, the Polish element had been eliminated, but the appointment of members made the ethos of these bodies essentially bureaucratic. Furthermore, only the gubernia assemblies held any power; on the uezd level, they were merely consultative.[44] Therefore, the appointed zemstvo merely aggravated local awareness of Russian landlord absenteeism, which, although diminished with passing generations, still remained a problem.

The bureaucratic solution to the west's problem had been necessitated by the historic domination of landholding and agriculture by technically advanced Polish landlords. By 1907, however, according to Ministry of Agriculture figures cited by V. V. Shulgin, the total number of *desiatiny* privately owned by Russians in the southwest gubernias of Kiev, Podol'e, and Volynia far exceeded that owned by Poles.[45]

	Russians	*Poles*
Kiev	1,540,000	616,000
Podol'e	1,126,000	619,000
Volynia	2,372,000	1,091,000

The pattern of large ownership by Poles and smaller tracts owned by Russians had also diminished. The amount of land held by Russians and Poles in allotments of more or less than 200 *desiatiny* (a figure that is Shulgin's point of distinction and has no special analytic meaning) broke down as follows:[46]

	In tracts above 200d.		*Below 200d.*	
	Russian	*Polish*	*Russian*	*Polish*
Kiev	1,027,663	725,289	2,194,774	24,763
Podol'e	756,040	788,821	1,839,546	33,499
Volynia	1,234,923	1,423,546	2,502,712	83,664

Even by the earlier figures of the 1897 census, Russian landlords owning more than 200 *desiatiny* had been slightly more numerous than
their Polish counterparts:[47]

	Russian	Polish
Kiev	660	501
Podol'e	766	691
Volynia	796	1,017

The real political distinction emerges, however, when the franchise
requirements of the electoral law are introduced. The number of *pomeshchiki* possessing sufficient property to meet the full census requirement (for participation directly in the district assemblies of the landowners curia) was markedly greater among the Poles than among any
of the Russians:[48]

	Russian	Polish
Kiev	341	355
Podol'e	179	495
Volynia	182	438

This predominance of large Polish property had its effect on the composition of the west's State Council delegation chosen by *special* noble
assemblies: all were Polish. Had the 1890 zemstvo law been introduced
into the borderland without alteration, Polish landlords would have
dominated local government.

Because of this area's high fertility and accessibility to the international grain market, production for profit rather than subsistence
was the rule. Land was either farmed by the *pomeshchiki* themselves
or rented on long-term leases to people who could run it profitably.
Often renters were light industrial firms involved in food processing.
Distilling and sugar beet refining were the most common such enterprises. Generally, agriculture in the borderland, particularly in the
southwest gubernias of Kiev, Podol'e, and Volynia, was characterized
by a well-developed capitalist economy. Much of this modernity is
explained by the existence of a commercial market more developed
than elsewhere in Russia. Market relations pushed the gentry of the
region, both Polish and Russian, into the modern capitalist world of
profit, competent bookkeeping, and efficient organization.[49] These
were not traditional noble characteristics, and the effect was unset-
tling. It deprived the landlord of the smugness, and the political passivity, that went with the absolute domination of the relatively self-
contained world of the traditional village untouched by the market.

Instead, the western *pomeshchiki* moved in the unfamiliar world of money-lenders, shippers, and other middlemen, whom they confronted in the towns of the borderland. The necessity of functioning in this urban economic context was particularly disturbing to Russian landlords, who had only recently left the far stabler and more secure environment of the bureaucracy. While their new environment made them feel more insecure than their central Russian counterparts, it also made them more open, by necessity, to comparatively modern approaches to both economics and politics.

There were few self-sufficient communes and dues-collecting landlords in the west. The profitability of farming was reflected in the high value of land, especially in the southwest. There land sold for an average of 128.7 roubles per *desiatin* in 1900, a figure exceeded in value only in the left-bank Ukraine and the southern steppe.[50] In addition, the borderland exhibited a higher concentration of land in the hands of large holders and a higher level of private landholding than the rest of Russia. Of this private land, 61.7 percent was owned by nobles and 13.3 percent by peasants.[51]

Significantly, noble landlords of the west had lost far less land over the course of the late nineteenth century than had their central Russian counterparts. Since Emancipation, the *dvorianstvo* of the empire had generally been losing its grip on the land, but the *pomeshchiki* of the southwest still retained 84 percent of what they had owned in 1877. The figure for Bielorussia was 88 percent, in comparison with a national average of 70 percent.[52] Much of this resilience is attributable to the performance of the more efficient Polish landlords, who had never been distracted by the necessity of state service, and many of whom had formally studied agronomy. While not always direct participants in agricultural activity, west Russian nobles nevertheless had a conception of agriculture that derived from the experience of their more advanced Polish competitors. For this reason among others, the Russian landlord of the west came to perceive agriculture as a modern productive force, which could bolster and indeed define his social position.

In Gaisin uezd of Podol'e roughly two-thirds of the holdings were managed by their owners. One-third had been rented out on long-term leases.[53] Little land was left fallow or given to peasant communes to cultivate in exchange for rent. Crop rotation had become more sophisticated in the west. In Gaisin 85 percent of the land was under multifield tillage, and the few individual holdings on which we have information were also multifield.[54] As noted above, the west had always been a fertile field for the growth of private peasant holding; yet ownership of most of the land was still firmly in noble hands. In Kiev gubernia, 14,304 private owners were members of the *dvorianstvo*, while only 2,673 peasants held land privately.[55] Aside from land ownership, in Kiev gubernia there were 53,113 people of the noble estate and 2,972,275 peasants.[56] In Volynia 47,024 *dvoriane* dominated the lives of 2,241,062 peasants.[57] These figures reflect the classic pattern of concentration of wealth in the hands of a relative few, but they also show that the ranks of the nobility were not miniscule: nobles were present in sufficiently large numbers to make up a sizable constituency to which the Nationalists would later feel accountable.

One finds leading Nationalist figures engaged in both renting and farming. Professor V. E. Chernov was vice-president and later president of the Kiev Club of Russian Nationalists. A medical specialist in the city of Kiev, Chernov had no time for agriculture despite his noble ancestry, and so rented his 1,068 *desiatiny* in Uman uezd to the Verniachsky sugar factory. Leaving the professor 52.3 *desiatiny* for *usad'ba*, the factory planted 786.6 *desiatiny* and left 214 as forest. 16 *desiatiny* were unusable.[58] The opposite pattern obtained for the Nationalist deputy, A. A. Pototsky. A member of one of the empire's wealthiest landowning families, Pototsky owned land in Podol'e and Kiev.[59] He had fifteen villages in Zvenigorod uezd of Kiev gubernia. Pototsky actually farmed 14,598 *desiatiny* while renting out 891. Of the land he worked, 8,305 *desiatiny* were planted, all of it in a ten-field system; 4,199 were left as forest; 296 were given over to raising hay; and the manor's *usad'ba* lands comprised 421 *desiatiny*.[60]

A more mixed approach was exhibited by Konstantin Konstantinovich Pototsky, who possessed some 30,625.7 *desiatiny* in Gaisin. Of this land, 5,260.3 *desiatiny* were managed by Pototsky while another 5,559.5 *desiatiny* were in forest land. The remaining 19,805.8 *desiatiny* were rented out on long-term leases to a variety of people. Of the land actually worked by K. K., 4,588.93 *desiatiny* were planted in a multi-field arrangement, 22.7 went for *usad'ba* and hay-raising land, 191.2 were rented to peasants, 178.5 was occupied by Pototsky's own sugar factory, and 1.2 were given over to a distilling plant.[61] Information on the estates of several relatives of Nationalist deputies reveals an even clearer pattern of agricultural modernity. Of nine such holdings, all but one were multifield, and the one three-field estate provided the grain for a large distilling operation. All the estates had either sugar beet refining or distilling factories; in some cases both.[62] This is concrete proof of the Nationalists' involvement in production for the market. This involvement in market relations had compelled these men to do business regularly in the city of Kiev, the economy of which was heavily geared to sugar and alcohol. This practical involvement in city life, in turn, had significant political and institutional consequences, which will be elaborated below.

While the future Nationalists exhibited a variety of patterns of land use, the limited number of our examples should caution us not to assume an automatic relationship between *specific* approaches to land-owning and the politics of the Nationalist party. But the tendencies toward activism and involvement with the market are clear. What is crucial is that agriculture in the west, regardless of the particular form of tenure, was capitalistically organized, and the importance and profitability of agriculture reinforced the commitment of Russian land-lords to retain their lands. Capitalist agriculture coupled with the confrontation of different nationalities created a particularly volatile political setting.

Because of their desire and ability to maintain their estates, the landlords of the west were extremely unsympathetic to peasant demands for land. Indeed their very success in holding onto their property had created an especially acute land shortage for the peasantry of the west. Many peasants had been forced off their allotments to work as wage laborers on the landlords' huge sugar plantations. Even most of those who held onto some land could not make ends meet, and they too had to seek employment, for piteously low wages, on the estates of the *pomeshchiki*. Thus the relationship between the land-lords of the west and those who worked their lands more closely resembled that of a capitalist and his employees than that of a traditional feudal landlord and his peasants. In contrast to much of the rest of Russia, something far more like a class of capitalist farmers confronted a class of agrarian laborers in an intense, bitter, and daily struggle.

Importantly, the landlords of the west did not have to search their memories to find proof of the seriousness of what could properly be called a class struggle on the land. In the course of the massive peasant revolts of 1905 and 1906, it was the southwest that had the highest per capita incidence of disturbances of any region. Bielorussia ranked third. Moreover, these were neither the elemental burnings and lootings nor the sporadic forest offenses typical of the rest of Russia. The peasants of the west engaged in well-planned, highly conscious strikes for higher wages and better working conditions. While this movement met with some initial successes, it eventually was brutally repressed by the autocracy's policemen and soldiers. By the end of 1907, the landlords had been reminded of their ultimate dependence on the state, and the peasants had once again been thwarted in their desires.

Excluding the provinces of Moscow and Petersburg, the southwestern gubernias had an especially large percentage of urban residents. By 1910 the city of Kiev had a population of just under half a million, which made it the third largest city in Russia.[63] Of a population of 4,200,354 in Kiev gubernia, 604,135 lived in towns larger than 10,000.[64] This is 15 percent, a figure higher than the national percentage of 13 percent, and particularly high if we eliminate the two capitals from our calculations.[65] In Volynia some 9 percent lived in towns, and in Podol'e the figure was 8 percent.[66] However, Kiev dominated the entire southwest, serving as the central city for landlords from Podol'e and Volynia, many of whom maintained houses or apartments there. Since the 1860s, when it had been an administrative and military center of 68,000, Kiev had experienced an astronomical demographic growth:[67]

1884—154,000
1897—247,723   (census)
1907—404,000
1908—450,000
1913—594,000

Industrial expansion had been enormous, especially during the 1890s. Much of it involved light industries closely related to agriculture. Sugar beet refining and distilling were the major industries. Railroads had played a crucial role in the city's growth: the agriculture products of the borderland found easy access to a newly revived European grain market. By 1907 this growth had somewhat slowed down and unemployment was a serious problem.[68] The political unrest of the previous two years had been suppressed, but the Nationalists' future supporters could not help but feel that they were sitting on a powder keg.

Urbanization also had a profound effect on the politics of the Nationalists. This aspect of the party's development distinguishes it sharply from the Octobrists. After eliminating from consideration the capitals, from which the Octobrists drew most of their bourgeois support, one is struck by the absence of large cities in areas that returned Octobrist deputies: Samara, Chernigov, Ekaterinoslav, Poltava, Voronezh, Tambov, Khazan, Kaluga, and Kharkov all elected large numbers of Octobrist deputies, but only the last even approached Kiev in size. Moreover, in those areas of Bielorussia that were least urbanized—Mogilev and Vitebsk—the Nationalists did not fare as well; whereas in

Minsk, which was roughly similar to the southwest, seven deputies who would become Nationalists were elected.

The precise influence of urban society on west Russian nobles was well delineated by V. V. Shulgin. I have cited Shulgin extensively because he can truly be said to reflect the views of the Russian landowning nobility of the western borderland, and it is, of course, the Russian gentry's perceptions that concern me here. In particular, Shulgin provides a highly revealing analysis of the effect of urban politics in the absence of elected zemstvos in the southwest.

Many descendants of the original *chinovnik* landowners had remained on their land to take up farming, yet there existed no institutional framework that brought them into regular contact with one another. Rarely seeing their neighbors, they lived isolated lives. Shulgin compared them to *dachniki*, who lived alone with their families in summer vacation cottages. Atomized in this way, they lacked any real community. This interpersonal alienation was compounded by a sense that farming was an inadequate form of self-objectification, or often simply boring. Public activity could offer a solution to this psychological problem, but given the absence of well-functioning zemstvos, no arena for this public activity existed in the countryside. To engage in public activity, it was necessary to go to the city:

> Often people meet each other, for example in Kiev, and find out to their amazement that they are close neighbors or even farm land in the same uezd. To such an extent did Russian landowning exist in isolation that men were kept in their little cells. It was clear that given such a situation people who wished to occupy themselves with public affairs . . . had no place in the countryside. They had to run to the city to find both gratification for their spiritual needs and a way to expend their energy. [Only] people of an exceptional nature remained on the land, either scorning society or feeling called to the land.[69]

Thus, the initial political experience of those who later became Nationalist leaders had unfolded in the cities of the west, particularly Kiev. Only in the towns and cities could they find the sort of personal involvement that they sought. As a result, their approach to party work came to be influenced by the urban political culture and social structure to which they had been exposed. Shulgin's chief complaint was the lack of a satisfactory institutional structure in the countryside. He sought a framework that would give the Russian landowners of the region the possibility of playing an independent local political role, freed of the tutelage of the bureaucracy. "The local population must think for itself and be able to help itself."[70] To be sure, the Russian landowners should organize to dominate the new local institutions, and thus to control local life. In this respect, the Nationalists' approach to the zemstvos was entirely different from that of nobles in central Russia. The elected zemstvo was not to be above party politics; rather, it was to be the arena for the struggle for power in the western borderland. Local elections were to be contested under the same party label as those that had emerged in the Duma.

The Electors

Until now, analyses of the electors have been drawn from incomplete and inconsistent newspaper accounts. These reports used a variety of terminologies and often did not corroborate each other.[71] There are available, however, statistical breakdowns of the Third Duma electors compiled by the Ministry of Interior's *Osoboe delo-proizvodstvo po vyboram*. While the categories used by the Ministry would not necessarily occur to the modern political analyst, the government's criteria are sufficiently clear to permit greater understanding of this level of the electoral process.

For purposes of comparison it is useful to look at certain of the national totals on all the electors. By *soslovie*:[72]

	Vyborshchiki of the Landowners' curia (2542)	*All vyborshchiki* (5150)
dvorianstvo	1542 (61%)	1896 (37%)
clergy	533 (22%)	631 (12%)
honorary citizens	117 (4%)	316 (6%)
kuptsy	121 (5%)	395 (8%)
meshchanstvo	47 (2%)	320 (6%)
peasants		1244 (24%)
others	119 (4%)	344 (7%)

By political tendency:[73]

	Landowners	*All vyborshchiki*
right	1569 (62%)	2432 (47%)
moderate	585 (23%)	1046 (20%)
left	97 (8%)	1118 (22%)
unknown	191 (7%)	552 (11%)

By education:[74]

	Landowners	*All vyborshchiki*
higher	943 (37%)	1473 (29%)
secondary	1197 (47%)	1474 (29%)
primary	402 (16%)	2201 (42%)

My concern here is to compare the results for areas that returned Nationalists with those that elected Octobrists, in order to determine if it is possible to draw still more precise distinctions between the two parties. I shall be comparing the six western gubernias that received zemstvos in 1911 (Kiev, Podol'e, Volynia, Minsk, Vitebsk, and Mogilev) first with other gubernias that chose future Nationalists (Bessarabia, Tula, and Pskov), and second with regions that went heavily Octobrist (Ekaterinoslav, Samara, Chernigov, and Poltava).[75]

Most striking is the numerical weakness of the nobility in the land-owners' curiae of the western gubernias. They do not constitute even half the landowners' curiae, the very category in which one would expect them to be dominant. This stands in marked contrast to other Nationalist gubernias and to Octobrist strongholds.[76]

	6 western gubernias	3 Nationalist gubernias	4 Octobrist gubernias
dvorianstvo	195	104	198
clergy	174	17	44
honorary citizens	12	5	10
kuptsy	5	10	18
meshchanstvo	15	2	8
peasants	10	0	6
others	8	11	10

The large number of priests in the west is the most salient feature of this comparison. It clearly demonstrates the severe problems that Russian landlords faced in these gubernias. While the soslovie distribution in the Octobrist and Nationalist Duma fractions was basically the same, this similarity did not carry over to the vyborshchiki who elected them. These statistics reveal the Nationalists to be the representatives of an especially weak segment of the landed nobility, which could not be secure in the belief that their wealth and position would assure them representation in the Duma. Instead it was necessary for them to do what nobles had not done previously: organize politically. As the statistics reveal, the clergy was to play a special role in the development of their political organization.

Priests were to act as a surrogate for Russian noble interests, a role with which they were not always happy, but one that they ultimately accepted and fulfilled. Had the priests' position been one of absolute independence, it is reasonable to assume that the number of clerics in the Nationalist fraction in the Duma would have been considerably larger than it was. The large number of clerical electors may partly explain the Nationalists' intense concern with religious questions during the course of the Duma. Yet it seems reasonable that the party's ideological predispositions and concern for nationality probably would have assured a strong interest in religious matters under any circumstances. What is really underscored here is the extreme precariousness of the west Russian landlords' position. Severely threatened, they were far less likely to play with such notions as legality and constitutionalism than were their central Russian counterparts. The Nationalist constituency concentrated first and foremost on safeguarding its most immediate interests.

The Russian nobles of the west had been more involved in state service and less in "public activities" than their Octobrist counterparts, a fact easily explained by the absence of zemstvos in the west. While this phenomenon affected the attitudes of those deputies who came from the borderland, its broader explanatory force is limited by the fact that the rate of participation in zemstvo work in Nationalist areas where such bodies did exist is roughly the same as that encountered in Octobrist regions. Indeed, the material presented on Octobrist electors and Nationalist electors outside the west reveals no major differences for any criterion save political tendency, the very factor I have sought to explain. Even the large number of so-called moderates (116) in the Octobrist strongholds requires qualification. In Samara and Ekaterinoslav "moderates" did dominate the assemblies, but in Poltava and Chernigov "right" electors were far more numerous. This similarity of characteristics makes the phenomenon of Nationalist strength outside the west difficult to explain.

But if there are not sharp "objective differences" between the electors of the Octobrist and future Nationalist deputies (except for the western provinces), what is to be made of the contrasts I have drawn above between the two Duma factions? One of the sharpest contrasts, it will be remembered, was in educational level. 45 percent of the Octobrist Deputies had gone to universities, as opposed to 25 percent of the Nationalist Deputies. When we exclude the peasant and church-affiliated deputies of both Duma factions from our calculations, the contrast between Octobrist and Nationalist Deputies becomes even more acute. Of the Octobrist Deputies, who were nobles, bourgeois, and professionals, 51 percent had had higher education; while the figure for the Nationalists was 39 percent. No such differences are discernible between the electors of the two parties, however; the national average of electors in the landowners' curia with university training was 37 percent. In the western gubernias, 35 percent of the electors in this curia were university educated, while in the other Nationalist strongholds, the figure was 40 percent, the same as the percentage that obtained in the Octobrists' strongholds. The pattern is clear: The Octobrist Deputies exhibited a higher educational level than the people who had elected them, while the Nationalists were more typical of their electorate. This finding would appear to reinforce my earlier contention that the Octobrist faction was less representative of its imputed social base than were the Nationalists.

The electors of the first city curiae repeat the pattern we discerned in the landowners' assemblies. The western gubernias show different results from both the nonwestern Nationalist and Octobrist provinces. These latter two groups of gubernias again are similar in all categories with the exception of political inclination. Outside the west, the electors of the first city curia were generally allied with the landlords. In the borderland, however, there were fewer nobles among the urban electors, and Jews tended to dominate the city assemblies. Their politics were decidedly left wing. The breakdown in the first city curiae:[77]

	western gubernias	Nationalist areas	Octobrist areas
By *soslovie*:			
dvorianstvo	14	10	16
clergy	0	2	2
honorary citizens	9	6	10
kuptsy	25	18	12
meshchantsvo	21	3	19
peasants	0	0	1
other	17	2	1
By nationality:			
Russian	17	34	40
Polish	8	0	1
Jewish	63	7	19
By politics:			
Right	11	20	10
Moderate	19	11	13
Left	49	10	33
Unknown	8	0	5

Quite clearly, alliances between electors from the landowners' curiae and those in the first city assembly did not occur in the west, forcing the local Russian gentry deeper into the embrace of the clergy. The fact that so much of both landed and commercial wealth was in the hands of aliens naturally reinforced the chauvinism of many Russian landlords, but it also gave to their particular form of nationalism a highly expedient and pragmatic character. While certain more romantic Russian nationalists were often willing to subordinate immediate interests to nationalist principles or to view nationalism as a supraclass ideology, the Nationalist party's principles were nearly always consistent with the most basic, pragmatic interests of their constituents.

The figures for the *vyborshchiki* amplify the suggestion, given by the profiles of the Duma fractions, that the Nationalists represented a less secure and historically established element of the *dvorianstvo*. The national divisions in the western borderlands further exacerbated this feeling. The insecurity of the landowners of the west goes far to explain the intransigence of the Nationalists' defense of what they perceived to be their immediate interests. The Nationalists were far less willing than the Octobrists to engage in a politics of compromise. The Nationalists' unswerving support of the Western Zemstvo Act, which introduced zemstvos into the borderland in 1911, is probably the most dramatic case of this attitude. In fact, it was around the demand for zemstvos in the borderland that the Nationalists coalesced during the first years of the Third Duma.[78] The campaign for control of local government in the west provided a broad basis for the development of the Nationalist Party. It was not a simple question of extending an institution to a region where it did not exist; rather, the western zemstvo issue highlighted all the party's fundamental concerns.

Basing their politics on concrete economic and political interests, the Nationalists evinced a modernity that carried over to the organizational forms they evolved during the course of the Third Duma. The party developed a network of local organizations, which maintained contact with, and had a strong influence upon, the Duma faction. Unlike other parties, these local groups sought to contest zemstvo and city Duma elections in terms of the same political affiliations that had emerged on the national level, and, perhaps most importantly, the Duma faction and the party's national center maintained constant contact with the localities. Thus, the Nationalists actually represented, in the truest sense of the word, the interests of a clearly defined constituency. Yet this specificity and modernity of organization owes much to the peculiarities of the western borderland. In the last analysis, one is drawn to the conclusion that the peculiar character of the Nationalist party was primarily a regional phenomenon.

It was the Nationalists' greatest failure that they could not extend their base in the west to the rest of Russia. The party had some success in central Russia in the Fourth Duma elections (1912), but it failed to increase the size of its Duma fraction (eighty-eight). Stolypin's absence from the scene does much to explain these mixed results. Some thirty nonwestern deputies who earlier might have joined the Nationalists affiliated instead with Krupensky's new center group. The Octobrists were reduced to less than one hundred deputies. Thus, in the years before the war the Fourth Duma was left with no consistent, working majority. The result was drift and apathy. The Nationalists were as much to blame for this state of affairs as anyone else, but, as their most vocal spokesman, A. I. Savenko, pointed out repeatedly, this political sloth only mirrored the indifference and aimlessness of the social classes represented in the Duma.

The war reanimated national politics. The autocracy's military and logistic failures reopened the gap between state and privileged society. The Nationalists, with ties to both state and society, found themselves caught in the middle. The creation of the clearly oppositional Progressive Bloc in the summer of 1915, with its call for a ministry of public confidence, forced them to take sides, which they were unable to do as a united group. For all their talk of modernity, many of the Nationalists still had not entirely forsaken the service tradition. Thus, they could not reach a common view on joining the Progressive Bloc. The result was a party split. Shulgin and V. A. Bobrinsky led thirty-six Nationalists into the Progressive Bloc, while the party's president, P. N. Balashev, continued to lead those of the Nationalist deputies who refused to follow the others. From this moment on, the Nationalists, as a party, ceased to be a significant force on the national political scene.

To recapitulate, there are four main factors that account for the Nationalists' political behavior in the western provinces:

1. The capitalist organization of borderland agriculture, the accompanying market relations, the high value of land, and production for profit rather than subsistence undermined traditional noble attitudes and intensified the desire of landlords to retain their lands. This provided a material basis for the evolution of class consciousness. To be sure, this is not a sufficient explanation given the presence of capitalist forms of agriculture in some areas of Octobrist strength. It is, however, the necessary first step for any understanding of the Nationalists. Had agriculture in the west been more traditional, they would have turned into a very different kind of political formation.

2. The division and conflicts of nationalities in the west contributed to a sense of precariousness among the Nationalists' supporters. The greater wealth and efficiency of Polish landlords made Russian noble landowners extremely insecure both economically and politically.

3. The greater wealth of the Polish landlords had made it impossible to introduce elected zemstvos in the borderland: according to the property requirements of the 1890 law, the zemstvo would have been dominated by Poles. It was politically impossible to allow local government in an area near Austria and Germany to be in the hands of unreliable aliens.

4. The absence of zemstvos made it necessary for Russian noble landlords interested in public activities to go to the towns, primarily Kiev, where they were exposed to a modern urban political culture in which the class struggle was a clear and unavoidable element of everyday reality. This contributed to a still greater sense of social conflict. It also provided the Nationalists with a whole new set of terms of reference about politics, which they proceeded to apply, along with the peculiar intensity of urban politics, to the politics of the countryside.

I should stress that these basic determinants cannot be viewed in isolation. No single one provides a sufficient explanation, nor is any one more important than the others. Taken separately, each can be said to apply to groups other than the west Russian gentry. It is only the combination of these factors, together with the political culture to which they gave rise, that explains the genesis and peculiar character of the Nationalist party.

NOTES

1. A. Ia. Avrekh, *Tsarizm i tret'eiunskaia sistema* (Moscow, 1966), p.16.

2. Samuel Harper, *The New Electoral Law for the Russian Duma* (Chicago, 1908). Fyodor Dan, *Novyi izbiratel'nyi zakon* (Spb., 1907). Alfred Levin, "The Russian Voter in the Elections to the Third Duma," *Slavic Review*, December 1962, pp.660–67, has valuable information on procedural aspects of the law, the text of which can be found in *Polnoe sobranie zakonov*, vol. XXVII, #29242. See also Geoffrey Hosking, *The Russian Constitutional Experiment* (Cambridge, 1973), pp.45–48, and Levin, *The Third Duma: Elections and Profile* (Hamden, 1975).

3. C. Jay Smith, "The Russian Third State Duma," *Russian Review* #3, 1958, pp.201–10.

4. E. D. Chermenskii, "Bor'ba partii i klassov v IV gosudarstvennoi duma (1912–1917 gg.)," t.I, Doctoral dissertation, Moscow, 1947, p.70.

5. Ibid., p.21.

6. Statistical compilations by the government, previously unused, provide the possibility for a more solid empirical basis for discussions of the 1907 election campaign. Ministerstvo vnutrennykh del, *Vybory v tretiu gosudarstvennuiu dumu* (hereafter *Vybory*) (St. Petersburg, 1911), p.171. Alfred Levin's "The Russian Voter . . ." (see note 4), "The Reactionary Tradition in

the Elections to the Third Duma," *Oklahoma State University Occasional Papers* (Stillwater, 1962), and his recent book *The Third Duma* are the only works on the elections themselves. Avrekh in *Tsarizm i tret'eiunskaia sistema* and in "Tret'eiunskaya monarkhia i obrazovanie tret'edumskogo pomeshchi-che-burzhuaznogo bloka," *Vestnik moskovskogo universiteta*, #1, 1956, pp.1–70, avoids the problem, offering neither an investigation of the election campaign nor a real analysis of its social significance. Hosking's discussion, pp.45–48, is also brief, though more insightful than that of Avrekh.

7. Dan, p.30.

8. Smith, p.202.

9. See note 6.

10. *Golos Moskvy*, November 1, 1907.

11. Avrekh, *Tsarizm* . . . , p.20.

12. Father Fiodr Nikonovich, *Iz dnevnika chlena gosudarstvennoi dumy ot Vitekskoi gubernii* (Vitebsk, 1912), p.11.

13. G. Iursky, *Pravye v tret-ei gosudarstvennoi dume* (Kharkov, 1912), p.3.

14. Levin, "The Reactionary Tradition . . . ," p.4.

15. *Kievlianin*, November 2, 1909.

16. *Tsentral'nyi gosudarstvennyi arkhiv Oktiabrskoi revoliutsii* (hereafter TsGAOR), fond 102, departamenta politsii, 4-Oe deloproizvodstvo, 1907, delo 164, list 302.

17. TsGAOR, f. 102, D.P., 4-oe deloproizvodstvo, 1907, d. 164, 11. 149–50.

18. TsGAOR, f. 102, D.P., 4-oe deloproizvodstvo, 1907, d. 164, 1. 191.

19. TsGAOR, f. 102. D.P., 4-oe deloproizvodstvo, 1907, d. 164, 1. 281.

20. Gosudarstvennaia Duma, 3-yi sozyv—*Portrety, biografii, avtografii* (hereafter *Portrety*) (St. Petersburg, 1910).

21. *Obzor deiatel'nosti Gosudarstvennoi Dumy*, tretyi sozyv, Chast'I, pp. 72–93.

22. *Okrainy Rossii*, no. 43, October 27, 1907; no. 47, November 24, 1907.

23. Avrekh, "Stolypinskyi bonapartizm i voprosy voennoi politiki v IIIei Dume," *Voprosy Istorii*, no. 1, 1956, p.20.

24. Avrekh, "Tret'a Duma i nachalo krizisa tret'eiunskoi sistem," *Isotoricheskie zapiski*, no. 53, p.53.

25. Avrekh, "Tret'eiunskaia monarkhia," *Istoria SSSR*, t. VI (Moscow, 1968), p.346.

26. *Portrety*.

27. Avrekh, "Tret'a Duma . . . ," p.54.

28. *Portrety*.

29. TsGAOR, f. 115, o.1., d. 34, 1.1.

30. Public Records Office (hereafter PRO), Foreign Office series 371, vol. 318, no. 27698, August 19, 1907.

31. PRO, FO 371, vol. 513, no. 31810, September 14, 1908.

32. *Portrety*.

33. Sir Lewis Namier, "Country Gentlemen in Parliament, 1756–84," in *Crossroads of Power* (New York, 1962), p.31.

34. PRO, FO 371, no. 30901, September 5, 1908.

35. *Portrety*.

36. Ibid.

37. Ibid.

38. Ibid.

39. V. V. Shulgin, *Vybornoe zemstvo v iugo-zapadnom krae* (Kiev, 1909), p.17.

40. Ibid., p.20.

41. These figures are from Mary Schaeffer, "The Political Policies of P. A. Stolypin," (doctoral diss., Indiana University, 1964), p.268. They are based mainly on the census of 1897.

42. Avrekh, "Vopros o zapadnom zemstve in bankrovstvo Stolypina," *Istoricheskie zapiski,* no. 70, 1962, pp.61–112. Edward Chmielewski, "Stolypin's Last Crisis," California Slavic Studies (3), 1964, pp.95–126, and *The Polish Question in the Russian State Duma* (Knoxville, 1970), A. S. Izgoev, *P. A. Stolypin* (Moscow, 1912). All three writers show a tendency to regard the Nationalists' concern with nationalism as an autonomous factor divorced from questions of class. See also Hugh Seton-Watson, *The Russian Empire 1801–1917* (London, 1967), p.674. Of all historians who cover this period, Seton-Watson appears to be the only nonspecialist who is sensitive to nationalism's broad political appeal. He draws a useful parallel to Germany, where nationalism, and later fascism, was strongest in southern border areas.

43. Chmielewski, *The Polish Question in the Russian State Duma,* p.82.

44. Shulgin, pp.25–32.

45. Ibid., p.50. In citing these figures from Shulgin, we are primarily interested in the kinds of information on which the Russian landlords based their opinions, for we are concerned here largely with their state of mind and less with the objective conditions of land ownership.

46. Ibid., p.56.

47. Ibid., p.36.

48. Ibid., p.37.

49. A. M. Anfimov, *Krupnoe pomeshchiche khoziaistvo evropeiskoi Rossii* (Moscow, 1969), p.167.

50. S. D. Kovalchenko, "Agrarnyi rynok i kharakter agrarnogo stroia evropeiskoi Rossii v kontse XIX—nachale XX veka," *Istoria SSSR,* no. 2, 1973, p.47.

51. N. A. Proskuriakova, "Razmeshchenie i struktura dvorianskovo zemlevladenia evropeiskoi Rossii v kontse XIX—nachale XX veka," *Istoria SSSR,* no. 1, 1973, p.61.

52. Ibid., p.64.

53. *Materialy po agrarno-ekonomicheskie issledovanie iugo-zapadnogo kraia* (hereafter *Materialy*) (Gaisin, 1908) p.v.

54. Ibid., p.3.

55. *Ves'iugo-zapadnogo kraya* (Kiev, 1907), p.9. A. I. Yaroshevich, *Ocherki ekonomicheskie zhizni iugo-zapadnogo kraya* (Kiev, 1908), p.12.

56. *Materialy,* p.4.

57. *Ves'iugo-zapadnogo kraya,* pp.7, 220.

58. *Materialy,* p.122.

59. *Anfimov,* p.394.

60. *Materialy,* p.148.

61. Ibid., p.7.

62. Descriptions of these estates were made by the Ministry of Agriculture. See *Kratkie spravochnye svedenia o nekotorikh russkikh khoziaistvakh, izdanie vtoroe, vypusk vtoroi* (St. Petersburg, 1901). It is necessary to be

extremely cautious about drawing direct political conclusions from this information. There is no way of specifying the precise relationships of these landlords to the Nationalist deputies, nor can one be certain of the extent and nature of communication that went on between family members. Obviously joint family membership is no definite determinant of shared political opinion, but as a general indication, this particular connection is, I think, meaningful. The estates mentioned in the *Kratkie svedenia* include additional information on the lands of A. A. Pototsky, p.182, and K. K. Pototsky, p.242. Others were the heirs of N. A. Bezak, p.177, P. E. and A. I. Suvchinsky, p.214, Praskovaia Aleksandrevna Urusova, p.188, Nikolai Petrovich Balashev, p.244, Nikolai Matveich Chikhachev, p.265. Finally, it should be noted that there is no guarantee that this group is in any way typical. It does, however, correspond to most general accounts of the nature of agriculture in the borderland.

63. Cited from *Goroda Rossii v 1910 godu*, compiled by the Central Statistical Committee of the Ministry of the Interior, cited in Seton-Watson, p.674.

64. *Ves'iugo-zapadnogo kraya*, p.7.

65. Ibid., p.218.

66. Ibid., p.453.

67. Institut istorii, akademia nauk USSR, *Istoria Kieva*, t. I (Kiev, 1965), pp.339–41, 464.

68. Ibid., p.462.

69. Shulgin, p.19.

70. Ibid., p.33.

71. See McNaughton and Manning, this volume. The same imprecision in zemstvo elections existed on the elector level in Duma elections.

72. *Vybory*, p.272, figures taken from various sections.

73. Ibid.

74. Ibid.

75. The choice of these particular gubernias requires some explanation. As noted before, the western provinces were the Nationalists' area of greatest strength. I have not included the northwest gubernias of Vilna, Kovno, and Grodno, all of which were eliminated from the original proposals for western zemstvos. The future Nationalists did well in Grodno, but *pravye* were chosen in Vilna and Kovno, where national curiae divided the regular assemblies, presenting figures that cannot be readily correlated with these other findings. Bessarabia and Pskov were selected for their proximity to the western borders, while Tula was included to represent the limited phenomenon of Nationalist success in central Russia. Ekaterinoslav (eight), Chernigov (nine), and Samara (nine) returned the largest delegations of Octobrists, with Poltava (seven) close behind. The last province also voted in four moderate rights and has been included both to prevent the Octobrist sample from being too pure and to counterbalance the impact of Vitebsk (where three Octobrists were chosen) on the statistics for the western gubernias.

76. *Vybory*, p.272.

77. Ibid.

78. Robert Edelman, "The Russian Nationalist Party and the Political Crisis of 1909," *The Russian Review* (January 1975), pp.22–54.

The Landed Nobility,
the State Council, and
P. A. Stolypin (1907-11)

ALEXANDRA SHECKET KORROS

Desperate to restore some semblance of normalcy to society in the wake of the disorders of 1905, the Russian government acceded to demands for a popularly elected legislative assembly (the State Duma). The early stages of the 1905 revolution had been marked by expressions of discontent from all strata of society, including the landed nobility, the commercial and industrial classes, and the ever dissident intelligentsia. However, by the end of the year most of the newly radicalized nobles found their ardor beginning to cool in the wake of the increased peasant disorders and the Moscow armed uprising. Thus, when the tsar's special conference met to discuss the electoral law for the new Duma, the government turned to the landed nobility as a means of buffering the power of what was expected to be a radical, if not revolutionary, institution.

In order to place this "buffer" within the framework of the limited constitutional order established by the Manifesto of 17 October, the reformers of Russia's governing institutions converted the bureaucratic *Gosudarstvennyi sovet* (State Council) into an upper house, a legislative chamber with powers equal to the popularly elected Duma.[1] In contrast to the Duma, which was to represent the entire Russian population without regard for estate (*soslovie*) origins, the membership of the State Council, beyond the bureaucratic elite of which it had traditionally been composed,[2] was to be limited to representatives of the "cultured" elements of Russian society.

To this end, the bureaucratic reformers decided to allocate six representatives to each of several important interest groups—commerce and

industry, the Academy of Sciences and the universities, and the Orthodox clergy—or a total of eighteen deputies. The remaining seventy-four
elected members were to come from the zemstvos (thirty-four representatives), the landowners of the nonzemstvo provinces (twenty-two),
and the nobility (eighteen representatives indirectly elected by the
local assemblies of nobility). By establishing high service and property
qualifications for those elected by the zemstvos and landowners, the
government virtually guaranteed that seventy-four of the ninety-eight
elected members of the State Council would be noblemen. As a result,
the Council became the institution in the new governmental structure
that most strongly represented noble interests.[3]

Loosely organized though they were, the landed noble representatives in the State Council had a considerable impact upon the government's policies. It is the purpose of this article to examine this group's
impact and, more generally, its political characteristics, focusing on
their awareness and defense of their estate interests. Of necessity, the
term "landed nobility" is here defined as the *Russian* landed nobility,
for, although there were Polish landed noblemen in the State Council,
their distinct national and historical identity caused them to pursue
very different concerns in the upper chamber and prompted them to
form their own political grouping, the Polish *kolo* (which usually supported the majority center faction).[4] The Russian landed noblemen
displayed no similar propensity to form a single political group representing their common interests, but they did display common patterns
of political behavior reminiscent of those of Russian noble organizations before the 1905 upheaval.

Since the reign of Catherine the Great, the Russian landed gentry
had been organized into district and provincial assemblies of nobility,
whose elected marshals represented and sought to reconcile the corporate interests of their estate with those of the State power. As a
result of the relatively high property qualifications for election, the
marshals tended to be large landowners,[5] who, because of their wealth
and unpaid status, remained relatively independent of the central bureaucracy. During the closing years of the nineteenth century, the
provincial assemblies, through their marshals, pressed the government
to safeguard their declining estate by conferring noble status on non-
noble landowners, and they also attempted to exclude from these
assemblies landless noblemen, who in large part were local bureaucrats
ennobled by the Table of Ranks. In addition, the marshals increasingly
emerged as champions of noble economic interests, demanding state
aid for the landed nobility whose fortunes had suffered serious de-

cline since the emancipation of the serfs. By 1896 provincial marshals had begun to meet annually to coordinate these activities and to attempt to influence state policies in their favor. But despite political concessions on the local level, including the 1890 Zemstvo Statute and the creation of the land captains (*zemskie nachal'niki*), government policy continued to support the industrialization of the country and to neglect the concerns of the agricultural sector, including those of the landed nobility. As a consequence, the imperial government was regarded as generally unresponsive to their demands.

The provincial and district zemstvos were the other principal center of noble activities. Created in 1864, the zemstvos were all-estate assemblies, dominated by noble landowners. The provincial and district assemblies were responsible for supervision of schools, hospitals, road construction, etc. in rural areas. Noblemen active in zemstvo affairs were frequently thought of as more "liberal" than their counterparts in the assemblies of nobility; however, the district zemstvo was presided over by the district marshal of nobility, who also frequently served as chairman of the zemstvo board (*uprava*). Thus, at the district level, these two centers of noble activity overlapped.[6]

It is important to emphasize that only a relatively small number of the noblemen in any given district or province were actively involved in zemstvo affairs. Few could afford the money or the time to travel to the district or provincial capital to participate fully and regularly in zemstvo assemblies. As a result, only a handful of nobles dominated zemstvo affairs, often giving a zemstvo a political character shaped by the concerns of a minority of its members.

Government policies under Nicholas II strengthened hostility among both the zemstvos and the assemblies of the nobility toward the central administration. Liberals discussed constitutional limitations on bureaucratic arbitrariness, while conservatives sought means to retain exclusive estate privileges. Both sides, however, viewed the state bureaucracy as insensitive to noble needs and were even more vocal and unrestrained in their criticism of the government.

However, before 1905 the vast majority of landed noblemen stood aside from political activity, although their ostensible political leaders—the marshals through their annual meetings and the zemstvo men through their congresses—had begun to draw more closely together. In the midst of the national crisis of 1905, many noblemen who had rarely, if ever, participated in zemstvos found themselves involved in political affairs for the first time. Initially led by liberal zemstvo men, the assemblies moved to the left in a wave of support for universal (though not direct) suffrage and constitutionalism. But after the peasant disorders in late summer 1905, the zemstvos began to return to "sanity," replacing the liberals of 1905 with leaders of much more moderate, if not conservative, persuasion.

The conservative noblemen, alarmed both by the spread of liberal ideas and by the liberals' initial success in the noble milieu, decided to establish their own organization. Early in 1906, they called a congress of provincial and district marshals, which led to the formation of the United Nobility, a political organization dedicated to the defense of noble interests. Throughout the succeeding years, the United Nobility became the principal spokesman and pressure group for the provincial nobility. It is significant that approximately one-third of the delegates to the First Congress of the United Nobility, and nine of its fifteen-member executive board (the Permanent Council), served as elected members of the State Council, and that all of these men gravitated toward the right wing of the chamber.[7]

The creation of the State Duma introduced a new element into Russian political life—the legal political party. Most of the noblemen who had been active in the moderate wing of the zemstvo congresses joined the Union of 17 October, a party committed to the principles of the October Manifesto. But the Octobrists attempted to represent the interests of both rural and urban property owners, expecting the noblemen to renounce their special estate privileges and fuse with property owners of other estates.[8] Such an expectation ran counter to the traditional attitudes of the landed nobility. Thus, the party to which more noblemen were initially attracted than any other could not represent their particular interests as an estate.

The State Council provided a forum for the articulation of these interests. All seventy-four seats that could be occupied by nobles were in fact filled by them. In choosing their representatives to the upper house, the nobility, the zemstvos, and the landowners of the west quite naturally gravitated to their traditional leaders—the marshals of the nobility and the chairmen of the zemstvo boards. At least thirty of the representatives elected to the State Council in 1906 were past or present marshals, while another six had chaired their local zemstvo boards.[9]

Although the noble delegates were numerous enough to form the second largest grouping in the chamber (second only to the appointed bureaucrats), the Russian landed nobles in the upper house did not form a single "nobles' group." Not surprisingly, the political divisions among the nobles' representatives in the State Council occurred over the same issues that had previously divided the local zemstvos and noble assemblies: support of constitutional government as outlined in the October Manifesto, rejection of the Manifesto in favor of the old order, or, in a few cases, advocacy of further constitutional concessions.

Yet, whatever their political affiliations or inclinations, Russian noblemen of all political factions in the Council approached government in a similar manner. Noble interests frequently conflicted with bureaucratic views of state interest. But while bureaucrats were accustomed to playing an active, if not always creative, role in implementing state policy, the nobles' representatives were not; they had always looked to the autocrat to enact changes on their behalf. Thus, their conception of state service was to implement whenever possible the wishes of the central authority, while protesting only those measures which interfered with their own estate interests. This was true, by and large, even of those noblemen in the State Council who had previously participated in the Liberation Movement. These self-professed "progressives" had, for the most part, adhered to the moderate rather than liberal wing of the zemstvo congresses, resisting demands for four-tail suffrage and a constitution. Later, in the upper house, they tended to go along with their more conservative colleagues in considering the noble estate the most loyal servant of the tsar and of the state. Thus, even they were not inclined to oppose government policies as long as these policies did not directly conflict with the concerns of their estate.

Within a few weeks of the convocation of the State Council, three groups emerged—the right, center, and left—of which the first two almost immediately became considerably larger than the third. The center attracted many Russian noblemen, particularly zemstvo representatives, as well as bureaucrats of moderate views (largely from the Ministries of Justice and Finance), some former senators, the representatives of trade and industry, and Polish and Baltic landowners. The right was composed of retired military men, bureaucrats, representatives of the Orthodox clergy and some noble and zemstvo representatives. The left included only the six academic representatives and five zemstvo men who combined to form the "liberal" opposition in the upper chamber. Generally, bureaucrats and landed noblemen were so intermingled in the major political groups of the State Council that individual allegiances appeared to be determined largely by personal opinions and attitudes.

Early in the second session, Stolypin turned to the center group for his base of support in the Council. The center was ostensibly the majority group in the upper chamber and sought to act as a genuine political party, playing an active role in passing legislation.[10] But while he had a group to which he could turn in the State Council, it was not until after the coup d'état of June 1907 and the issuance of the new electoral law that the prime minister was able to begin developing his base in the Duma. The first and second Dumas had been radical assemblies, spurring reactionaries to hope that Stolypin would abolish the Duma entirely. Instead, he altered its composition to permit the domination of large property owners. When the State Council met in the fall of 1907, many of its members had changed their attitude toward the lower chamber. The dominance of the moderate property-owning elements made it possible for moderates of the State Council to cooperate with the Duma, forcing the advocates of a return to the old order to face for the first time the prospect of effective representative government.

However, while Stolypin could look now to the Union of 17 October for a somewhat stable base of Duma support, he found that the center of the State Council was not a "sure thing." The Octobrists could enforce some degree of group discipline in the Duma, but discipline was nearly impossible in the State Council. Members of the upper chamber were not dependent on their group or party affiliation for election and reelection; rather, group affiliation was entirely voluntary, and by the end of the Council's second session, the center as much as admitted that it could do little to make its members abide by group decisions.[11] Many of the center's landed noble members refused to heed leadership decisions and, in so doing, formed a right wing, which was to plague the group throughout the period under discussion.

In his first speech to the State Council as Chairman of the Council of Ministers, Stolypin outlined the areas of reform he envisioned.[12] Most significant was the introduction of new institutions of local government at the *volost'* (district) level. He sought to make the district the basic unit of administration—to establish zemstvos, courts, and other necessary local institutions at this level, thereby permitting local residents maximum participation in their own government. Stolypin also outlined a program rationalizing Russian administration, eliminating many problems that had led to discontent in 1905. He promised to carry out his programs without eliminating or displacing those already in power.

The reforms entailed extensive restructure of local government, particularly at the next level, the uezd (county). The county zemstvo was to be reorganized through the abolition of restrictions on peasant and urban suffrage. The basis for determining the franchise would be the amount of taxes an individual paid rather than the amount of immovable property he possessed. Supervision of the zemstvo would be limited to the legality of its actions rather than the expediency of its decisions. A county council would be created to coordinate government offices in the area, the head of which would be appointed by the Ministry of Interior. In sum, proposals were designed to substitute bureaucratic for noble control in the county, reducing the role of the county marshal of nobility to that of estate representative.[13]

The proposals prompted an immediate reaction from the Council of the United Nobility. A. A. Naryshkin, a member of the Council from Orel', met with Stolypin on February 27, 1907, to warn the Prime Minister that the passage of his "democratic" proposals would bring the "third element" into zemstvo work at the expense of the nobility. Naryshkin emphasized that the "virtual replacement of the county marshals would undermine the authority of the nobility," and he asked Stolypin to submit his proposals for discussion to the zemstvos and assemblies of nobility.[14]

In defending his program, Stolypin maintained that the "estate principle" had lost its meaning and had to be rooted out of local government. He contended that the "third element" presented no threat to the zemstvo and refused to submit the bill to noble scrutiny before its introduction into the State Duma, fearing that only a "purposeless mass of written materials" would result.[15] But Stolypin later reconsidered and allowed the nobility in their zemstvos and noble assemblies to discuss and review the government projects while they were being considered by the Duma.

The United Nobility formed a special committee to deal with the various aspects of the proposals and the organization retained its interest in Stolypin's local reforms long after the abrupt dismissal of the Second Duma on June 3, 1907. In particular, the report presented to the Congress of the United Nobility in March of 1908 gave the nobility the opportunity to exact maximum pressure on the government.

The threat of local government reform was the dominant theme of the 1908 Congress, and all its discussions related directly or indirectly to the subject. Even the first topic, the need to increase the number of noble representatives in the State Council, bore on this issue.[16] Many noblemen felt that their estate was insufficiently represented in the upper house, particularly in comparison to the zemstvos. Everyone agreed that a change was necessary, but several points of difference emerged: about at whose expense, if anyone's, this increase should be made; about the nature of temporary election changes until the increase had been achieved; and finally, about when such a petition should be presented to the tsar. The last point brought the ominous reform proposals into the discussion.

V. L. Kushelev of Pskov suggested that the best time to petition the tsar would be in connection with the projected zemstvo reform. All the zemstvo representatives, he observed, were noblemen, but it was unlikely that all postreform zemstvo representatives would continue to be noblemen. Since the State Council had to be "a conservative institution, restraining those impulses beyond the strength of the state, and it is this which we are constantly required to prove to the emperor and the government," Kushelev suggested that if the local government reforms were passed, the eighteen noble members would be a "drop in the ocean." Thus the nobility could not "lay aside" its estate interests or postpone "the expansion of the conservative element in the State Council."[17]

S. M. Prutchenko of Novgorod agreed with Kushelev but advised the Congress to wait until the reform had been adopted by the government before presenting its petitions. The nobility would then have a valid basis for its arguments that democratization of the zemstvo would mean democratization of the State Council. He suggested that the organization rephrase its request for an increase in noble representation in order to enable the legislative institutions "to hold off the approaching attack of radicalism . . . and . . . to call to the emperor's attention the desirability of increasing the number of noble representatives in the State Council, especially in view of the approaching zemstvo reform."[18]

Closely tied to the zemstvo proposals (which had not yet been submitted to the Duma) were the other proposed reforms of local government, to which the Congress devoted the remainder of its sessions. F. D. Samarin, one of the two Moscow noble representatives in the State Council, reported on the special committee's criticism of the reforms. The committee, he emphasized, had opposed the reforms, not as a threat to estate interests, but as measures objectively unsuited to Russian conditions at this moment. He urged the Congress to deal with them in a similar manner, stressing that the government had not yet surrendered on the reforms in the face of the committee's opposition, although it had not yet resubmitted the proposals to the Third Duma. Samarin claimed that if the first two projects for local court reform were approved, the others would pour into the legislative chambers.[19] He outlined the manner in which the marshals of nobility would lose their powers and how local court reform was designed to deprive land captains of their judicial powers. Samarin conceded that changes were needed, but he insisted that reform should be gradual lest its telescoping lead to a series of drastic projects exceeding Russia's financial means.

The Congress condemned the reforms and affirmed the intrinsic worth of the existing elective local institutions dominated by the noble estate. In its resolution against the county reforms, the Congress concluded that "such a measure, resulting mainly from the desire to structure all local institutions on a nonestate principle, cannot be justified either by the characteristics of the county marshals' . . . activities, or by any considerations of a practical character."[20]

Several leaders of the Congress were members of the State Council's right and had frequently opposed Stolypin's policies, so their vehement protests were not unexpected. But when P. V. Dicheskul', a former marshal of nobility and the Bessarabia zemstvo representative in the State Council, voiced his opposition, it was quite another matter. Dicheskul' belonged to the center group; indeed he was a leader of its right faction and his views were probably representative of many of his colleagues. His comments were scathing.

> I believe that the nobility desires to reform all that can be reformed . . . but it does not believe that what is being offered . . . will be any better than, and fully replace, what already exists. . . . I am for the retention of land captains . . . and against the administration's pernicious influence. . . . Thus, we cast our votes not against reform and partial change . . . but against the bureaucratic structure. . . .[21]

Dicheskul's remarks, reflecting traditional noble opposition to bureaucratic control, indicated that if the more moderate noblemen were opposed to the proposals, it would be a difficult task to muster a majority on their behalf in the State Council.

Toward the conclusion of the Congress, Ia. A. Ofrosimov of Vitebsk, later a member of the State Council, reminded the noblemen that their most important task was the preservation of the marshals' powers, and that all other aspects of the reforms were secondary. If justices of the peace replaced land captains, they would still be appointed by provincial or county marshals. "On that," Ofrosimov concluded, "we must insist."[22]

The press thoroughly reported the proceedings of the Congress, publishing several accounts of the debates and carefully noting the opposition to the Stolypin proposals.[23] The prime minister could not be unaware of the poor reception accorded his reforms.

The proceedings revealed the full extent of the nobles' opposition to what they regarded as encroachments on their estate interests. The proposed reforms were an overwhelming threat to the nobility's position in the countryside, particularly if the powers of local elective leaders—the provincial and county marshals—were reduced. All factions of the nobility opposed the reforms—not only Stolypin's traditional opponents, but his supporters as well.

The prime minister had been subjected to noble pressure against the reforms from the moment they had been announced. He had responded to the pressure by reorganizing the Ministry of Interior's Council on the Affairs of Local Economy (*Sovet po delam mestnago khoziastva*) in October of 1907, five months before the Congress of the United Nobility. Various provincial zemstvos sent their representative (usually the provincial marshal) to the council, and almost all of them rejected the reforms, particularly the one altering the district zemstvo.

S. E. Kryzhanovskii, Deputy Minister of Interior and architect of the reforms, wrote that Stolypin dropped the zemstvo reform as a result of the defeat in the Congress of the United Nobility.[24] Geoffrey Hosking cites the Congress's resolutions and observes: "It is certain that the combination of these with those passed in the Council on the Affairs of Local Economy constituted a crushing blow for the local reforms. . . . In fact, little more was heard of the provincial and *uyezd* zemstvo reforms."[25] The reforms previously submitted to the Duma did not come up for legislative action until 1910, and then again in 1913. The State Council did not discuss them until 1913, but by then, the projects were so altered that they conformed to noble demands— land captains and marshals had had their power restored, although in altered form.[26] Thus, conscious of his need to maintain the landed nobility's support, Stolypin was forced to postpone the enactment of his local government reforms and to reevaluate the considerations that had prompted them.

After his setback on local government, Stolypin apparently chose to refrain from encroaching on noble estate interests. However, the center group on which he relied was still unable to provide the prime minister with the base of support he needed to ensure passage of his legislation in the State Council. Although it ostensibly remained the largest single group in the Council, the center's numbers continued to decline. The combination of declining size, tenuous noble loyalty, and lack of group discipline increased Stolypin's need to find new allies in the upper chamber.

In March of 1909 the State Council barely passed a bill funding the Naval General Staff and approving a list of naval appointments, which had been included in the bill by the Duma. The bill's opponents argued that the latter section violated the tsar's prerogatives, but a small majority, composed of parts of the center, the left, and seven ministers, contended that this section was an exception and that, rather than force the Naval General Staff to go without funding, the bill should be passed.[27] Its passage precipitated the first major political crisis of the Stolypin era.

During most of April, rumors spread throughout Petersburg that Stolypin would be forced to resign and be replaced by a prime minister with strong right-wing sympathies. Stolypin was accused of associating with liberal elements and seeking to increase his own power at the expense of the autocrat. After nearly a month's speculation, the tsar refused to sign the Naval Staff bill but retained Stolypin as prime minister. Having squelched the intrigues against him of the State Council right Stolypin emerged from the crisis determined to disassociate his policies from "liberal" elements. In May 1909, in his first State Council appearance after the resolution of the crisis, the prime minister endorsed a proposal designed to increase Russian representation from the nine western provinces in the upper chamber at the expense of the Polish majority. In supporting this plan, the Pikhno proposal, sponsored by thirty-three members of the right and named after D. I. Pikhno, an archrightist appointed member of the upper house and the editor of the nationalist newspaper *Kievlianin*, Stolypin set out on a new course—supporting Great Russian nationalism.[28] He sought to establish a new majority in the State Council, one that would include not only the center but also the nationalists in the Council, breakaway members of the center and right who had begun to emerge as an important element in nationalist organizations since 1908.[29]

Several prominent State Council nationalists were landed noblemen active in the right faction of the center group. One of them, Stolypin's brother-in-law, A. B. Neidgardt, the zemstvo representative from Nizhnii Novgorod and a former provincial marshal of nobility, was a member of the Permanent Council of the United Nobility. Neidgardt emerged as the leader of the center's right faction, a group numbering between fourteen and nineteen members largely composed of landed noblemen.[30] They became the strongest supporters of government policy in the State Council after Stolypin's move to the right.

Throughout the Council's fifth session (1909–10), Stolypin seemed to be gaining some measure of legislative success with his new policy. The government modified its 1906 stand on a bill liberalizing the position of the Old Believers, and the prime minister personally sponsored a bill severely curtailing the autonomous powers of the Finnish Sejm.[31]

By advocating these invasions, Stolypin apparently succeeded in neutralizing his opponents on the Council's extreme right wing. He sponsored bills that encouraged nationalist aims, and enjoyed the tsar's enthusiastic support, making it impossible for the rightists opposing him to block legislation.

Yet another barometer of Stolypin's growing support was the attitude of the right-wing press. *Novoe vremia,* a paper that had been severely critical of the prime minister, especially during the ministerial crisis of 1909, now praised Stolypin's farsighted policies and condemned the shortsighted members of the State Council who seemed to oppose him. The nationalist journal *Okrainy Rossii,* the organ of the Russian Borderlands Society (*Russkoe okrainnoe obshchestvo*), lauded the government and Stolypin personally, where only months before it had entirely ignored him.[32]

Attitudes in the State Council, particularly among the landed noblemen, were now characterized by two basic trends: an important nationalist group, led by Neidgardt, Pikhno, Stishinskii, and others, warmly supported Stolypin's new policy; in contrast, some landed noblemen, members of the center's so-called basic group (i.e., that group of the center, approximately forty-seven members, who faithfully followed the decisions of the group's bureau) supported nationalist legislation so long as it did not affect their immediate concerns. After the second session, the center's leaders tried to *support* government policy as much as possible, and the "basic group" followed them.

Stolypin's opponents on the right also had to assume supportive posture, but against their will. These men, a majority of whom had been career bureaucrats or military men, were reluctant to vote against legislation enjoying the tsar's endorsement. Nevertheless, they continued to oppose Stolypin personally, consistently seeking new ways to undermine his position at Court, in the legislative chambers, and in the public eye.

The prime minister's adoption of nationalism seemed to serve him well: it provided him with support outside government circles as well as in the legislative chambers. In 1910 the government submitted a bill introducing the zemstvo into the six southwestern provinces. The bill, known as the Western Zemstvo bill, sought to bring these institutions under Russian domination, a goal to which Russian nationalists had long aspired. In order to accomplish this aim, the proposal included a section establishing national curiae so designed as to enable Russian landowners in the region to obtain a sufficient number of votes to outnumber their larger and more powerful Polish counterparts. A

Duma amendment further guaranteed Russian dominance by cutting the property qualification for direct participation in the western zemstvos in half. These two modifications had major implications for the structure of the zemstvo. The national curiae, in effect, eliminated election by estate social group as the chief characteristic of zemstvo structure, while the lowered property qualification permitted much greater peasant participation than was currently the case in most zemstvos.

Stolypin correctly assessed that the nationalists would be so anxious to attain domination of the western zemstvos that they would be willing to forsake some measure of noble preponderance for this purpose. But while the nationalists were willing, less committed members of the State Council displayed great reluctance to support these aspects of the bill. Consequently, these two sections of the bill, and especially the national curiae, were the most controversial. But Stolypin underlined the importance of the national curiae by declaring the Western Zemstvos a meaningless bill without their inclusion,[33] an opinion strongly seconded by the nationalists in the Council.

The Western Zemstvo act encountered strong opposition from the outset. Its passage was delayed from spring 1910 until the beginning of the sixth session that fall. When the bill was introduced in the Council in November, the Duma's amendments, particularly the lowered property qualification, caused such an outcry that it had to be returned to committee. Only in January of 1911 was the bill finally brought before the Council.

As expected, the Polish *kolo* and the left strongly opposed the bill, and they were joined by the Baltic noblemen and many Russian zemstvo noblemen. The zemstvo noblemen approved of the idea of extending the zemstvo to the southwest, and many of them also believed that Russian domination of the zemstvo was worthwhile. However, they objected to the specific means chosen to effect this goal: the national curiae and lowered franchise.

A. A. Donetskii, a landowner from the Don region, emphasized this point. Identifying himself as an "old zemstvo man," he asserted that the bill's other provisions were sufficient to guarantee Russian domination of the zemstvo. "It is self-evident that such a situation, created by the bill, which deviates from basic principles of self-government, and is in direct breach of fairness, cannot but hinder the Poles' activities and ruin Russo-Polish relations, resulting in extremely harmful consequences for local as well as state interests."[34] Donetskii concluded that the proposed zemstvo structure was basically inequitable, giving dominance to those paying lower taxes. The bill thus violated the basic nature of the zemstvo, setting a precedent that could spread throughout Russia.

Another opponent was V. F. Trepov, an appointed member of the extreme right. Trepov had advocated the dissolution of the First Duma and continued to oppose the Duma's existence despite the changes wrought by the electoral law of 3 June 1907. He now voiced his opposition to the zemstvo bill, even though his fellow rightists, unsure of the tsar's position, seemed reluctant to do so. Trepov accused Stolypin of playing a "game" designed to tamper with the Empire's most fundamental institutions, noting that the courts, navy, schools, and church were among the "cards" that had already been played. "The conservative, monarchical principle of the zemstvo has been placed on the board today—true, only in six western provinces—but it is not necessary to be a prophet to predict that this game will be extended to include the all-Russian zemstvo and in this game the card will be played out."[35]

Trepov's remarks emphasized the close relationship between the bill's two controversial sections. He opposed the introduction of zemstvos into the western provinces because they would be dominated not by the landowning nobility but by peasants who just happened to be Russian. The government argued that the goal of this legislation was to establish a Russian zemstvo, but the bill in reality would allow the peasants to dominate the zemstvos. Such a precedent, if extended to central Russia, would make the zemstvos a potential base for revolutionary agitation. Trepov's fellow rightists remained silent throughout the debate since they did not know to what degree the tsar supported the legislation. Only a few felt they had nothing to lose in defying the tsar's apparent wishes.

Thus, when the bill was voted on its first reading, 103 members supported considering it article by article, while 56 opposed any further discussion.[36] On this occasion, Stolypin succeeded in forming a new majority in the State Council, the right and most of the center, bridged by the nationalists, having fallen into line. It appeared that opposition would be minimal when the individual sections of the proposal were examined by the Council at the second reading in early March.

When the national curiae section was brought up at the second reading, Prince P. N. Trubetskoi, a leader of the center and chairman of the special committee considering the bill, emerged as the leading opponent of the section, reiterating Trepov's earlier objections. He admitted that introduction of the zemstvo was important to the southwest's development, but urged that the zemstvos be based on principles identical to those that applied in the rest of Russia. Trubetskoi feared the national curiae would politicize the zemstvos, exacerbating rather than reducing national antagonisms.[37]

Another noble landowner and member of the center, N. P. Balashev, agreed with Trubetskoi. While concurring that the zemstvo had to be a Russian institution, he asserted that there were ways to achieve this goal other than the national curiae. The curiae, Balashev insisted, were both extraneous and dangerous; they were needed only in Poland and Finland.[38]

As Balashev's remarks indicate, the Polish and Russian noblemen differed greatly in their reasons for opposition to the Western Zemstvo project. The Russians feared for their estate's dominance in the zemstvos if the national curiae should become a precedent for zemstvo organization. They suggested that it would be easier to guarantee Russian dominance by stipulating that the zemstvos and their boards be composed of a majority of Russians. The Poles protested that their loyalty to the Russian Empire had been called into question and claimed, even more vociferously, that passage of the national curiae would create further national antagonisms in the southwest.

It appeared from the debate that the core opposition to the national curiae had remained unchanged since the January vote. The left, the Poles, the trade and industry group, and some Russian landed noblemen opposed the form in which the zemstvo was to be introduced, while the right, with a few exceptions, kept silent. However, when the vote was taken, provision for a national curiae was defeated by a vote of 92 to 68—[39]a stunning setback for Stolypin's new policy.

The crucial shift in the balance of votes had come from the unexpected defection of the right. P. N. Durnovo and V. F. Trepov, two of the group's leaders, had conspired to defeat the bill. On the eve of the voting on the curial system, Trepov had asked for an audience with the tsar and returned from the interview to inform his rightist colleagues that the autocrat wanted them to be guided in this matter only by their "conscience," i.e., to vote as they wished.[40] Thus freed of their commitment to support unquestioningly a policy favored by the throne, the members of the right supplied the margin of defeat for the national curiae. To be sure, the right would not have been able to muster a majority in the State Council without the support of landed noblemen usually loyal to Stolypin. As we have seen, these men opposed the Western Zemstvo bill because the establishment of the national curiae might have a dangerous effect on their own estate interests and privileges. Thus Stolypin was undone by a combination of bureaucratic and estate interests.

The outraged prime minister refused to accept his defeat. He prorogued the two chambers and enacted the Western Zemstvo under the emergency provisions of Article 87 of the Fundamental Laws.[41] In so doing, Stolypin damaged beyond repair his image as a "constitutionalist," enraging both legislative chambers and losing much of his moderate support. It was clear after his gamble on the Western Zemstvo that his power was on the wane: that he had lost credibility both with the tsar and with the legislative chambers. Indeed, the Western Zemstvo crisis marked the end of Stolypin's political career.

It is understandable that the landed nobility had played an important role in Stolypin's political demise, for although from the outset he had looked to it for support, he had failed to understand its most basic social attitudes. Whatever their ostensible political position, landed noblemen continued to regard themselves as belonging to a special group within the Russian social order, whose rights it was their duty to safeguard.

The political divisions among the landed noblemen, after all, were relatively new—products of the general politicization of Russian society during the 1905 crisis. Few noblemen had really managed to break out of their older estate orientations, and fewer still among the elite who became members of the reformed State Council. Stolypin was repeatedly baffled, and eventually defeated, when these men united against policies that appeared to threaten the predominant position of their estate in national life.

NOTES

1. In his report to the tsar on October 9, 1905, Count S. Iu. Witte wrote: "It is most important to reform the State Council to allow an elected element to participate prominently in it. Only in this way will it be possible to establish normal relations between this institution and the State Duma." Cited in Sidney Harcave, *First Blood* (New York: Macmillan, 1964), p.291.

At the secret December Conference called by the tsar to discuss the Duma electoral law, Witte commented: "The Council must be the second chamber and emerge as the necessary counterweight to the Duma, as a moderator. . . ." See "Tsarskosel'skiia soveshchaniia, Protokoly sekretnago soveshchaniia pod predsedatel'stvom byvshago imperatora po voprosu o rashirenii izberatel'nago prava," in *Byloe*, no. 3, Sept. 1917, p.245.

2. The State Council was created in 1810 by Tsar Alexander I. Until its restructuring in 1906, its members were appointed by the emperor from the ranks of the highest levels of the bureaucracy and military.

3. Although the bureaucrats represented in the State Council were of noble rank and many were indeed hereditary noblemen, in this particular context we are referring primarily to that part of the landed nobility which was involved in the local zemstvos and assemblies of nobility. In order to be elected to the State Council from the zemstvo, an eligible candidate had to possess three times the full property requirement for direct participation in the county zemstvo, or he had to own the full property qualification *and* to have served for at least two elected terms as either a provincial or county marshal of nobility, a chairman of the provincial or county zemstvo board, a mayor of a town, or a justice of the peace.

The landowner assemblies of Poland and the western provinces elected their representatives from among those who were entitled to participate directly in Duma elections in their district and who had owned three times the full property qualification for three years. They were exempt from the requirement of local officeholding since no local elective institutions existed in these provinces. The marshals of the western provinces were essentially bureaucrats, appointed by the central government. In Poland, electors possessing three times the property qualifications chose six representatives to the State Council from among themselves at a special assembly convoked in Warsaw.

The only qualification for election as a representative of the noble corporations was membership in a local assembly of nobility. See *Polnoe Sobranie Zakonov*, Series III, Vol. 26, Feb. 20, 1906, #27425: Article 1, section 6 for election of noble representatives; Article VII for election of zemstvo representatives; Article VIII, sections 1 and 2 for election of landowner representatives.

4. Polish noblemen in the State Council came from the Kingdom of Poland and from the nine western provinces, where a significant proportion of the larger landowners were Poles, even though a majority of local landowners were Russian. The *kolo* was made up of fifteen Poles. Because of the strong Polish influence, the western provinces were not allowed to elect their own marshals of nobility, who were appointed instead by St. Petersburg.

5. In 1905 thirty of the thirty-one marshals of the nobility of the zemstvo provinces owned over 500 *desiatiny* of land. The sole exception—M. A. Stakhovich of Orel province—came from a large and wealthy family with vast holdings in his home province. See Roberta Manning, "The Russian Provincial Gentry in Revolution and Counterrevolution, 1905–07" (doctoral diss., Columbia University, 1975), p.61.

6. A. P. Korelin, "Rossiskoe dvorianstvo i ego soslovnaia organizatsiia (1861–1904gg)," *Istoriia SSSR*, no. 5, 1971.

7. Fifty-five of the 133 elected delegates and 10 of the 61 coopted delegates at the First Congress of the United Nobility were State Council representatives. TsGAOR, f. 454, op. 1 d. 5/4, 1906 g., 11. 278–82; *Ob'iavlenia soveta ob'edinennykh dvorianskikh* (St. Petersburg, 1906); *Entsiklopedicheskii slovar'* (Granat & Co.), vol. 23. I would like to thank Roberta Manning for supplying me with this information.

8. Michael C. Brainerd, "The Octobrists and the Gentry, 1905–1907: Leaders and Followers?" This volume, p.69.

9. See Russia. Council of the Empire. *Stenograficheskie otchety* (here-

after *GSSO*), Session II. (St. Petersburg: Gosudarstvennaia tipografiia, 1907), pp.1–14 of the Supplement.

10. *Birzhevye vedomosti*, #9783, March 3, 1907.

11. *Birzhevye vedomosti*, #9825, June 2, 1907.

12. *GSSO*, Session II, meeting 4, pp.27–42.

13. Geoffrey A. Hosking, "Government and Duma in Russia (1907–1914)," (doctoral diss., King's College, Cambridge, England), pp. 214–16.

14. Ibid., p.216.

15. Ibid., pp.215–16.

16. Ibid., p.216.

17. *Trudy IV s'yezda upolnomochennykh dvorianskikh obshchestv', 1908.* 32 provinces. March 9–16, 1908. (St. Petersburg, 1909), pp. 23–24.

18. Ibid., pp.50–51.

19. Ibid., pp.54–55. In fact, only two government projects for local reform ever reached the State Council: the district zemstvo and the district court bills, the first of which was considered only in 1913.

20. Ibid., pp.234–35.

21. Ibid., p.314.

22. Ibid., p.322.

23. *Rossiya*, March 11 and 13, 1908.

24. S. E. Kryzhanovskii, *Vospominaniia* (Berlin, 1938), pp.218–19.

25. Hosking, p.225.

26. Ibid., pp.227–28.

27. For details of the crisis created by the passage of the Naval General Staff bill, see Geoffrey A. Hosking, *The Russian Constitutional Experiment: Government and Duma, 1907–1914* (London: Cambridge University Press, 1973), and Edward Chmielewski, "Stolypin and the Ministerial Crisis of 1909," in *California Slavic Studies*, Vol. IV, 1965. In Russian, see A. Ia. Avrekh, "III-ia Duma i nachalo krizisa treteiun'skoi sistemy," in *Istoricheskie zapiski*, Vol. 53, 1955. For more details, see Alexandra D. Shecket, "The Russian Imperial State Council and the Policies of P. A. Stolypin, 1906–1911: Bureaucratic and Soslovie Interests versus Reform" (doctoral diss., Columbia University, 1974), Chapter V.

28. During the crisis over the Naval General Staff bill, the right group developed a proposal altering the election laws to the State Council from the nine western provinces. There were rumors that they sought to embarrass the Stolypin government with this proposal, which guaranteed that a majority of the State Council representatives from the western provinces would be Russians. The Stolypin government had never taken a strong stand on nationalist questions, but quite unexpectedly Stolypin spoke favorably on the issue, promising to present a bill enacting a zemstvo dominated by Russian elements in the west. See *GSSO*, Session IV, meeting 34, May 8, 1909, cols 1933–1944. The press perceived a very important change in Stolypin's policies, as evidenced in such articles as "Na pravo!" [To the Right!] in *Birzhevye vedomosti*, #11096, May 9, 1909.

29. Among the nationalists in the State Council Right were A. S. Stishinskii and D. I. Pikhno, whose interests coincided with those of such prominent members of the center as A. B. Neidgardt and V. I. Deitrikh. See *Rossiya*, Nov. 29, 1907; *Birzhevye vedomosti*, #10226, November 29, 1907; *Rossiya*,

June 12, 1908. All are articles pertaining to the formation of the Russian National Party.

30. See A. N. Naumov, *Iz utselevskikh vospominanii, 1868–1917*, Vol. II (New York: Izdanie A. K. Naumovoi i O. A. Kussevitskoi, 1955), p.145: "Despite their relatively small numbers, they played a very important role in the fate of a whole series of State Council proposals, often emerging during the balloting as the deciding factor, depending upon with which of the two basic groups the "Neidgardtsy" voted. This gave them weight in the legislative life of the State Council, particularly when Stolypin was in power."

31. In 1910 the government introduced a bill to limit the powers of the Finnish Sejm by curtailing its right to approve or reject legislation passed in St. Petersburg. For further details, see A. Ia. Avrekh, *Stolypin i tret'ia Duma* (Moscow: "Nauka," 1968), pp.23–58. See also Shecket, op. cit., Chapter VI.

32. See *Novoe vremia*, Jan. 1, 1911, for the editorial commenting on the "quiet year," and the nationalist journal *Okrainy Rossii* throughout 1911.

33. *GSSO*, Session VI, meeting 25, March 4, 1911, cols. 1240–41.

34. *GSSO*, Session VI, meeting 18, Jan. 28, 1911, cols. 835–839.

35. Ibid., col. 927.

36. Ibid., col. 979.

37. Ibid., meeting 25, cols. 1199–1203.

38. Ibid., cols. 1209–1212.

39. Ibid., col. 1256.

40. For details of the intrigue, see V. N. Kokovtsov, *Iz moego proshlago* (Paris: Izdanie zhurnala Illiustrirovaniia Rossiia, 1933), Vol. 1, pp. 451–55; V. M. Andreevskii, *Biograficheskie sosedeniia o zhizni i deiatel'nosti* (Unpublished ms., Columbia University Russian and East European Archive), pp.78 d and e; A. Ia. Avrekh, *Stolypin i tretaia Duma*, pp.330–34; and Shecket, Chapter VII.

41. When Stolypin learned of the intrigue that had led to the defeat of the Western Zemstvo, he persuaded the tsar to allow him to prorogue the Duma and State Council and enact the bill under Article 87 of the Fundamental Laws. Article 87 stipulated that while the legislature was out of session, the government could enact emergency laws, which would then be approved by the Duma and State Council. Stolypin's action enraged the Duma and the State Council, and both chambers proposed very strong interpellations against the Prime Minister. Although the State Council interpellation failed (by two votes; a two-thirds majority was necessary), it was clear that Stolypin no longer retained his authority. On Sept. 1, 1911, Stolypin was assassinated in Kiev. Although his killer, one Bogrov, was caught, no adequate explanation of how he had gained access to the Prime Minister, who was attending an Imperial performance at the Kiev Opera House, was ever forthcoming. See Shecket, Chapter VII.

What Was the
United Nobility?

GEOFFREY A. HOSKING and
ROBERTA THOMPSON MANNING

Recent Soviet historians seem to agree that the so-called United Nobility had a strong influence on Stolypin's government. E. D. Chermenskii describes it as the "initiator and inspirer" of the June Third coup,
while A. Ia. Avrekh sees it as "the guiding ideological center" of all the
"Black Hundred–monarchist organizations." More recently V. S. Diakin has shown that it also exercised great influence in *opposing* Stolypin's policies. We have tried in our own researches to indicate that it
played a major role in both establishing and then frustrating the Third
of June system.[1]

No one, however, has yet attempted to describe what the United
Nobility actually was, how it came into being and how it operated.
Was it a federation of the provincial nobles' associations? In some
ways, yes, since most of those associations were represented at its
regular congresses, but not entirely, since some were not. In any case,
many of the leaders of the United Nobility repudiated the idea that
their political powers were dependent on the associations. Was it a
landowners' union? Again, in some ways, yes, since its members were
large landowners,[2] and much of its activity was directed to the defense of private landed property. Yet the United Nobility never succeeded in developing an agricultural or commercial side to its activity,
nor did its members accept to their ranks the growing class of private
landowners who were not nobles. Perhaps, then, it was really a kind
of political party? The United Nobility certainly had policies on a
wide range of political issues and tried to influence the government
in favor of those policies. But it never put itself forward as a party

at the ballot, nor did it associate itself electorally with any of the Duma parties. In fact, as a body, the United Nobility is exceedingly difficult to classify, and it is symptomatic that it had no proper name: "United Nobility" is only an appellation of convenience. The published reports of its congresses appeared under the unwieldy title of "Proceedings of the nth *Congress of Delegates of 29* (or whatever) *Nobles' Associations."*

It may help us to understand the peculiarities of the United Nobility if we compare it with a German political organization that at first sight looks rather similar, and that some members of the United Nobility took as their model—namely, the *Bund der Landwirte* or Agrarian League, as it is often known in English.

The *Bund der Landwirte* was established in Berlin in 1893 as a direct reaction to the German government's policy of lowering tariffs on imported grain. This step weakened both Junkers and peasant farmers at a time when their economic position was already declining as a result of the growth of industry and international finance. The *Bund* had, at its height, 200,000–300,000 members organized in an elaborate hierarchical network of provincial and local branches; it had its own internal newsheets and strong influence over one of the most important national daily newspapers, the *Deutsche Tageszeitung;* and it was closely associated with a Reichstag party, the Conservatives, for whom it provided an organization, mass membership, and publicity. Its outlook was monarchist and conservative, but its published program was confined mainly to economic questions, leaving the political ones to the Conservatives. Its members were landowners and farmers of all kinds, the great majority of them medium and small peasants, but the leadership was always firmly in the hands of the large estate owners, who used the organization successfully for their own purposes. It pursued some purely economic and commercial ends, such as the promotion of cheap credit, the arrangement of bulk purchasing, and the provision of insurance and agricultural advice; and, in fact, it absorbed a number of existing regional agrarian associations.[3]

As we explore the structure of the United Nobility, it will become apparent that it was a very different type of organization. Some preconditions of these differences immediately suggest themselves. The economic position of the landed nobility was much weaker in Russia than in Germany, where the Junkers had generally adjusted well to the demands of commercial agriculture, hiring local peasants as wage laborers. Some Russian landowners, especially in the west, had made a similar adjustment as the economic pressures of the post-Emancipation era forced increasing numbers of noble proprietors to involve themselves personally as never before in agriculture and the daily management of their family estates. But the large majority still ran their estates by semifeudal practices, with the peasants rendering labor services of one sort or another or renting areas of the estate to work on short leases.[4]

The political role of the Russian nobility was a curious mixture of autonomy and dependence. Although the nobility in Russia had possessed their own local corporate associations since the charter granted to them by Catherine the Great, these organizations did not play much of an independent political role before 1905, having no right to concern themselves with general political questions or to coordinate their activities on the national level. In fact, the associations of the nobility were actually integrated into the state apparatus, since the main elective officials of these bodies, the provincial and county marshals of the nobility, were required by law to perform a number of important administrative functions in the localities. The marshals served as members *ex officio* of all the main local bureaucratic committees; moreover, at the county level, the marshal was—until the end of the Old Regime —the senior ranking official as well as the only administrative figure capable of coordinating governmental functions, since he alone was included by law on *all* governing bodies from the zemstvo to the local draft board.[5] The overall effect of these arrangements was that the Russian nobility combined administrative experience, responsibility, and pride in state service with almost total political passivity.

The nobility's traditional indifference to politics outside the state administration was, however, undermined by the economic decline, which assumed crisis proportions around the turn of the twentieth century. In 1896 the marshals of the nobility began to convene annual conferences to discuss the economic problems of the nobility and to put political pressure on the national government to intervene in their behalf; and in 1904–1905 the marshals and many local noble assemblies, like most other segments of Russian society, were carried away by the Liberation Movement, adding their voice to the general clamor for the establishment of representative government in Russia. Yet, despite this brief foray into the political arena, the Russian nobility in 1906 was far more accustomed to administrative intrigues than to the more open give-and-take of modern electoral politics.

Finally, the Russian nobility was not only far weaker and accustomed to very different political practices than its German counterpart; the political situation in the two countries was completely different. By the

1890s Germany had had nearly half a century's experience with parliaments of one sort or another, whereas the United Nobility was created in the middle of a revolution, an upheaval with economic implications, certainly, but beyond everything else an event that threatened the whole social and political fabric. The United Nobility—as its organizers readily admitted—was created to combat revolution, not to counter an unfavorable tariff policy.

The organizational antecedents of the United Nobility were three-fold:

1. noblemen of a conservative bent in and out of the government, who began to organize themselves in the course of 1905 to combat the then dominant liberal and constitutional tendencies;

2. the congresses of landowners that arose in the wake of the 1905 peasant disorders to demand more government protection for landed property;

3. the semiofficial gatherings of the provincial marshals of the nobility, which had convened annually since 1896.

To be sure, all of these streams overlap to some degree. As we shall see, the same names appear repeatedly throughout our discussion. The men who were later to become the United Nobility experimented with several political forums before finding one that was viable and that suited their needs.

The first political group to anticipate the methods of the United Nobility and to contain a significant number of its future leaders was the St. Petersburg–based Patriotic Union (*Otechestvennyi soiuz*). This organization arose in the spring of 1905, soon after the government had capitulated to the demands of the Liberation Movement by promising in the February 18 Rescript to convene a national representative assembly. Seeking to defend the prerogatives of the autocrat and the privileges of the nobility from the dominant reformist element in the state bureaucracy, the Patriotic Union advocated the foundation of a purely consultative—not legislative—assembly, elected by estates (thus preserving the power of the tsar and ensuring a political role for the numerically small nobility).[6]

In spite of its well-formulated political program and occasional public appeals, the Patriotic Union was in no sense a political party but, rather, a small, select gathering of thirty to forty prominent society figures and high officials, especially former officials of the traditionally conservative Ministry of the Interior, many of whom had recently been dismissed or demoted by Sviatopolk-Mirskii, Pleve's liberally inclined

successor as Minister of the Interior. All the men concerned had been
previously associated with the anti-Witte salon of K. F. Golovin. They
now met regularly in the sumptuous home of Count A. A. Bobrinskii,
the former long-term provincial marshal of St. Petersburg and the future chairman of the United Nobility.[7] Like Bobrinskii, most of these
men—or their close relatives—were to be associated in some way with
the United Nobility. In fact, the dominant leadership of the nobles'
organization virtually throughout its existence—the two chairmen of
the United Nobility in the 1906–16 period (Bobrinskii and A. P.
Strukov) as well as their chief assistant, A. A. Naryshkin—were veterans of the Patriotic Union, while its bureaucratic members did not
hesitate to cooperate with the nobles' organization from their high
positions in the government or the State Council. As far as we can tell,
the members of the Patriotic Union were all large landowners, if not
actual landed magnates, owners of enormous latifundia of more than
5,000 *desiatiny*. Many came from families that had been prominent
in Russian politics since the eighteenth century, if not earlier. All were
accustomed, by virtue of their family position as well as by the offices
they held, to move in the highest reaches of St. Petersburg society and
the state bureaucracy. Quite a few of them held high court appointments or worked in the court administration in addition to their many
official positions. Consequently the Patriotic Union should be regarded
as the last organized beachhead of aristocratic influence in a political
order increasingly dominated by professional bureaucrats recruited
from outside the hereditary landed nobility.[8]

The social composition of the Patriotic Union greatly influenced its
mode of operation. It did not seek public support but attempted to
influence privately the delicate operations of the autocratic-bureau-
cratic government. After sending a deputation to the emperor in June
1905 and submitting its program to the Peterhof Conference, which
met in July to discuss the election law for the new national assembly,
a number of the members of the Union (Bobrinskii, Naryshkin, Strukov,
N. A. Pavlov, A. S. Stishinskii and Prince A. A. Shirinskii-Shikhmatov)
were invited to participate in the conference. Here they argued vigorously—though unsuccessfully—for an estate-based electoral system. We
see here a foreshadowing not only of the leadership of the United Nobility and its political program but also of its political methods—the
use of highly placed persons and institutions to influence government
policy.

In addition to the Patriotic Union, another of the ephemeral right-
wing groups of 1905, the Union of Russian Men (*Soiuz russkikh liudei*),

is of interest. For this organization, too, attracted many men subsequently associated with the United Nobility, including two of Russia's largest landowners, Count P. S. Sheremetev and Prince A. G. Shcherbatov; S. F. Sharapov, a publicist well known for his spirited defense of noble agricultural interests; and the marshals of Moscow and St. Petersburg provinces, Prince P. N. Trubetskoi and Count V. V. Gudovich. The Union of Russian Men espoused a somewhat more moderate political program than the Patriotic Union, welcoming the February 18 Rescript as the first step toward the establishment of a *zemskii sobor*, a purely advisory body based on the traditional estates of Russian society, through which the tsar could resume the communication with his people long obstructed by the bureaucracy.[9] The Union of Russian Men, like the Patriotic Union, hoped to limit the power and the electorate of the new national assembly, and, indeed, some of its members joined the Patriotic Union in a deputation to impress these views on the emperor in the summer of 1905.[10] But the Union of Russian Men tended to operate quite differently, seeking support not only in government circles and at the imperial court but also in the local zemstvos and noble associations. Such tactics, too, were to enter the political repertory of the future United Nobility.

Another major contributor to the formation of the United Nobility was the All-Russian Union of Landowners. The initiative for the formation of such an organization came from provincial landowners in Samara and Saratov provinces, among them A. A. Chermodurov, N. A. Pavlov, and the Saratov provincial marshal, N. F. Mel'nikov—all men who were to play prominent roles in the future nobles' organization. Living in one of the most unruly areas of the empire, they were naturally primarily concerned with the defense of their estates against the peasant movement, which culminated in the massive disorders of October–November 1905. After a series of local and regional meetings, a national conference of landowners under the chairmanship of Prince A. G. Shchertbatov was convened in Moscow from November 17–20, at the very height of the 1905 agrarian unrest.[11]

This congress attracted 203 landowners from 33 provinces, including many names subsequently associated with the United Nobility. This was the first gathering of noble landowners to declare itself in favor of ending official support for the peasant land commune (*obshchina*), advocating instead the encouragement of private peasant landholdings as a remedy for peasant land hunger. In this way, the Union of Landowners blazed a trail that the United Nobility and the government would later follow; and they did so at a time when a number of important state officials, including Prime Minister Witte and his Minister of Agriculture, Kutler, as well as the influential D. F. Trepov, were recommending the compulsory expropriation of all private lands now rented out to peasants as the only means to curb agrarian unrest. While a few participants in the congress also accepted such measures, the overwhelming majority of the delegates affirmed the inviolability of private property as an absolute principle.[12] The meeting went on to condemn the government for its inactivity in the face of the peasant rebellions and recommended the stationing of cavalry and mounted police in the countryside and the punishment of entire peasant communities from which peasant rebels were known to have come.[13]

Although primarily concerned with the land question, this congress nevertheless took its place among the right-wing political gatherings of 1905, accepting Orthodoxy, Autocracy, and Nationality as its basic political principles, "not open to dispute or discussion." It also received greetings from the new Union of Russian People and the Russian Assembly (*Russkoe sobranie*); and Prince Shcherbatov announced that the Union of Landowners would affiliate itself with the All-People's Russian Union, the right wing's counterpart to the Union of Liberation, which was established in the autumn of 1905 to coordinate the activities of all political groups engaged in combating the revolution.[14] Indeed, two representatives of the Union of Landowners—Chermodurov and Pavlov—participated in a deputation sent by the All-Russian Union to the emperor, which condemned the Duma as the brainchild of the westernized Petersburg bureaucracy and recommended instead the convocation of a *zemskii sobor*. The emperor, while listening to the deputation "with sympathy," nevertheless maintained that the October Manifesto represented his irrevocable will.[15]

The second congress of the Union of Landowners met in February 1906 and publicly attacked the Kutler land reform program by name, calling it "not only an act of unprecedented violence to the broad class of landowners who are faithful to Your Throne but also a threat to the peasants and the exchequer." The congress, following in the footsteps of a number of local noble associations, petitioned the Emperor to reaffirm the sanctity of private property and to dismiss Kutler's protector, "the all-powerful bureaucrat Witte."[16]

After this congress, the Union of Landowners gradually fizzled out, only surviving long enough to distribute copies of Stolypin's land decree of November 9, 1906 (wholly in keeping with its own anticommunal ideals) to a number of peasants. To be sure, there were periodic attempts on the part of the United Nobility in the 1906–1908 period to revive this organization. But the Union at best lived a shadowy existence, attracting by 1908 no more than fifty-three members nationwide.[17] In his memoirs, N. A. Pavlov, one of its founders, blamed himself for the decline of the Union of Landowners, attributing its early demise to the number of nonlandowning elements that he had invited to the first congress in hope of profiting from their political influence. Because of their presence, he argued, the congress bogged down in fruitless political controversies and never got on with the essential *economic* task of developing private agriculture.[18] This is certainly true and rendered the Union swiftly redundant.

There was another anomaly in the Union of Landowners. In theory it was intended to be an all-estate body, uniting noble landowners with landed proprietors from other estates of Russian society, with the aim not only of political agitation but also of promoting good husbandry. Initially, considerable efforts were made—at least verbally —to attract non-noble landowners, especially peasants. Indeed, the United Nobility became involved in efforts to prop up the Union in hopes of contributing to the emergence of a Russian counterpart to the *Bund der Landwirte*.[19] However, the social tensions between the landed nobility and the peasantry after the 1905 agrarian disorders greatly complicated the problems of founding a landowners' association along the lines of the German model. While the peasantry as a whole was quiescent after 1907, and *individual* peasants were quite willing to enter traditional client-patron relationships with neighboring noblemen for their own personal advantage, considerable peasant hostility toward the landed nobility persisted after 1905; and many peasants remained committed to a "black partition," as was quite evident from the numerous demands for a more favorable allotment of lands made by peasant deputies in the Third Duma.[20]

As long as such deeply rooted peasant land hunger existed, there was simply no way for the nobility and peasantry to unite in defense of their other, common economic interests. Therefore, it is not surprising that nobody who was not in fact a nobleman attended any of the congresses of the Union of Landowners. But if the Union of Landowners was to remain predominantly or entirely noble in composition, then it was duplicating functions that could be performed by the noble associations, by themselves and for their own benefit.

Consequently, the political side of the work of the Landowners' Union gave way to a broader initiative aimed at bringing together the uncoordinated noble associations in defense of the interests of the noble estate as a whole. At their annual meetings the provincial marshals had, in spite of the official prohibition, sometimes discussed general political problems; and in any case the decrees of February 18, 1905, implictly annulled the prohibition, so that the marshals were able to assume an overtly political role.[21] They reacted to the confused situation of the spring of 1905 by trying to reach among themselves some kind of consensus to present as the view of the nation's "leading estate." On March 26, twenty-six of them met in Moscow to discuss a memorandum prepared by D. N. Shipov, Prince P. N. Trubetskoi, and M. A. Stakhovich: this document was based on the minority opinion of the Zemstvo Congress of November 1904 and rested on the principle that there should be a purely consultative popular assembly selected by a limited franchise favoring the nobility.[22] The marshals approved the memorandum and sent the emperor an address requesting further reforms and emphasizing their loyalty and desire to work with the government. In June, after the Tsushima debacle, twenty-five provincial marshals met in St. Petersburg and decided to back the petition of the recent May Coalition Zemstvo Congress with a far more critical address that projected a picture of a general loss of confidence in the government, which had "come to represent something alien, hostile, and unbearable." Trubetskoi and Gudovich presented this statement to the emperor, and Trubetskoi allowed himself some rather sharp remarks. This incident—and the marshals' apparent willingness to coordinate their activities with those of the far more liberal Zemstvo Congress— appears to have caused some segments of the nobility to regard Trubetskoi and Gudovich as politically unreliable and possibly even constitutionalists at heart (a suspicion strengthened by the well-known views of Trubetskoi's brother Sergei, the liberal rector of Moscow University).[23]

One influential local figure who felt this way was A. N. Naumov, the recently elected marshal of Samara province and the founder of the Samara Party of Order. In November 1905 Naumov and Prince V. N. Volkonskii, a county marshal in Shchatsk (Tambov province), both of whom were members of the executive board of the Union of Landowners, urged Trubetskoi to take steps to establish some kind of union of the *entire* landowning nobility.[24] Trubetskoi was sufficiently impressed to call a national conference of marshals, county as well as provincial, which met in Moscow on January 7–11, 1906. Although this congress endorsed a moderate Octobrist-like political program calling for the speedy convocation of the State Duma, firm measures against revolutionary unrest, and the preservation of the territorial integrity of the Russian Empire, the attention of the marshals was clearly focused on the agrarian question. Meeting in a city still under martial law and dominated by the memory of the recent workers' insurrection and street fighting,[25] the congress took its cue from the Union of Landowners. They responded to Trubetskoi's revelations that the Minister of Agriculture, Kutler, was preparing a bill for the expropriation of all private lands now rented to peasants by dismissing any idea of compulsory expropriation and insisting that only the elimination of the peasant land commune could solve the agrarian question in Russia.[26] Since the resolution of the congress won the favorable attention of the emperor, and both Kutler and his patron Witte were soon dismissed from their posts, the January conference of marshals and the meetings of the Union of Landowners were important turning points in the determination of the government's agrarian program.[27]

The marshals, however, took no action on the issue that had inspired their conferences in the first place—the need for the establishment of some more permanent form of nobles' organization. Indeed, this question was not even raised by the marshals in January, and there is evidence that their inactivity reflected the opposition of at least their leaders to the political organization of the nobility. Immediately after the marshals dispersed, a call for the convocation of a national nobles' congress was issued once more in the localities—this time by the Tambov and Kursk noble assemblies. This appeal was rapidly endorsed by nine other noble associations, while only five reacted negatively to the idea.[28] Nevertheless, the marshals, who continued to meet periodically throughout the spring of 1906 to plan for the nobility's first elections to the State Council, still managed to avoid acting on the issue by referring the matter back to the provinces, on the grounds that the voice of the local nobility had yet to be heard.[29] Only in early April, after twenty-six of the thirty-five provincial noble associations considering this issue had expressed themselves in favor of a nobles' congress and had already begun electing representatives to such a meeting, did the marshals reluctantly give in and sanction in principle the formation of a permanent nobles' union.[30] Even then, no actual steps to convene such a congress were taken until the end of the month, on the very eve of the opening of the First State Duma.

The motives of the marshals in obstructing the political unification of the nobility were quite complex. While the marshals rightly feared the emergence of a potential organizational rival that might usurp their role as the traditional spokesmen of the nobility, their opposition to the organization of what was to become the United Nobility was more political than institutional in character. From the very first, the movement to unify the nobility was directed against the political role the provincial marshals had played in 1905. In this way, the foundation of the United Nobility should be regarded in part as the nobility's counterpart to the rank-and-file revolt against the leadership of the Liberation Movement currently under way in the zemstvos. For throughout 1905, the marshals, albeit with some reservations, had generally adhered to the liberal opposition to the Old Regime. Their most prominent national leaders—Trubetskoi, Gudovich, and Stakhovich— were political moderates who had long favored the establishment of representative government in Russia and strongly supported the new political order established by the October Manifesto. Indeed, Gudovich and Stakhovich were members of the Central Committee of the new Union of 17 October. And Trubetskoi, while never a member of the party, was a close personal friend of the Octobrist leader Guchkov: at the January conference of marshals, he tried—unsuccessfully—to persuade his colleagues to adhere formally as a group to the Octobrist Union.[31]

The most vociferous champions of the unification of the nobility in the winter of 1906 were men of quite a different political complexion. If we have to pin a political label on them, that of "reactionary" or "far right" may well be the most appropriate. Certainly they were opponents of the new political order as it currently existed. Though they generally favored the existence of representative institutions to offset the power and influence of the hated bureaucracy, many of them feared that the recent October Manifesto had conferred far too much power on the State Duma, and they were most uneasy about the recent expansion of the Duma electorate (the law of December 11, 1905). Their fears were not groundless, for the new legislative chamber selected under the December 11 franchise was predominantly peasant in its social composition and overwhelmingly committed to a new allotment of land for the peasantry. Thus it is not surprising that the proponents of a nobles' congress hoped to use the new organization as a political counterweight to the Duma, a rival "State Nobles' Duma," as one of them described the coming congress.[32] Accordingly, the chief advocates of a national nobles' association among the Tambov nobility, Prince D. N. Tsertelev and V. N. Snezhkov, argued that the nobles' congress should assemble *before* the Duma convened so that the nobility might "raise its voice among the hubbub while there are still no elected representatives." That way, they maintained, the nobility might be able to influence state policies on a number of key issues (which were clearly in the Duma's domain), such as the agrarian question and the preservation of "the leading influence" of the nobility in local government.[33]

Consequently, it is not surprising that the liberals and moderates among the marshals, under the leadership of Trubetskoi, Gudovich, and Stakhovich, spared no efforts in attempting to delay the organization of the nobility until well after the Duma had convened, maintaining that the expression of "the real feelings" and "one-sided views" of the nobility would be "untimely," if not outright "dangerous," in view of the Duma elections, which were currently under way. Stakhovich in particular feared that the political intervention of a conservative nobles' congress might encourage anti-Duma forces within the government.[34] Even after the elections were over and the marshals capitulated to provincial pressures and actually convened a steering committee on April 20 to make the final preparations for the congress, Trubetskoi and Gudovich continued to try to divert the nobility from a political confrontation with the Duma. Under their influence, the nobles' congress was scheduled to meet in Moscow, well away from the center of government, and participants were strictly limited to the elected representatives of the local noble associations, who they hoped would be a more moderate lot than the many right-wing spokesmen currently attempting to use the organized nobility for their own political ends.

At this point, however, a number of right-wing noblemen managed to intervene and take over the steering committee of the nobles' congress. To do this, they utilized a new political organization, the Circle of Nobles Loyal to Their Oath (*kruzhok dvorian vernykh prisiage*). This association, whose curious name refers to the oath to the monarch taken by all those entering state service, first arose in Moscow in early February as a purely local organization committed to the unification of the nobility around a conservative political program.[35] In the wake of the general reorganization of the right after its disastrous defeat in the Duma elections, the Circle was converted by the Kursk marshal, Count V. F. Dorrer, and a number of other noble activists close to the Monarchical Party into a national organization, a rallying point and pressure group for the more conservative noblemen.[36] By conveniently scheduling the first national congress of the Circle of Nobles to overlap with the first meeting of the steering committee of the nobles' congress,[37] the Circle leaders were able to overwhelm the committee with an influx of new members, forcing Trubetskoi by its second session to turn over the chairmanship to Prince N. F. Kasatkin-Rostovskii, a member of the Patriotic Union and a close political associate of Count Dorrer.[38]

Under the leadership of Kasatkin-Rostovskii, the committee immediately reversed all its previous decisions. Setting at long last a final date for the congress (May 21), the committee turned its back on noble traditions and decided to move the site of the congress from Moscow (where the marshals had traditionally met) to St. Petersburg, the seat of the government and the legislative organs; and it decided to co-opt members and invite to the congress "persons not elected in the localities who can be useful to the cause of the congress."[39] Exercising its new powers, the bureau forthwith co-opted several members of the former Patriotic Union—Count A. A. Bobrinskii, Senator A. A. Naryshkin and K. F. Golovin—[40] while pointedly denying the provincial marshals of the nobility the right to attend the congress as official delegates unless specifically elected for this purpose in the localities. Subsequently, a number of other members of the Patriotic Union were invited to the congress. These men, who were noted more for their connections at the imperial court and among high officialdom than for their ties with the provincial nobility, were to play a disproportionately large role in the affairs of the United Nobility. The Nizhnii Novgorod zemstvo activist and secretary to the Permanent Council of the United Nobility, A. I. Zybin, went so far as to maintain that "if these people had not been allowed to attend the first congress, then the unification of the nobility would not have taken place."[41]

The organization known as the United Nobility was, in spite of its generally accepted name, never representative of the nobility *as a whole*. This is true in particular of the first congress, even if one excludes the sixty-one co-opted delegates, who were divided equally among noble agrarian experts (all known opponents of the peasant land commune), high officials and ex-officials largely from the Ministry of the Interior, and prominent conservative activists of noble origins who could not manage to get elected in their home provinces (Bobrinskii and V. M. Purishkevich are good examples of this latter type).[42] Only twenty-nine of the thirty-nine provincial noble associations with elected marshals (and hence eligible to participate in the congress) were represented. Six provincial associations refused to send delegates as they disapproved of the congress's being called at all,[43] while four others simply ignored the invitation.[44] Since the abstaining provinces were generally located on the borderlands of the empire or in the forest belt of the Central Industrial and Lake districts, the congress, its debates, policies, and executive organs were dominated by the nobles of the Central Agricultural Region, Novorossiia, and the Volga, the very areas that had borne the brunt of the recent peasant disorders.

Sociologically, the United Nobility appears to have been a political alliance between prominent absentee magnates from St. Petersburg (Bobrinskii and Co.) and larger provincial landowners, many of whom were actively involved in the public affairs of their home provinces.[45] M. Menshikov, the well-known columnist for the moderate daily *Novoe vremia*, described the participants in the first congress of the United Nobility quite accurately as "our aristocracy."[46]

Almost all the delegates for whom we have data came from the top 10–20 percent of the landed nobility in regard to landed wealth, and over half of them from the top 4 percent (see table 1).[47]

TABLE 1.

Distribution of the personal landholdings of participants in the First Congress of the United Nobility and those of the landed nobility as a whole, compared.

Amount of land owned	Participants in the First Congress of the United Nobility		Distribution of noble landholdings (as of 1905)	
	No.	%	No.	%
over 5,000 des.	26	24%	1,319	1.2%
2,000 to 5,000 des.	30	28%	2,923	2.7%
1,000 to 2,000 des.	20	19%	5,092	4.8%
500 to 1,000 des.	24	22.5%	8,768	8.2%
300 to 500 des.	7	6.4%	8,604	8.0%
less than 300 des.	0	0%	80,141	75%
Total	107	100%	107,247	100%

Sources: TsGAOR fond 434, op 1, del 5/4 1906, pp.278–82; TsGIA fond 1283, op 1 (1906); *Vsia Rossiia* (St. Petersburg, 1903 and 1912); *Statistika zemlevladeniia 1905 g: Svod dannykh po 50-ti gubernii Evropeiskoi Rossii* (St. Petersburg, 1905) p.78; and the sources listed in table 1 in Roberta Thompson Manning, "Zemstvo and Revolution," this volume, p.34.

The half dozen or so exceptions to this general rule were overwhelmingly members of large landowning families in their home provinces. Thus the nobles' congress brought together quite a few members of the top "one hundred" landowning families of the Russian Empire, the power elite of the Old Regime, who collectively owned 40 percent of all noble landholdings and now contributed such founding figures of the United Nobility as Count A. A. Bobrinskii, A. A. Naryshkin, A. P.

Strukov, Count P. S. Sheremetev, Prince S. S. Abamalek-Lazarev, and N. P. Sukhomlinov.[48]

Thus, most of the delegates to the first congress not only originated from the provinces most affected by agrarian unrest, but they represented the stratum of the landed nobility (large proprietors with more than 500 *desiatiny* of land) who appear to have been the chief victims of these disorders.[49] It is not surprising, therefore, that the provincial delegates as well as those co-opted were staunchly conservative, if not outright reactionary.[50] Nevertheless no *public* offensive against the Duma was undertaken at this time. This restraint was due to, in the words of the Permanent Council (the executive organ of the congress), "the respect for the *principle* of a legislative institution," which prevailed among the congress participants.[51] Also, most delegates apparently greatly feared the political consequences of the dissolution of the Duma, which they all assumed would lead to a revival of the mass worker and peasant disorders of the previous autumn.[52]

However, the Duma and "its one-sided composition" were vigorously criticized from the podium of the nobles' congress; and the meeting did not hesitate to take sides in the mounting political conflict between the national assembly and the Goremykin government. The congress strongly asserted its support for the government, openly hailed the emperor as "Autocrat" (thus reaffirming his power over the national assembly), and established a commission to work out a new Duma electoral law, "which would secure the representation of the real needs of the people, especially landowners."[53] The delegates then concentrated their attention firmly on the agrarian question, the issue of prime importance to the peasant-dominated First Duma. Stressing the economic contributions of the agricultural enterprises of the nobility and totally rejecting the compulsory expropriation schemes favored by all Duma factions, even the nobles among them, the United Nobility demanded instead what was to become known as the "Stolypin" land reform—the abolition of the peasant land commune.[54]

Quite naturally under these conditions, the conflicts with the liberal and moderate marshals that preceded the formation of the United Nobility carried over into the congress itself. Prince P. N. Trubetskoi made one last-ditch attempt to delay the political unification of the nobility, by objecting to the organizational proposals of the steering committee. Most notably, he objected to the establishment of a strong executive organ, the Permanent Council, which was to be endowed with the right to co-opt members and make representations to the government on all matters. Maintaining that such a strong executive body would usurp the powers of the local noble associations, Trubetskoi insisted that these proposals should be thoroughly discussed in the localities before being accepted by the congress. Judging from Trubetskoi's past political actions, it is quite likely that he was in fact opposed not so much to a strong executive organ as such as to the political uses to which it might be put. His apprehensions were not misplaced, for the Permanent Council elected by the First Congress was dominated by men of *extreme* right-wing political persuasions, who provided eight of the fifteen-man Council; and the body did play an important part in the events leading to the dissolution of the First Duma. However, the general sentiment of the nobles' congress was clearly against Trubetskoi. The meeting adopted the steering committee's plan of organization without referring the matter back to the provincial associations on the grounds that the nobility must act rapidly, having been so slow to unite in the past and being now the least politically organized of any social group in Russia.[55]

Late in the proceedings, the moderate marshals mounted a counterattack. A group of twenty-three of them, predominantly county marshals, led by Gudovich, attempted to undermine the political influence of the congress by casting doubts on its representative nature. Charging that the delegates had been selected in a most haphazard fashion and that eight provincial noble associations were not represented at all,[56] the twenty-three maintained that the congress lacked a mandate to consider political issues and should simply concentrate its energies on the establishment of a formal organization for the nobility, referring all matters of substance back to the noble associations in the localities.[57] The protesters, who were overwhelmingly Octobrists (mainly on the party's left flank), their close associates, or members of the moderate Octobrist-oriented center group of the State Council, were apparently seeking once again to prevent a conflict between the organized nobility and the legislative chamber.[58] These men, whose ranks included a number of First Duma deputies (including the sole Kadet at the nobles' congress, the Kharkov provincial marshal G. A. Firsov) insisted that the congress should not take any substantive stand at all on the key agrarian question but should confine itself to a request that the agrarian project drafted by the Duma be submitted for the consideration of the local noble associations before being enacted into law.[59]

In the end, however, all the marshals got for their pains was a barrage of attacks, both for their "liberalism" during 1905 and for their recent efforts to delay the unification of the nobility. In the course of these attacks, N. E. Markov of Kursk and S. S. Bekhteev of Kazan went so far as to maintain that only the newly founded United Nobility, not "the self-appointed marshals," had the right to speak out in the name of the nobility,[60] whereupon Trubetskoi withdrew from the congress in protest, and fourteen other highly conservative provincial marshals (including Markov's political associate Count Dorrer) came to the defense of their office, forcing Markov and Bekhteev to apologize in public for their remarks.[61]

After this apology, a majority of the provincial marshals present decided to remain in the nobles' congress "in the interest of . . . creating a united Russian nobility."[62] But the tension between the United Nobility and the marshals did not immediately subside. While the marshals were given the right to attend sessions of the Permanent Council, they were initially allowed to vote only on matters concerning the province they represented.[63] Nevertheless, the conflict gradually abated by the end of the year. The marshals tacitly accepted their position as local agents of the Permanent Council; in return in November 1906 they were given full voting rights at Council meetings.[64] By this time, however, most of the liberal and moderate marshals of 1905–1906 had come up for reelection and were being replaced by far more conservative men,[65] thus removing the political differences between the marshals and the nobles' congress that had inspired the conflict in the first place. Those few moderates who remained in office after 1907 were generally won over to the goals and methods of the United Nobility through the flow of political events, most notably the peasant disturbances accompanying the agrarian debates in the first two Dumas, the impunity with which the government was able to dissolve the First Duma, and the experience of the elections to the Second Duma, when moderate and conservative elements, despite improved organization, failed to make significant gains over the first elections. The dissenting and abstaining provincial noble associations, too, gradually accepted the leadership of the Permanent Council. The last holdout—St. Petersburg—joined the United Nobility at the end of 1911.[66]

Thus, the United Nobility eventually achieved a semblance of unity and organization (as great, perhaps, as that achieved by any noble-dominated political group during the Duma monarchy). Each year, through 1915, a congress of its members, elected as seemed appropriate to each local association, would meet in St. Petersburg in February or March to debate the major political issues of the day. The congresses were often conveniently scheduled to coincide with major political events, such as the sessions of the Council on the Local Economy. Protocols and resolutions of these conferences were meticulously published and presented to the emperor, while some of the keynote speeches and reports were printed separately as brochures. All of this material was widely disseminated among the provincial nobility and provided a valuable political resource for conservative noblemen, enabling this generally inarticulate stratum to express their ideas more forcibly and coherently in zemstvo and legislative debates (thus possibly contributing to the growth of right-wing influence among the provincial nobility after 1905). In a deliberate move, the Permanent Council also distributed its reports and congress proceedings to high government officials, people prominent in the social world of St. Petersburg, and members of the royal family (including the Dowager Empress and the Grand Dukes).[67] In addition, the congresses were always widely reported in the press. The United Nobility could, no doubt, have sought a broader base for its public relations if it had published its own newspaper (and this was frequently discussed during the early years),[68] but the idea was eventually dropped for lack of funding.

Besides, the United Nobility evidently did not require mass support, to judge by the extraordinary number of measures they espoused that were subsequently adopted by the government. In 1906–1907 alone, the political interventions of the United Nobility contributed to the dissolution of the First Duma, the Stolypin agrarian decrees, the establishment of roving military tribunals in areas of agrarian unrest, and, finally, the promulgation of the new electoral law of June 3, 1907. Of course, it is exceptionally difficult to prove beyond any doubt that these acts resulted from the interventions of the United Nobility, since the decisive battles were waged not in the press or public meeting places but in the cabinets of ministers, the salons of St. Petersburg, and the reception halls of the imperial court, places where public records were rarely kept. In fact the full impact of the organization on the course of Russian politics may never be definitely determined. What is known, however, is that the Permanent Council and individual members of the United Nobility, both in public statements and private communications, liked to claim credit for these governmental acts;[69] and the acts concerned often closely followed the political intervention of the nobles' organization. The timing is most suggestive in the case of the dissolution of the First Duma, for the Permanent Council as a body visited key government figures (both the Minister of the Interior Stolypin and Prime Minister Goremykin) to discuss agrarian matters between June 14 and 19, shortly before the government issued its June 20 communiqué on the land question, prohibiting any form of compulsory expropriation and thus provoking the final confrontation with the Duma.[70] The memoirs of the future prime minister, Count V. V. Kokovtsev (then Minister of Finance), indicate that the government's final decision to dissolve the First State Duma, instead of attempting to meet its demands, was made precisely during this period—in the interval between June 15 and June 20.[71] Certainly the timing of these interventions alone suggests at the very least that the United Nobility was *one* of the forces pushing the government toward dissolution.

The United Nobility was in large part able to achieve such notable success because of the tactical flexibility conferred on the organization by the nature of its membership. Thus, it could, with equal facility, exert behind-the-scenes pressure on the central government, place political pressure on the government from without by mobilizing the local zemstvos and noble associations behind a common program of political demands, and/or work within the established legislative institutions, especially the upper house of the Russian parliament, the State Council. All these political tactics were utilized by the nobles' congress at one time or another.

Elite pressure—i.e., a direct appeal to the emperor or a high government official on the part of the nobles' congress or its Permanent Council—appears to have been utilized most frequently, although not exclusively, in the early period of the organization's existence (especially 1906). Beginning in 1910 the noble organization's access to the emperor was actually formalized. In that year the nobles' congress began to adopt loyal addresses to the tsar on an annual basis, which were personally transmitted to Nicholas II by the Chairman of the Permanent Council, who then proceeded to inform the monarch of the deliberations and opinions of the United Nobility.[72] With this rather ritualized exception, such an approach to politics was usually reserved for times of political crises, when the United Nobility and its members felt themselves particularly threatened by measures under consideration and immediate action was of utmost importance. It appears, however, that if such elite interventions were to be effective, the United Nobility required highly placed associates within the imperial government willing to work for them. These were provided for the nobles' congress by the personal connections of its members, particularly those men who had come from the now defunct Patriotic Union. In 1906 two former members of the Patriotic Union—A. S. Stishinskii, Kutler's successor at the Main Administration of Agriculture and Land Settlement, and V. I.

Gurko, Deputy Minister of the Interior and the architect of the future "Stolypin" land reform—were actual members of the Goremykin government.

Notwithstanding their high posts, the two men, who were among the members of the government most adamantly opposed to political concessions to the Duma, continued to maintain intimate relations with their former political associates (such as Count Bobrinskii), who now stood at the head of the nobles' organization. Stishinskii went so far as to allow the First Congress of the United Nobility to meet in his office at the Main Administration of Agriculture,[73] while Gurko graced the congress with his presence and received a standing ovation for his recent tough rejoinder to the Duma on the land question.[74] Such ties between government figures and groups in society had been an integral feature of bureaucratic politics in Russia from the period of the Great Reforms, if not earlier. Since the support of groups in society could greatly strengthen an official's political hand and advance his program and/or career, government officials occasionally even sought out such alliances. Relationships of this kind enabled the United Nobility to demand—and usually immediately receive—interviews and audiences with the most highly placed government officials.[75] Furthermore, these contacts also enabled the nobles' organization to know when its political interventions on a given matter could be most effective.[76] The political interventions of the United Nobility were never haphazard but were carefully coordinated with parallel campaigns conducted by the organization's current political allies in the government. Whenever the latter deemed it "inopportune" to continue to press for particular policies, the Permanent Council of the nobles' congress would prudently refrain from launching a political offensive on that front no matter how inflamed were the opinions of its provincial constituents. The best example of such calculated restraint was the refusal of the Permanent Council in the autumn of 1906 to press on with its campaign for further revisions of the Duma electoral law, although a large majority of Council members favored such revisions, and many local noble associations were clamoring for action.[77]

When it was impractical to undertake elite interventions with the government, the organization tended to rely more heavily on its provincial components.[78] At such times, the nobles' union rather self-consciously resorted to the tactics of the now defunct Liberation Movement, striving to influence the government from without by mobilizing the local zemstvos and noble associations behind its political demands. Such activities on the part of the United Nobility were most characteristic of the organization in the early Stolypin years (especially 1907). At this time, the United Nobility's allies, Stishinskii and Gurko, had been removed by Stolypin from the government, and it seemed to many in the nobles' association that their main opponent was not so much the revolutionary movement as a reformist-minded government bent on reaching a political accommodation with the Duma.[79] For the new Stolypin administration not only prepared a large body of reform measures, which it then proceeded to introduce in the Duma, but it also allowed the second national assembly—to the surprise of many noble activists—to continue in operation somewhat longer than its predecessor. Therefore, the nobles' organization in this period generally refrained from making direct representations to the government, preferring to concentrate their forces on a public campaign within the zemstvos and noble associations against the Prime Minister's local reform projects.

The local reform projects were selected by the United Nobility as the target for their campaign partly because "the preservation of the leading influence of the nobility in the localities" was one of the main aims of the nobles' organization from its very inception, but also because these bills represented one of Stolypin's most far-reaching efforts to cooperate with moderate reformers in the Duma. Therefore, a campaign launched by the United Nobility in coordination with the State Council right to have these bills withdrawn from the Duma for preliminary consideration by local zemstvos and noble associations struck at the heart of the prime minister's relationship with the national assembly. Moreover, the campaign against the local reforms culminated in the convocation of the 1907 Zemstvo Congress, an assembly that many members of the United Nobility hoped would go beyond the local reforms and draft a new electoral law for the national assembly, if the Duma were not dismissed by the time the congress convened.[80] In this way, the involvement of the United Nobility in the organization of this congress contributed to the dissolution of the Duma (which occurred two days before the zemstvo congress was originally scheduled to meet) and to the immediate publication of a new electoral law by government fiat to forestall any possibility of the zemstvo congress's assuming this task.

The nobility's campaign against Stolypin's local reforms did not stop with the June Third coup d'état. The government's reform projects were soundly criticized by the two sessions of the 1907 Zemstvo Congress in June and August, and the campaign for preliminary consideration continued in the zemstvo and noble associations until Stolypin capitulated to their demands on November 16 by establishing within the Ministry of the Interior the Council on the Affairs of the Local Economy,[81] empowered to review all bills on local government *before* they were submitted to the Duma. This quasi-legislative body included elected representatives of the thirty-four provincial zemstvos and selected provincial governors (to which some marshals of the nobility and city duma representatives were subsequently added). Thus, the political pressures of the nobility also helped bring about the foundation of a pre-Duma, if not a third legislative house in the Russian political order.

With the June Third coup d'état and the foundation of the Council on the Affairs of the Local Economy, the political activity of the United Nobility entered a new phase. Henceforth, the organization primarily —but not exclusively—sought its political ends through the existing legislative organs. Initially, it appears that the organization staked many hopes on the Third Duma and its new composition. The Permanent Council went so far as to maintain in the autumn of 1907 that "future legislative work should remain in the hands of the legislative institution—the State Duma," an evaluation of the political situation that left remarkably little scope for the usual behind-the-scenes machinations of the nobles' organization.[82] But relatively few members of the United Nobility—only twenty-two of the participants in the First Congress—were elected to this five hundred–man chamber.[83] Consequently the organization could exert little influence within the Duma[84] and soon directed its attention elsewhere.

At first the nobles' organization possessed only a little more influence within the Council on the Local Economy than it had in the Duma. The original thirty-four delegates elected to this body from the zemstvos were evenly divided between people close to the Octobrist Union and men of the right (at least ten of the latter were members of the United Nobility). Under these conditions, the Council, which included twenty-two members appointed by the government, was inclined initially to accept the essence of Stolypin's local reform projects (i.e., the replacement of the current estate-based electoral system with a more democratic suffrage), although they did want to substitute a rather low landed-property qualification for voting in place of the tax-based franchise favored by the government.[85] However, after the Fourth Congress of the United Nobility (meeting in March 1908) passed a resolution denying that *any* basic changes in local institutions were necessary or desirable and sent a special delegation to convey these sentiments to the emperor,[86] a number of provincial marshals of the nobility—at least eight, possibly more—were suddenly added to the Council. Since all the marshals concerned were active members of the United Nobility and apparently acted as a solid bloc, they provided a nucleus of leadership for the opposition to the government.

At any rate, after the addition of the marshals, the only way that the government could salvage any part of its reform program was through the mobilization of *all* the appointed members on the Council, who were then pressured to vote for the government's project. This was done in December 1908 in order to pass Stolypin's project on the *uezdnyi nachal'nik*, an appointed official who was to supersede the marshal of the nobility as the chief administrative figure in the county. The bill was passed over the opposition of a majority of "public" members of the Council from the nobility (all the marshals and a solid majority of the zemstvo delegates). The twenty-seven dissenting delegates immediately issued a protest,[87] which was endorsed by the Fifth Congress of the United Nobility,[88] after which nothing more was heard of this project. When Stolypin's county zemstvo bill was brought up for a vote in March 1909, the marshals were present in full force, and a number warned against "the bureaucratization" of the zemstvo, which they maintained this measure would entail. This time, the opposition won a majority in the Council, leaving Stolypin, who had presided over the proceedings, to storm furiously out of the chamber.[89] Although the Council continued to meet throughout the Stolypin period, it played thereafter a far less crucial political role and was formally dissolved by the Kokovtsov administration.[90]

Therefore, the most reliable and important of the United Nobility's weapons in the post-1907 period was the influence of its members in the State Council. As a result of the reform of the State Council in 1906, the nobility from the first enjoyed a dominant position in the elective half of the chamber, occupying almost three-quarters of the seats (seventy-two out of ninety-eight). The close interrelationship between the United Nobility and the State Council can be appreciated from the following figures: members of the nobles' congress accounted for between a third and a fifth of the total membership of the upper house throughout the 1905–17 period (sixty-five members in 1906, forty-four in 1912, forty-six in 1914, for example).[91] This was a striking degree of dominance of a major state institution for an organization that could be regarded as only a faction within the nobility. The members of the United Nobility in the upper house did not form a special group, however, but took their place in both the right and center groups, especially the right-wing subgroup of the center, which coalesced in 1907 around Stolypin's brother-in-law, A. B. Neidgardt, a member of the Permanent Council of the United Nobility. Members of the nobles' organization were also prominent among the founders of the right group in the State Council, which included such stalwarts of the United Nobility (and previously the Patriotic Union) as Prince Kasatkin-Rostovskii, F. D. Samarin, O. R. Ekesparre, Count D. A. Olsuf'ev, A. P. Strukov, and A. A. Naryshkin.[92] Here they were joined by other veterans of the Patriotic Union from among the appointed members of the Council, such as A. S. Stishinskii and V. F. Stiurmer, who had already cooperated with the nobles' organization in its 1907 campaign against Stolypin's local reform projects.[93]

While divided among the political groups of the chamber, members of the United Nobility in the State Council continued quite naturally to keep in touch with one another, and occasionally they acted in concert on issues of vital concern to the landed nobility along lines previously indicated by the nobles' congresses. Indeed, the existence of such ties between Council members, cutting across factional lines, was one of the factors that prevented the emergence of a fully developed party system in the upper house. Because of the composition of the State Council, the nobles' organization found it easiest of all to work through members close to the government. We find the United Nobility represented by former veterans of the Patriotic Union among the appointed members of the upper house, most of whom had served in the Ministry of the Interior under Pleve. The most notable of these was A. S. Stishinskii, a man associated with the introduction of the land captains and other administrative counterreforms of the 1890s.

The debates on local government in the State Council provide a good illustration of how the United Nobility functioned in the upper house on issues of vital concern to the provincial nobility. Stolypin's defeats in the Council on the Affairs of the Local Economy did not wholly predetermine the fate of his local reforms, since in many cases the Duma enthusiastically restored incisions that the government had made in these bills at the suggestion of the Council. This was most noticeably the case in the reform of local justice and the establishment of a district (*volost*) zemstvo, both of which came before the State Council in a form that the United Nobility at its congresses had already declared unacceptable. In the case of local justice, the Duma recommended over the adamant objections of the Fourth Congress of the United Nobility[94] that both the district peasant court and the judicial powers of the land captains be abolished, and their functions

turned over to new justices of the peace, elected by the county zemstvos. When the Duma's bill came up for discussion in the State Council in 1911, the United Nobility's reluctance to see the district court
abolished was reasserted in the Judicial Committee of the upper house
under the leadership of A. S. Stishinskii.[95] In the face of this opposition, Stolypin unexpectedly capitulated and, reversing his previous
policy, publicly spoke out in favor of the peasant district court. Under
these conditions, the State Council substantially revised the Duma's
bill, and in the end, the peasant district court was not abolished but
merely somewhat reformed.[96]

The United Nobility was, however, less successful in its attempts
to preserve the judicial powers of the land captain, quite possibly because this time the organization was unable to win over the government to its views. The quality of the land captains had been deteriorat-
ing rapidly in recent years as the economic decline of the nobility
sharply reduced the ranks of noble landowners from whom these officials were traditionally selected, and it was apparent to the government
that it was in the state interest that some of the tasks of the land captains be delegated to other institutions. Since the government, especially in the Stolypin period, controlled the votes of a sizable proportion of the appointed members of the State Council, who were subject
to annual reappointment, the nobles' organization had little chance
to prevail. Nevertheless a number of members of the United Nobility
(Prince A. N. Lobanov-Rostovskii, A. A. Naryshkin, Ia. N. Ofrosimov,
M. Ia. Govorukho-Otrok, and of course Stishinskii) spoke out vigorously on this issue, insisting that the land captain's unique mixture of
judicial and administrative functions was essential for the preservation of order in the countryside.[97] But the government won out in the
end: the majority of the upper house voted to strip the land captain
of his judicial functions, thus reestablishing the principle of the separation of powers in the localities.[98] In short, it would seem that the
support or opposition of the government was sometimes a crucial factor
in determining the political success or failure of the United Nobility
in the upper house.

The United Nobility was more fortunate in its opposition to the
district zemstvo bill, which was passed by the Duma in 1912. Makarov
and Maklakov, Stolypin's successors at the Ministry of the Interior,
who were generally reluctant to interfere in the deliberations of the
upper house or to infringe on the vital interests of established groups
in Russian society, did not actively intervene to salvage this bill.[99]
The bill, passed by the Third Duma, would have transformed the

purely peasant district administration into an all-estate body, representing all local inhabitants and possessing considerably more independence from the local administration than the current institutions, which were subject to the administrative tutelage and manipulation of the noble land captains. Such an independent, all-estate, but still peasant-dominated district government would have exercised considerable powers (including that of taxation) over local noble landowners. Consequently, it is not surprising that the Eighth Congress of the United Nobility, meeting in 1912, declared the measure "unacceptable" in its entirety, and that members of the United Nobility, spearheaded once again by their highly vociferous spokesman, Stishinskii, led the attack on this bill on the floor of the upper house. A few members of the United Nobility (Gurko, D. V. Kalachov, and Count D. A. Olsuf'ev) wanted to see the bill proceed to a second reading in view of the manifest deficiencies of the existing district administration. But the other members of the nobles' organization speaking on this bill (I. E. Rakovich, D. D. Levshin, Neidgardt, Strukov, V. I. Karpov, and Bobrinskii) called for its immediate rejection on the grounds that the proposed institutions would readily fall into the hands of the radical third element, since the nobility's ranks were rapidly thinning, and the new independent peasant proprietors (presumably being created by the Stolypin land legislation) had not yet appeared in sufficient numbers to provide the district zemstvo with reliable personnel.[100] Thereupon the house without further ado rejected the Duma's bill by a fairly slim majority (seventy-seven to seventy-one),[101] members of the nobles' organization obviously providing the margin of defeat. Hence, it would not be much of an exaggeration to say that thanks to the intervention of the United Nobility, the land captains and village elders under their supervision continued to rule the Russian countryside until the fall of the Old Regime.

The extent of the United Nobility's influence over education reforms, another area of interest to moderate reformers like Stolypin, is more questionable. Yet here again we find the nobles' organization conducting a spirited campaign against the proposed reforms, which was widely publicized in the press, while its members in the State Council, speaking in close accordance with the resolutions of the nobles' congresses, helped alter the course of the reforms. The introduction of compulsory primary education was particularly hard fought, even after it had been piloted through the Duma by the enthusiastic Octobrists, with the initial support of the Ministry of Education and most sections of urban public opinion. What worried the United Nobility about the

program as it emerged from the Duma was, first, the secularization of
education entailed in the Duma's subordination of the existing parish
school network of the Orthodox Church (currently controlled by the
Holy Synod) to new local school councils under the Ministry of Education. Second, the nobles' organization objected to the Duma's provision for elementary education in local languages in non-Russian
areas. They were also concerned with the mounting costs of education
envisioned by the bill (which proposed to raise the credits allocated
to the Ministry of Education by ten million roubles annually) and by
the Duma's proposal to allow graduates of primary schools to transfer
automatically to higher levels of education without having first to pass
an entrance examination.[102] According to V. M. Purishkevich, this latter measure would allow "the simple peasant to stray from his own
background, to become a crow in peacock's feathers and then a revolutionary."[103]

In the State Council, members of the United Nobility appeared less
united over these issues than over those concerning local government,
presumably because their own estate interests were less directly involved. Nevertheless, *most* of the speakers associated with the nobles'
congress expressed themselves in ways predictable from these resolutions, although they did not address themselves to all issues of concern
to the United Nobility. For example, only Count D. A. Olsuf'ev spoke
against allowing students to transfer directly from primary to secondary
schools without an intervening examination, despite the inflated rhetoric that had greeted this proposal at the nobles' congress. In addition,
a co-opted member of the United Nobility, N. A. Zverev,[104] the official
reporter for the Education Commission of the upper house, introduced
a series of amendments to the Duma's legislation along lines previously
suggested by the nobles' organization. Two amendments, supported
by all United Nobility members speaking on this bill and ultimately
adopted by the State Council, limited education in native languages
to the first two years of schooling and reserved 1.5 million roubles of
the annual 10-million-rouble increment for the schools of the Holy
Synod.[105] In both these cases of political success, the nobles' organization had received support from elements within the government. The
first amendment, interestingly enough, was endorsed by the Minister
of Education, Kasso, whose recent repressive policies toward Moscow
University were enthusiastically backed by the United Nobility, while
Prime Minister Kokovtsev supported the second amendment. The alteration of this bill by the upper house meant that the legislative chambers of the Old Regime never enacted universal primary education

into law, since the two houses were unable to work out an acceptable compromise version.[106]

In agrarian, local government, and educational matters, then, the United Nobility can be said to have exercised definite, though varying, degrees of influence on state policies. It is doubtful whether they did so in other areas. They never discussed military or foreign affairs, even when these raised controversial issues and were debated in the legislative chambers. Perhaps they were restrained here by the conviction that these questions lay outside the nobility's jurisdiction, falling entirely within the emperor's prerogatives. Even in areas where the United Nobility's influence was clear, however, it is possible to overestimate it and to misunderstand its nature. The nobles' organization never "dictated to" or "manipulated" the government; they simply worked within the Russian political system as it had evolved over the years (both before and after 1905), articulating the political interests of the upper strata of the landed nobility and throwing their support to elements favoring similar policies within the government. In the process both the United Nobility and its bureaucratic allies profited from this alliance of mutual convenience at the expense of the legislative institutions, especially the Duma.

Yet the political successes of the United Nobility led to the gradual abandonment of its extraconstitutional role, as the State Council took over the function of aggregating and articulating right-wing views with the advantage of its legislative authority. Thereafter the United Nobility, while remaining a focus for the respectable right wing of the landed nobility, ceased to make an independent political contribution. After the death of its adversary, Stolypin, attendance at the nobles' congresses declined markedly, while their members appeared increasingly unsure of the scope and nature of the political role that the organization could play[107] or even precisely whom it should represent. At its last congresses, the United Nobility began to discuss whether successful landowners of other estates should not be admitted to augment the ranks of the now rapidly declining nobility.[108] Perhaps having attained its original goals, the United Nobility would eventually have faded away, had not the World War and its new political challenges intervened.

It also appears that the United Nobility was always much less effective on economic questions than on political matters. To be sure, the Stolypin land reform was passed at the nobility's instigation, and the government in the end did take effective measures to restore law and

order in the countryside after the 1905 peasant rebellions. But the
United Nobility never did succeed in changing the policies of the
Peasants' Land Bank, which was held accountable by many noblemen for the extreme rapidity of the economic decline of the nobility
after 1905. Nor did the nobles' organization ever manage to obtain
government compensation for the victims of the agrarian disorders[109]
or a reduction in the import tariff, which they felt discriminated against
the agricultural sector and made it more difficult to find foreign cus-
tomers for their agricultural produce. These issues, one would think,
were of utmost importance to the membership of the United Nobility,
who, by virtue of their large landholdings, were among the leading
exporters of agricultural products, the chief victims of the agrarian
unrest, *and* the group most likely to engage in mass panic land sales
after 1905.[110] The congresses did indeed take up these matters[111] and
repeatedly appealed to the government. But the economic decline of
the nobility proceeded more rapidly than ever during these years,
leaving the last prewar congress to discuss once more "the crisis of
private agriculture" with virtually no achievements to its credit in
this sphere. The sole source of relief for noble landowners after 1905
came from a direction never mentioned at the congresses of the United
Nobility—the vast sums of state funds poured into agriculture via the
noble-dominated zemstvos.

Why was this so? In part, we think the United Nobility's relative
lack of economic success reflects the nature and aims of the organization. Its political preoccupations always outweighed its economic concerns, as can be seen from the much greater amount of time that the
congresses devoted to political as opposed to economic issues. Nevertheless, the idea of an economic union of landowners, not necessarily
only nobles, never entirely faded. Even after the original Union of
Landowners had collapsed, despite the support rendered it by the
nobles' organization, N. A. Pavlov produced another scheme for an
economic union at a meeting of the Permanent Council in 1910. By this
time, the economic position of the nobility was the subject of annual
debates at the nobles' congresses. While most members of the United
Nobility—true to the established principles of the organization—felt
that the best way to improve the position of the nobility was to influence government financial policies, Pavlov maintained that with good
organization and well-conducted husbandry, noble landowners could
themselves overcome many of their problems. Inspired by the example
of the *Bund der Landwirte,* he recommended that the United Nobility
set up a nationwide agricultural cooperative to arrange cheap credit

on flexible terms, organize the grain trade without relying on middle-men, undertake the bulk purchasing of agricultural machinery from abroad, and make available agricultural advice, legal aid, and insur-ance.[112] He also announced that the foreign banking firm of van Setters was prepared to offer the United Nobility up to four million roubles at 4½ percent interest to get such a union under way.

However, the nobles' organization, particularly its leadership, re-acted rather coolly to this scheme. Even many partisans of an economic union of some sort, like V. N. Snezhkov of Tambov, thought such ac-tivities were better left to the zemstvos, which possessed the requisite capital (thanks to the influx of state funds mentioned above) and an all-estate composition.[113] Although Pavlov's idea was approved *in principle* by two congresses (the Seventh and the Eighth), it was never implemented. On the suggestion of the Permanent Council, Pavlov's proposal was constantly referred back to the localities (where it aroused little enthusiasm) or to a commission for further refinement. Consequently, nothing more came of the proposal, and Pavlov with-drew from the nobles' organization to his estate to write his highly polemical memoirs in hopes of converting the younger generation of noble proprietors to his ideas.

In part, the opposition to Pavlov's scheme stemmed from the fact that his plans were ill formulated and highly confusing. Pavlov ap-parently was not at all clear in his own mind about the future goals and composition of his union. Although he originally conceived of it as a purely economic association, Pavlov subsequently began to stress the political tasks that it could perform, seeing a union of landowners as the only group in Russia able effectively to combat the growing militancy and organization of the proletariat through its control over food supplies for the cities.[114] Likewise, he sometimes talked of a union of purely *noble* landowners, only to contradict himself at other times by maintaining that his union would include persons of "all estates."[115] The only thing that was clear was that Pavlov's plans for a union in 1910–12 did *not* include ordinary peasants, unlike the plans of his original 1906 union and the practices of his professed model, the *Bund der Landwirte*. He insisted that only those possessing a capital of at least three hundred roubles would be allowed to join: by his own esti-mate, those meeting this qualification would have to be at least "me-dium proprietors."[116] This is another example of the distrust that still existed between the Russian nobility and peasantry as late as 1912.

There is another basic reason why the noble's organization did not implement Pavlov's scheme: he was advocating a mode of activity

that the United Nobility found foreign to their nature. Their political
method *par excellence* was discreet pressure on the government through
the use of personal contacts and elite institutions. In his proposals for
a union, Pavlov was asking them to do something quite different, to
break their ties to the government and launch out on their own in a
world of purely economic values. To be sure, such values had come
to play an ever larger role in the lives of Russian noblemen as the
economic conditions of the post-Emancipation era forced increasing
numbers of them to renounce traditional careers in state service and to
involve themselves directly in agricultural affairs. Nevertheless, much
of the traditional value system and thought patterns of the service
estate, "the Petersburg psychology" as Pavlov disdainfully dubbed
them in his memoirs, continued to influence noble landowners under
the new conditions of life. Noble proprietors were by and large simply
not the independent and self-reliant types that Pavlov's plans for a
union of landowners required. Rather, they continued to look to the
state, which their ancestors had traditionally served, rather than to
themselves for their salvation; and even the most agriculturally oriented among them continued to regard public service of some sort,
even if only in local elective office, as no less important than their
agricultural concerns.[117] Such attitudes were especially entrenched
among the absentee magnates (Bobrinskii and Co.) who dominated
the executive organs of the United Nobility; but they were also shared
by the more provincially oriented members of the nobles' organization. Therefore, Pavlov was politically and psychologically out of step
with the nobles' organization when he told them forthrightly: "We can
expect nothing from anyone."[118] The whole organization of the United
Nobility was geared to get things from people in the government: that
was its *raison d'être*, and that is why it found Pavlov's scheme unat-
tractive.

Returning to our initial comparison with the *Bund der Landwirte*,
we think a number of conclusions can be stated that summarize the
characteristics of the United Nobility. First, the organization was set
up in response not so much to economic challenges as to political ones:
the 1905 Revolution, the attacks on noble landed property, the weakened position of the nobility in the new political order of 1905–1906.

Thus, its economic aims were subsidiary and its main drive was
always in the political field. On the other hand, while the United Nobility had a tolerably coherent conservative and monarchist outlook
and policies on a broad range of issues, it was not a political party.
Indeed, it avoided close association with any political party in an

attempt to preserve its character as a traditional estate corporation. It exerted its influence through elite contacts, particularly in the Ministry of the Interior, and state institutions, especially the State Council. For this reason the United Nobility had no organization other than the Permanent Council and the annual congresses. It did not generate a system of mass communications through a newspaper or even an internal newsletter, confining itself to the publication of the proceedings of its congresses and to personal contact with bureaucratic elites and figures around the imperial court. Its membership tended to come from the upper strata of the landed nobility. Moves to attract non-nobles or smallholders and to make the United Nobility into the nucleus of an agrarian union were all abortive. Nor did the organization ever succeed in developing a purely commercial and agricultural side to its activities.

The United Nobility reflected, in fact, the ambiguous and transitional phase through which the Russian social and political order was currently passing. In a genuine autocracy, it would not have existed at all. In a full-blown parliamentary system, it would either have had to become purely a farmers' lobby or to have sought a mass base in some political party. In a society still based on traditional estates, it would have represented the noble estate unambiguously; in a society where estates had disappeared altogether, it could have represented a class-based economic interest. But Russia was in transition from an autocracy to a parliamentary form of government and from an estate-based to a class-based social order, with all the ambiguities which that transition entailed. These ambiguities were faithfully reproduced in the curious organization that has gone down in history as the United Nobility.

NOTES

1. E. D. Chermenskii, *Istoriia SSSR (period imperializma)*, 2d edition (Moscow, 1965), pp.318–19; A. Ia. Avrekh, *Tsarizm i tret'eiiunskaia sistema* (Moscow, 1966), p.17; V. S. Diakin, "Stolypin i dvorianstvo," in *Problemy krest'ianskogo zemlevladeniia i vnutrennei politiki Rossii* (Leningrad, 1972); G. A. Hosking, *The Russian Constitutional Experiment: Government and Duma, 1907–14* (Cambridge, 1973), esp. chapters 2, 3, and 6; and Roberta T. Manning, "The Russian Provincial Gentry in Revolution and Counter-revolution, 1905–07" (Ph.D. diss., Columbia University, 1975), esp. chapters 5–8.

2. In this essay, we adhere to the standard Soviet definition of "large land-owner," regarding any individual who possessed 500 *desiatiny* or over as a large landed proprietor.

3. On the *Bund der Landwirte*, see S. R. Tirrell, *German Agrarian Politics after Bismarck* (New York, 1952); Thomas Nipperdey, *Die Organisation der deutschen Parteien vor 1918* (Düsseldorf, 1961), pp.249–50; Hannelore Horn, *Der Kampf um den Bau des Mittelland-kanals: eine politische Untersuchung über die Rolle eines wirtschaftlichen Interessenvervandes im Preussen Wilhelms II* (Köln, 1964), pp.8–33.

4. Manning, "The Russian Provincial Gentry," pp.4–47.

5. For the role of the marshal of the nobility, see M. A. Katkov, *Rol' uezdnykh predvoditelei dvorianstva v gosudarstvennom upravlenii Rossii. K voprosu o reforme uezdnogo upravleniia* (Moscow, 1914).

6. The advocacy of such a program on the part of the Patriotic Union was by no means an act of political opportunism, provoked by the events of 1904–1905. Many members of this organization had favored the establishment of a similar representative body with the same limited powers and electoral base since the early 1880s. See K. F. Golovin, *Vospominaniia* (St. Petersburg, 1908–11), vol. II, pp.114–18.

7. Apart from Bobrinskii (who was to become a Deputy Minister of the Interior and a Minister of Agriculture), this organization included: Senator A. A. Naryshkin (an Orel zemstvo deputy and former provincial governor), A. P. Strukov (a former and future provincial marshal of the nobility in Ekaterinoslav and the head of the Office on the Affairs of the Nobility in the Ministry of the Interior), S. S. Bekhteev (head of the zemstvo section of the Ministry of the Interior, 1902–1904), V. I. Gurko (a Deputy Minister of the Interior in 1906), N. A. Khvostov (Oberprokurator of the Second Department of the Senate and the father of a future Minister of the Interior), A. D. Zinoviev (provincial marshal of the nobility in St. Petersburg, 1897–1903; former St. Petersburg Governor and Deputy Minister of the Interior, 1902–1904), A. S. Stishinskii (former Deputy Minister of the Interior, 1899–1904), Prince A. A. Shirinskii-Shikhmatov (Governor of Tver Province), N. A. Pavlov (Saratov landowner; provincial correspondent for *Moskovskie vedomosti* and *Grazhdanin;* and a special duty clerk in the Ministry of the Interior until the end of 1904), F. D. Samarin (a uezd marshal of the nobility and zemstvo deputy in Moscow province and a member of the Bulygin Commission), N. F. Kasatkin-Rostovskii (former Kursk marshal of the nobility, 1890–94). In addition, many of these men served in the Senate or on the State Council. The reader should note that both the provincial governors and the marshals of the nobility were subordinated to the Ministry of the Interior. The Patriotic Union was originally founded by V. F. Stiurmer (Director of the Department of General Affairs of the Ministry of the Interior), but he soon left the organization (when, according to Gurko, he found that he could not use it to advance his candidacy for the premiership). Hence the authors believe that the Patriotic Union may have grown out of the anti-Witte (or pro-Pleve) clique in the Ministry of the Interior and their allies in St. Petersburg society and among the provincial nobility. This group apparently maintained remarkable continuity as a distinct faction within the Russian government, from the 1890s to the fall of the Old Regime. Therefore it merits closer study, for this group may not only have played a role in the counterreforms of 1889–90 but also have provided the nucleus of the opposition to the policies of the reformist Prime Minister, P. A. Stoly-

pin (1906–11), as well as some of the "dark forces" operating on the monarchy in the last days of the Old Regime, when many veterans of the Patriotic Union or their close associates were appointed to cabinet posts. V. I. Gurko, *Features and Figures of the Past: Government and Opinion in the Reign of Nicholas II* (Stanford, 1939), pp.383–85); *Petergofskie soveshchaniia* (Petrograd, 1917); "Dnevniki A. A. Polovtseva," *Krasnyi arkhiv*, vol. IV, p.108; and P. P. Mendeleev, *Svet i teni v moei zhizni 1864–1933: obryvki vospominanii* (mss. in the Columbia University Russian Archive), notebook III, pp.49–50.

8. A. P. Korelin, "Dvorianstvo v poreformennoi Rossii (1861–1904 g.g.), *Istoricheskie zapiski*, vol. 87, pp.91–173; N. A. Rubakin, "Rossiiskoe dvorianstvo v tsifrakh (Iz etiudov o chistoi publike," *Trudovoi put*, 1907, nos. 11 and 12; N. A. Rubakin, *Rossiia v tsifrakh* (St. Petersburg, 1912).

9. V. Levitskii, "Pravye partii," in *Obshchestvennoe dvizhenie v Rossii v nachale XX veka* (edited by L. Martov and others) (St. Petersburg, 1909–11), II, pp.366–70; Hans Rogger, "The Formation of the Russian Right," *California Slavic Studies*, vol. III (1964), pp.80–83. On Shcherbatov, see L. P. Minarik, "Proiskhozhdenie i sostav zemel'nykh vladenii krupneishikh pomeshchikov Rossii kontsa XIX veka-nachale XX veka," *Materialy po istorii sel'skogo khoziaistva i krest'ianstva SSSR*, vol. 6 (1965), p.393.

10. The programs of the two organizations appear to have differed slightly, although the difference is a subtle one. The Union of Russian Men seemed much more sincerely committed to the foundation of a national assembly than the Patriotic Union, even though they, too, wished to preserve the autocratic powers of the emperor. They were also willing to base elections on something other than estates, advocating curiae of "customary groupings," determined by actual life style rather than by outmoded legal definitions (such a system, however, would have resembled an estate-based franchise in many ways).

11. *Zhurnal zasedaniia s"ezda uchreditelei vserossiiskogo soiuza zemlevladel'tsev 17 noiabria 1905 g.* (Moscow, 1906), p.6.

12. Ibid., pp.20–30.

13. Ibid., pp.10–11, 30–33.

14. Ibid., pp.7, 9, 37.

15. Ibid., pp.37–40; *Zhurnal zasedanii s"ezda vserossiiskogo soiuza zemlevladel'tsev, 12–16 fevralia 1906 g.* (Moscow, 1906), pp.8–9; and Rogger, "The Formation of the Russian Right," p.83.

16. *Zhurnal zasedanii . . . 12–16 fevralia 1906 g.*, pp.140, 142–43.

17. *Novoe vremia*, nos. 10884–10886, Jul. 3 (16)–5 (18), 1906, and no. 10893, Jul. 12 (25), 1906, pp.3–4, and *Zhurnal zasedaniia soveta vserossiiskago soiuza zemel'nykh sobstvennikov 14-go maia 1908 goda* (St. Petersburg, 1909).

18. N. A. Pavlov, *Zapiski zemlevladel'tsa* (Petrograd, 1915), pp.248–49.

19. *Trudy vtorogo s"ezda upolnomochennykh dvorianskikh obshchestv 31 gubernii 14–18 noiabria 1906 g.* (St. Petersburg, 1906), pp.122–28.

20. Only one of the fifty peasant deputies who spoke on the Stolypin land legislation failed to maintain that the abolition of the land commune in itself would not remedy peasant land hunger unless it were accompanied by a new allotment of land. Russia: *Gosudarstvennaia duma. Stenograficheskie*

176 HOSKING AND MANNING

otchety. Tretii sozyv sessiia II, ch. i, 171–1666, ch. ii, 705–2303 and sessiia III, ch. i, 105–252.

21. A. P. Korelin, "Rossiiskoe dvorianstvo i ego soslovnaia organizatsiia," *Istoriia SSSR,* 1971, no. 5, p.80.

22. TsGAOR fond 434, opis 1, delo 1/303, 11. 15–16. See also Hosking, *The Russian Constitutional Experiment,* pp.30–32.

23. See Manning, "The Russian Provincial Gentry," pp.223–26; O. Trubetskaia, *Kniaz' S. N. Trubetskoi: vospominaniia sestry* (New York, 1953), pp. 149–50; S. Iu. Witte, *Vospominaniia* (Moscow, 1960), vol. II, p.390; A. N. Naumov, *Iz utselevshikh vospominanii* (New York, 1954–55), vol. II, p.45; D. N. Shipov, *Vospominaniia i dumy o perezhitom* (Moscow, 1918), pp.297 et seq.; Gurko, pp.380–81.

24. Naumov, II, pp.45–46.

25. Ibid., p.63.

26. The congress was even highly reluctant to accept the steering committee's suggestion that compulsory expropriation might be permissible under certain conditions to allow access to waterholes, etc. At any rate, the congress initially rejected this point, accepting it only after the issue had been raised once more by the leadership of the congress. TsGAOR fond 434, opis 1, delo 1/303, p.19–20.

27. Ibid., pp.15–16. See also Hosking, *The Russian Constitutional Experiment,* pp.3–32.

28. Three other noble associations took no official position on this question. TsGAOR fond 434, opis 1, delo 2/1, 1906 11. 9–10 and 23–129; TsGIA fond 1283, opis 1, delo 12 (1906), 11. 34–35.

29. TsGAOR fond 434, opis 1, delo 2/1, 1906, pp.9–19.

30. Ibid., 21–23.

31. Ibid., delo 1/303 11. 3–4.

32. *Kruzhok dvorian vernykh prisiage: otchet s"ezda 22–25 aprelia 1906 goda s prilozheniiami* (Moscow, 1906), p.15.

33. TsGAOR fond 434, opis 1, delo 2/1, 1906, pp.121–31. See also the report that Snezhkov submitted for the consideration of the First Congress of the United Nobility. *Kruzhok dvorian: Znachenie dvorianstva v sovremennoi Rossii* (Moscow, 1906). Similar views were also expressed by other spokesmen for a nobles' congress in the localities, especially the Kursk nobility, which had already as early as June 1905 petitioned the emperor for an advisory Duma elected by estates. Levitskii, p.361.

34. TsGAOR fond 434, opis 1, delo 2/1, 1906, 11. 9–19.

35. *Novoe vremia,* no. 10739, Feb. 5 (18), 1906, p.2. The relationship between the Circle and the Patriotic Union is unclear, although there was some overlap of membership.

36. *Kruzhok dvorian vernykh prisiage otchet,* pp.6, 10.

37. The Circle was aided in this endeavor by the casual nature of the membership of the steering committee. Prince Trubetskoi on April 6 had called upon the local noble associations to send delegates to the committee, but he failed to specify precisely how these delegates were to be selected. Consequently anybody from an unrepresented province could simply declare himself a delegate from that region. TsGAOR fond 434, opis 1, delo 1/2, 1906, p.23.

38. Ibid., delo 3/3, 1906, pp.17–24 and *Doklady sobraniia predvoditelei i deputatov dvorianstva S-Peterburgskoi gubernii 18 fevralia 1907 g.* (St. Petersburg, 1907), pp.7–12.

39. Zhurnal podgotovitel'noi kommissii in *Trudy 1-ogo s"ezda upolnomochennykh dvorianskikh obshchestv 29 gubernii* (henceforth cited as *Trudy pervago s"ezda*), 2d edition (St. Petersburg, 1910), pp.177–80.

40. TsGAOR fond 434, opis 1, delo 10, pp.141, 143.

41. Ibid., delo 76, 1906, p.85.

42. For a list of the participants in the First Congress of the United Nobility, see Ibid., delo 5/4, 1906, pp.278–82.

43. The provinces concerned were Vladimir, Kostroma, Novgorod, Orel, Penza, and Estland.

44. The noble associations concerned were those of Voronezh, Tver, Kurland, and Orenburg. Non-Russian nobles (except from the Baltic) were not invited to the nobles' congress. It is interesting that the internal opposition to the policies of the Permanent Council tended to come from roughly the same geographic region as most of the dissenting or abstaining noble associations.

45. On the basis of woefully incomplete biographical data (covering approximately half the delegates), we found seventy uezd marshals of the nobility, thirty-three provincial marshals, forty-eight zemstvo deputies, and thirty-seven justices of the peace among the participants in the First Congress of the United Nobility.

46. *Novoe vremia*, no. 10854, June 3/16, 1906, p.4.

47. The attentive reader has, no doubt, noted that this table compares two different quantities—the distribution of *landed wealth* among members of the United Nobility and the distribution of landed *estates* owned by noble proprietors. Individual nobles, especially the more wealthy, could and frequently did own more than one estate. However, as far as we know no aggregate data exists on the distribution of total landholdings among noble proprietors, and the table that we have compiled does clearly establish in any case that members of the United Nobility tended overwhelmingly to come from the wealthiest Russian landowners.

Landholding data were available for 107 of the 221 men attending the First Congress (including 98 of the 133 elected delegates). Our sample seems to have been a fairly typical cross section of the congress, not necessarily only the wealthiest participants, since we have no landholding data for a number of men (like F. D. Samarin and Count P. S. Sheremetev) whose families are known to have owned tens of thousands, if not hundreds of thousands, of *desiatiny* of land. Also, our information may very well show many of the participants to be less wealthy than they actually were. For *Vsia Rossiia*, one of our major sources for the landholdings of the nobility, is a list of addresses of landowners and only lists the size of the estate on which a landowner actually resided, eliminating all other holdings (which were often not inconsiderable, since the Russian nobility was renowned for its many, scattered landholdings). Finally, we have made no attempt to take into account family holdings, although these, no doubt, are of great importance in determining which strata of the landed nobility a particular individual belongs to.

48. Our list would be far longer had we possessed sufficient data to trace the cadet branches of the one hundred families. For a description of this group, see L. P. Minarik, "Kharateristika krupneishikh zemlevladel'tsev Rossii kontsa XIX-nachala XX v.," *Ezhegodnik po agrarnoi istorii vostochnoi evropy 1963 g.* (Vilna, 1964), pp.693–708; "Proiskhozhdenie i sostav zemel'nykh vladenii krupneishikh pomeshchikov Rossii kontsa XIX-nachala XXv," *Materialy po istorii sel'skogo khoziaistva i krest'ianstva SSSR*, sbornik 6 (Moscow, 1965), pp.356–95; and "Sostav i istoriia zemlevladeniia krupneiskikh pomeshchikov Rossii," in ibid., sbornik 7.

49. S. N. Prokopovich, *Agrarnyi krizis i meropriiatiia pravitel'stva* (Moscow, 1912), pp.113–18.

50. *Novoe vremia*, no. 10850, May 30/June 12, 1906, p.3.

51. *Zapiska soveta ob"edinennykh dvorianskikh obshchestv ob usloviiakh vozniknoveniia i o deiatel'nosti ob"edinennago dvorianstva* (St. Petersburg, 1907), p.13.

52. See, for example, *Trudy pervago s"ezda*, pp.7, 67, 79, 72–73, 77–78, 81–82.

53. Ibid., pp.84, 116–18; TsGAOR fond 434, opis 1, delo 3/304, 1906, p.7; *Zapiska soveta*, p.14; *Ob"iavleniia soveta ob"edinennykh dvorianskikh obshchestv* (St. Petersburg, 1906), p.2; and *Novoe vremia*, no. 10843, May 23/June 5, 1906, p.3.

54. *Svod postanovlenii I-X s'ezdov upolnomochennykh ob'edinennykh dvorianskikh obshchestv 1906–14 g.g.* (Petrograd, 1914), p.1–4, 92.

55. *Trudy pervago s"ezda*, pp.11–12.

56. The First Congress of the United Nobility, however, appears to have been more representative than most of the 1905 congresses of this sort. Many noble associations selected their representatives to the congress at the time of the State Council elections; others chose their delegates less systematically. TsGAOR fond 434, opis 1, delo 1/2, pp.56–115, 148–62, and delo 5/4, 1906, pp.1–5.

57. *Trudy pervago s"ezda*, p.8; and *Novoe vremia*, No. 10845, May 25/June 7, 1906, p.4.

58. The signatories of this protest can be divided as follows:

1. The Petersburg group: Count V. V. Gudovich, the provincial marshal of St. Petersburg and member of the Octobrist Central Committee; N. Shubin-Pozdeev, uezd marshal of St. Petersburg; Lev Aleksandrovich Zinoviev, marshal of Peterhof uezd; Evgenii N. Shvarts, marshal of Novoladozhskii uezd; Count G. N. Sivers, marshal of Iamburg uezd; N. P. Pykhochev, representative of the Shlissel'burg nobility;

2. The Chernigov group: Count V. A. Musin-Pushkin, marshal of Sosnitskii uezd, member of the Octobrist party; V. I. Krinskii, Kozeletskii uezd marshal; P. P. Markovich, Glukhovskii uezd marshal; Vasilii Khanenko, Starogubskii uezd marshal; Pavel Aleksandrovich Abalashev, Novozykhovskii uezd marshal;

3. First Duma deputies: M. A. Stakhovich, Octobrist, Orel marshal; Prince I. A. Kurakin, Octobrist, Iaroslavl marshal; Nikolai N. Andreev, Octobrist, Vologda marshal; N. A. Khomiakov, Octobrist, Sychevskii uezd marshal (Smolensk); Count P. A. Geiden, Octobrist, Opochetskii uezd marshal (Pskov); Prince N. S. Volkonskii, Octobrist, Riazan' representative; G. A. Firsov, Kadet, Khar'kov marshal;

4. The State Council Center: Prince P. P. Golitsyn, Novgorod marshal; I. N. Leontovich, Lubenskii uezd marshal (Poltava), Octobrist; Prince P. N. Trubetskoi, Moscow marshal; Prince Repnin, Kiev marshal;

5. Other: P. A. Belevich, Kremenchug uezd marshal (Poltava), may very well have been an Octobrist or have possessed close ties with them, for a number of prominent Octobrist families (the Leontovich, Kapnists, and Lizogubs) resided in his uezd.

59. This protest may very well have been rooted in social and geographic differences among the nobility as well as political ones. The protesters (like the provinces abstaining from joining the United Nobility) tended to come from provinces to the north of Moscow, where peasant land hunger—and agrarian disturbances—were much less severe. The exceptions mainly came from Chernigov and Poltava, regions renowned for the large concentration of petty noble proprietors residing there, who, some maintained, were not at all adverse to seeing peasant land hunger satisfied through the compulsory expropriation of the lands of their larger, more prosperous neighbors. See, for example, the letters of Count A. A. Uvarov to *Novoe vremia*, no. 10859, May 30/June 12, 1906, p.3 and no. 10854, June 3/16, 1906, p.4. The protesters collectively, however, appear to have been no less wealthy than the remainder of the congress.

60. *Trudy pervago s"ezda*, pp.12–14.

61. TsGAOR fond 434, opis 1, delo 4/304, 1906, 1. 2.

62. *Trudy pervago s"ezda*, pp.16–17.

63. Ibid., p.27.

64. *Svod postanovlenii*, p.83.

65. Manning, "The Russian Provincial Gentry," pp.460–62.

66. It is quite possible that St. Petersburg was the last noble association to join the United Nobility because it included in its ranks many highly placed officials, opposed to the formation of a national nobles' organization capable of intervening at a moment's notice in the intricate power plays of bureaucratic politics.

67. TsGAOR fond 434, opis 1, delo 250, 1906, p.169, and delo 93, 1906, p.37.

68. Ibid., delo 76, 1906, pp.11–12, 16, 28–29, 69–70, and delo 10, pp.11, 103–104.

69. For example, see ibid., delo 15/10, pp.1–2, delo 93–94, 1906–1907, p.38; *Zapiska soveta ob"edinennykh dvorianskikh obshchestv ob usloviiakh vozniknoveniia i deiatel'nosti ob"edinennago dvorianstva* (St. Petersburg, 1907), pp.11–24; V. Snezhkov, *Ob"edinennoe dvorianstvo* (St. Petersburg, 1909); *Russkiia vedomosti*, nos. 5–6, Jan. 9–10, 1906; nos. 10–14 (Dec. 30, 1906–Jan. 5, 1907) and no. 16 (January 9, 1907) pp.1–2; *Rech'*, Jan. 4, 1907; and *Postoiannyi sovet ob"edinennykh dvorianskikh obshchestv: Materialy po voprosam voznikshim na s"ezde gubernskikh predvoditelei 5–7 ianvaria 1907 goda* (no date). See also the remarks made by Martov and Pavlov at the Seventh Congress of the United Nobility in 1911. Quoted in Maxim Kovalevskii, *Chem Rossiia obiazana soiuzu ob"edinnennago dvorianstva* (St. Petersburg, 1914), pp.23–25.

70. TsGAOR fond 434, opis 1, delo 75/305, pp.9–15, and delo 15/10, 1908–1909, p.1.

71. The government's decision to dissolve the Duma was by no means a

foregone conclusion even at this late date. On June 15 Nicholas II showed Kokovtsev a list of new government ministers who, he had been assured by the Court Minister Baron Fredericks and D. F. Trepov, the Court Commandant, could get along with the Duma better than the present government. Nicholas seemed genuinely undecided what to do about this list, which consisted in the main of prominent members of the Kadet Party. The appointment of such a government would have gone a long way to meet the Duma's demand for a responsible ministry and would have probably changed the political history of Russia. Kokovtsev, I, pp.197–211.

72. *Svod postanovlenii*, pp.17–22, and A. A. Bobrinskii, "Dnevnik," *Krasnyi arkhiv*, vol. XXVI (1928), p.147.

73. Naumov, II, p.76.

74. *Trudy pervago s"ezda*, p.18.

75. In the first eighteen months of its existence, the Permanent Council of the United Nobility was formally received by Prime Ministers Goremykin and Stolypin (the latter when he was still only Minister of the Interior), V. A. Vasil'chikov, Stishinskii's successor at the Main Administration of Agriculture, and by the management of the Peasant's Land Bank. TsGAOR fond 434, opis 1, delo 75/3–5, pp.9–16, and delo 76, 1906, pp.45–46, 111–12.

76. The leaders of the United Nobility appear to have been extremely well informed about developments within the inner circles of the government. In fact, they were sometimes better informed than officials who occupied important positions of power in the public eye. For example, Stolypin's successor as prime minister, Count V. V. Kokovtsev, first learned of his impending dismissal from the premiership in early 1914 from the former permanent chairman of the United Nobility, Count A. A. Bobrinskii, at this time a leader of the right faction in the State Council. Earlier Kokovtsev had heard insistent rumors of his impending forced retirement but he could not bring himself to believe any of them until he heard the same thing from Count Bobrinskii, "a man," according to Kokovtsev, "who never shoots the breeze [*nikogda ne govoriashchago na veter*] . . . and who has reliable sources of information." Kokovtsev, II, p.275.

77. Ibid., p.6, and delo 75/305, 1906–1907, p.16.

78. Precisely at the time the United Nobility began to adopt such tactics, the role of its provincial component was vastly strengthened. The provincial marshals of the nobility were granted full voting rights in the Permanent Council, and the practice of co-option was severely limited to no more than ten persons per congress. When the Circle of Nobles protested against this move in the name of "landless nobles," who had no political rights in the zemstvos and noble associations and hence were useless to the nobles' organization in its new phase of activity, the Circle was told firmly that the United Nobility was an organization of the *landed* nobility. See Manning, "The Russian Provincial Gentry," pp.458–61.

79. See, for example, the remarks of Prince Tsertelev to the Permanent Council. TsGAOR fond 434, opis 1, delo 76, 1906, p.95.

80. These events are discussed in some detail in Manning, "The Russian Provincial Gentry," chapter 7.

81. *Zhurnaly tverskago ocherednogo gubernskago zemskago sobraniia sessii 1907 goda (18–19 dekabria) i chrezvychainago sobraniia 16–17 maia 1907*

goda i prilozheniia k nim (Tver, 1908), pp.15–16, and *6–i material po vo-prosu o mestnoi reforme: postanovleniia chrezvychainykh i ocherednykh gubernskikh dvorianskikh sobranii po voprosu o mestnoi reforme* (St. Petersburg, 1908).

82. TsGAOR fond 434, opis 1, delo 15/10, 1908–1909, pp.1–2.

83. The organization did little better in the Fourth State Duma. Only twelve participants in the First Congress of the United Nobility served in that chamber.

84. Nonetheless, the United Nobility never turned against the reconstituted Duma, adamantly refusing to follow the lead of its permanent council chairman, Count A. A. Bobrinskii, who wanted the nobles' organization to retaliate in 1910 for the many attacks on the landed nobility made from the Duma podium by launching a public offensive against that chamber, including demands for further revisions in the Duma electoral law. Quite possibly the United Nobility's reluctance to take the offensive can be explained by the fact that the authority of the Duma could easily be curbed by the other legislative institutions (in which the nobles' organization possessed considerably more influence). Avrekh, pp.491–94.

85. See the report of council member P. Koropochinskii on the activity of the council before the marshals were added. *Reforma mestnago samoupravleniia po rabotam Soveta po Delam Mestnago Khoziaistva: Doklad XXXIV ocheredomy Ufimskomu gubernskomu zemskomu sobraniiu predstavitelia Ufimskago zemstva P. Koropochinskago* (Ufa, 1909).

86. In addition, the congress resolved that the consideration of the local reform projects by the Council on the Affairs of the Local Economy could not be considered an adequate substitute for the review of these projects by the local zemstvos and noble associations. *Svod postanovlenii*, pp.333–35. The deputation sent by the Fourth Congress of the United Nobility consisted of Bobrinskii, Naryshkin, and two provincial marshals of the nobility (A. D. Samarin of Moscow and S. M. Prutchenko of Nizhnii Novgorod), both of whom were subsequently added to the Council. *Kratkii obzor deiatel'nosti upolnomochennykh dvorianskikh obshchestv za 1907–1908 i 1909 gody Upolnomochennago Moskovskago Dvorianstva grafa Chernysheva-Bezobrazova* (St. Petersburg, 1909), p.21.

87. TsGAOR fond 434, opis 1, delo 19/69, p.50.

88. *Trudy piatago s"ezda upolnomochennykh dvorianskikh obshchestv 32 gubernii s 17 fevralia po 23 fevralia 1909 g.* (St. Petersburg, 1909), pp.110–31, 281–84.

89. Naumov, II, pp.133–38.

90. N. Mel'nikov, *19 let na zemskoi sluzhbe (avtobiograficheskiia nabroski i vospominaniia)* (unpublished mss. in the Columbia University Russian Archive), p.348.

91. Members of the United Nobility virtually monopolized the elections from the nobility to the State Council in the 1906–14 period, accounting for eighteen out of the eighteen delegates in 1906, sixteen out of eighteen in 1912, and fourteen out of eighteen in 1914. They usually provided about half of the zemstvo representatives to this body. However, it would be wrong to regard this interlinking membership simply as the result of the single-minded infiltration of a state institution on the part of the nobles' orga-

nization. The members of the United Nobility were in the main men of considerable political experience with both bureaucratic and provincial connections. Most of them would no doubt have been elected to the State Council even had the United Nobility not existed.

92. "Dnevnik A. A. Polovtseva," *Krasnyi Arkhiv* No. IV (1923), pp.107–108, 116–17.

93. As far as we can tell, Stishinskii and Shtiurmer were the first to call for the preliminary consideration of Stolypin's local reform projects in the zemstvos and noble associations. They were also appointed to the United Nobility's commission on local reforms. TSGAOR fond 434, opis 1, delo 76, 1906/07, 88–92, and *Svod postanovlenii*, p.30.

94. Ibid., pp.48–52, and *Trudy chetvertago s"ezda upolnomochennykh dvorianskikh obshchestv 32 gubernii s 9 po 16 marta 1908 g.* (St. Petersburg, 1909), pp.151–226.

95. Stishinskii was a leading figure on the judicial committee of the State Council.

96. Russia. Council of the Empire. *Stenograficheskie otchety* (St. Petersburg, 1911–12) sessiia 7, esp. cols 1756–60 (henceforth cited as GSSO) and Naumov, II, pp.161–62.

97. GSSO 7 (1911–12), cols 1773–88, 1846–55, 1903–17, 1925–33, 1965.

98. It is possible that members of the United Nobility might have been included in this majority; but without voting lists that were not available to us, we cannot tell. Ibid., 1846–55, 1903–17, 1925–33, 1965.

99. Hosking, pp.168–69. Earlier the government had supported the district zemstvo bill.

100. GSSO 9. (1913–14), 2200–12, 2238–47, 2261–66, 2308–19, 2217–26, 2302–8, 2319–25, 2332–27.

101. Ibid., 2394.

102. *Svod postanovlenii*, pp.59–61, and *Trudy piatago s"ezda*, pp.110–33, 282, 315–37.

103. *Trudy shestago s"ezda upolnomochennykh dvorianskikh obshchestv 33 gubernii s 14 marta po 20 marta 1910 g.* (St. Petersburg, 1910), p.388.

104. N. A. Zverev is yet another official who had served in the Ministry of the Interior under Pleve (as head of the Chief Administration on the Affairs of the Press) and who proved willing to work with the nobles' organization. He came from a peasant family in Novgorod province and was given an education by the Khotiainintsev family, local landowners who were closely associated with the United Nobility. Gurko, pp.88–89 and 638.

105. GSSO 7, 2695–2714, 2999–3010, 3019–30, 3048, 1149–59, 1218–28, 1344.

106. Hosking, p.178.

107. *Rech'*, no. 68, Mar. 10, 1912, p.6, and *Trudy vos'mago s"ezda upolnomochennykh dvorianskikh obshchestv 37 gubernii s 5 marta po 11 marta 1912 g.*

108. Ibid., pp.150–94 and *Trudy deviatago s"ezda upolnomochennykh dvorianskikh obshchestv 39 gubernii s 3 marta po 9 marta 1913 g. (St. Petersburg, 1913)*, pp.31–52.

109. The most the victims of the disorders ever received were government loans under the Law of March 15, 1906. These, however, had to be

repaid, and the United Nobility deserves no credit for this measure, which was adopted before the nobles' organization came into existence. TsGAOR fond 434, opis 1, delo 227/22, pp.3–13.

110. S. N. Prokopovich, *Agrarnyi krizis i meropriiatiia pravitel'stva* (Moscow, 1912) pp.113–18, and I. G. Drozdov, *Sud'by dvorianskago zemlevladeniia v Rossii i tendentsii k ego mobilizatsii* (Petrograd, 1917), pp.49–71.

111. *Trudy pervago s"ezda*, pp.127–35; *Trudy vtorago s"ezda*, pp.82–85, 108–109; *Trudy tret'iago s"ezda upolnomochennykh dvorianskikh obshchestv 32 gubernii s 27 marta po 2 aprelia 1907 g.* (St. Petersburg, 1907), pp.210–92; *Trudy chetvertago s"ezda*, p.138; *Trudy piatago s"ezda*, pp.43–95, 155–308, 12–26; *Trudy shestago s"ezda*, pp.98–112, 301–25; *Trudy vos'mago s"ezda*, pp.211, 262–81; *Trudy desiatago s"ezda upolnomochennykh dvorianskikh obshchestv 39 gubernii s 2 marta po 6 marta 1914 g.* (St. Petersburg, 1914), p.14.

112. TsGAOR fond 434, opis 1, delo 80/307, pp.42–43; Pavlov's report to the Permanent Council, November 12, 1910. See also his *Zapiski zemlevladel'tsa, Trudy sed'mago s"ezda*, p.226.

113. Snezhkov had long been advocating such a zemstvo organization. See his report to the Fourth Congress of the United Nobility. V. Snezhkov, *Zemstvo i zemlia* (St. Petersburg, 1907); TsGAOR fond 434, opis 1, delo 93/94, 1906–12, pp.201–37, and *Trudy vos'mago s"ezda*, p.23.

114. Ibid., pp.17–21.

115. *V sovete ob"edinennago dvorianstva* (no date); *Zhurnal zasedaniia komissii dlia vyrabotki ustava po proektu N. A. Pavlova ob ob"edinenii dvorianstva na pochve ekonomicheskoi 16-go maia 1911 goda* (St. Petersburg, 1912), and *Izvlechenie iz perepiski N. A. Pavlova s sovetom* (no date).

116. *Trudy vos'mago s"ezda*, p.371. Also it seems that he wanted the nobles to fight the unionization of agricultural laborers.

117. Manning, "The Russian Provincial Gentry," pp.48–49.

118. Pavlov, *Zapiska*, 7. Pavlov's motives in urging the nobility to be independent of the government are unclear. Having grown up in "the milieu" of St. Petersburg, as he put it, he left the capital at a rather young age (nineteen) to devote himself full time to agriculture, a pursuit in which he ultimately attained reasonable success. Hence, his provincial roots were far deeper than those of many other United Nobility leaders. Also, he was almost alone among the members of the Permanent Council in never serving in the legislative chambers, and he was much less involved in the affairs of his local zemstvo and noble association than one would expect from a man in his position. However, he had not always been as wary of the government or indifferent to officeholding as he was in 1910–12. In the opening years of the century, he had served as a special duty clerk (without a salary) in the Ministry of the Interior, flooding the government with a long series of proposals and suggestions, none of which were accepted, according to Gurko. Perhaps his views of the government were influenced by this experience, coupled with the events of 1905, when the government proved itself incapable of defending the property of noble landowners from the peasant rebellions. See Gurko, pp.213, 643, and Pavlov, op. cit.

The Crisis of the Third of June System and Political Trends in the Zemstvos, 1907–14

RUTH DELIA MacNAUGHTON and
ROBERTA THOMPSON MANNING

The Manifesto of October 17, 1905, called into being a new form of political organization in Russia: the legal political party. Historians concerned with Russia's political evolution in subsequent years have devoted the greater part of their attention to the development of these parties, their functioning in the four State Dumas, and their inability to form a workable majority in opposition to the government.[1] Focusing narrowly on the Duma, political histories of the post-1905 period have generally neglected parallel developments within a predecessor of the Duma as a multiclass elective institution—the zemstvos, the local organs of self-government established in the countryside during the "great reform" era of Alexander II.

In this neglect, historians of the post-1905 period have merely followed in the footsteps of liberal contemporaries, who generally maintained that with the creation of the State Duma, the zemstvos had fulfilled their essential function by contributing to "the crowning of the constitutional edifice" through their participation in the Liberation Movement.[2] Accordingly, after 1905 the zemstvos were expected to pass unnoticed from the political scene, concentrating their energies and attention on purely routine local matters. Meanwhile, with the convocation of a multiclass Duma, the landed nobility, which effectively dominated the zemstvos under the 1890 estate-based election law, was to be superseded in the national political arena by men of diverse social origins.

Despite liberal expectations, neither the zemstvos nor the landed nobility were reduced to a secondary political role after 1905. On the contrary, with the defeat of the Revolution of 1905–1907 and the adoption of the Third of June electoral law, the landed nobility emerged as *the* leading social force in the new political order, providing approximately half of the deputies to the Third and Fourth State Dumas[3] as well as almost all the elected representatives to the State Council, the upper house of the new Russian parliament.[4] At the same time, the zemstvos came to exert greater influence on national affairs than ever before. The zemstvos not only elected the largest single block of deputies to the State Council but also provided the bulk of the public representatives on the Ministry of the Interior's Council on the Affairs of the Local Economy (*sovet po delam mestnago khoziaistva*). Many contemporary observers considered this unduly neglected body a preparliament or even a third legislative chamber within the post-1907 political order, since it was endowed with the power to review— and hence also to revise—all the government's legislative proposals relating to local government *before* such bills were submitted to the Duma.[5]

Consequently, no historical evaluation of the Imperial Russian government and its policies after 1907 is complete without a survey of the political attitudes of the zemstvos and their noble constituency, especially as these attitudes developed during the premiership of P. A. Stolypin, the most creative statesman of the post-1905 period. A study of the zemstvos at this time is all the more warranted because the ultimate collapse of the tsarist regime and the victory of the Russian Revolution are often attributed to the Imperial Russian government's reluctance to give responsible public forces, especially the zemstvo men, a meaningful voice in national affairs.[6]

This failure was not shared by the Stolypin government.[7] In the first place, Stolypin was not a career bureaucrat but, rather, a longtime provincial landowner and marshal of the nobility. He left his native Kovno province to serve as governor of Saratov in 1904, only two years before his appointment as Minister of the Interior and Chairman of the Council of Ministers.[8] He therefore tended quite naturally to identify with the noble landowners of the provinces. Early in the course of the Revolution of 1905, he concluded that Russia needed above all else "the formation of a landed party, rooted in the nation, which opposed a theoretical approach to politics and which might counteract and neutralize what is harmful in the third element [i.e., the intelligentsia]."[9] Consequently, in the hope of aiding the emergence of such a political formation, he actively cooperated with moderate conservative elements in the legislative chambers.

He also attempted to collaborate with such men in the local zemstvos, consulting with the zemstvos on all legislation that might affect them through the zemstvo representatives in the Council on the Local Economy. In addition, he utilized these institutions to administer key portions of his reform program in the localities, especially in the fields of education and agriculture. In the course of Stolypin's administration, the zemstvos were encouraged to become actively involved in his land reform program by establishing special programs to improve the economic practices of the new private peasant proprietors who left the land commune under the Stolypin land legislation. In this way, the zemstvos were a vital part of Stolypin's plans for the future of Russia, and his success or failure as a statesman must be gauged at least in part by political developments in these institutions and his changing relationships with them.

A survey of the political attitudes of the zemstvos at this time can serve other purposes as well. It can provide us with insights into the local roots of the political behavior of the landed nobility, the dominant element within the new post-1907 political order. In the course of our study we will be forced to consider whether the new national political parties, which quite often developed directly out of the zemstvo movement,[10] exerted a reciprocal influence on provincial affairs or whether local politics tended to follow the sound of a different drummer, shaped by concerns other than national political alignments. A study of the political tendencies among the zemstvo nobility can also illuminate the limitations within which Russian statesmen were compelled to operate, on both the national and local levels. For during this period the zemstvos and their noble constituency not only played an unprecedented role in national affairs but also continued to exert a critical influence on precisely those areas of activity upon which Stolypin turned the full force of his reformist zeal: economic relations in the countryside and the expansion of the role of non-noble elements in local elective institutions.[11]

Of necessity our inquiry will focus heavily on the zemstvo elections of 1909–10, since official returns are most complete for these elections. From these elections we can gauge the political mood of the provincial nobility—and other elements of the population—midway through the Third Duma period. Only a detailed scrutiny of the returns of these elections held near the end of the Stolypin era can reveal whether the political reaction in the zemstvos that set in at the end of 1905[12] was finally reversed after political stability was restored in Russia, allowing liberals and reformers to assume their previous position of preeminence and authority within the zemstvos. A move to the left was quite likely in view of earlier, pre-1905 zemstvo experiences. Time and again in the past, the liberals had suffered setbacks similar to those of 1906–1907 in individual provinces and regions, only to stage a political comeback in subsequent elections.

Before turning to the electoral results, however, we would like to point out that there are considerable problems in evaluating the available statistical data on zemstvo elections. In the first place, given the necessary limitations of this essay and our primary interest in the political evolution of the provincial nobility, four of the thirty-four zemstvo provinces—Vologda, Viatka, Olonets, and Perm—will have to be excluded from our discussion, since relatively few nobles resided in them, and the local zemstvos evolved along different lines from the noble-dominated assemblies.[13] Furthermore, in order to facilitate our task, the greater part of our attention must be focused on the provincial zemstvo assemblies—one in each of our thirty remaining provinces —rather than on the 322 county assemblies. This approach is also the more useful, since by tradition political tendencies were developed more fully at the provincial level, while parochial interests tended to prevail within the smaller units.

Also, any comparison of the results of the 1909–10 elections with those of 1906–1907 will be hindered by the fact that the official returns of the 1906–1907 elections compiled by the Main Administration on the Affairs of the Local Economy of the Ministry of the Interior are incomplete. For the government gathered information on the political alignment of the zemstvos in the spring of 1907, on the eve of the June 3 coup d'état, midway through the current round of zemstvo elections. At this time only fifteen of the thirty-four provincial zemstvos had been reelected.[14] The resulting gap in official electoral statistics was only partially remedied by B. B. Veselovskii, the well-known expert on zemstvo affairs, in his monumental history of the zemstvos published in 1909–11. In this work Veselovskii analyzed the political trends in the zemstvos after 1905 by comparing the political affiliation of the provincial zemstvo board chairmen elected in 1903–

1904 with those elected in 1906–1907.[15] The problem with Veselovskii's figures is twofold. First, the political affiliation of the board chairman might not necessarily reflect the predominant political tendency prevailing in any given assembly as a whole. While the 1906–1907 elections were quite probably the most politicized in the entire history of the zemstvos,[16] personal factors, such as bonds of kinship and friendship, which traditionally played a large role in provincial politics among the landed nobility, continued to influence the outcome of the elections no less than purely political considerations.[17]

The second difficulty with Veselovskii's analysis of the elections coincides with the third problem that we encounter in attempting to comprehend the results of the zemstvo elections: the problem of political classification. While Veselovskii discussed political tendencies among the provincial board chairmen largely in terms of affiliation to one or another of the new legal political parties—the Kadets, "progressives," Octobrists, or "rights"—the Ministry of the Interior both in 1907 and again in 1909–10 classified the political alignment of the local zemstvos according to three more general categories: "rights," "moderates," and "lefts."[18] Such a classification of the outcome of the 1909–10 elections may seem surprising. By 1909–10 the new national legal political parties that had formed in response to the October Manifesto and the establishment of representative government in Russia were no longer novelties. One might thus reasonably expect that the new round of zemstvo elections would reveal even more clear-cut political allegiances than had been displayed three years earlier. But the government was not alone in using this vaguer political classification. The contemporary press, too, used identical terms to describe the results of the 1909–10 elections, while frequently confusing matters even further by adding a fourth category to the government's three—that of "progressive."

The terms "right" and "left" present fewer difficulties than the terms "moderate" or "progressive." In contemporary political literature, with certain qualifications to be discussed later, the term "zemstvo left" was commonly employed as a catchall phrase to refer to Kadets and Kadet sympathizers, as well as to those zemstvo men whose political views might rank them closer to the Social Democrats and Social Revolutionaries than to the liberals, but we should realize that there were certainly only negligible numbers of this latter group, particularly after 1906–1907. Nor did anyone ever claim that the term "zemstvo rights" was more than a convenient way to refer to anyone who stood to the right of the Octobrists.[19] However, given the general recognition of a strong strain of Octobrism in the post-1905 zemstvo,[20] it is reasonable to inquire why the press and the government continued to refer to the center of the zemstvos' political spectrum as "moderates" rather than "Octobrists."

On the basis of a survey conducted by its provincial correspondents in the spring of 1909, the liberal Moscow newspaper *Russkoe slovo* advanced a straightforward answer to this question. "Octobrists as any sort of organized force," the editors concluded, "do not appear in the provinces even during city duma and zemstvo elections." Assigned the task of sampling the attitudes of local Octobrists toward the activity of the Duma faction in general and Guchkov in particular, correspondents from Ufa, Odessa, Baku, Smolensk, Kharkov, and other localities reported themselves unable to complete the assignment because of the lack of any bona fide Octobrists to question. Although the official Octobrist organ, *Golos moskvy*, made a halfhearted, albeit strongly worded, attempt to discredit the survey's findings, the journal in the end was forced to concede that the party's work "is concentrated in the parliamentary faction and in the central committee."[21]

Earlier accounts of attempts by the Kadets as well as the Octobrists to establish provincial branches indicate that the majority of these organizations collapsed almost as soon as they were founded.[22] Evidently the conditions of life in the countryside, particularly in those remote areas commonly referred to as "deep in the provinces," were not conducive to the establishment of formal party organizations. Those seeking to organize party chapters among the landed nobility in these areas did not only have to contend with the primitive condition of transportation and communication and the premodern ties of friendship and blood in all social interactions. They also had to face the all-pervasive authority of the generally highly conservative marshals of the nobility, to whom their fellow noblemen tended traditionally to defer. The marshals, though always important figures, appear to have played a more active role in provincial politics after 1905, taking the lead in ousting the liberals from the zemstvos and dominating the zemstvo contingents in the State Council and the Council on the Local Economy.[23]

Hence, it is not surprising that even by 1909–10 the number of zemstvo members who possessed formal party ties was so insignificant that the press and the government had no choice but to resort to less specific terminology to describe the general political inclinations of the provincial nobility. Moreover, those relatively few provincial noblemen who did join political parties apparently did not fully adhere to the views of their representatives in the Duma. Writing in *Sovremennyi mir*, the publicist I. Larskii noted in 1909 that "provincial Octobrists are somewhat more conservative than their counterparts in the capital."[24] In the countryside, political distinctions were blurred, and individuals quite often subscribed to the most unlikely assortment of political tenets.[25] Nevertheless, national issues could not help but impinge occasionally on zemstvo life and in 1909–10 the press continued to associate rather broadly the term "zemstvo left" with Kadets and "zemstvo moderates" with the Octobrists as a device of admittedly limited usefulness to group the zemstvo membership according to their attitudes toward the government, the recent national upheaval, the land question, etc.[26]

This brings us to still another source of confusion in dealing with political terminology. In addition to the new national partisan connotations of these terms, the terms "rights," "moderates," and "lefts" continued within the context of the zemstvo to retain their original meanings, which were based primarily on local rather than national issues. To be sure, liberal publicists frequently argued with some justification that local and national issues were inseparable. While "zemstvo rights" traditionally tended to advocate fiscal austerity—and hence lower taxes —out of a sense of their own "class" interests, the "zemstvo lefts" tended to promote the expansion of zemstvo services out of a quasi-populist conviction that "the zemstvo cause is a commitment to satisfying the needs of the lower classes of the population, a commitment to the cultural uplifting and education of the people."[27] Those political observers discussing the "zemstvo lefts" in 1909 and 1910 could hardly have been referring to the Kadets or Kadet sympathizers alone, so few now were their numbers in the zemstvos. Hence, as employed in contemporary political literature, the term "left" or "progressive" clearly had a meaning of its own within the confines of the zemstvo, being applied to any zemstvo man who could be termed an "activist" in promoting the extensive development of the cultural and economic services provided by his zemstvo. Expanded zemstvo programs necessarily entailed higher taxes and the hiring of more zemstvo employees, both of which were likely to provoke opposition from more conservative elements.

In addition, "zemstvo rights" and "zemstvo lefts" also held divergent views of the zemstvos' immediate priorities. The more right-wing assemblies tended to display a strong interest in such endeavors as road building and the construction of telephone networks while neglecting local medical and education programs.[28] One would assume that schools and doctors came well ahead of roads on the peasants' list of priorities, since the Russian peasantry largely lived in a subsistence, not a market, economy. Certainly telephones, while advantageous for the nobility residing in the countryside, were of no use whatsoever to the peasants.[29]

Nevertheless, the distinction between the conservatives who swept to power in 1906–1907 and the *praktiki* of the "old zemstvo" is far from being as clear as contemporary liberal journalists often suggested. At least initially, they were correct in noting that the "new" conservative zemstvo men manifested greater talent for destructive rather than creative work. Yet, like their liberal predecessors, many of the new zemstvo men, at least after immediate political passions had cooled, found a strong sense of personal fulfillment in devoting their energies to "practical" zemstvo work.[30] Consequently, by the end of 1908 and early 1909 there were signs that a revival of zemstvo economic and cultural work was well under way. In the course of the regular 1908–1909 winter sessions of the provincial zemstvo assemblies, many vital zemstvo services eliminated in 1906–1907 were restored or even expanded by the local zemstvos, to the delight of many liberals who had earlier expressed alarm over the enormous budgetary cutbacks of 1906–1907.[31] By 1909 most local assemblies were beginning once more to allocate substantial sums to education, agronomy, and medicine, the three fields most drastically curtailed by the zemstvo reaction of 1906–1907; and several of the more conservative assemblies even proceeded to implement a number of projects initiated by liberal zemstvo boards and voted down in 1906–1907.[32] Yet in most cases, the resumption or expansion of zemstvo activities was undertaken under the pressure of outside developments, not the spontaneous initiative of the local assemblies concerned.[33]

This was certainly true of the dramatic expansion of zemstvo-sponsored educational and agricultural services. These activities were directly stimulated by the Stolypin government, which allocated vast sums to the zemstvos to develop universal primary education and to bolster the faltering economic undertakings of the peasantry, particularly those who had left the land commune under the Stolypin agrarian reform (see, for example, table 1).[34] Evidently the government, which had come to depend on the zemstvos to perform a great number of basic services in the localities, must have been deeply concerned about

TABLE 1

Government subsidies to zemstvo agricultural enterprises in the prewar years.

Year	Amount allocated by the government
1906	3,898,000 roubles
1907	4,040,000 roubles
1908	4,596,000 roubles
1909	5,365,000 roubles
1910	7,495,000 roubles
1911	16,365,000 roubles
1912	21,880,000 roubles
1913	29,200,000 roubles

SOURCE: V. E. Brunst, "Zemskaia agronomiia," in B. B. Veselovskii and Z. G. Frenkel, *Iubileinyi zemskii sbornik 1864–1914* (St. Petersburg, 1914), p.328.

the curtailment of zemstvo activities in 1906–1907, since the proper functioning of zemstvo programs was crucial to Stolypin's policies of "pacification" in the countryside.

As a result, grants from the central government accounted for about 10 percent of the total expenditures of the local zemstvos by 1910, and the ready availability of such funding was stimulating an expansion of zemstvo services every bit as rapid as the great advance of the 1890s.[35] In the key area of agriculture, the zemstvos of this period displayed an unprecedented degree of vitality. Indeed, never before in zemstvo history had the agricultural programs of the zemstvo expanded at such a rapid pace as in the years of "reaction" after 1905 (see table 2).

The zemstvos' recovery, however, even to the extent to which it was self-initiated, did not necessarily indicate that partisan rivalries or political discord had been significantly reduced among zemstvo

TABLE 2

Number of agronomists employed by the zemstvos, 1877–1909.

Year	Number of agronomists on the zemstvo payrolls
1877	1
1885	8
1890	29
1895	86
1900	197
1905	422
1908	1,820
1909	2,363

Derived from the same source as table 1.

men. Once undertaken, the restoration of zemstvo programs could itself be a source of continuing and even intensified conflict among
zemstvo activists. The construction of an extensive network of new
schools, for instance, was hardly a noncontroversial issue: the all-
important questions of teacher training and curriculum remained to
be decided by the zemstvos in consultation with the government. In
an effort to influence zemstvo educational policies, the United Nobility, whose members were quite active in zemstvo affairs, would
have a good deal to say throughout this period on "the preparation
of a cadre of teachers acceptable to the nobility."[36] Nor was the long-
standing controversy over whether the zemstvos should subsidize the
parish schools of the Russian Orthodox Church instead of construct-
ing their own educational establishments a dead issue. Secular schools
were most likely to be staffed by religiously indifferent, if not outright
anticlerical, instructors who might possibly also harbor other types of
"subversive" ideas. Therefore, secular education for the peasantry was
anathema to the generally highly religious right wing of the landed
nobility.[37] Bitter disputes over this issue resurfaced during the 1909
sessions and again in 1910, when the government's—and Duma's—
new educational program, which was based on secular control and
direction of the existing parish schools, was the chief topic of discussion.[38]

Likewise, Stolypin's appeals to the zemstvos for aid in promoting
his land reform schemes aroused strong opposition among the few
remaining liberals. Liberal zemstvo men tended to believe that *all*
peasants, whether members of land communes or owners of individual
holdings under Stolypin's land reform law, were equally deserving
of zemstvo aid.[39] The more conservative zemstvo men, however, generally responded enthusiastically to Stolypin's proposals.[40] As always,
any discussion of zemstvo aid to agriculture prompted a lively exchange of opinions. Zemstvo men of a quasi-populist slant—and hence
usually "lefts" or "progressives"—wanted zemstvo agricultural services
in the main to benefit the peasantry, while more conservative zemstvo
members were quite often intent on channeling some of the enormous
sums allocated to the zemstvos by the government for agriculture in
these years to aid their own faltering economic ventures.[41]

The revival of zemstvo activities in 1908–10 demonstrated that "zemstvo rights" could be as interested in, and capable of, promoting "practical" zemstvo work as "zemstvo lefts," particularly if such work could
be used to advance their own ideological—and personal—objectives.
Still we should keep in mind the tendency of many liberal journalists

to associate the "zemstvo left" with superior practical skills when we turn to a discussion of the zemstvo elections of 1909–10, since we are dependent, except for government statistics, on liberal sources. While the zemstvos may have been nonpartisan in terms of official party organizations, they were not apolitical; and the labels "right," "moderate," "progressive" and "left" must be understood in terms of both the vague associations with national political parties and also (when we deal with press accounts) the zemstvos' internal life, for which such classification schemes were still more meaningful.

The special use of the term "left" by the press to include those zemstvo men, regardless of actual political affiliation, most active in expanding zemstvo services, may explain why the liberal press generally concluded that the new round of voting in the zemstvos had merely reinforced the status quo of the past few years.[42] Official government statistics on the 1909–10 elections displayed an even further shift toward the right, compared to the 1906–1907 elections. Evidence of further victories for the zemstvo right is unmistakable whether we compare the official results for our thirty noble-dominated provinces with the government's survey of the political alignment of the provincial zemstvos in the spring of 1907 or with Veselovskii's contemporary figures on the political affiliation of the board chairmen (see table 3).[43] Fourteen of the thirty assemblies appeared to have shifted to the right since the spring of 1907, while the composition of twelve others remained essentially unchanged. In four zemstvos, the political balance was somewhat redressed in favor of the left. The changes appear to have been fairly evenly distributed nationwide, although four of the fourteen assemblies for which there are indications of a shift to the right were located in the Central Agricultural Region, where the shift to the right had already been the most pronounced in the 1906–1907 elections.

To be sure, gains for any one group generally involved small numbers of seats, especially in the provincial assemblies, and the changes usually fell far short of the transformation of zemstvo politics that had occurred three years earlier. One significant exception was Kostroma, the only provincial zemstvo in the Central Industrial Region whose left majority had survived the test of 1906–1907. In 1910 gains by rights produced an electoral shift in Kostroma similar to that which had taken place in most localities in the previous elections, although the reconstituted assembly still remained in the "moderate" camp.[44]

TABLE 3

*Results of the elections to the provincial zemstvo assemblies
in the thirty noble-dominated provinces, 1903–10.*

Political tendency of the assembly majority	Left	Left-moderate (or progressive)	Moderate	Moderate-right	Right
Veselovskii's analysis of the political affiliation of the provincial board chairmen elected in 1903–1904	13	6	11*		0
The Ministry of the Interior's survey of the political alignment of the provincial zemstvos in May 1907	3	2	10	6	9
Veselovskii's analysis of the political affiliation of the provincial board chairmen elected in 1906–1907	1	3	17*		9
The Ministry of the Interior's figures on the political alignment of the provincial zemstvo assemblies after the 1909–10 elections	1	1	5	9	14

* Veselovskii's analysis contains no term equivalent to the "moderate-right" category used by the government. No doubt some of his Octobrist board chairmen, particularly after the completion of the 1906–1907 elections, were actually representing coalitions of moderates and rights within their assemblies.

sources: Veselovskii, *Istoriia zemstva*, IV, 58, and TsGIA fond 1288, op 2, del 2–1907 and del 46–1909.

The conservative victories in the zemstvo elections of 1909–10 occurred despite renewed attempts on the part of the liberals to redress the political imbalance within the zemstvos in their favor. One might assume that with the foundation of a national representative assembly, liberal political energies and attention would be totally absorbed by the seemingly more significant political struggles under way in the State Duma. But such was not at all the case in the Stolypin period. In the course of 1907 and 1908, the Kadet party, aided by leading activists who formerly had stood on the right wing of the old, pre-1905 zemstvo movement (such as D. N. Shipov and Prince E. N. Trubetskoi), repeatedly called "conferences of progressive zemstvo men." The purpose of these meetings was to encourage the now miniscule left wing of the landed nobility to remain active in local affairs no matter how "hopeless" the liberal cause currently appeared in the provinces.[45]

Liberal political strategy in the 1909–10 elections was essentially defensive and proceeded along two fronts. First, the liberals quite often did not even attempt to regain control of the zemstvos but threw their support to "Octobrists and moderates" in order to defeat the most offensive "rights." Although such procedures did result in the defeat of certain individual conservatives, as in the often cited case of Saratov county, even here the composition of the assembly as a whole generally "remained just about the same as before."[46] Elsewhere, most notably in Tver and Moscow, the liberals attempted to build electoral alliances with townsmen and peasants who voted in the second and third curiae of the zemstvos. Such efforts, however, were ultimately self-defeating. Under the 1890 electoral law, the limited representation accorded non-noble elements[47] ensured that even if all the small landowners, townsmen, and peasants elected to the zemstvos were overwhelmingly "progressive," they were rarely able to provide the margin of difference that would determine the political cast of an assembly's ruling majority. The weakness of such elements was particularly striking in the provincial zemstvo assemblies. While zemstvo members from the nobility constituted an absolute majority of the deputies in all but a small minority of county (uezd) zemstvos, their rule was virtually unchallenged in the provincial assemblies, where the landed nobility provided 89.5 percent of the deputies nationwide (including the four "peasant" provinces).[48] Thus, in 1909–10, a number of rightist victories occurred, by our calculations, despite alliances between "progressive" noblemen and voters from other social classes.[49]

To be sure, there were a few scattered liberal victories in the 1909–10 elections. In individual counties of Moscow, Saratov, Tver, and Novgorod provinces, several famous "old zemstvo men" ousted in 1906–1907 were returned to zemstvo work.[50] In Novotorzhskii county (Tver), the home of the renowned Bakunin brothers, a group of "progressive" nobles, led by Professor E. V. de Roberti, well known for his radical speeches at the 1905 zemstvo congresses, managed to overturn the rightist majority voted in in 1906, and their victory allowed a lesser known Petrunkevich (Mikhail Ivanovich) to become chairman of the county zemstvo board.[51]

Despite these few and highly isolated victories, the elections generally terminated in a further rout of zemstvo liberalism. At this time not only most of the remaining Kadets in the zemstvos but also an unspecified number of "progressives" were voted down in the nobles' curia. Neither did the zemstvo moderates fare well in the 1909–10 elections.[52] Even those Octobrists who remained within the zemstvo movement after the elections usually stood "decisively to the right" of their Duma representatives.[53] To be sure, given the low turnover rates that prevailed among the noble deputies in 1909–10, the apparent movement to the right in the elections stemmed as much from the growing conservatism of men already in the zemstvos as from the influx of new elements. There were, however, some major upsets in the 1909–10 elections, the most outstanding being, of course, the defeat of the well-known progressive D. N. Shipov, the long-time chairman of the Moscow provincial zemstvo board and the leader of the moderate zemstvo minority in 1905. Even though only twelve voters showed up in the first (nobles') curia in Shipov's home county of Volokolamsk (Moscow province) to elect fifteen zemstvo members, Shipov was soundly defeated in the elections. For the grand old man of the pre-1905 zemstvo movement, only recently considered the most outstanding zemstvo leader in all Russia by men of virtually all political factions, was the victim of a remarkably vicious personal vendetta waged by the Volokolamsk nobles and supported, if not actually instigated, by the influential marshal of the nobility of Moscow province, A. D. Samarin.[54]

The ouster of zemstvo progressives like Shipov and the eclipse of the moderates in the zemstvo movement is much more puzzling than the repudiation of the Kadets three years earlier. After all, the Kadets had been purged from the zemstvos for their espousal of the compulsory expropriation of noble landholdings and their political alliance with the peasantry in the first two State Dumas. While progressives like Shipov—and many moderates as well—had participated in the Liberation Movement alongside the Kadets, they surely posed no comparable threat to noble interests four years later. It is possible, however, that the presence of a progressive like Shipov in the zemstvos aroused fears among the extreme right of a possible revival of the Liberation Movement.[55] For Shipov, after breaking decisively with the Octobrists at the end of the First Duma, attempted to forge an electoral alliance with the Kadets against the zemstvo right in 1908–1909; and he was more than willing to cooperate with the Kadets and Kadet sympathizers in opposing key right-wing political initiatives,

like the 1907 Zemstvo Congress.[56] But most zemstvo moderates, including the Octobrists, had overwhelmingly supported the 1907 Zemstvo Congress. Indeed, they had been among its prime organizers, and
the Octobrists had taken the lead in purging the Kadets from the
zemstvos at the end of 1905. Since then they had firmly supported the
government of P. A. Stolypin in its attempts to promote the far-reaching
political and economic reconstruction of Russian society. In fact, the
moderates—particularly the Octobrists—had become virtually identified
with the policies and program of the Stolypin government, and they
actively cooperated with the prime minister not only in the State Duma
but in the local zemstvos as well.

Hence, it is in the policies of the Stolypin government that we must
seek the reasons for the decline of the influence of the moderates in
the zemstvos. For much of the prime minister's reform program appeared to threaten the provincial nobility's political control of the
countryside, if not a revival of the 1905 disorders. This was particularly true of Stolypin's attempts to end the political segregation of the
peasantry and to expand the role of non-noble elements in local self-
government, of his attacks on the extensive powers of the marshals of
the nobility, and of his efforts to foster universal primary education
among the recently rebellious peasantry through the construction of
a network of potentially subversive secular schools. Despite the Prime
Minister's intentions—we have seen that he was quite friendly toward
the nobility—his political program would have created a modern secular society in which the landed nobility would have ultimately lost its
privileged position.

Consequently, noble elements repeatedly criticized Stolypin's program in the United Nobility and the Council on the Local Economy,
and increasingly such complaints were heard in the legislative chambers as well.[57] By 1909 some men in both the Duma and the localities
were beginning to drift away from the Octobrist party over the party
leadership's firm espousal of such policies,[58] thus contributing to the
decline of moderate forces in the country. In this way, the zemstvo
elections of 1909–10 reflected in part growing dissatisfaction with Stolypin's policies among the provincial nobility, the leading social element in Stolypin's own Third of June system, which had so recently
hailed the prime minister as their salvation from further revolution.[59]
The election results also sharply reduced the prime minister's influence within his own government. For the move to the right in the
zemstvos in the 1909–10 elections heralded a rightward shift in the
zemstvo contingents in the State Council and the Council on the Local
Economy, institutions that had already proved themselves willing and

capable of blocking major legislative initiatives of Stolypin, including his all-important local reforms.

Furthermore the zemstvo elections of 1909–10 revealed much about the changing alignment of social forces in the countryside. Although the results of the elections in the first (nobles') curia determined to a large extent the assembly's ultimate political composition, other social groups did participate in the elections, and their political conduct often departed significantly from that of the nobility. Not surprisingly, the percentage of rights elected in thirty-three provinces[60] from the nobility was higher (56.8 percent) than the corresponding proportions for the third or peasants' curia (51.98 percent) or for the second curia (40.47 percent). The second curia was composed of an odd assortment of non-noble landowners, urban representatives, and noble proprietors possessing less than the minimum property qualification for voting in the first curia. Even more striking was the discrepancy in the turnover rates among the three curiae. Far more incumbent noble landowners were reelected to the county assemblies (65.24 percent) than townsmen and non-noble landowners (36.8 percent) or peasants (26.06 percent).[61]

The turnover rate among noble representatives to the county zemstvos in the 1909–10 elections appears especially low (35 percent) when compared to an overall turnover rate of more than 50 percent in the usually far more stable provincial zemstvo assemblies in the previous elections.[62] This development reflected the current crisis of noble land-ownership, the precipitous economic decline of the landed nobility that followed the 1905 peasant disorders.[63] By 1910–12, mounting land sales by the nobility and corresponding purchases by the peasantry and other social groups had resulted in a growing economic disparity among the three zemstvo curiae, displayed in table 4.

TABLE 4

Landholdings of the three zemstvo curiae in the thirty-four zemstvo provinces, 1890–1910/12.

Curia	Amount of land owned (in millions of desiatiny)	
	1890	*1910–12*
First	52.25 (33.03%)	29.25 (17.32%)
Second	20.4 (12.89%)	43.4 (25.70%)
Third	85.5 (54.06%)	96.2 (56.97%)
Total	158.15 (100%)	168.85 (100%)

SOURCE: B. Veselovskii, "Ocherednyia zemskie zadachi," *Sovremennik*, May 1913, p.302.

The loss of noble landholdings—and the concomitant decline in the number of men eligible to vote (and be elected) in the first curia—contributed to a nationwide membership shortage of 14 percent in the provincial and county zemstvos after the 1909–10 elections, with the nobles' curia accounting for almost all the vacant seats. In some localities the membership shortage reached crisis proportions. For example, in Saratov county, where one hundred noble landowners had qualified to vote in the first curia in 1906, only twenty so qualified in 1909,[64] while some county zemstvos, like the Nikolaev assembly (Samara province) were actually disbanded at this time because of the lack of nobles qualified to stand for elections.[65]

Given the marked decrease in the number of eligible voters, highly contested first curia elections were the exception rather than the rule in 1909–10, since in most cases, according to Aleksandr A. Savel'ev, the former Kadet chairman of the Nizhnii Novgorod provincial zemstvo board, "Nearly every eligible noble who wishes can become a zemstvo deputy."[66] Under these conditions, the continued exclusion of the zemstvo left and the withering of the influence of the moderates and progressives was all the more remarkable. Evidently, despite the absence of formal party organizations in the countryside, political passions still ran so high among the provincial nobility that in some localities, like Shipov's Volokolamsk county, noble voters actually preferred to leave some of their allotted seats in the zemstvo assemblies unfilled rather than to allow a political opponent to occupy them.[67] Nevertheless, in many regions, the nobles displayed a scant interest in the elections, so confident were they of their invulnerability, and voter turnout was generally substantially lower than the record levels set in 1906–1907.[68]

While the shrinkage of the nobles' curia was a major factor in both the low turnover rate for zemstvo members from the nobility and a corresponding continuity in personnel between the reconstituted assemblies and those elected in 1906–1907, the second and third curiae were prevented by their restrictive representation from exerting a comparable impact on the outcome of the elections. Nonetheless, eligible townsmen, non-noble landowners, and peasants (particularly the latter) were unusually active participants in the new round of voting in the zemstvos.

The heightened interest on the part of the peasantry in the zemstvo elections of 1909–10 was directly related to new electoral procedures established under the Law of October 5, 1906.[69] This law ensured the independence of peasant elections by abolishing a provision of the

1890 statute requiring all zemstvo members from the third curia to receive gubernatorial confirmation. The old system of indirect voting in two stages was retained, but whereas previously the peasant members of each county zemstvo had been selected by the local governor from among a list of candidates chosen by the district (volost) assemblies, the peasant candidates, like those of other curiae, were now given the right to meet independently and elect zemstvo representatives from their own midst. In addition, the new law permitted peasants who met the specified property requirement to vote in the second curia as small landowners.[70] Local authorities, of course, remained free to interfere with third curia elections through the traditional devices of voiding them for alleged "irregularities" and occasionally resorting to the arrest of "undesirable" candidates.[71]

Still, the new law offered the peasantry the hope, if not always the reality, that their votes would count for more than in the past; and the peasants generally responded by displaying a vivid interest in the elections and by taking advantage of the new law to vote incumbents out of office, thus accounting for the extremely high (75 percent) turnover rates in the third or peasants' curia. Although the liberal press generally maintained that the large majority of the newly elected peasant deputies were "progressives" or even "lefts,"[72] government figures present a different picture of the elections, classifying approximately half of the county deputies elected by the peasantry in 1909–10 as "rights," a little more than a third as "moderates," and only 10 percent as "lefts."[73] Nonetheless, it seems that these new right-wing or moderate peasant members of zemstvo assemblies tended to be rather independent types, beholden to no local landowners or officials as in the past. For the prime targets of the peasant voters in the 1909–10 elections were the protégés and clients of the local gentry land captains (*zemskie nachal'niki*), who had traditionally represented the local peasants in the zemstvos under the old electoral system. Occasionally the peasants even replaced such men with peasants who possessed some sort of organizational experience, perhaps in a cooperative, or even with members of the local intelligentsia of peasant origins.[74] As a result, despite their generally conservative political affiliations, the new peasant representatives in the zemstvos, like their counterparts in the State Duma, were steadfast defenders of peasant group interests, although they, too, lacked the ability to form a cohesive political force on their own.

The inequity of the zemstvo tax burden was one of the major grievances of the peasants in the elections,[75] although after 1907 they no

longer continued the widespread tax boycott of the noble-dominated
zemstvo characteristic of the revolutionary period. The new peasant
deputies appeared determined that the zemstvo should not continue
to be run solely in the interests of the nobility. Instead the zemstvos
should face the fact that the peasantry bore a disproportionately large
share of the tax burden and provide them at last with a fair share
of zemstvo services.[76] In order to pursue these goals, the new peasant
deputies tended to cooperate in the zemstvo assembly with townsmen
and the now miniscule left wing of the landed nobility.[77] Needless to
say, the election of independently minded peasant representatives
prone to defend peasant interests in the zemstvos in alliance with what
remained of a "zemstvo left" was not likely to encourage right-wing
noblemen to temper their opposition to zemstvo reform.

In many localities voters in the second curia, although to a lesser
degree than the peasants, also displayed an unusually active interest
in the zemstvo elections of 1909–10. Possessing the smallest share of
the representation, townsmen and non-noble landowners had traditionally been the most indifferent to the elections and proceedings of
the zemstvo assemblies.[78] In 1909–10, as before, absenteeism in the
second curia was substantial and even extreme in some regions;[79] but
far more common were cases of "unusually full electoral assemblies"
and even examples of an "unprecedented turnout."[80] (A major factor
promoting such a turnout, as we have indicated, was the addition of
new electors from the ranks of private peasant landowners who were
given second curia voting rights under the Law of October 5, 1906.)

In 1910, during the second round of the elections, there were scattered indications that growing class consciousness on the part of
Russia's urban population was penetrating zemstvo life. In some counties of Vladimir, Perm, and Ekaterinoslav provinces, and elsewhere in
the south (more so than in the north), industrialists and other townsmen banded together at the second curia electoral assemblies in a con-
certed and ultimately highly successful effort to vote down all or most
of the landowners (largely non-nobles) included in this curia. As in the
case of the peasantry, the tax question was the major stimulus for the
new activity on the part of the townsmen,[81] since urban elements, like
the peasants, were always allocated a disproportionate share of zemstvo taxes.[82]

Within the second curia, the urban elements were apparently taking
precedence over the agrarian elements in an effort to seize for their
own uses whatever limited influence the group as a whole could com-
mand. Yet while the townsmen and industrialists held an increasingly

clear perception of their interests, as well as the determination and boldness necessary to defend them, such characteristics were lacking among the small landowners. Zhilkin observed that "among the petty nobles[83] and small landowners, class interests are undefined and of little weight." Such landowners could not help but be intimidated by their position in the zemstvos, a position caught "between two groups with defined, strongly and passionately hostile class interests: the large [landowning] nobility and the peasantry."[84]

The zemstvo elections of 1909–10 presented a picture of social relations between the various groups included in zemstvo life that differed radically from the vision that had been held by broad layers of society during the early period of the institution's existence. In the 1860s, there had been widespread expectations that the day-to-day "practical" work of the zemstvo would somehow promote a spirit of harmonious co-operation and even eventually a *rapprochement* among the various estates (*sosloviia*) that took part in the zemstvos.[85] Indeed, for several decades, noble predominance together with the general indifference of other estates had served to minimize incidence of open conflict. By 1909–10, however, the peasantry, merchants, and industrialists were no longer quiescent. Having emerged from the experiences of 1905 with a new awareness of their specific interests, they were increasingly demanding a greater voice in the zemstvos, as well as the concrete satisfaction of their own needs—neither of which the large majority of the noble activists in the countryside were apparently willing to allow them. Consequently, no one by this period was advancing the old argument that class conflict was alien to the principles of the zemstvo, particularly now that its liberal Kadet leadership had been replaced by nobles who clearly made no pretense of sharing their predecessors' official dedication to an "all-class" point of view.

In this way, the 1909–10 elections in the zemstvo underscored the existence of deep-seated political weaknesses within the political order of the Third of June, which appeared long before the untimely demise of the system's architect, P. A. Stolypin. First, the elections clearly revealed that the antagonisms among the various strata of the Russian population that had emerged in the course of the Revolution of 1905 were not declining as the prime minister had intended, but, on the contrary, were persisting and—at least in regard to the townsmen's attitudes toward nobles and other landowners—actually growing stronger. Moreover, the considerable political interest and abilities displayed by both townsmen and peasants in the zemstvo elections could only aggravate these antagonisms by increasing the landed nobility's already exaggerated fear that any meaningful form of zemstvo reform would ultimately entail its political eclipse in the zemstvos. Such fears not only impeded the prime minister's efforts to reduce class conflict by integrating peasants and other non-noble elements into local political life but also contributed to the Western Zemstvo crisis of 1911, the major political crisis of the Stolypin period. This crisis was set off when a number of politically moderate zemstvo and noble representatives in the State Council, who normally supported government law projects, joined the far right of the chamber to vote down Stolypin's bill establishing elected zemstvos in the western provinces of the Russian Empire. Most of these men voted with the right at this time because this bill based electoral curiae not on estates but on national groups and property holdings. At the same time the bill lowered the property qualification for voting in the zemstvos to such a degree that many believed that the landed nobility would be swamped by the peasantry if an electoral system along similar lines were introduced in the old zemstvo provinces of central Russia.[86]

The zemstvo elections of 1909–10 also demonstrated that even after four years of quasi-representative government in Russia, no national political parties had yet emerged that commanded the allegiances and loyalties of the most important social element within the political system—the noble landowners of the central Russian provinces. Since modern legislative chambers rest in the final analysis on the functioning of a well-defined party system, the absence of formal partisan ties to national political groupings among the provincial nobility contributed to the constant political fragmentation of the existing parties that was already well under way by 1909–10. This fragmentation impeded the emergence of a stable working majority within the Duma.[87]

Finally, the zemstvo elections of 1909–10 contributed not a little to an ongoing process that the Soviet historian A. Ia. Avrekh has called "the crisis of the Third of June system."[88] This progressive crisis within the Stolypin administration was marked by the gradual breakdown of the tentative political alliance between the prime minister and his hitherto most enthusiastic supporters within the legislative chambers —the Duma faction of the Octobrist party. By the autumn of 1909 the Octobrists began to recognize that their support of Stolypin was a political liability in view of the growing conservatism of the provincial nobility and the growing militancy of Russia's urban population, as demonstrated by the recent zemstvo elections. At this time, the Octobrist leadership publicly denounced the State Council as an obstacle to further reforms and launched a major drive to persuade the government to push its original reform program—including basic zemstvo reform—far more vigorously than before.[89]

By then, however, Stolypin was scarcely in a position to respond favorably to the initiatives of his erstwhile Octobrist allies. The new round of voting in the zemstvos had greatly eroded Stolypin's ability to maneuver within the confines of his own constitutional order. For the passage of legislation under the current political system required the approval of *both* houses of the Russian parliament—the Duma *and* the far more conservative State Council. By 1909 the latter body had experienced a substantial decline in the numbers and influence of its previously dominant moderate Center Faction, which, like the Octobrists in the Third Duma, had generally supported the reform program of the Stolypin government. In the 1906–1909 period, the number of right-wing members of the State Council had noticeably increased not only among the appointed members of the Council (who were subjected to annual reappointment by the tsar)[90] but also among the elected half of the Council.[91] This was especially true of the zemstvo representatives returned since 1906 both in by-elections and in the regular triannual State Council elections held in the spring of 1909, well *before* the start of the new round of zemstvo elections (see table 5).[92] Admittedly, the changes that took place in the zemstvo contingent in the upper house were not great, but minor shifts in political inclination could prove decisive in a chamber like the State Council, in which a relatively few votes not infrequently provided the margin between defeat and victory for major legislative projects.[93] Moreover, the conservative victories in the 1909–10 zemstvo elections, which followed the 1909 State Council elections, ensured the continuation of the political status quo, if not an even greater evolution to the right among the zemstvo members of the Council in the future. Since the State Council had already demonstrated a marked ability to defeat major government-sponsored law projects,[94] it now seemed clear that the remains of Stolypin's reform program—and possibly the prime minister's hold on political power as well—hung in jeopardy. Certainly the shrinking political options available to Stolypin after the 1909 elections contributed to the growing breach between the government and the Octobrists.

Consequently, almost immediately after the completion of the 1909 State Council elections, Stolypin turned away from his previous exclusive reliance on the declining Octobrists to forge new political ties with the emerging Nationalist party, which offered Stolypin several

Table 5

State Council elections from the zemstvos, 1906–1909.

Political tendency	Composition of the zemstvo representatives in the State Council, elected in 1906	Composition of the zemstvo representatives in the State Council, re-elected in the 1906–1909 period[a]	Composition of the zemstvo representatives in the State Council after the 1909 elections
Kadets	6	1 (4)[b]	3
Progressives	3	1 (2)	2
Moderates (including Octobrists)	13	2 (5)	10
Right	12	14 (7)	19
Total	34	18[a]	34

[a] By the end of the spring of 1909, eighteen of the thirty-four provincial zemstvos had reelected their representatives to the upper house. The provinces concerned were Bessarabia, Vladimir, Vologda, Viatka, Ekaterinoslav, Kostroma, Kursk, Moscow, Novgorod, Orel, Riazan, Samara, Tambov, Tver, Tula, Ufa, Kharkov, and Iaroslavl.

[b] The figures in parentheses show the political composition of the representatives from these provinces *before* the new elections.

sources: Veselovskii, *Istoriia zemstva*, IV, 36; A. D. Stepanskii, "Politicheskie gruppirovki v gosudarstvennom soveta v 1906–07 g.g.," *Istoriia SSSR* 1965, no. 4, pp.52–55; *Novoe vremia*, no. 10808, April 11 (24), 1906, p.2; Naumov, II, 86; Tsgia fond 699 (the diary of the Third Duma deputy I. S. Kliuzhev); and XXXV *chrezvychainoe riazanskoe zemskoe sobranie 12 aprelia 1906 goda* (Riazan, 1906) p.10.

advantages. Not only were the Nationalists from the very first able to enlist—at least in their home base in the western provinces—the support of the local Russian landowners, which the Octobrists clearly failed to elicit.[95] But the introduction of zemstvo institutions into the western provinces, favored by this group, provided Stolypin with an opportunity to strengthen the declining moderate element in the upper house, thereby increasing his own influence in that chamber.[96] For the Western Zemstvo Act was expressly designed to replace the Polish landowners, who currently represented the western provinces in the upper house and who generally voted with the small left-wing opposition to the government, with Russian landowners, who presumably would adhere to the relatively moderate Nationalist party.[97] Both Stolypin and the State Council extreme right considered his attempt to alter the political balance in the upper house so important that the right openly defied government orders and voted against the Western Zemstvo Act, while the prime minister moved willingly to provoke a major constitutional crisis over this issue by resorting to the use of Article 87 of the Basic Law of the Russian Empire in order to enact this bill immediately into law by administrative decree.

In the end, however, not even the adoption of the Western Zemstvo Act by government fiat was able to salvage the remains of Stolypin's original political program. Within a few months of the Western Zemstvo Crisis, Stolypin was assassinated under mysterious circumstances. He was replaced by men without his vision and drive, who were content to administer the country on a day-to-day basis without aspiring to any political or social transformations that might alienate established social groups and turn them against the government. Yet even had Stolypin survived, it is doubtful that all his energy and abilities could have saved his program of political reforms. For the introduction of moderate Nationalist representatives from the western provinces in the State Council failed to alter the balance of political power in the upper house of the Russian parliament, which continued to reject —or revise beyond recognition—all major reform efforts of the Duma in the prewar period.

Subsequent zemstvo elections merely reinforced the political status quo in the State Council. To be sure, with the demise of Stolypin, many of the political tensions characteristic of the post-1905 period gradually disappeared from zemstvo life. The Ministry of the Interior, in recording the results of the last zemstvo elections held before the war, those of 1912–13, merely listed the names of the newly elected zemstvo deputies and members of the zemstvo executive boards. No reference whatsoever was made to the political affiliations of these men or to the dominant tendency of the assembly as a whole,[98] so irrelevant had partisan politics become to the zemstvos. The liberal press, however, hopefully noted that the elections had returned a number of old zemstvo "progressives" of the pre-1905 vintage to the zemstvos.[99] Yet liberal commentators were the first to maintain that the addition of these individuals did not alter the general conservative character of the post-1905 zemstvo or indicate any developing liberal trend among the zemstvos' predominantly noble electorate. Rather, the return of some "progressives" in the 1912–13 elections was the result of the interplay of several factors, all of which were contributing to the gradual depoliticization of zemstvo life.

First, the conservatives who took over the zemstvos in 1906–1907 had generally refrained from affiliating themselves with any of the national political parties, being content as country gentlemen merely

to represent themselves, their estate (soslovie), and their county. By
1912–13 they no longer felt threatened by the liberals in the zemstvos,
so confident were they of their invulnerability under the 1890 election law. Indeed, by then no vestiges of a genuine left-wing alternative
remained in the zemstvos. Press accounts of the 1912–13 elections did
not even mention a "zemstvo left" in discussing the political tendencies
in the zemstvos.[100] Those "progressives" still active in provincial politics among the landed nobility in 1912–13 had definitely abandoned
political goals, preferring, like their conservative counterparts, to concentrate their energies on the purely "practical" side of zemstvo work.
Hence, the dominant conservative element among the zemstvo nobility no longer feared to allow these few "progressives" who still desired
to do so to play a role in zemstvo affairs. The return of the "progressives" to the zemstvos was also facilitated, as we have seen, by the
economic decline of the landed nobility after 1905, which greatly reduced the available pool of noble landowners eligible to participate
in the first curia of the zemstvos. At the same time, the decline of
political tensions in the zemstvos and the disappearance of the zemstvo
left resulted in a substantial increase in electoral absenteeism on the
part of noble voters. As a result, virtually no first curia elections were
contested in 1912–13. In fact, "almost all" the zemstvo members returned by the landed nobility in these elections were actually self-
appointed, and an increasing number of seats allotted noble landowners remained unfilled.[101]

In addition, the political challenge presented to the nobility by other
social groups in the 1909–10 elections was not renewed in 1912–13. The
new round of voting in the zemstvos was marked by widespread indifference and substantial electoral absenteeism on the part of second
and third curiae voters, in marked contrast to the vivid interest and
record turnouts of these elements in the previous elections.[102] When
pressed to explain the reasons for their absenteeism, abstaining voters
in the second and third curiae inevitably pointed to their lack of influence on zemstvo affairs under the current electoral system.[103] The decline of public interest in the zemstvos was reflected in the press,
which significantly curtailed its coverage of the 1912–13 elections compared to previous electoral contests in the zemstvos. Those few journalists still following zemstvo affairs in 1912–13 increasingly limited
their comments to a discussion of what was beginning to be called
"the crisis of the zemstvo," i.e., the problems created by the growing
inability of the landed nobility to staff the zemstvos and the waning

interest of other social groups in these noble-dominated institutions. The only positive note ever sounded in these discussions was a general recognition of the rapidity with which zemstvo services were developing and the growing importance of these services for Russia.

Yet the very fact that so many vital public services were entrusted to an institution dominated by a small and rapidly declining social group indicates the existence of serious weaknesses in the Imperial Russian political order. These weaknesses could not be easily remedied within the confines of the Third of June system. For the zemstvo nobility was able to ward off all attacks on its privileged position in the localities through its inflated political influence in national affairs. All attempts on the part of the Duma to expand the zemstvo electorate in the 1911–14 period ultimately went down to defeat at the hands of the now dominant right wing of the State Council, whose ranks included many representatives of the zemstvo nobility. In this way, the noble-dominated zemstvo survived until the fall of the Old Regime, perpetuating the ongoing crisis of the Third of June system and leaving the country without local institutions capable of commanding the loyalty and allegiance of the overwhelming majority of the population.

NOTES

1. See, for example, A. Ia. Avrekh, *Stolypin i tret'ia duma* (Moscow, 1968); A. Ia. Avrekh, *Tsarizm i tret'iiun'skaia sistema* (Moscow, 1966); Geoffrey A. Hosking, *The Russian Constitutional Experiment: Government and Duma 1907–1914* (Cambridge, 1973); Alfred Levin, *The Third Duma: Election and Profile* (Hamden, Conn., 1973); Ben Cion Pinchuk, *The Octobrists in the Third Duma 1907–12* (Seattle and London, 1974); Alfred Levin, *The Second Duma: A Study of the Social Democratic Party and the Russian Constitutional Experiment* (New Haven, 1940); E. D. Chermenskii, *Burzhuaziia i tsarizm v revoliutsii 1905–1907 g.g.* (Moscow, 1939 and 1970); and S. N. Sidelnikov, *Obrazovanie i deiatel'nost' pervoi gosudarstvennoi dumy* (Moscow, 1962). Two notable recent exceptions to this general tendency are V. S. Diakin, "Stolypin i dvorianstvo (proval mestnoi reformy," *Problemy krest'ianskogo zemlevladeniia i vnutrennoi politiki Rossii: Dooktiabr'skoi period* (Leningrad, 1972), pp.231–74 and Terence Emmons, "The Russian Landed Gentry and Politics," *The Russian Review*, XXXIII, No. 3, pp.269–283.

2. I. P. Belokonskii, *Zemstvo i konstitutsia* (Moscow, 1910) and Prince D. Shakhovskoi, "Politicheskie techeniia v russkom zemstve," in B. B. Veselovskii and Z. G. Frenkel, *Iubileinyi zemskii sbornik* (St. Petersburg, 1914), pp.466–67.

3. See Warren B. Walsh, "The Composition of the Dumas," *Russian Review*, VIII, no. 2 (1949), pp.111–16 and Roberta T. Manning, "The Russian

Provincial Gentry in Revolution and Counter-revolution, 1905–1907" (Ph.D. diss., Columbia University 1975), pp.610–613.

4. See the article by Alexandra Shecket-Korros, this volume.

5. For evaluations of this institution and brief summaries of its activities, see Hosking, *The Russian Constitutional Experiment,* pp.122, 150, 160; Diakin, op. cit., N. A. Mel'nikov, *19 let na zemskoi sluzhbe* (unpublished mss. in the Columbia University Russian Archive), pp.334–48, and *Reforma mestnago samoupravleniia po rabotam soveta po delam mestnago khoziaistva. Doklad XXXIV ocherednomu ufimskomu gubernskomu sobraniiu predstavitelia ufimskago zemstva P. Korapachinskago* (Ufa, 1908). The stenographic proceedings of the Council, which ceased to meet after Stolypin's death, can be found in the personal archives of S. A. Panchulidze. TsGIA fond 1625, delo 5–13.

6. See, for example, George F. Kennan, "The Breakdown of the Tsarist Autocracy," in Richard Pipes (ed.), *Revolutionary Russia* (Garden City, N.Y., 1969), pp.7–11.

7. Mel'nikov, pp.158–59, 346–48; Prince A. D. Golitsyn, *Vospominaniia* (mss. in the Columbia University Russian Archive), pp.290–91; and George L. Yaney, "Social Stability in Pre-Revolutionary Russia: A Critical Note," *Slavic Review,* XXIV, no. 3 (Sept. 1965), pp.521–27. Yaney maintains that the expanded role played by the zemstvo men in national affairs after the Revolution of 1905 was an important source of political and social stability for the existing regime. This essay will demonstrate that the increase in the political influence of the zemstvo men was a serious obstacle to the peaceful reform and modernization of the country.

8. Stolypin, to be sure, was an *appointed,* not an elected, marshal, since elected zemstvo and noble institutions had not yet been introduced in the western *guberniia,* including his home province, because of the large number of politically active Polish landowners in that region. However, the ethos of such appointed marshals (and many *zemskie nachal'niki* as well) appears to have been far closer to that of elected public activists than that of persons pursuing a traditional career in the state bureaucracy. Hosking, pp.21–22.

9. Baron A. Meiendorf, *A Brief Appreciation of P. Stolypin's Tenure in Office* (mss. in the Columbia University Russian Archive), p.15. See also Bernard Pares, "Conversations with Mr. Stolypin," *Russian Review* II, no. 11 (1913), p.106, for an identical comment by the Prime Minister.

10. E. D. Chermenskii, *Burzhuaziia i tsarism v revoliutsii 1905–1907 g.g.* (Moscow, 1970), pp.158–210.

11. For a discussion of Stolypin's local reforms, see Diakin, op. cit., and Hosking, 150–77.

12. For a discussion of the post-1905 reaction in the zemstvos, see the essay by Roberta Thompson Manning, this volume.

13. There was no nobles' curia at all in Viatka, Olonets, or Perm, or in seven of the ten counties of Vologda. See Section 32, Zemstvo Statute of June 12, 1890 *Polnoe sobranie zakonov Rossiskoi imperii,* sobranie tretee Vol. X otdelenie pervoe no. 6927.

14. These figures were compiled by the government in May 1907, on the eve of the Stolypin coup d'état. TsGIA fond 1288, op. 2, delo 2–1907, pp.1–52.

15. B. B. Veselovskii, *Istoriia zemstva za sorok let* (St. Petersburg, 1909–11), vol. IV, 58.

16. V. A. Avevskii, "Zemstvo i zhizn (zapiska predsedatelia zemskoi upravy)," *Istoricheskii vestnik* CXXVII (Jan. 1912), pp.180–81.

17. A good example of this phenomenon was the moderate M. A. Stakhovich, who served numerous terms as marshal of the nobility of Orel province, although he was far more liberal than the majority of his constituents. V. I. Gurko, *Features and Figures of the Past: Government and Opinion in the Reign of Nicholas II* (Stanford, 1939), p.210.

18. See TsGIA fond 1288, opis 2, delo 2–1907, and delo 46–1909.

19. Indeed, in this case, the term was quite accurate. None of the various monarchist parties, for example, claimed a nationwide following. Even in the Duma, members of the right faction for the most part did not adhere to any political parties but simply called themselves "rights." Melnikov, p.131.

20. Veselovskii, for one, maintained in 1906 that a majority of the members of the local zemstvos had "gone over to . . . the program of the Union of the Seventeenth of October." B. B. Veselovskii, "Koe chto o nastroenii zemlevladel'tsev," *Obrazovanie*, April, 1906, p.21. This is also the opinion of the future rightist chairman of the Moscow provincial zemstvo board, V. F. Shlippe. V. F. Shlippe, untitled memoirs (mss. in the Columbia University Russian Archive), p.86.

21. In this polemic *Russkoe slovo* was supported by a number of other provincial newspapers, which also failed to find any Octobrists in their localities. See A. Petrishchev, "Khronika vnutrennei zhizni," *Russkoe bogatstvo*, August 1909, pp.58–60.

22. See, for example, the experiences of the Kadet D. D. Protopopov in Samara and the Octobrist Count P. A. Geiden in Pskov. D. D. Protopopov, "Iz nedavniago proshlago (Samara v 1904–1905 g.g.)," *Russkaia mysl*, XXVIII, No. 12 (December 1907), p.5 and V. B., "Opochetskii vospominaniia o gr. P. A. Geidena (Episod iz istorii osvobozhditel'nago dvizheniia v glukhoi provintsii)," in *Ibid.*, XXVIII, no. 11, p.73, and no. 12, p.46.

23. For the powers and influence of the marshals of the nobility, see Veselovskii, *Istoriia zemstva*, III, 215–17 and A. P. Korelin, "Rossiskoe dvorianstvo i ego soslovnaia organizatsii (1861–1904 g.g.), *Istoriia SSSR*, 1971, no. 5 (Sept.–Oct.), pp.56–81; N. N. Kissel-Zagorianskii, *Les Mémoires du Général Kissel-Zagorianskii* (mss. in the Columbia University Russian Archive), pp.170–71; TsGAOR fond 434, opis 1, delo 19/69, 1. 50, and the essay by Alexandra Shecket Korros, this volume.

24. I. Larskii, "Voprosy tekhushchei zhizni: zemskie vybory," *Sovremennyi mir*, 1909, no. 10, p.89.

25. During one trip through the countryside, the *Vestnik evropy* correspondent I. Zhilkin even encountered a member of the black hundreds who ardently supported the Kadet demand for a responsible ministry! I. Zhilkin, "Khronika: provintsial'noe obozrenie," *Vestnik evropy*, XLIV, no. 5 (May, 1909), p.368.

26. The publicists themselves frequently complained about the limitations of the political terms at their disposal. See, for example, V. S. Golubev, "Zemskie vybory," *Moskovskii ezhenedel'nik*, no. 31, August 8, 1909, p.7.

27. V. G. Kuzmin-Karavaev, "Oppositsiia i partiinost v zemstvo," *Vestnik evropy,* vol. III, no. 5 (May 1909), pp.206–208 and Vas. Golubev, "K zemskim vyboram," *Moskovskii ezhenedel'nik,* no. 24, June 19, 1910, pp.1–4.

28. P. Chizhevskii, "Vliianie sostava zemskikh sobranii na rezultaty zemskoi deiatel'nosti," *Vestnik evropy,* August 1909, pp.577–91 and V. N. Lind, "Zemskiia sobraniia tekhushchago goda," *Russkiia mysl,* XXX, no. 6 (June 1909), pp.141–42.

29. Quite possibly the interest in road building was stimulated by the spread of automobiles among the more prosperous of the landed nobility at this time. See A. N. Naumov, *Iz utselevshikh vospominaniia 1868–1917* (New York, 1954), vol. II, p.54.

30. See, for example, the memoirs of Golitsyn, pp.24–25; Naumov, I, p.309; Shlippe, pp.54–57, 128; Kissel-Zagorianskii, pp.30–31, 39–41, 91–94; Mendeleev, pp.81, 160; Mel'nikov, pp.268–70; and Vladimir Mikhailovich Andreevskii, *O moei sel'skom khoziaistve* (mss. in the Columbia University Russian Archive).

31. See, for example, "Iz obshchestvennoi khroniki," *Vestnik evropy,* XL, no. 2 (February 1909), pp.898–99; V. N. Lind, "Zemskaia sobraniia tekhushchago goda," *Russkaia mysl,* XXX (June 1909), pp.139–40; Prince E. N. Trubetskoi, "K okonchaniiu zemskoi sessii," *Moskovskii ezhenedel'nik.* 1909, no. 4 (January 24), pp.18–20; D. N. Shipov, *Vospominaniia i dumy o perezhitom* (Moscow, 1918), pp.536–37; Vas. Golubev, "Samoupravlenie v Rossii," *Russkaia mysl,* XXXI, no. 11 (November 1910), pp.152–53.

32. For example, the Tver zemstvo adopted an insurance program, originally proposed by its former liberal leadership, while the Saratov, Viatka, and Tula zemstvos resumed statistical work only recently eliminated as a "subversive" activity. I. V. Zhilkin, "Provintsial'noe obozrenie," *Vestnik evropy,* XVIV, no. 5 (May 1909), p.359.

33. For example, the rapid growth in zemstvo medical services at this time was a response to a cholera epidemic that broke out in 1907 and raged uncontrolled over a large part of central Russia until 1911, when most of the medical personnel and services eliminated by the zemstvos in 1906–1907 had been restored. Ibid., XLI, no. 10 (October 1910), pp.353–67; Z. G. Frenkel, "Osnovnoi nerazreshennyi vopros zemskoi meditsiny," in B. B. Veselovskii and Z. G. Frenkel (eds.), *Iubileinyi zemskii sbornik* (St. Petersburg, 1914), pp.412–22; and A. Petrishchev, "Khronika vnutrennoi zhizni," *Russkoe bogatstvo,* no. 8 (August 1910), pp.78–81.

34. A good example of the initiative taken by the government in this regard is the telegrams dispatched by Stolypin on the eve of the annual county zemstvo sessions in the autumn of 1909 and again in 1910. In these Stolypin warned the local marshals of the nobility, who chaired all zemstvo meetings *ex officio,* that "the success or failure" of his land reform depended on "the most rapid development of improved methods of cultivation among the newly organized *khutora* and *otruba* [individualized peasant holdings formed under Stolypin's land reform program]." In this endeavor, he continued, "I have now decided it necessary to turn to aid . . . to the zemstvos which have always been so responsive to popular needs." Text in I. Zhilkin, "Pro-

vintsial'noe obozrenie," *Vestnik evropy*, XL, no. 12 (December 1909), p.777. See also his telegram of the following year in I. Petrishchev, "Khronika vnutrennoi zhizni," *Russkoe bogatstvo*, November 1910, p.105.

35. The government law project of February 10, 1907, and the Stolypin-sponsored laws of May 3, 1908, June 10, 1907, and June 14, 1910, attempted to establish compulsory primary education in Russia. Veselovskii, *Istoriia zemstva*, IV, pp.95–97, 149–50; B. B. Veselovskii, "Vseobshchee obuchenie i zemstvo," *Iubileinyi zemskii sbornik*, 391–92; V. E. Brunst in ibid., pp.327–28; Vas. Golubev, "Samoupravlenie v Rossii," *Russkaia mysl*, XXXI, no. 12 (December 1910), p.164; Golubev, in *Moskovskii ezhenedel'nik*, 1910, no. 24 (June 19), p.3; I. Zhilkin, "Provintsial'noe obozrenie," *Vestnik evropy*, XLIV, no. 11 (November 1910), p.338; and "Iz obshchestvennoi khroniki," ibid., no. 2 (February 1910), pp.888–89.

36. See, for example, *Svod postanovleniia I-X s"ezdov upolnomochennykh ob'edinennykh obshchestv 1906–1914 g.g.* (Petrograd, 1915); *Trudy vi s"ezda upolnomochennykh dvorianskikh obshchesty 33 gubernii 14 marta po 20 marta 1910 g.* (St. Petersburg, 1910), pp.73–93, 376–444; *Novoe vremia* (nos. 12542–12544), February 10–12, 1911; *Trudy vii s"ezda upolnomochennykh dvorianskikh obshchestv 37 gubernii s 5 marta po 11 marta 1912 g.* (St. Petersburg, 1912), pp.45–83; and *Trudy x s"ezda upolnomochennykh dvorianskikh obshchesty 39 gubernii s 2 marta po 6 marta 1914 g.* (St. Petersburg, 1914), pp.74–101. No doubt, the United Nobility considered this question repeatedly in an attempt to influence zemstvo opinion on the subject as well as the attitudes of the government and the legislative chambers.

37. The issue of parish schools vs. secular education was one of the main issues dividing nobles who adhered to the Octobrists in the State Dumas from their more conservative colleagues in the national assembly. Although these men otherwise tended to share virtually identical backgrounds of agricultural involvement and public service in the localities, the Octobrists among them tended to serve on secular school boards, while men to the right of the Octobrists were usually members of parish school boards. See *Tretyi sozyv gosudarstvennoi dumy, Portrety, biografii i avtobiografii* (St. Petersburg, 1910), and *Chetvertyi sozyv gosudarstvennoi dumy khodozhestvennyi fototipicheskii al'bom s portretami i biografiiami* (St. Petersburg, 1913).

38. V. N. Lind, "Zemskiia sobraniia tekhushchago goda," *Russkaia mysl* XXX (June 1909), p.153. In 1910 the zemstvos' interest in this issue quickened as the Duma began debate on a project that would transfer the parish schools from the jurisdiction of the Holy Synod to that of the Ministry of Education, thus ending the role of the Orthodox Church in public education. See "Khronika vnutrennoe obozrenie," *Vestnik evropy*, XLV, no. 11 (November 1910), pp.359–61.

39. For the zemstvos' responses to Stolypin's appeals, see A. Petrishchev, "Khronika vnutrennei zhizni," *Russkoe bogatstvo*, November 1910, pp.104–107; Vas. Golubev, "Zemstvo i zemleustroistvo," *Moskovskii ezhenedel'nik*, no. 30, July 31, 1910, pp.1–7; I. Zhilkin, "Provintsial'noe obozrenie," *Vestnik evropy*, XLIV, no. 12 (December 1909), pp.776–87. Since many liberal jour-

nals, especially those inclined towards populism like *Russkoe bogatstvo,* were highly critical of the Stolypin land reform, one should use these accounts with the utmost caution.

40. I. Zhilkin, "Provintsial'noe obozrenie," *Vestnik evropy,* XLV, no. 11 (November 1910), p.333. The United Nobility also enthusiastically supported the Stolypin land reform as an alternative to the compulsory expropriation schemes of the First and Second Dumas. See the paper by Hosking and Manning, this volume.

41. A. N. Anfimov, the leading Soviet expert on Russian agriculture in the early twentieth century, maintains that most of the money allocated to the zemstvos by the government for agricultural services actually went to finance projects that benefited noble agriculture far more than the economies of the local peasantry. A. N. Anfimov, "Krest'ianstvo Rossii v 1907–1914 g.g." (unpublished paper delivered to the 1971 annual convention of the American Historical Association), p.28.

42. See, for example, B. Veselovskii, "Ocherednyia zemskii zadachii," *Sovremennik,* May 1913, p.301; I. Zhilkin, "Provintsial'noe obozrenie," *Vestnik evropy,* XLIV, no. 9 (September 1909), p.339; and Vas. Golubev, "Zemskie vybory," *Moskovskii ezhenedel'nik,* August 8, 1909, p.8.

43. We have taken the liberty of converting Veselovskii's political labels of Kadet, progressive, Octobrist, and right into left, moderate-left, moderate, and right so that his figures might be more easily compared with official government statistics on the 1909–10 elections. The discerning reader should remember, however, that Veselovskii is referring to the political affiliation of the *board chairman,* not the political alignment of the assembly majority as a whole.

44. Veselovskii, *Istoriia zemstva,* IV, pp.316, 456.

45. Tsgaor fond 102, opis 9, delo 35–1908, pp.4–6, 24–27, 261–66. D. N. Shipov, *Vospominaniia i dumy o perezhitom* (Moscow, 1918), pp.519–21.

46. Vas. Golubev, "Nakanune zemskikh sobranii," *Moskovskii ezhenedel'nik,* no. 34, August 28, 1909, p.4.

47. One searches in vain in the contemporary press for evidence of attempts on the part of dissident zemstvo men to organize like-minded *nobles,* however few they may be.

48. L. G. Zakharova, *Zemskaia kontrreforma 1890 g.* (Moscow, 1968), pp.151–61.

49. I. V. Zhilkin, "Khronika–provintsial'noe obozrenie," *Vestnik evropy,* XLIV, no. 5 (May, 1909), p.360; Vas. Golubev, "K itogam zemskikh vyborov," *Rech,* no. 248, September 10, 1909; B. B. Veselovskii (ed.), *Istoricheskii ocherk deiatel'nosti zemskikh uchrezhdenii Tverskoi gubernii (1864–1913)* (Tver, 1914), p.586, and Tsgia fond 1288, opis 2, delo 46–1909.

50. Larskii, op. cit., p.87, and Vas. Golubev in *Moskovskii ezhenedel'nik,* no. 34, August 28, 1909, p.1.

51. Veselovskii, *Istoriia zemstva,* IV, 571. See also Golubev in *Rech,* September 10, 1909.

52. Golubev in *Moskovskii ezhenedel'nik,* no. 34, August 28, 1909, p.3; Shipov, pp.537–38; and T. I. Polner, *Zhiznennyi put Kniazia Georgiia Evgenievicha L'vova* (Paris, 1932), pp.127, 175–77.

53. Larskii, p.89.

54. Shipov received only four votes (including his own) from the twelve noble voters who showed up for the first curia elections. However, he was ultimately reinstated in the zemstvo in February 1910 after a complicated series of maneuvers and appeals. The Volokolamsk zemstvo, meeting as a whole and containing progressive peasants and townsmen, overrode noble opposition and elected Shipov to a nonsalaried post on the county zemstvo board. This appointment allowed him to be elected to the Moscow provincial zemstvo. The local bureaucracy, however, tried to prevent this by denying Shipov administrative confirmation of his new position on the zemstvo board. When this ploy failed, A. D. Samarin filed a protest against Shipov's election to the provincial zemstvo with a local office of the Ministry of the Interior. As might be expected, that office ruled against Shipov; but this ruling was ultimately overturned in his favor by a decision of the Senate, the supreme court of Old Regime Russia. Shipov, pp.537–38; "Iz obshchestvennoi khroniki," *Vestnik evropy*, VLIV, no. 8 (August 1909), p.877 and Vas. Golubev, "Zemskie vybory," *Moskovskii ezhenedel'nik*, no. 31, August 8, 1909, p.8.

55. See, for example, N. A. Pavlov, *Zapiska zemlevladel'tsa* (Petrograd, 1915), pp.28–29, 35.

56. TSGAOR fond 102, opis 165, delo 49, p.203. We are deeply grateful to Professor E. D. Chermenskii of Moscow State University for kindly allowing one of the authors of this paper to use his notes on this fond. See also *Samoupravlenie*, no. 22, May 22, 1907, p.18.

57. See the paper by Alexandra Shecket Korros, this volume, and the proceedings of the Council on the Affairs of the Local Economy of the Ministry of the Interior in TSGIA, fond 1288, opis 2–1905, delo 7, and fond 1652, op 1, delo 5–13.

58. Hosking, pp.85–91, 97–104.

59. See, for example, the almost idolatrous attitude toward Stolypin displayed by the delegates to the 1907 Zemstvo Congress and by the local zemstvo assemblies in the summer of 1906. *Golos moskvy*, no. 135, June 12, 1907, p.2, *Novoe vremia*, no. 11224, June 13 (26), 1907, p.2 and Hosking, p.30.

60. All except Perm, for which no statistics are available.

61. TSGIA, fond 1288, opis 2, delo 46–1909.

62. See Manning, "The Russian Provincial Gentry," pp.469–72.

63. See the paper by Roberta Thompson Manning, this volume, p.36.

64. A. Petrishchev, "Khronika vnutrennei zhizni," *Russkoe bogatstvo*, August 1909, p.55.

65. When local zemstvos were dissolved for lack of properly qualified candidates for office, existing zemstvo programs were taken over by a board appointed by the local administration. B. Veselovskii, "Ocherednyia zemskiia zadachi," *Sovremennik*, May 1913, p.302.

66. Al Savel'ev, "Zemskie vybory v nizhnegorodskoi gubernii," *Rech*, September 18, 1910.

67. Four seats allotted to the nobility in the Volokolamsk zemstvo remained unfilled at the time that Shipov was voted down. Shipov, pp.537–38.

68. I. Zhilkin, "Provintsial'noe obozrenie," *Vestnik evropy*, XLIV, no. 9 (September 1909), p.333.

69. The electoral reform of October 5, 1906, was promulgated in most

provinces for the first time in 1909–10. Only a few provinces were affected by the law in the previous elections.

70. Larskii, op. cit., p.79, and S. Lisenko, "Krest'iane v zemstve (Nekotorye itogi i perspektivy)," *Russkaia mysl*, XXIX, no. 8 (August 1909), p.111. The impact of the Law of October 5 was, however, significantly reduced by a series of Senate interpretations including one that specifically denied the new second curia voting rights to those peasants who had separated from the land commune and established separate holdings (*khutora*) under the Stolypin land reform. Veselovskii, *Istoriia zemstva*, IV, 178.

71. In 1909, for example, circulars from the provincial governors directed the noble land captains (*zemskie nachal'niki*) to prepare lists of any "undesirable elements" among the peasantry who were seeking election to the zemstvos. Larskii, op. cit., p.79 and Petrishchev in *Russkoe bogatstvo*, August 1909, p.53.

72. Vas. Golubev, "K itogam zemskikh vyborov," *Rech*, No. 246, September 3, 1909. Golubev also pointed out, however, that the new enthusiasm occasionally produced negative consequences. In a number of counties, each of the peasant electors in the final stage of the elections, wanting to see himself elected, refused to vote for other candidates, resulting in the failure of the assembly to elect the full quota of zemstvo members to which it was entitled.

73. Veselovskii, "Zemskiia nastroeniia," *Obrazovanie*, November 1906, p.52.

74. Such as schoolteachers, technicians, etc. Larskii, p.85.

75. The landed nobility, which elected 55 percent of the deputies to the county zemstvo assemblies and provided over 89 percent of the members of the provincial zemstvos, paid only 11 percent of all zemstvo taxes, although nobles eligible to vote in the first curia alone owned 17.3 percent of the land in 1910–12. N. I. Larevskii, "Zemskoe izbiriatel'noe pravo," in *Iubileinyi zemskii sbornik*, pp.66–67.

76. Vas. Golubev, "K zemskim vyboram," *Moskovskii ezhenedel'nik* 1910, no. 24, June 19, 1910, p.3.

77. For examples of such cooperation, see Mendeleev, pp.170, 177, and Shipov, 538.

78. Veselovskii, *Istoriia zemstva*, IV, pp.180–82.

79. For example, in Briansk county (Orel), only four of the fifty-three eligible electors appeared, and new elections had to be called. Golubev in *Rech*, no. 246, September 8, 1909.

80. Ibid.

81. Vas. Golubev, "Samoupravlenie v Rossii," *Russkaia mysl* XXXI, no. 11 (November 1910), p.154, and Golubev in *Moskovskii ezhenedel'nik*, no. 24, June 19, 1910, p.4.

82. Veselovskii, *Istoriia zemstva*, I, pp.13–33. The inequitable distribution of zemstvo taxes accounts in part for the adamant opposition of a considerable part of the landed nobility to Stolypin's proposals for zemstvo reform, especially his original projects, which attempted to base the property qualification for voting in zemstvo elections on the amount of zemstvo taxes paid.

83. Small noble landowners voted in the second curia if they could not

meet the property qualification for voting in the first curia.

84. I. Zhilkin, "Provintsial'noe obozrenie," *Vestnik evropy,* XLIV, no. 9 (September 1909), p.339.

85. Veselovskii, *Istoriia zemstva,* III, pp.57–58.

86. A. A. Bobrinskii, "Dnevnik," *Krasnyi arkhiv,* vol. 26 (1928), p.139.

87. Hosking, pp.97–105.

88. Avrekh, *Stolypin i tret'ia duma,* pp.275–76.

89. The Octobrists were also prompted to move by Stolypin's failure to deliver his political promises to them, which was most evident in the wake of the tsar's veto of the Naval General Staffs Bill in the spring of 1909.

90. See the paper by Alexandra Schecket Korros, this volume, p.126. The appointed Council members were usually selected from a list presented the tsar by the extreme right-wing president of the upper house, M. G. Akimov.

91. The large majority of the State Council representatives from the nobility already tended to adhere to the right rather than to the center faction. See Naumov, II, 151, and Manning, "The Russian Provincial Gentry," p.373.

92. We base our calculations of the political affiliations of the State Council representatives elected in 1906 on those which prevailed at the *moment of their election.* Consequently, our figures differ slightly from those given by Veselovskii in *Istoriia zemstva,* IV, 36. Veselovskii tended to cite the political tendency of the men concerned as that which prevailed at the time of his writing (1909–10). Many of these representatives had moved substantially to the right since their election to the upper house in 1906.

93. For example, the Naval General Staffs Bill was passed in March 1909 by an eight-vote majority. Hosking, p.85.

94. Ibid., pp.84–85, 151–81.

95. Robert Edelman, "The Russian Nationalist Party and the Political Crisis of 1909," *The Russian Review,* Vol. XXXIV, no. 1 (January, 1975), pp.33–53.

96. It is clear that Stolypin was currently very interested in curbing the rightward drift of the State Council from the way that he resolved his conflict with Nicholas II over the Naval General Staffs Crisis. The prime minister essentially agreed to give up his sponsorship of the bill in dispute in return for control of the appointments list of State Council members for the coming year. Ibid., pp.42–43.

97. To ensure such an outcome of these elections, the government decided to confine the introduction of elected zemstvos to only the six southernmost of the nine western provinces. In this way, the new elected zemstvos would be established only in known Nationalist political strongholds, excluding the three northwestern provinces where local Russian landowners generally supported the far right. Ibid., p.49.

98. TsGIA, fond 1288, opis 2, delo 46.

99. Data on the political results of the 1912–13 zemstvo elections is rather sparse. The government failed to record any information on the political leanings of the newly elected assemblies, while the press neglected the 1912–13 elections in the zemstvos. Nonetheless the woefully incomplete press accounts all indicate that "progressives" made some gains in Chernigov, Nizhnii Novgorod, Poltava (especially Krememchug county), and Tambov provinces (in the latter, the "progressives" were especially strong in Kirsanov, Kozlov, Usman, and Tambov counties). They also did well in

the Griazovets (Vologda), Nerekhets (Kostroma), and Volkov county zemstvos. I. Zhilkin, "Provintsial'noe obozrenie," *Vestnik evropy*, XLVIII, no. 12
(December 1913), pp.385–88, and B. Veselovskii, "Ocherki mestnago samoupravleniia," *Sovremennik*, November 1913, p.231, and September 1913,
p.304.

100. Kadet commentators on the elections were generally so glum that
it is difficult to imagine that many of their fellow party members managed
to enter the zemstvos under the rubric of "progressive." Although a few isolated individual Kadets did continue to participate in zemstvo affairs, especially at the county (uezd) level, they ceased to pursue their political goals
in the zemstvos. See, for example, A. Shingarev, "Zemskoe i gorodskoe samoupravlenie," *Ezhegodnik gazety Rech na 1914* (St. Petersburg, 1914, esp.
pp.224–27).

101. I. Zhilkin, "Provintsial'noe obozrenie," *Vestnik evropy*, XLVIII, no. 6
(June, 1913), pp.335–37; A. Petrishchev, "Khronika vnutrennoi zhizni," *Russkoe bogatstvo*, no. 12 (December 1913), p.347; B. Veselovskii, "Ocherednyia zemskiia zadachi," *Sovremennik*, May 1913, p.303, and "Ocherki mestnago samoupravleniia," in ibid., September 1913, p.305.

102. See especially I. Zhilkin, "Provintsial'noe obozrenie," *Vestnik evropy*,
XLVIII, no. 8 (August 1913), pp.333–41. The withdrawal of urban voters
from the zemstvos was especially striking in view of the fact that these elements were concomitantly enthusiastically participating in city duma elections, which resulted in the selection of a record number of "politically undesirable" city officials who were promptly denied administrative confirmation
by the government. See Veselovskii in *Sovremennik*, September, October,
and November, 1913.

103. Some electoral assemblies in the third (peasants') curia even passed
resolutions in favor of far-reaching zemstvo reform. However, the peasantry
was generally unable to unite to resist the very widespread government interference in the elections that occurred in 1912–13. As a result, many more
village elders and zemstvo incumbents, i.e., men who were likely to have
developed some sort of client-patron relationship with local officials, were
elected to the zemstvos in 1912–13 than in 1909–10. Also, an increasing
number of electoral assemblies were so divided among themselves that they
were unable to select a delegate to represent them in the zemstvos. Hence a
rising number of seats allotted to the peasants remained unfilled. Ibid., September 1913, p.305.

The Russian Peasantry
and the Elections to the
Fourth State Duma

EUGENE D. VINOGRADOFF

The subject of this article is the voting behavior of the agricultural peasantry of European Russia and Siberia during the elections to the Fourth State Duma in 1912.[1] Its objective is to examine the political mentality of the peasantry—their political conceptions and capacity for unity and discipline, as well as their positions on specific issues and their attitudes toward various groups of peasants and nonpeasants.

An examination of the political mentality of the peasantry in 1912 tests the two major historiographical schemata that have developed on the basis of research about peasant politics. According to the first schema, socioeconomic differentiation was dividing the peasantry during the early twentieth century into two mutually antagonistic classes, a peasant "bourgeoisie" and a peasant "semiproletariat." The development of these classes was being accelerated by the Stolypin land reform program, and these two new classes were engaging in an increasingly serious intrapeasantry class struggle, while the older struggle between the peasantry as a whole and the gentry was continuing.

According to the second major historiographical schema, on the other hand, intrapeasantry strife was minimal. Socioeconomic differentiation, although significant, was accompanied by no significant political consequences. Instead of revealing increasing divisions, the peasantry was continuing to display great political cohesion because the landed gentry, its ancient opponent, continued to be predominant in the coutryside.[2]

The test of these historiographical analyses on the basis of the 1912 election is facilitated by the fact that a proponent of the first schema

219

has already studied these elections. In the only previous examination of peasant voting patterns in 1912, the Soviet historian E. D. Chermenskii concluded that they provided evidence of a sharp class conflict between the wealthy and the poorer peasants. "Almost half of the peasant [Duma] deputies [who won election in 1912] were rich kulaks," Chermenskii wrote. They owed their election to the fact that "the government to a significant extent succeeded in falsifying the elections in the peasants' curia. At least half of the peasant deputies did not reflect the genuine interests of the peasant masses," whom Chermenskii identified as the emerging peasant "semiproletariat."[3]

The evidence to be reviewed in the present article contradicts Chermenskii's conclusions, and it also contradicts the conclusions one would expect to draw on the basis of the second historiographical schema. It indicates that class divisions among the peasantry were politically significant in a few regions, as Chermenskii argued, but insignificant in the great majority of regions, as the second historiographical schema would suggest. In other words, there were two fundamentally different sets of political attitudes and conceptions among the peasants in 1912, and the line of demarcation between them was one of region rather than one of class.

In the Baltic littoral, Kovno province, and, to a lesser extent, Siberia, peasants manifested one set of political attitudes and conceptions. They expressed interest in a wide variety of political, economic, and cultural issues—in civil liberties and in the autonomy of local governments; in the land question, rural wage rates, and agricultural development; in education and, where peasants were non-Russian and non-Orthodox, in national cultural and religious autonomy. In addition, as Chermenskii maintained, the peasants of these regions took different positions on these issues, which corresponded to differences in their socioeconomic positions. Finally, these peasants shared the attitudes and conceptions of some groups of nonpeasants, and they affiliated with political parties and otherwise joined together to defend their political attitudes and conceptions. Because the socioeconomic status of these peasants was correlated with the positions they took, their political mentality will here be called a "class" political mentality.

In all the other regions of the empire, the peasants manifested a different set of attitudes and conceptions. They expressed interest in only one issue, the land question, and they took a single radical position on that question despite great differences in their socioeconomic positions. Moreover, although they held a common position on this one issue, these peasants proved to be incapable of united or even disciplined action. Indeed, instead of affiliating with political parties or otherwise uniting with one another, they affiliated with individual gentry or official patrons, their principal antagonists on the land question. Because the political attitudes and conceptions of these peasants were correlated only with their membership in the legal peasant estate (*krest'ianskoe soslovie*) and not with differences in their socioeconomic positions, their political mentality will here be called an "estate" political mentality.

In summary, then, the evidence poses problems for both of the arguments that were outlined above. Neither of them is valid for the peasantry of the empire as a whole, and neither of them provides an explanation for the inability of peasants who shared a common position on the land question to act with unity and discipline.

The bulk of this article will be devoted to presenting the evidence of the regional variations in the political mentality of the peasants. Its major historiographical objective is to demonstrate that the existing schemata are inadequate; it is not to prove a new schema. Nevertheless, since the evidence calls for a closer examination of regional variations in social and economic conditions that might have shaped the political mentality of the peasants, the article will conclude with such an examination, revealing that regional variations in the peasants' political mentality roughly coincided with regional variations in the peasants' agrarian system. This suggests that possible relationships between political mentality and agrarian system are worthy of further study.

The elections to the Fourth State Duma were governed by the electoral law of June 3, 1907, which divided the empire's population into several electoral curiae, defined on the basis both of legal and of socioeconomic status. During the elections each of these curiae elected electors (*vyborshchiki*) from among its own ranks, and the electors from all curiae then jointly elected the Duma deputies from among their own ranks. Although the law required that one of the peasant electors from each province be elected a Duma deputy, one of its most important consequences was to discriminate severely against the peasantry: for example, it took the votes of 261 members of the peasants' curia to equal the vote of one member of the landowners' curia.[4] Nevertheless, for the purpose of investigating the political mentality of the peasantry, what is critical is not the law's discrimination; rather, it is that the law did allow an important segment of the peasantry to voice and even to act upon its political attitudes and conceptions.

With specific regard to the peasants' curia, the first important aspect of the law was that it effectively limited the peasant electorate to a particular group of the agricultural peasantry, male heads of households. It did this by denying the franchise to a large number of other groups: all women; all persons who belonged to the legal peasant estate but otherwise had little in common with the agricultural peasantry (i.e., most workers, many rural professionals, and a significant number of townsmen); and those agricultural peasants who did not own land or who happened to be away from their villages while the elections were taking place (i.e., members of households other than heads, in whose names title to land was vested; heads of landless households; and peasants who were engaged in migratory labor). Furthermore, although the law was tailored to heads of households, it made the participation of the great majority of them extremely indirect: it stipulated that the peasant electorate consist of members of district assemblies (*volostnye skhody*) who met the criteria outlined above, which meant that most heads of households participated only by virtue of having elected the members of the district assemblies in earlier, local elections.[5] In short, under the various stipulations of the electoral law, the peasant electorate consisted of peasant heads of households who had strong ties to their villages, who earned some if not all of their income from land, and who enjoyed sufficient status among their neighbors to have been elected members of district assemblies.

The second important aspect of the electoral law is that it opened the way to extensive landowner influence over the elections among the peasants. It did this in two ways: it provided local officials, who were elected by landowners, with numerous opportunities to try to prevent the election of "undesirable" peasants, and it permitted landowner electors to participate directly in the election of the peasant Duma deputies.

Officials were provided with opportunities to try to prevent the election of individual peasants, and in some cases of entire groups, by the complex three-stage process in which the peasants voted. In the first stage, members of district assemblies voted for representatives (*upolnomochennye*) from their own ranks; in the second stage, these representatives assembled at the county (uezd) level and elected electors (*vyborshchiki*) from their own ranks; and in the third stage, the peasant electors, together with the electors from all other curiae, met in the provincial electoral assembly and elected Duma deputies from among their ranks by majority vote of all of the electors.

The first two stages in this process were chaired by landowner officials—land captains (*zemskie nachal'niki*) in the first stage and county marshals of the nobility (*predvoditeli dvorianstva*) in the second stage. Although the balloting was secret, these officials knew more about the peasants of the district assemblies than did any other nonpeasants, which meant that they knew which individuals, villages, or even districts tended to be troublesome. If "undesirable" peasants won election in the first or second stage, officials could try to prevent their election to the next stage in several ways. First, they could seek technical violations on the basis of which to invalidate an election (e.g., inconsistent spellings of a peasant's name). In practice, formal invalidations were rare and were usually directed against oppositional members of former Dumas who had become particularly obnoxious to high officials in the capital. Second, officials could engage in obstructionism, which was a somewhat more frequent practice: they could fail to inform an "undesirable" peasant of the names of his colleagues or of the time and place of an electoral assembly; they could schedule the assemblies at inopportune times and places, reschedule them on short notice, etc.[6] Most often, however, the land captains and marshals of the nobility had merely to advise the peasants about "desirable" candidates in order to produce satisfactory results, for they exercised enormous powers over the district assemblies in the course of their routine affairs. In fact, both the peasants and the officials viewed the latter's role in the elections as so similar to their routine functioning that their actions were rarely described in detail; the best descriptions came from the relatively few provinces in which neither land captains nor marshals of the nobility had been instituted. One such province was Volynia, whose chief of police cited the absence of land captains as the reason for his inability to supply a firm prediction of how the peasants would vote: ". . . in Volynia province the peasant institutions . . . are deprived of that indispensable influence from the side of administrative authority which can be attained in those provinces with land captains. As a result, the peasant institutions are inert, undependable and, in the great majority of cases, are given over, so to speak, to the spontaneous arbitrariness of the little-cultured masses."[7] As will be evident in the pages that follow, local officials succeeded in preventing "spontaneous arbitrariness" in the great majority of regions.

While gentry influence was exercised by landowner officials during the first two stages of the electoral process, it was exercised even more directly by landowner electors during the third and final stage. As noted above, the electoral law of June 3 stipulated that all Duma deputies were to be elected by majority vote of the provincial electoral assembly, which was composed of all electors from all curiae. In the overwhelming majority of provinces, these provincial electoral assemblies were so apportioned as to give electors from the landowners' curia roughly 50 percent of the votes and electors from the first city curia (that composed of the wealthiest townsmen) another 12–20 percent; peasant electors, by contrast, usually had between 15 percent and 25 percent of the votes.[8] Clearly, then, if the landowner and first city electors were reasonably well united, they would constitute the majority in a provincial electoral assembly. Subject to two important limitations imposed by the electoral law, they would be free to elect whichever deputies they preferred.

The first important limitation upon the freedom of the majority of a provincial electoral assembly to elect deputies of its choice was the requirement that at least one of the electors from each of the major curiae be elected a deputy. In almost all provinces, the law stipulated that the assembly first elect one of the peasant electors a deputy (he became the so-called curial peasant deputy), and that it then elect, in turn, a deputy from among the landowner electors and one or two deputies from among the city electors (the five largest cities of the empire elected their own deputies and thus sent no electors to the electoral assemblies in their provinces). In addition, in several provinces with large concentrations of workers and/or Cossacks, a worker and/or a Cossack deputy was similarly mandated. Finally, in the few non-Russian provinces with substantial Russian minorities, at least one of the deputyships was reserved for Russians, and the Russian electors were sometimes entitled to hold separate electoral assemblies. After an assembly had elected all of its various curial or mandated deputies, it was free to elect the remaining deputies to which its province was entitled without regard to curia (deputies elected in this fashion will here be called "at-large" deputies).[9] In short, although the electoral law gave landowners and first city electors a majority in most of the provincial electoral assemblies, it allowed them completely free use of their majority only in the election of at-large deputies; in the election of the other deputies, it required them at least to choose candidates who belonged to the appropriate curiae.

The second important limitation upon the freedom of the majority of a provincial electoral assembly was the seemingly inoffensive requirement that each nominee for a deputyship declare his willingness to stand for election.[10] Coupled with the requirement that a curial peasant deputy be elected in the great majority of provinces, this provided the peasant electors of each province with one sure means of maintaining their control over the election of the curial peasant deputy: if they could agree unanimously on one of their number as their nominee, they could compel his election by refusing to accept nominations themselves. Indeed, even if all the nonpeasant electors opposed the peasants' nominee, they could not prevent his election; all that they could do was to compel a second ballot, for the law stipulated that if no candidate received an absolute majority on the first ballot, the candidate who received the highest number of favorable votes (a relative majority) on a second ballot would be considered elected.[11]

In summary, then, the electoral law discriminated against the peasants and opened the way to extensive gentry influence, but it did allow an important segment of the peasantry to express its political attitudes and conceptions. It placed an extremely high premium on unity and political discipline, for if the peasant electors were sufficiently well united, they could guarantee their control over the election of their curial peasant deputy. Moreover, if they were united while the electors from other curiae were not, they could even gain control of a provincial electoral assembly and play the major role in the election of the other deputies, and especially of the at-large deputies who could be chosen from electors belonging to any curia.

The elections to the Fourth State Duma took place during the late summer and early autumn of 1912, a tranquil period in all the rural regions of the Russian Empire. The last reverberations of the revolutionary turmoil of 1905–1907 had been stilled four years earlier, and neither the Stolypin land reform program nor the new upsurge of strike activity among the workers, which had commenced in the spring of the year, were producing any discernible echoes of unrest among the peasantry. In a few villages, to be sure, disorders were under way; in a few others, rumors about the partitioning of nonpeasant lands were circulating; and in a few others still, the disruptions produced by a crop failure and mild famine continued to be felt.[12] But phenomena such as these merely constituted the norm during periods of tranquility.

Despite the overall tranquility, regional differences among the peasants were already apparent as the date of the elections approached. Peasants in all regions except the Baltic remained completely apathetic:

they did and said nothing about the elections; no peasant candidates emerged; and they were ignorant of, or indifferent to, the activities of the previous State Duma.

In the Baltic region, on the other hand, peasants were interested both in the activities of the Third Duma and in the elections; several candidates emerged; indeed in Lifland province two Estonian peasant candidates were engaged in a primary campaign that was attracting the attention of townsmen and *intelligenty* as well as of peasants.[13]

In regions other than the Baltic, Kovno province, and Siberia, the apathy of the peasants resulted not only from the general tranquility in the countryside. It stemmed as well from the peasants' indifference and hostility to the Duma itself—from feelings that had begun with disillusionment in 1907 and that had been reinforced by the five years' "inactivity" of the Third Duma.

The creation of the Duma in October of 1905 had initially evoked an enthusiastic response from the peasants. In most regions they had hoped that it would carry out a "black partition," that is, that it would divide up all nonpeasant lands among the peasants. The peasants had traditionally pinned their desires for such a drastic resolution of their problems on the tsar, and they were now confusing, or equating, the tsar and the new Duma. During the spring of 1906, for example, as the date of the convening of the Duma drew near, "in many provinces . . . the peasants . . . were expecting 'Joy' from the Tsar. 'Joy'—the allotment to each man of five *desiatiny* of land."[14]

But the peasants' enthusiasm had rapidly given way to disillusionment when neither the First nor the Second Duma produced a radical resolution of the land question. Their disillusionment had then been compounded when the electoral law of June 3, 1907, drastically altered the balance in Duma elections between themselves and the landowners, reducing the number of peasant electors by more than 50 percent while increasing the number of landowner electors by more than 25 percent. This had left the landowners in control of the vast majority of the provincial electoral assemblies, as has been explained above, and the result was a tremendous decline in the number of peasant Duma deputies (for example, from approximately 199 in the First Duma to only 74 in the Fourth Duma) and a commensurate increase in the number of landowner deputies.[15]

By the autumn of 1908, when the Third Duma began its debate on the Stolypin land reform program, the peasants had already grown completely indifferent to it. Their attitude was succinctly summarized by some peasants in Tver province, who, when asked whether the

Duma should be retained in its present form, reformed, or abolished altogether, replied: "Although [we] are indifferent, [we] see no reason . . . [to reform the Duma], for . . . no matter what kind of Duma there is, [we] still won't get the land for nothing."[16] And the peasants had remained indifferent from 1908 through 1912, for none of the Duma's actions, including its passage of the Stolypin land reform program in 1910 and of a bill to facilitate enclosures in 1911, had had anything in common with their desire for a black partition.

In summary, then, the peasants of the great majority of the regions of the empire—of those regions which are here being called "estate" regions—had viewed the Duma with indifference or hostility since 1907, the year in which political tranquility had been restored in the Russian countryside. Indeed, the peasants' disillusionment with the Duma had been merely one of the signs of the restoration of tranquility, like the decline in the number of agrarian disturbances in 1907. The onset of tranquility, the disillusionment with the Duma, and the decline in the number of disturbances had all resulted fundamentally from the dashing of the peasants' hopes for a black partition. This had been their constant and almost exclusive objective; when it had begun to appear unattainable, they had responded by lapsing into apathy, not by shifting their attention to lesser, more readily attainable objectives.

In the Baltic region, Kovno province, and Siberia, on the other hand, the peasants had never focused exclusively on the land question. Even during the revolutionary upsurge of 1905 and 1906, the peasants of these "class" regions had sought such goals as civil liberties, autonomy for local governments and for minority cultures and religions, increased rural wage rates, and improved agricultural marketing conditions. Moreover, they had sometimes sought these goals with as much fervor as they sought land. In the post-1907 atmosphere of tranquility, the peasants of these regions continued to pursue many of these objectives, and they continued also to view the Duma as a means by which some of these objectives might be attained.

During the 1912 elections themselves, the regional distinctions among the peasantry were revealed very clearly. They were evident even from aggregate data summarizing the party affiliations of the peasant deputies who were elected, despite the fact that the national party labels tended to disguise them to a certain degree.

In all, seventy-four peasant deputies were elected to the Duma in 1912, fifty-four of whom were curial deputies and twenty of whom were at-large deputies. Their breakdown by party in the two major types of regions is illustrated in table 1.[17]

The deputies from the class regions stood considerably to the left of the deputies from the estate regions. All of the former belonged to liberal or revolutionary parties, while most of the latter belonged to conservative or moderate parties and none to a revolutionary party.

Although the aggregate figures reveal that there was *some* distinction between the peasants of the two types of regions, they mistakenly suggest that it was a distinction only of degree. That is because the party names in the table appear to represent a single political continuum, and the distribution of peasant deputies along it implies that a single continuum existed among them too. In fact, however, there was no single continuum, for the party labels meant very different things to the peasants of the two types of regions. Thus, the apparent overlap between the class and estate peasants who joined liberal parties is misleading; as we shall see below, peasants from class regions who joined liberal parties did so because they held liberal positions on a number of political issues, while peasants from estate regions who joined liberal parties did so only because they were

TABLE 1

Party distribution of peasant Duma deputies by types of regions.

Party	Estate regions		Class regions		Totals	
	Total	Percent	Total	Percent	Total	Percent
Rightist	15	23.1	—	—	15	20.3
Nationalist	17	26.2	—	—	17	23.0
Centrist	4	6.2	—	—	4	5.4
(Subtotal for rightist bloc)	(36)	(55.4)	(—)	(—)	(36)	(48.6)
Belorussian-Lithuanian-Polish Group	1	1.5	—	—	1	1.4
Octobrist	13	20.0	—	—	13	17.6
(Subtotal for moderate bloc)	(14)	(21.5)	(—)	(—)	(14)	(18.9)
Moslem	2	3.1	—	—	2	2.7
Progressist	8	12.3	1	11.1	9	12.2
Kadet	5	7.7	4	44.4	9	12.2
Trudovik	—	—	4	44.4	4	5.4
(Subtotal for leftist bloc)	(15)	(23.1)	(9)	(99.9)	(24)	(32.4)
Totals	65	100.00	9	99.9	74	100.2

clients of gentry patrons who happened to be liberals. Similarly, the
apparent political diversity among the estate peasants who joined
such a wide range of parties is equally misleading; these peasants
shared a common desire for a radical resolution of the land question
and a common indifference to other issues, but they joined a range of
parties because the local landowners, whom they obediently followed
so long as the general political atmosphere seemed to preclude a black
partition, led them into a range of parties. An examination of the electoral results in several provinces will illustrate these points.

Let us look first at the overlap between the class and estate peasants
who joined the liberal Progressist and Kadet parties. Two examples
will indicate how different liberal peasants were in the two types
of regions.

A typical liberal peasant from a class region was the Kadet Iu. M.
Oras of Estonia, whom the local governor described as follows:[18]

> Oras . . . is the chairman of a district court and a prominent member
> of the local agricultural and all other privately organized societies. . . .[19]
>
> Until the outbreak of disorders in the area in 1905–1906. Oras was a
> teacher in . . . [a] district school. With the outbreak of disorders he be-
> came one of the prominent agitators, took an active part in meetings,
> and, with the arrival of punitive detachments, went into hiding in Fin-
> land. From there he returned in 1907. Presently he belongs to the left
> wing of the Estonian Progressist-Nationalists. Among the local Estonian
> population he enjoys great trust and respect and, being an active mem-
> ber of various societies, exercises a prominent influence on the public
> life of the local peasant population. . . .
>
> His election to the Duma was the result of a decision of a pre-electoral
> assembly organized by electors [belonging to] the Estonian Progressive
> group, which nominated him as the candidate from the peasantry. In
> view of this decision, the other peasant electors—including, by the way,
> the member of the Third Duma [A. Ia.] Teras—refused to permit them-
> selves to be nominated at the [Provincial] Electoral Assembly.

Two aspects of this report deserve emphasis, the first of which per-
tains to Oras and the second to his fellow Estonian peasants. According to the report, Oras himself, although an agricultural peasant with
only an elementary education,[20] was virtually indistinguishable from
many members of the intelligentsia. He was dedicated to rational improvements in both the economic and the cultural life of the peasantry,
and he was equally dedicated to political liberty. His political activities, moreover, had undergone a transition between 1905 and 1912 that
was typical of those of many members of the intelligentsia, and of
many Kadet *intelligenty* in particular: a revolutionary in 1905, he had

become a liberal in the years after 1907 and had confined himself to legal activities that helped develop a liberal constituency.

The second aspect of the governor's report that deserves emphasis concerns the other peasants of Estonia. In compelling Oras's election by refusing nominations themselves, they displayed both a thorough understanding of the electoral law and a capacity for unity and discipline that was matched only by industrial workers during the 1912 elections.[21] Other reports strongly suggest, in addition, that not only peasant but also urban electors had participated in the preelectoral assembly that had nominated Oras, and this would indicate that the Estonian peasants concerned had joined together politically with certain groups of nonpeasants as well as with one another.[22]

In summary, the Estonian peasants (or at least this particular group of them) were "conscious" liberals. They understood political liberty in the same sense in which many townsmen understood it, and they associated it with economic and cultural development. To achieve their aims, they could unite among themselves and with others, and they could manipulate provisions of the electoral law to their advantage.

Let us examine now a typical liberal peasant deputy from an estate region. Such a deputy was the Progressist A. A. Sychev of Ufa province, whom the governor of Ufa described as follows:

Sychev . . . does not work directly in agriculture, but serves in the county zemstvo as agent for road construction. Earlier, Sychev was elected to a term as member of the zemstvo board (1900–1903), and then, when the chairman of this board, Koropachinskii, became chairman of the Provincial Zemstvo Board, he was elected chairman for the remainder of [Koropachinskii's] term. However, the hopes placed upon him were not fulfilled, [for he] displayed extremely little activity in this post; this was noted by the . . . next zemstvo assembly session in 1903, which did not find it possible to re-elect him to this post and made him only a member of the board. But even in this post Sychev earned such a reputation for inactivity that, when he was again elected by the district assembly as a candidate for the zemstvo assembly . . . in 1906, my predecessor [as governor] . . . did not find it possible to confirm him. . . . [My predecessor also] failed to confirm his election . . . in 1909.
    Sychev has no significance whatever in the life of the local public institutions, and plays no active role with respect to politics. If he was elected a member of the [zemstvo] assembly and then to responsible posts in the . . . zemstvo, it was thanks exclusively to the support of the Chairman of the Provincial Zemstvo Board Koropachinskii, an influential public figure and landowner in Zlatoustovskii county who became his patron.

Displaying no political activity, Sychev even has scarcely any serious, thorough acquaintance with the programs of the political parties; but he was elected a member of the Duma by the Kadetish [*kadetstvuiu-shchie*] zemstvoites [who formed] an oppositional majority, and by all accounts will join the Constitutional-Democratic fraction or the Progressive Group in the Duma.[23]

Unlike Oras, Sychev had displayed no initiative whatsoever in local politics; indeed, he could distinguish the liberal parties from the conservative parties only with difficulty, if at all. The sum and substance of his political career was his client-patron relationship with the landowner Koropachinskii—a relationship so strong that it had survived revolution and counterrevolution alike. Inert and passive, Sychev was a liberal only because his gentry patron was a liberal. An obedient client, he presumably joined the Progressist party at Koropachinskii's direction, for, although Koropachinskii himself remained in Ufa as chairman of the provincial zemstvo, two of his fellow gentry zemstvoites were elected to the Duma, and both were Progressists.[24]

Significantly, the attitude of the other peasants toward Sychev was not mentioned by the governor or by anyone else who reported on the elections. In fact, the reports mentioned only one other peasant at all, and they mentioned him only because he too was elected to the Duma. This was the Moslem party deputy G. Kh. Baiteriakov, who was supported by the liberal bloc under the terms of its electoral alliance with the Moslems. Like Sychev, Baiteriakov was the obedient client of a powerful landowner patron, the Moslem nobleman K. B. Tevkelev, a member of the First, the Second, and the Third Dumas, who was reelected in 1912.[25]

It is clear, then, that the other peasants of Ufa province played no significant role in the elections. Perhaps they followed the directives of their local landowner electors as obediently as Sychev and Baiteriakov followed their patrons. It is evident, in any case, that Sychev's affiliation with the Progressist party meant nothing more to the other peasants than it did to Sychev himself.[26] "Peasant liberalism" in Ufa was not the same thing as "peasant liberalism" in Estonia. Indeed, "peasant liberalism" in Ufa reflected nothing whatsoever about the peasantry there, except that they were subservient to landowning noblemen, some of whom happened to be liberals.

This raises the broader question of what political parties in general meant to the peasants of the estate regions, and thus introduces the second misleading implication of the aggregate figures summarizing the results of the elections. As these figures showed, the peasants of the estate regions joined a wide range of parties, which at first glance would imply that they held a wide variety of political attitudes and conceptions. An examination of the views of several moderate and conservative peasant deputies from estate regions, however, will demonstrate that they all held the same political attitudes. Like Sychev and Baiteriakov, they joined parties not on the basis of their own views, but rather on the basis of the views of local landowners and officials.

A typical moderate peasant deputy was the Octobrist G. G. Mazurenko of Kherson province. A thorough investigation of his background by local officials revealed that he had "occupied the post of District Elder . . . for fifteen years and enjoy[ed] great respect in his milieu. . . . By his political convictions, [he] belong[ed] to the moderate right." Nevertheless, the governor who was reporting this information felt constrained to warn:

> It is difficult to say with assurance what position he will take in the Duma, in view of the attraction of the peasants to the left parties [because of] the land question, which is central to them. However, after the elections he promised the [other] members of the Duma from Kherson province not to sit to the left of them in the Duma.[27]

This was a promise that he kept, for he joined three of the landowner deputies from his province in the Octobrist party, and none of the other deputies from Kherson sat to the left of the Octobrists. It might be tempting to assume that Mazurenko chose the Octobrists because he knew that they were to the left of the Centrists and the Rightists, the other two parties to which his fellow Kherson deputies belonged, but there is no evidence for this in the reports.[28] In all probability, he chose the Octobrists simply because he was more familiar with the particular landowners in that party than with those in the Centrist or Rightist parties; in any case, it is clear that the three parties held essentially identical conservative positions on the land question, which was the only issue of concern to Mazurenko.

Five Rightist party peasant deputies, including one who was a member of the Union of Russian People, were elected in Volynia province, and their election capped the biggest single conservative victory among the peasants during the 1912 elections.[29] The governor, understandably pleased with this success, paused during an otherwise enthusiastic report, however, to warn that the Rightist party peasants were not altogether reliable. "In deciding questions connected with the ownership of the land," he wrote, "they will be ready during balloting to join with the opposition."[30] The governor did not mean that they might endorse a *liberal* agrarian program, such as the Kadets' old program of the compulsory alienation with compensation of gentry lands; he meant that they favored a black partition.[31]

In summary, then, the party affiliations of the peasant deputies from the estate regions, which emerged only upon their election to the Duma, indicated nothing of significance about their political attitudes and conceptions.[32] Whatever parties they joined, they expressed profound interest only in the land question, and all but two or three of them favored a black partition.[33] When joining a party they did not consider its position on the land question or on any other issue; the only thing that they did consider was the party preference (or preferences) of the local landowners and officials who were so important in their everyday lives.

Before leaving the topic of the party affiliations of estate peasants, it would be useful to look more closely at the kinds of peasant-landowner relationships that determined them. As we have already seen in the case of Sychev and Baiteriakov of Ufa province, many of the estate peasants were bound to landowners by strong client-patron relationships. These peasant clients automatically affiliated with the parties of their patrons, even when to do so meant to break with the other peasant deputies from their own provinces.

Although almost all the peasant deputies and most of the peasant electors from the estate regions were clients,[34] many had patrons who were not personally involved in the electoral process. Instead of exercising relatively greater independence in choosing a political party, however, these peasants in effect chose new patrons to guide their activities in the Duma at the same time that they chose a party. They aligned themselves with the most powerful and most benevolent group of landowner electors during the balloting at the provincial electoral assemblies and then joined whichever party the landowner deputies preferred.[35] How they determined which group of landowners was the most powerful and benevolent is illustrated by the following report, which explains why rightist peasant electors in the Don region defected to the opposition:

> . . . on the eve of the elections the rightists [i.e., mostly landowner and clerical electors] controlled 45 purely party votes, the opposition only 40, and the remaining votes belonged to the Octobrists . . . and the non-party Cossacks and peasants, who were more inclined to support the right. . . . However, the leaders of the rightist parties . . . not only did not further the success of their party, but on the contrary aided its

complete defeat. While the [opposition] advanced to the struggle in complete discipline . . . the rightists concerned themselves only with the success of personal candidacies, and of discipline there was not a trace. Things reached such an absurdity that all 45 rightists announced their candidacies, and as a result received some 3–4 votes each. . . . Moreover, the rightists behaved extremely scornfully towards the German [colonist] Octobrists, the Cossacks and the peasants, . . . as a result of which the Germans, the peasants and a small group of the Cossacks went over to the opposition.[36]

This produced an oppositional majority that had no trouble electing its slate of candidates, including the Kadet peasant deputy A. G. Afanas'ev.[37] "Rightist" peasant electors, surprised by the apparent weakness of the conservative landowners and offended by their scornful treatment, had readily aligned themselves with the more powerful and more considerate oppositional landowners. In so doing, they had displayed not the slightest interest in the political views of either group of landowners.

One other relationship between peasants and landowners deserves mention here. Ethnic and religious affinities could sometimes have an effect upon the party affiliations of the peasant deputies in estate regions. In the Right-Bank Ukraine and White Russia, for example, conservative Russian Orthodox landowners were confronted by oppositional blocs composed predominantly of Polish Catholic landowners and urban Jews. The peasant electors of these regions, who were overwhelmingly Orthodox and who identified themselves on official records as Russians rather than as Belorussians or Ukrainians,[38] always aligned themselves with the Russian Orthodox landowners during the balloting at electoral assemblies, and the peasant deputies who were elected always joined whichever party these landowners preferred.[39] That religious and ethnic affinities played a role in their choice is clear from some of the reports,[40] but that they played a very large role is doubtful. For one thing, the Russian Orthodox landowners of these regions exercised unusually good discipline within their own ranks and treated the peasants very generously (e.g., they frequently supported peasants for at-large deputyships).[41] For another thing, a solidly rightist group of peasant electors in Tauride province quickly defected to the opposition as a result of what the governor called the "agitational talents" of the Kadet leader Solomon S. Krym. Krym, who was Jewish, was a large landowner and an elector from the landowners' curia, and he was personally acquainted with "the majority" of the electors, both rural and urban, through his activities in the zemstvo and the city duma. The peasants' willingness to follow him, without receiving any at-large deputyships and without being propelled by rightist bungling, demonstrates that a personable land-owner leader could overcome religious and ethnic differences.[42]

Finally, it is important to note that the various types of peasant-landowner relationships discussed above were the *only* important determinants of the party affiliations of the peasants of estate regions. Socioeconomic and other important distinctions among the peasants themselves were completely unrelated to their party affiliations, as table 2 illustrates (bloc membership rather than party membership is used here for the sake of simplicity).[43] Clearly, there was no tendency for the poorer peasants to cluster toward the left end of the political spectrum or for the wealthier peasants to cluster toward the right.

TABLE 2

Socioeconomic status of peasant deputies in estate regions correlated with their political orientation.

Socioeconomic status	Conservative bloc		Moderate bloc		Oppositional bloc		Totals	
	Abso-lute	Per-cent	Abso-lute	Per-cent	Abso-lute	Per-cent	Abso-lute	Per-cent
Poor	1	100.0	—	—	—	—	1	100.0
Middle	16	61.5	3	11.5	7	26.9	26	99.9
Rich	19	52.8	9	25.0	8	22.2	36	100.0
Extremely Rich	—	—	2	100.0	—	—	2	100.0
Totals	36	55.4	14	21.5	15	23.1	65	100.0

In summary, then, the most important factor in determining the party affiliations of the peasants of the estate regions was the party preferences of local landowners and officials—or more precisely the preferences of those landowners and officials who appeared to the peasants to be the most powerful and benevolent. Religious and ethnic affinities also played some role in determining which landowners peasants would follow, and thus also which parties they would join. The political positions of the parties themselves played no role, nor did the peasants' own position on the land question, which was the only issue of profound significance in their eyes. Socioeconomic and other important distinctions among the peasants also played no role.[44]

In the class regions, on the other hand, the peasants selected their parties on completely different grounds. We have already seen that the Kadet deputy Oras of Estonia province was a "conscious" liberal, whose political biography closely resembled that of many Kadet *intelligenty*. Let us here add a second example, the Trudovik deputy A. I. Ryslev of the Amur region, whose party selection involved the weighing of some rather complex considerations.

Like Oras, Ryslev had been an active participant in the Revolution of 1905; he had then been a railroad clerk in Irkutsk province, a post from which he was dismissed because he participated in "disorders" and was suspected of being affiliated with the Social-Democratic party. In the years following 1905, the program of the Social-Democrats continued to appeal to him in most respects, but he had one serious reservation about it—one that he related quite openly to the governor after his election in 1912:

> Ryslev sympathizes with the Social-Democratic Party, but in personal conversations he declared to me that he would remain non-party [in the Duma], since the discipline of any party could, on many issues, conflict with the interests and needs of the [Amur] region.

Arriving in St. Petersburg, Ryslev found the Trudovik fraction both sufficiently flexible to permit him to espouse the local interests with which he was concerned and sufficiently radical to accord with his general programmatic desires. He therefore joined it (nevertheless, it is noteworthy that he was mistakenly listed as a Social-Democrat at one point in the Duma's official index, and he was the only deputy about whom that rather serious error was made; perhaps he continued to express his general support of Social-Democratic positions).[45] Thus, although Ryslev was the only Fourth Duma peasant deputy who found it difficult to choose between two revolutionary parties, he closely resembled the other deputies from the class regions in the sophistication with which he approached the question of party affiliation.

On a more general level, it was noted earlier that all nine of the deputies from class regions joined either liberal or revolutionary parties. Suffice it to add here that the issue of economic reforms, and of the land question in particular, was the watershed between the liberal and the revolutionary deputies from these regions: those who favored radical economic reforms joined the Trudovik party, and those who opposed them joined the Kadets or, in the case of one extremely wealthy deputy, the Progressists. The Trudovik deputies tended to be relatively poor, to have only elementary educations, and to be relatively uncommitted to religion (one was even an atheist); the Kadets and the Progressists, on the other hand, tended to be wealthy, to be highly educated, and to be more deeply committed to religion.[46]

In addition to having different conceptions of political parties and different reasons for joining them, the peasants of the estate and class regions differed with respect to their ability to act in a unified, disciplined fashion during the electoral process. In the estate regions, the peasant electors could act in unison only when they were following a unified group of landowners or officials, i.e., only when they were being subservient and passive. When they were acting independently —landowners and officials sometimes permitted them some independence—or on the very rare occasions when they acted aggressively, they were unable to maintain unity and discipline. In the class regions, on the other hand, the peasant electors almost always acted independently and aggressively, and yet they were able to maintain unity and discipline as well. Several examples will illustrate this difference.

In Vladimir province, eleven of the peasant electors were permitted to act independently and immediately began quarreling with one another. These eleven peasants had all been adherents of the rightist bloc, and the governor reported that the rightist and the oppositional blocs would be nearly equal in strength when the provincial electoral assembly convened. The Octobrists would therefore hold the balance, and the governor arranged a rightist-Octobrist meeting at which the two factions agreed to support a common slate of candidates. "Since . . . [the] eleven peasant electors were participating, it was decided to support [as the peasant deputy] whichever candidate they nominated."[47]

The reason for this "democratic" treatment of the peasants was clear enough: they were a sufficiently large bloc of electors to have been able to tip the balance in favor of the opposition if they took offense at the conservatives. But the "democratic" treatment had some consequences that the governor had not foreseen. Knowing that one of them would receive the support of the majority of the nonpeasant electors and would thus be elected to the curial deputyship, "each of the peasants at first tried to get elected . . . [and they all voted against each other], and the peasant deputy [who finally won] was unable to obtain an absolute majority."[48]

After the peasant deputy had finally been elected, the peasant electors began to quiet down. They voted for the next conservative candidate who had been slated in the Octobrist-rightist agreement (this was the deputy from the landowners' curia). But a rightist landowner who had not been nominated for a deputyship decided to try to obtain one by taking advantage of the peasants' instability, and the entire conservative majority threatened to disintegrate:

> The elector Gvozdev . . . began to try to convince the peasants not
> to elect the priest [who had been slated for the at-large deputyship],
> but to elect a peasant or a person sympathetic to the peasants; he put
> forward the peasant-born factory owner Malinin as such a candidate.
> . . . Then, in place of these suggestions, Gvozdev tried to persuade the
> peasants to vote for [the Kadet A. A.] Ern [as the deputy from the city
> curiae, who was being voted upon as this suggestion was being made].
> Behind this combination was hidden some hope on Gvozdev's part to
> put forward his own candidacy [for the at-large deputyship], once the
> balloting had been thrown into chaos by these methods.
>
> Gvozdev's hopes were realized in part. On the first ballot [for the
> deputy from the city curiae] Gvozdev, Malinin, and three or four pea-
> sants defected from the bloc, and the bloc's candidate and Ern received
> almost the same number of votes. . . . On the second ballot, either sev-
> eral more peasants or several priests also went over to Ern, and he re-
> ceived 45 votes [an absolute majority], while [the bloc's candidate]
> received 42.[49]

Before the at-large deputy, which Gvozdev hoped to become, could
be elected, there remained a workers' deputy to elect. It was a foregone conclusion that he would be the Bolshevik F. N. Samoilov, for
all the worker electors supported him and none would accept a nomination. However, the conservative leaders had planned to vote against
him anyway, simply to register their own convictions, even at the cost
of taking more time than necessary over the workers' deputy by compelling a second ballot. But for some reason this plan miscarried and
"the nucleus of rightist electors voted leftist," thereby helping to elect
Samoilov quickly. The governor interpreted this as a sign that the disarray in the rightist camp was continuing.[50]

There then remained the at-large deputyship to fill, and

> . . . it became clear at once that the intrigues of Gvozdev had succeeded:
> the [slated] candidate of the clergy, the archpriest Speranskii, received
> only 35 votes. A whole series of candidates then put forward, some by
> the rightist bloc and some by the leftists, failed to obtain a majority
> either on the first or on the second ballots. But Gvozdev himself, seeing
> such a mood in the assembly, decided not to run. At last the rightist bloc
> candidate Markov received 42 votes, and . . . the assembly, seeing the
> futility of further balloting, declared him elected.[51]

When all was said and done, then, the gullibility and instability of
the peasant electors had cost the conservative bloc only one deputyship. The bloc had otherwise managed to hold together, but only barely.

The contrast between the behavior of the peasant electors and the
behavior of the worker electors was striking indeed. The peasants,
knowing that they could nominate their own Duma deputy, all ran

against each other, while the workers, like the class peasants of Estonia, unanimously agreed upon a candidate of their own and refused further nominations in order to compel his election. Later, at least three or four peasants broke ranks with their fellows and broke their agreement with other conservatives when an intriguing landowner tempted them to run again for a deputyship—a deputyship in which the landowner himself was transparently interested. The workers, on the other hand, remained so steadfast in their unity that they convinced rightist leaders to vote for a Bolshevik so as not to spend any more time than necessary on the election of a workers' deputy. In general, the peasants were viewing the deputyships purely in terms of the advantages they might bring to the individuals who held them, while the workers were viewing the deputyships purely in terms of the advantages they might bring to a party or a class.[52]

When invited to nominate their candidate independently, then, the peasants of Vladimir had responded with anarchic rather than with disciplined political behavior. In other provinces, too, instances of peasant "independence" during the elections were usually initiated by landowners rather than by peasants, and they were usually marked by similarly anarchic behavior on the part of the peasants. However, in two or three provinces of the estate regions, peasants tried to exercise a more genuine and aggressive kind of independence: they tried to oppose dominant blocs of landowners in order to gain something for themselves. But even these peasants were unable to maintain unity and discipline. Their demonstrations of opposition were very short-lived and ineffectual, and their unity was very easily shattered when landowners from the dominant bloc offered to support one of them for a deputyship.

One of these oppositional demonstrations occurred in Tula province, where all the peasant electors initially aligned themselves with the opposition:

> . . . eighty-five [electors] were present at the [provincial electoral] assembly, and were distributed by group as follows:
> *rightists*—25, and clergy—19; in all, 44 votes.
> *leftists*—25, and peasants—16; in all 41 votes. (The peasants' votes went to the leftists because they [i.e., the peasants] are undependable and easily give way to any absurd promises from [the leftists]).[53]

In this case, then, the peasants' opposition had not been entirely independent; it had been instigated by oppositional leaders who made "absurd promises." It is unfortunate that the chief of police, from whose report the above quotation was taken, did not specify what the promises were, for without knowing what they were it is impossible to determine what the peasants hoped to gain by siding with the opposition. In all probability, the promises involved at-large deputyships, for the oppositional leaders were almost certainly liberal rather than revolutionary "leftists." Still, one cannot completely dismiss the possibility that the promises involved the offer of oppositional support for a radical resolution of the land question, because no policeman in the realm would have called the promise of extra deputyships "absurd."

Whatever it was that the peasants hoped to gain, they did prove willing to oppose a well-disciplined conservative bloc of landowner electors who completely dominated the assembly. From among their own ranks, these landowners elected two Nationalists and one Rightist to the Duma, and they succeeded in leading a clerical deputy into the Rightist party after his election.[54]

However, the law also required that a peasant deputy be elected ahead of all the others, which meant that the conservative landowners had to select one of the sixteen "leftist" peasants. Their choice fell upon A. M. Sinitsyn, who promptly defected to the conservatives during his own election (he was joined by two other oppositional electors, but it is unclear whether they were peasants[55]) and then rejoined his fellow oppositional peasants while the remaining Duma deputies were being elected. When the elections were over, Sinitsyn switched once more, joining the landowner deputy and the priest in the rightist party and thereby completing the conservative sweep of the Tula deputyships.[56] Clearly, then, Sinitsyn's instability closely resembled that of the gullible peasants of Vladimir, for both he and they viewed deputyships only in terms of the personal advantages they entailed.

That Sinitsyn should have resembled so closely his fellow estate peasants is remarkable, for he was one of the few who had availed himself of the full possibilities of the Stolypin land reform program. The governor described him enthusiastically:

> [He] was the first peasant in [his] county to remove his allotment land from the commune in order to form a separate *khutor*.* With the assistance of the land reform commission, [he] established a model farm [on it], which without doubt will be of benefit to the surrounding peasant population.[57]

* A *khutor* is an enclosed farm with the farmer's house and buildings located on it; an *otrub* is an enclosed farm with the farmer's house and buildings located elsewhere (usually in a nuclear village). The formation of *khutors* was the maximal objective of the Stolypin land reform program.

The governor's assessment was, at the very least, premature. The model farm's "benefit" had not prevented Sinitsyn's fellow peasants from voting against him, nor had the model farmer himself acted any differently during the elections than the ordinary communal peasants of the estate regions.

Even the most aggressive peasants of the estate regions, then, were unable to maintain unity in their effort to obtain whatever benefits they were seeking in the elections. The peasants of the class regions presented a sharply contrasting picture.

We have already seen how the peasant electors of Estonia united in favor of the Kadet Oras and compelled his election by refusing the nominations that the Octobrist majority offered them. Reports from Lifland province suggest that peasant electors used the same tactic there, but it was in Kovno province that peasant electors reaped the largest rewards from maintaining unity and discipline. They exercised the decisive voice in electing all of that province's deputies, and they managed to win all of the at-large deputyships for peasants.

Although it is unclear from the reports whether the Kovno peasant electors displayed complete unanimity, it is evident that a very solid bloc of at least ten to twelve revolutionary and liberal peasant electors dominated the assembly.[58] Their votes gave the opposition a one-vote majority over the conservatives and enabled it to elect its slate. With the exception of the landowners' deputy and the deputy from the city curiae, whose elections were required by law, the oppositional slate consisted exclusively of peasants, and one Kadet and two Trudovik peasant deputies were elected.[59]

The participation of the Kadet deputy in the peasant bloc is worthy of special note because, like Sinitsyn of Tula province, discussed above, this Kadet deputy had formed a *khutor* under the Stolypin land reform program. The Kadet was M. M. Ichas, and aside from his *khutor*, he had nothing in common with Sinitsyn. Ichas had remained a steadfast liberal and disciplined adherent of the peasant oppositional bloc throughout the elections, whereas Sinitsyn had first joined the opposition together with his fellow peasants, then deserted the opposition when conservative landowners nominated him for the peasant deputyship, then rejoined the opposition while the other deputies were being elected, then finally deserted it again when he joined the Rightist party after the elections. A more general difference was that Ichas was an *intelligent*—he had a law degree from Tomsk University and published extensively in cultural and religious journals—while Sinitsyn, who had only an elementary education, was a typical estate peasant client.

Finally, Ichas's involvement in the Stolypin land reform program had resulted from his popularity among his fellow peasants, who had requested his legal services when they decided *en masse* to enclose their lands, while Sinitsyn's involvement had probably resulted from the wishes of an official patron and, in any case, had not prevented his fellow peasant electors from voting heavily against him.[60] In short, the political mentalities of the Stolypin *khutoriane* differed as sharply in the two types of regions as did the political mentalities of the ordinary peasants.[61]

In summary, the peasants of the class regions could almost always act in a unified, disciplined fashion, but the peasants of the estate regions could not. This was true, moreover, despite the fact that the peasants of the class regions differed profoundly over a number of political objectives—some of them, as we have seen, were revolutionaries, and some were liberals, while the peasants of the estate regions almost all held the same position on the only political objective of significance to them, a black partitionist position on the land question. On the basis of their programmatic objectives, therefore, one might well have anticipated unity among the estate peasants and disunity among the class peasants, rather than the reverse.

This completes the list of the major differences between the political mentality of the class peasants and that of the estate peasants. Let us recapitulate them briefly. In the class regions, as we have seen, the peasants took different positions on cultural, political, social, and economic issues, and their different positions corresponded to differences in their socioeconomic positions. In the estate regions, on the other hand, the peasants took the same position on a single issue despite great differences in their socioeconomic positions. Similarly, in the class regions peasants shared the attitudes and conceptions of some nonpeasant *intelligenty,* workers, and townsmen, and they united both among themselves and with these nonpeasants in order to defend their political positions. In the estate regions, on the other hand, peasants affiliated with individual landowners and officials, their principal antagonists on the one issue in which they were profoundly interested, and otherwise failed to act with unity or political discipline.

As a first step in identifying regional variations in social and economic conditions that might have influenced the political mentalities of the peasants, the boundaries of the class and the estate regions should be delineated as precisely as possible. This well help eliminate some regional social and economic variations that might, at first glance, appear to have been significant, and it will also permit some attention to be paid to the "borderland" areas in which peasants displayed a mixture of class and estate political characteristics.

The three Baltic provinces and Kovno province of Lithuania formed a class region, as has been evident from the examples presented above. What is particularly worthy of note here is that these four provinces were the only provinces in the northwestern area of the empire in which peasants manifested a class political mentality. Other peasants with a class mentality were to be found not in the adjacent Russian, Belorussian, or even Lithuanian provinces; instead, they were to be found in Siberia.

The Siberian peasant deputies—two were Trudoviks and one was a Kadet—closely resembled the peasant deputies from the Baltic region and Kovno province. As we have seen, they shared the same relatively sophisticated conception of political parties, and the same liberal-revolutionary split appeared among them and among their constituents. In addition, they were deeply interested in civil rights and in the autonomy of local governments (in particular, they sought the introduction of zemstvos in Siberia), in cultural issues such as popular education, and in a number of economic issues in addition to the land question. Finally, they too were capable of united and disciplined political activity and of making strong alliances with certain groups of non-peasants (especially with workers and townsmen).

However, whereas the peasant deputies of Siberia displayed all the characteristics of a class political mentality, it is important to note that their peasant constituents did not. Most of the Siberian peasant electors were much less politically sophisticated than either the Siberian deputies or the peasant electors of the Baltic provinces. It will be recalled that in several of the Baltic provinces all or almost all of the peasant electors belonged to political parties, and in Estonia and Lifland they had unanimously supported the peasant candidates nominated by their parties. In Siberia, on the other hand, the majority of the peasant electors were reported to be nonparty moderates and a number were reported to be nonparty rightists; only the relatively few oppositional electors belonged to parties.[62] It was from among these oppositional electors that the competing Kadet and Trudovik candidates for the peasant deputyships emerged, and the other peasant electors apparently rallied around one or the other of these candidates during the balloting. Whether they did so "consciously" is impossible to determine, for the right wing of the political spectrum in all of the Siberian provinces was represented by the Kadets (with the exception of the rightist peasant electors themselves). Hence, had there been substantial groups of conservative landowners, it is conceivable that some of the Siberian peasant electors might have preferred to vote with them, as their counterparts from the estate regions of European Russia had done. It is clear in any case that the nonparty and the rightist peasants did display some estate characteristics, such as indifference to the elections and, in some cases, subservience to the strongest and most benevolent bloc at the provincial electoral assembly.[63]

In summary, then, the peasants of Siberia displayed a much wider range of political attitudes than did the peasants of the regions surveyed earlier. Some of them, including the peasant deputies who won election, resembled the class peasants of the Baltic and Kovno province, while others, such as the nonparty rightist electors, resembled the estate peasants of most of European Russia. In this respect, Siberia can be regarded as a "borderland" territory in which the two types of political mentalities were mixed.

A second territory with some "borderland" characteristics was Arkhangel province in the northern region. The peasant deputy there, P. A. Levanidov, struck the chief of police "as a commonplace peasant, little developed, a rightist," which is to say that he appeared to resemble the majority of Siberian peasant electors or the estate peasants of most of European Russia. Nevertheless, he joined the Kadet party after his election, and he did so in alliance with a deputy from the second city curia. There were very few landowners in Arkhangel, so Levanidov's decision might not seem significant; however, there were equally few landowners in neighboring Vologda province, but the peasant electors there proved to be as subservient to those landowners as their counterparts were in the estate regions of European Russia.[64] The boundary between the class and the estate regions, then, roughly coincided with the boundary between Arkhangel and Vologda provinces.

Finally, one of the peasant deputies from the Lithuanian province of Grodno displayed an unusually clear mixture of class and estate attitudes. He was exceptional, for his two fellow peasant deputies were typical estate peasants, and so was the deputy from the neighboring province of Vilno.[65] The attitudes of this deputy are nevertheless worthy of note, for he was the third and final *khutorianin* elected to the Fourth Duma. He was V. F. Sidoruk, a wealthy peasant who was described in part as follows: "Serving in the post of district elder during the years 1905 and 1906 he had enormous influence on the peasants, holding them back from demonstrations on the agrarian question."[66]

Even before the enactment of the Stolypin reform program, then, Sidoruk had developed a conservative position on the land question —a position that clearly distinguished him from estate peasants. Nevertheless, Sidoruk remained subservient to local landowners, following their directives during the elections and joining the landowner deputies in the Nationalist party after the elections were completed,[67] and his subservience clearly distinguished him from class peasants. He thus fell between the two types. Similarly, he occupied a position midway between the two other *khutoriane* who were elected to the Fourth Duma: like M. M. Ichas of Kovno province, Sidoruk was a conservative on land, but he shared none of Ichas's deep commitment to political liberalism; like A. M. Sinitsyn of Tula province, he was subservient to landowners but displayed none of Sinitsyn's willingness to join ranks with communal peasants over the land question.

This combination of political attitudes made Sidoruk the truly "ideal" peasant from the point of view of the architects of the Stolypin land reform program. By the same token, it made him a member of a very small minority among the Russian peasantry as a whole, and it made him a minority of one among the peasant deputies who were elected to the Fourth Duma. What is of most significance for our purposes is that the particular combination of attitudes that Sidoruk possessed could be found only in a peasant from a unique borderland region.

This completes the delineation of the boundaries between the class and the estate regions, so let us summarize them. A class political mentality was displayed by almost all the peasants of Estonia, Lifland, Kurland, and Kovno provinces, and by some of the peasants of Siberia; a mixture of class and estate mentalities was displayed by most of the peasants of Siberia and the northern part of the Northern region, and by a few peasants of the Lithuanian provinces other than Kovno; and an estate mentality was displayed by almost all the peasants of the other regions of the empire.

The regional distribution of class and estate peasants cut across several well-known regional variations in social and economic conditions, which suggests that these particular social and economic conditions had little to do with the shaping of the peasants' political mentalities. First, the regional distribution cut across ethnic and religious lines. As we have seen, some Lithuanian Catholic and Protestant peasants displayed a class mentality while others displayed an estate mentality; some Russian Orthodox peasants displayed a class mentality while others displayed an estate mentality; etc. While it is true that all the peasants who belonged to a few ethnic and religious groups, such as the Moslem Tatars of the Middle Volga region or the Orthodox Moldavians of Bessarabia, displayed only one type of political mentality, it is difficult to attribute much significance to this in view of the political diversity among the peasants of the larger ethnic and religious groups.

The regional distribution of class and estate peasants also failed to correspond with another well-known regional variation in the rural social structure, the relative strength or weakness of landowning gentry. As we have seen, the peasants of most regions of European Russia displayed an estate mentality, and the landowning gentry were predominant in these regions; however, peasants also displayed an estate mentality in Vologda province of the Northern region, where there were scarcely any landowning gentry. Among the class regions, landowning gentry were strong in Estonia, Kurland, Lifland, and Kovno, but almost totally absent in Siberia.

Similarly, the regional distribution of class and estate peasants was unrelated to the degree of urbanization in particular locales. In the two most heavily urbanized provinces, St. Petersburg and Moscow, the peasants displayed an estate mentality, with the significant but still only partial exception of those from the immediate vicinity of the city of St. Petersburg itself;[68] in Lifland, Kurland, and Estonia provinces, which were also heavily urbanized, peasants displayed a class mentality. In the majority of European Russian provinces, which had small urban populations, peasants displayed an estate mentality, but in Kovno province and Siberia, which also had very small urban populations, they displayed a class mentality or a mixture of the two types.[69]

Finally, the regional distribution of class and estate peasants corresponded very imperfectly to regional variations in the degree of peasant marketing activities. Peasant agriculturalists marketed relatively large portions of their products not only in the Baltic region, Kovno province, and Siberia, but also in New Russia, the Lower Volga region, and the north. In the other regions, they marketed relatively little. Moreover, the peasants in the commercial group of regions marketed voluntarily, so to speak, because they enjoyed relatively stable prices and favorable terms of trade, while peasants in the second group of regions were sometimes forced to market more than they wished in order to meet their annual tax and other cash obligations.[70]

In all the class regions, then, marketing activities were well developed, and that is a correlation of at least some significance. However, marketing activities were also well developed in the New Russian and the Lower Volga regions, and in both these regions the peasants manifested an estate mentality. The mere fact that peasants marketed a large share of their production, then, could not have determined whether they would display a class or an estate mentality.

However, the regional distribution of class and estate peasants did correspond to regional variations in one economic factor: the methods by which peasants farmed, that is, what may generically be called the peasants' agrarian systems. In all the class regions, peasants farmed by relatively complex, multifield rotational systems;[71] in all the estate regions, they farmed by the simpler and much older three-field system.[72] Furthermore, in borderland territories, such as Siberia or Arkhangel province, complex systems and the three-field system coexisted.

The question of the relationships between agrarian systems and the types of political mentality that peasants manifested is obviously complicated—too complicated to be fully explored here.[73] Nevertheless, some possible relationships can be outlined briefly. First, the different programmatic objectives of the estate and class peasants might have reflected their different agrarian systems. The three-field system of the estate regions produced only grain as a principal product, and only one variety of grain at that (winter rye was the principal grain in the northern and central regions, and winter or spring wheat in the southern and eastern regions). Furthermore, the tight interrelationships among the major components of the system made it impossible for the peasants to substitute new crops for their principal grain or to employ new techniques in producing it, unless they simultaneously changed all of the system's major components. As a result, peasants could attempt to increase their production in only one way, by acquiring additional land. This might have been the basis of the estate peasants' single-minded concern with a radical resolution of the land question.

The complex, multifield systems of the class regions, on the other hand, produced both crops and livestock as principal products, and they produced several varieties of each (e.g., several kinds of grains, potatoes and nitrogen-fixing food and fodder crops, as well as mutton, wool, dairy products and beef). As a result, peasants of these regions could attempt to increase their production in a variety of ways: they could substitute one crop for another or one livestock product for another; they could try a different rotational system, new implements, or new techniques; and, of course, they could try to acquire more land. This might have been the basis of the class peasants' concern with a range of economic issues in addition to the land question.

Second, the presence of a correlation between peasants' programmatic objectives and their socioeconomic status in the class regions, and the absence of such a correlation in the estate regions, might have reflected certain other aspects of their differing agrarian systems, in addition to those that were just described. In the regions with multifield systems, a peasant's capacity for increasing his production was a function of his wealth (and, of course, of the correctness of his investment decisions), for he could earn a return on a number of different investments. A wealthy peasant might therefore have had no interest in radical economic reforms or in a radical resolution of the land question, while a poor peasant might have had an interest in such measures.

In the three-field regions, on the other hand, the tight interrelationships among the major components of the system prevented a return on more than a few units of investments, except for investments in land. Furthermore, a number of social and economic mechanisms, which functioned to insure stable per capita production from year to year, vested control over the capital of individual peasants not in themselves, but in their villages or communes.[74] As a result, a peasant's capacity for increasing his production was not a function of his wealth alone; in addition, it was a function of the per capita landholdings of his village or commune. On this basis, a wealthy and a poor peasant would have shared a common interest in a radical resolution of the land question.

Finally, the different levels of political sophistication among the class and estate peasants, including their different capacities for unity and political discipline during the elections, might have reflected sociopsychological characteristics engendered by the different agrarian systems. Under the multifield systems of the class regions, peasants had to make numerous economic decisions during the course of each annual cycle, and they could make different decisions from one another or from year to year. In this sense, they governed their lives in the same fashion in which townsmen governed theirs, and they could develop the same conception of human nature that townsmen developed—the conception that the individual has the power and the authority rationally to order his life and the world around him. Possessing this conception, they could readily comprehend the legislative function of the Duma, and they could define and maintain independent political positions throughout the electoral process.

Under the three-field system, on the other hand, peasants had to do the same things during the course of each annual cycle that they had done during the previous cycle, and they had to do the same things that their fellow villagers were doing; to deviate from the past or from one's neighbors meant to incur the risk of famine. In this sense, the three-field peasants did not govern their own lives, for the rules by which they lived could not be altered by the peasants themselves. On this basis, they might have held a different conception of human nature—the conception that the power and authority to order human lives was superordinate, and that the role of the ordinary mortal was to submit. Possessing such a conception, they would not have been able readily to comprehend the legislative function of the Duma, and they would have had difficulty in defining and maintaining political positions independently of nonpeasants who seemed to be powerful and authoritative.

In conclusion, the most significant political division among the Russian peasantry in 1912 was one of region, not one of class. In the majority of regions, peasants were interested only in the land question, and they took a common radical position on it. Yet they were unable to act with unity and political discipline during the elections; instead of joining together, they followed the lead of powerful local landowners, their principal antagonists on the land question. In a few regions, on the other hand, peasants were interested in a number of issues, and the positions they took corresponded to differences in their socioeconomic status. Moreover, despite their programmatic differences, they acted with unity and discipline during the elections.

Neither of the two major existing historiographical schemata about peasant politics can account for these regional differences. Since regional variations in agrarian systems closely corresponded to these regional variations in the political mentality of the peasants, while regional variations in other social and economic conditions did not, the possible relationships between agrarian systems and political mentalities should be further explored.

NOTES

1. This article presents in condensed form some of the major conclusions of the author's doctoral dissertation, "The Russian Peasantry and the Elections to the Fourth Duma: Estate Political Consciousness and Class Political Consciousness" (doctoral diss., Columbia University, 1974). For a more detailed exposition of these conclusions and for more detailed evidence, see the dissertation.

2. Despite important differences between Soviet and emigré or Western scholars, it is interesting to observe that these conflicting historiographical conceptions reflect two scholarly generations rather than two ideological traditions. Thus, the older conception found both Soviet and emigré and

Western proponents, the most noteworthy of whom were S. M. Dubrovskii, P. N. Pershin, Geroid Tanquary Robinson, and Lazar Volin. Similarly, the new historiographical conception has also found both Soviet and Western proponents. However, the two groups tend to emphasize different factors to explain the political cohesiveness of the peasantry (since the discussion is still barely beginning, one can thus far speak only of "tendencies"). Soviet scholars tend to emphasize the continued domination of the landed gentry and their continued reliance on "feudal" or "traditional," rather than on "capitalistic" or "modern" methods of exploiting their land and the peasant labor force. Western scholars, on the other hand, tend to emphasize social and economic processes within the peasantry itself and within the peasants' agrarian system, i.e., what in Marxist terms might be called the "relation-ships of production." Major Soviet exponents of the new historiographical conception are A. M. Anfimov and A. V. Shapkarin. The only major Western exponent of the new conception to date is Teodor Shanin, but it has ap-peared in articles by Maureen Perrie and the present author.

3. E. D. Chermenskii, *Bor'ba klassov i partii v IV Gosudarstvennoi Dume (1912–1917 gg.)* (2 vols.; unpublished doctoral diss., Moscow University, 1947), vol. 1, pp. 123–24.

4. This is calculated on the basis of the number of electors allotted to each curia and the number of voters belonging to each curia. See F. I. Kalinychev, comp., *Gosudarstvennaia Duma v Rossii v dokumentakh i materialakh* (Moscow: Gosudarstvennoe izdatel'stvo iuridicheskoi literatury, 1957), p.342. For a copy of the law, see pp.357–95.

5. Most of the stipulations specifically applying to peasants were contained in Article 37 of the electoral law. For it, see ibid., p.364.

It should be noted that the exclusion of migratory laborers was not explicit; rather, it followed from the fact that no provision was made for absentee balloting.

In the few provinces in which district assemblies did not exist, the closest analogous institutions were substituted for them (see Articles 38–41 et passim in ibid., pp.364–65 et passim).

It should also be noted that peasants who earned portions of their income from nonagricultural activities were not excluded, so long as they earned at least some income from agriculture and/or landownership.

6. Obstructions of these types were usually directed at regional groups of peasants who were believed to be oppositional. Several examples are presented in Chermenskii, *Bor'ba klassov i partii*, vol. 1, pp.108–10.

7. Tsentral'nyi Gosudarstvennyi Arkhiv Oktiabr'skoi Revoliutsii (hereafter TsGAOR), f. 102, 1912 g., op. 104, d. 130, ch. 13, 1. 120b. A report from the governor of Vladimir province explicitly credited the land captains, the marshals of nobility "and partly . . . the police officials" with having successfully counteracted the leftist influence of the workers on the peasants in all counties except two. Tsentral'nyi Gosudarstvennyi Istoricheskii Arkhiv (hereafter TsGIA), f. 1327, 1912 g., op. 1/1430, d. 33, ch. 1, 11. 55–56.

8. In the forty-eight European Russian provinces in which landowner and peasant electors can be directly compared, landowner electors numbered 2,515 and peasant electors numbered 1,078. For the apportionment of each

of the electoral assemblies among electors from the various curiae, see the Appendix to Article 8 of the electoral law in Kalinychev, *Gosudarstvennaia duma,* pp.393–95 (it should be noted that the Don region was excluded in calculating the totals given above because the number of landowner electors in that region was omitted because of a misprint). Only in the northern and Siberian provinces, where gentry landowners were very few, did the apportionment of the assemblies leave the election of the peasant deputy largely in the hands of electors who belonged to the peasant estate (some of these were electors from the peasants' curia and some were electors from the landowners' curia).

9. See Articles 2 and 123 of the electoral law and the "List of Numbers of Members of the State Duma" appended to Article 5 in ibid., pp.357, 377–78, 389–92.

10. See Article 127 of the electoral law in ibid., p.379.

11. See Articles 124 and 126 of the electoral law in ibid., p.378.

12. Serious research about the peasant revolt movement during this period has been carried out by proponents of the two conflicting historiographical schemata discussed above. Researchers belonging to both groups agree that 1912 (as opposed to 1910 and 1911) was a tranquil year. For a summary of the views of researchers belonging to the older group, see Dubrovskii, *Stolypinskaia zemel'naia reforma,* pp.530–33 et passim. Dubrovskii here argues that there was an upsurge of disturbances resulting from the Stolypin reform program in 1911, but his data show them to have been dying away thereafter. For a summary of the views of researchers belonging to the younger group, see Shapkarin, ed., *Krest'ianskoe dvizhenie,* pp.21–23. Shapkarin attributes only minimal significance to the Stolypin reform program in accounting for peasant disturbances. His most complete data (pp.492–623) do show an increase in disturbances in 1911 and, to a lesser extent, 1912, but not a very significant one. Moreover, his data are generally unreliable (as, for that matter, were Dubrovskii's): from a check of his data against the archival sources, it is evident that his compilers omitted as many disturbances as they included (the check covered four provinces for 1912; for it, see Vinogradoff, *Peasantry and Elections,* pp.14–16).

For rumors in 1912 of the repartition of nonpeasant lands, see Dubrovskii, op. cit., p.531.

For information about the crop failure and famine of 1911, which was most severe in Western Siberia, see ibid. and Arcadius Kahan, "Natural Calamities and Their Effect upon the Food Supply in Russia (An Introduction to a Catalogue)," in *Jahrbücher für Geschichte Osteuropas,* Sept. 1968, p.375. For a report about the effects of the famine in Tobolsk province, which were still quite notable in June of 1912, see a letter from the governor in TsGAOR, f. 102, 1912 g., op. 104, d. 130, ch. 76, 1. 30b.

13. The sources for this article consist almost entirely of police and governors' reports about the behavior of the peasants during the elections and about the characteristics of the peasants who were elected at the various stages of the electoral process (the three-stage electoral process will be outlined below). Contemporary newspapers, the only other major sources of information about the elections, reported very little about the peasantry (they

confined themselves largely to landowners, townsmen and workers); more-over, when they did occasionally mention the peasants, they were often un-reliable and sometimes even purposefully misleading in order to stir opposi-tional sentiments among peasant electors while purporting to report their actual behavior.

The reports explicitly describe peasants as indifferent to the Duma in forty-seven provinces as the date of the elections approached. Reports from eleven provinces fail to state that peasants were indifferent, but they also fail to indicate that peasants were displaying any interest in the elections. Only in Iur'ev county of Lifland province, where Estonian *intelligenty* and peasants began organizing jointly for the elections during the summer, was there any sign of a genuine electoral campaign by and among peasants. The immediate reasons for their interest were the emergence of two competing peasant candidates and the desire of Estonians to nominate Estonian candi-dates (in the Third Duma elections, Latvians had played the dominant role). See TSGAOR, f. 102, 1912 g., op. 104, d. 130, ch. 37, 11. 7–12.

14. Petr Maslov, *Agrarnyi vopros v Rossi* (vol. 2; St. Petersburg: "Ob-shchestvennaia pol'za," 1908), p.266. Maslov notes that the connection be-tween the date of the "Joy" and the date of the convening of the Duma was first pointed out in *Russkie vedomosti*.

For a discussion of the peasantry's "naïve monarchism" in general and their more programmatic desires from the tsar in particular, see Daniel Field, *Rebels in the Name of the Tsar* (Boston: Houghton Mifflin Company, 1976), pp.1–29.

15. Under the electoral law of August 6, 1905, which governed the elec-tions to the First and Second Dumas, peasants could elect 2375 electors to the provincial electoral assemblies of fifty provinces of European Russia, and landowners could elect 1945 electors. Under the electoral law of June 3, 1907, peasants could elect only 1078 electors, while landowners could elect 2515 (see Kalinychev, *Gosudarstvennaia duma*, pp. 50–52, 393–95. It should be noted that Arkhangel province was excluded in calculating the numbers of peasant and landowner electors under the 1905 law because the land-owners' curia was combined with the city curia in that province, and that Arkhangel, Stavropol, Tobolsk and Tomsk provinces were excluded in calcu-lating the numbers of peasant and landowner electors under the 1907 law for the same reason; in addition, the Don region was excluded from the calcu-lations under the 1907 law because the number of landowner electors to which the region was entitled was omitted because of a typographical error).

By giving landowner electors control of most of the provincial electoral assemblies, the 1907 law allowed them to elect landowners rather than pea-sants to the "at-large" deputyships and thus to produce the decline in the number of peasant deputies that was noted. In both the First and the Fourth Dumas, for example, there were 53 or 54 curial peasant deputies (the num-ber varies depending upon how one counts a peasant deputy from the Amur region, in which the peasants' curia and the city curia were combined); how-ever, there were 145 or 146 "at-large" peasant deputies in the First Duma and only 20 or 21 in the Fourth Duma.

For information about deputies of the First Duma, see Gosudarstvennaia duma, *Ukazatel' k stenograficheskim otchetam. 1906 god. Sessiia pervaia. Zasedaniia 1–38 (27 aprelia–4 iiulia 1907 g.)* (St. Petersburg: Gosudarstvennaia tipografiia, 1907), pp. 3–17, and Knigoizdatel'stvo "Vozrozhdenie," *Gosudarstvennaia Duma pervago prizyva: Portrety, kratkiia biografii i kharakteristiki deputatov* (Moscow: 1906), pp.5–110; for information about the peasant deputies of the Fourth Duma, see Vinogradoff, *Peasantry and Elections,* pp.196–315.

16. TsGAOR, f. 102, 1907 g., oo, d. 615, 1. 91. The question was put to the peasants by a police interviewer as part of a questionnaire on peasant attitudes towards the Duma. (In addition to Tver province, the questionnaire was circulated in Orel, Bessarabia and the Nikolaev region.) The questionnaire originated in the Petersburg Committee of the Russian Social Democratic Labor Party, which intended that it be circulated by local S-D committees. No local S-D committees appear to have received it, however, and, through a series of bureaucratic misunderstandings, police in the above-named regions circulated it by mistake and reported the responses to their superiors. For a summary of the questionnaire and responses, which constitute the only direct evidence of rank-and-file peasants' attitudes towards the Duma between 1907 and 1912, see Vinogradoff, *Peasantry and Elections,* pp.48–63.

17. The parties are listed from right to left. As noted earlier, the "class" regions include the three Baltic provinces, Kovno province, and those Siberian provinces with a significant number of agricultural peasants (specifically, the Amur region and Eniseisk, Irkutsk, Tobolsk and Tomsk provinces); "estate" regions include all other European Russian provinces. Polish, Caucasian, and steppe electoral districts have been omitted.

The information used in compiling the table is from Gosudarstvennaia duma, *Ukazatel' k stenograficheskim otchetam (Chasti I–III). Chetvertyi sozyv. Sessiia I. 1912–1913 gg. Zasedaniia 1–81 (15 noiabria 1912 g.–25 iiunia 1913 g.)* (St. Petersburg: Gosudarstvennaia tipografiia, 1913) (hereafter *Ukazatel' . . . Chetvertyi sozyv, sessiia 1-aia*), pp.9–24. See also Vinogradoff, *Peasantry and Elections,* pp.348, 359–72.

18. TsGIA, f. 1327, 1912 g., op. 1/1430, d. 33, ch. 3, l. 177.

19. The public career that the governor was here summarizing included the following particulars: elector to the Third Duma in 1907; chairman of district court (1908–12); secretary of the local agricultural society and board member of another agricultural society; board member of a credit association; and board member of a dairy cooperative. See Vinogradoff, op. cit., p.266.

20. *Ukazatel' . . . Chetvertyi sozyv, sessiia 1-aia,* p.162, and Izdanie N. N. Ol'shanskogo, *4-i sozyv Gosudarstvennoi Dumy. Khudozhestvennyi fototipicheskii al'bom s portretami i biografiiami* (St. Petersburg, 1913) (hereafter *Chetvertyi sozyv . . . al'bom*), k tablitse 37; see also Vinogradoff, op. cit.

21. In fact, the unity of the Estonian peasant electors was even more noteworthy, for a large Octobrist majority at the Provincial Electoral Assembly actively tried to prevent the election of Oras by convincing one of the other peasant electors to accept a nomination. As a result, Oras was elected only on the second ballot, and then only by the relative majority of sixteen in favor

and twenty-five opposed. For the majority, see TsGIA, f. 1327, 1912 g., op. 1/1430, d. 35, ch. 2, 1. 109; for reports on the Octobrist leaders O. R. Brashe and K. Iu. von Brevern, who easily won the other two deputyships from the province, see *Ukazatel'* . . . *Chetvertyi sozyv, sessiia 1-aia*, pp.18, 21–23, 73.

22. A joint peasant-urban nominating assembly seems to be what the governor meant by "a pre-electoral assembly organized by electors [belonging to] the Estonian Progressive group," for the Estonian Progressists were strong among townsmen (e.g., in addition to the four peasant electors, they also had twelve electors from other curiae, as Oras's majority indicated). For additional information about the Estonian Progressists, see TsGAOR, f. 102, 1912 g., op. 104, d. 130, ch. 88, 1. 6. It is also noteworthy that Estonian peasants and townsmen had united politically in Lifland province, where they conducted a joint primary; see TsGAOR, loc. cit., ch. 37, ll. 70b-12.

23. TsGIA, f. 1327, 1912 g., op. 1/1430, d. 33, ch. 3, ll. 116–117 ob; see also Vinogradoff, op. cit., pp.296–97.

24. The two Progressist landowner deputies were N. V. Katanskii and A. P. Mel'gunov. For reports on them, see *Ukazatel'* . . . *Chetvertyi sozyv, sessiia 1-aia*, pp.17, 23, 116, 146, and *Chetvertyi sozyv* . . . *al'bom*, k tablitse 33.

25. See TsGIA, f. 1327, 1912 g., op. 1/1430, d. 35, ch. 2, 1. 155 for the governor's report. For additional reports on Baiteriakov, see *Ukazatel'* . . . *Chetvertyi sozyv, sessiia 1-aia*, p. 66, and *Chetvertyi sozyv* . . . *al'bom*, k tablitse 33; see also Vinogradoff, op. cit., pp.200–201. For reports on Tevkelev, see *Ukazatel'* . . . *Chetvertyi sozyv, sessiia 1-aia*, p.198, and *Chetvertyi sozyv* . . . *al'bom*, k tablitse 33.

26. The other Moslem peasant electors did play a significant role in Baiteriakov's election: none of them were willing to accept a nomination, which left Baiteriakov as the only candidate. However, this did not signify their support of Baiteriakov, whose election was already assured by an agreement between Tevkelev and other Moslem leaders, on the one hand, and Koropachinskii and other liberal leaders, on the other; rather, it signified only their complete indifference to the Duma. On this basis, the governor reported that Baiteriakov had been "elected to the Duma accidentally"; for his report, see TsGIA, loc. cit.

27. TsGIA, loc. cit., ch. 3, 1. 147; see also Vinogradoff, op. cit., pp.92 and 251.

28. Of the nine deputies elected from Kherson, one (Mazurenko) was a peasant, one was a German colonist, and seven were noblemen (some from the landowners' and some from the city curiae). Mazurenko, together with three of the noblemen and the German colonist, joined the Octobrist party; three noblemen joined the Centrist party; and one nobleman joined the Rightist party.

29. The conservative victory was overwhelming among the peasant electors as well as among the peasant deputies: forty of the total of forty-two electors were rightists or nonparty conservatives. For a report on the electors, see TsGAOR, f. 102, 1912 g., op. 104, d. 130, ch. 13, ll. 17–240b.

30. Cited in Chermenskii, *Bor'ba Klassov i partii*, vol. 1, p.123.

31. This is evident in part from the fact that the Volynian peasant electors and deputies had shown themselves undisposed to defend wealth in general,

let alone a conservative position on land in particular. This they did, in part, when they defeated the popular Third Duma peasant deputy G. A. Andreichuk only because "they openly recognized that [he] had gotten rather wealthy" (TsGAOR, loc. cit., l. 14); see also Vinogradoff, op. cit., pp. 85–86.

32. Even the more general political labels attached to the peasant electors in estate regions indicated nothing of significance about their views. A high official summarized the results of the second stage as follows: " . . . almost all peasants, especially those holding official posts, are categorized as 'rightists.' Whether they will all turn out to be rightists at the provincial electoral assemblies as well, that is, whether or not they will cast their votes for the left, is difficult to say in advance." See TsGIA, f. 1276, op. 1, ed. 35, ll. 23–30 (this contains a confidential report on the Fourth Duma elections prepared for the Ministry of the Interior, attributed to I. Ia. Gurliand), cited in Gibert Doctorow, "The Government and the Fourth Duma" (unpublished article).

33. The most significant exception was V. M. Tiatinin, a Rightist party peasant deputy from Nizhnii Novgorod province who was "completely reliable even on the land question" (the quote is from the governor and is cited by Chermenskii in *Bor'ba klassov i partii*, vol. 1, pp.116–117). Tiatinin, however, was an innkeeper with no reported landholdings or agricultural income (see Vinogradoff, op. cit., pp.303–304). He was thus not representative of agricultural peasants, and his election probably violated the provisions of the electoral law cited about (see pp.221–22).

In addition to Tiatinin, P. M. Makagon, an Octobrist peasant deputy from Ekaterinoslavl province, was reported to oppose "the peasants' being allotted state and crown lands without compensation," but what is most significant about this quotation is the omission of gentry lands from it (the quotation is from the governor; for it, see TsGIA, f. 1327, 1912 g., op. 1/1430, d. 33, ch. 1, l. 182; see also Vinogradoff, op. cit., p.247).

Finally, V. F. Sidoruk, a Nationalist peasant deputy from Grodno province, was reported to be a conservative on the land question, but he was a very unusual type of peasant, as will be explained below.

34. Although direct descriptions of client-patron relationships were not numerous, the holding of an administrative or zemstvo post by peasants can be taken as a rough indicator of their client status. All except one of the peasant deputies from the estate regions had held an administrative or zemstvo post prior to his election, and more than 50 percent of the peasant electors were reported to hold such posts (and it is clear that there was some under-reporting of posts held by electors). See Vinogradoff, op. cit., pp.150–53, 350, 373–402.

35. For tables illustrating the alignment of peasant deputies with the largest, or at least with a large group of landowner deputies, see Vinogradoff, op. cit., pp. 352–56.

36. The report was from the ataman (the equivalent of a provincial governor). See TsGIA, f. 1327, 1912 g., op. 1/1430, d. 33, ch. 1, l. 219.

37. For a summary of the reports about Afanas'ev, see Vinogradoff, op. cit., pp.197–98.

38. All the peasant deputies elected to the Duma from these regions

listed their religion as Orthodox and their nationality as Russian on the forms used in compiling the *Ukazatel'* . . . *Chetvertyi sozyv, sessiia 1-aia;* see pp.57–224.

39. In Volynia, as we have seen, the landowners' party was the Rightist party. In all other provinces except Smolensk, it was the Nationalist party, and in Smolensk it was the Octobrist party.

40. In Volynia province, for example, the police reported even before the first stage of the elections that "alien ethnics [*inorodtsy*], German colonists and Czechs, will not be elected representatives at the district assemblies because of the native mass's antagonism towards them and because of their desire to reserve for themselves the salaries of the deputies, which enrich the peasants." See TsGAOR, f. 102, 1912 g., op. 104, d. 130, ch. 13, l. 120b.

41. Ten of the twenty at-large peasant deputies who were elected to the Fourth Duma came from the Right-Bank Ukraine and White Russia. See *Ukazatel'* . . . *Chetvertyi sozyv, sessiia 1-aia,* pp.57–224, and Vinogradoff, op. cit., pp.197–315.

42. For the governor's account of the provincial electoral assembly, where Krym's "agitational talents" were employed, see TsGIA, f. 1327, 1912 g., op. 1/1430, d. 33, ch. 3, l. 24.

43. For a table correlating socioeconomic status and party membership, see Vinogradoff, op. cit., pp.358–72 (also the source of the present table).

The principal criterion used for distinguishing between the different socioeconomic categories of peasant deputies was the amount of land held. Allowance for regional variations in both the norms held and the productivity and market accessibility of land was made by comparing a deputy's holding only to the holdings of other peasants within the same province, as follows: a "poor" peasant was considered to be one who held less than half the average amount of land per peasant household in his province; a "middle" peasant was one who held from one-half to twice the average amount of land per household; and a "rich" peasant was one who held more than twice the average amount.

When additional information about a deputy's socioeconomic status indicated that he had substantial nonland holdings or that he derived a substantial portion of his income from nonagricultural activities, it was used to supplement the information about his landholdings and occasionally to change the category into which he would fall on the basis of landholdings alone.

On the basis of these criteria, the socioeconomic status of two deputies was so far above the norm for "rich" peasants that a fourth category, "extremely rich," was added.

The information about landholdings, other holdings, and nonagricultural incomes of the deputies was taken from Vinogradoff, op. cit., pp.196–315. Data on the number of peasant households and amounts of allotment and privately owned land per province were taken from Dubrovskii, *Stolypinskaia zemel'naia reforma,* pp.570–73, and from Oganovskii, *Sel'skoe khoziaistvo Rossii,* pp.20–21, 54–58 (the data in the former were derived from the 1905 agrarian census and in the latter from the 1905 and 1916 agrarian censuses).

44. In addition to varying with respect to socioeconomic status, the pea-

sants varied with respect to what might be called their "political experience." In particular, some peasants had held posts in the administration, some had held posts in the zemstvo, and a very few had held no posts in either institution; further, within the administrative and zemstvo groups, some had held high posts and some had held minor posts. None of these distinctions, however, was related to the peasants' party affiliations; for a table illustrating this, see Vinogradoff, op. cit., pp.373–402.

Finally, these peasants did not vary significantly with respect to level of education, except that some had had no formal education while others had had elementary educations. Again, this distinction was not related to their party affiliations (see ibid., pp.196–315).

45. Most of this information about Ryslev is from the governor's report on his election; for it, see TsGIA, f. 1327, 1912 g., op. 1/1430, d. 33, ch. 3, ll. 241–42. For his mistaken listing as a Social-Democrat in the Duma, see *Ukazatel'* . . . *Chetvertyi sozyv, sessiia 1-aia*, p.182. For these and other reports, see Vinogradoff, op. cit., pp.282–83.

46. For available reports about these nine deputies, see Vinogradoff, op. cit, pp.212–13 (for A. A. Durov of Tomsk); 220–21 (for Ia. I. Gol'dman of Kurland); 224–25 (for N. O. Ianushkevich of Kovno); 226–27 (for M. M. Ichas of Kovno); 235–36 (for F. O. Keinis of Kovno); 266–67 (for Iu. M. Oras of Estonia); 277–78 (for I. M. Ramot of Lifland); 280–81 (for M. S. Rysev of Tobol'sk); and 282–83 (for A. I. Ryslev of the Amur region).

47. TsGIA, f. 1327, 1912 g., op. 1/1430, d. 33, ch. 1, ll. 560b–57.

48. The victor in this free-for-all was P. V. Tarutin, who was elected after repeated balloting by the relative majority of 40 to 48. See TsGIA, loc. cit.; for Tarutin's majority, see TsGIA, loc. cit., d. 35, ch. 1, l. 38.

49. TsGIA, loc. cit., d. 33, ch. 1, ll. 57–570b.

50. Ibid.

51. Ibid., ll. 570b–58.

52. The peasants' view of the deputyships as sources of only personal advantages was manifested in many provinces and sometimes had ludicrous consequences. During the early stages of the elections, for example, no peasants at all would come forward in some districts as candidates for representatives, but all representatives elected then would "campaign" for elector with the hope of eventually winning the deputy's salary. As a result, each representative would sometimes receive one vote, his own, and none could be elected electors. For an example, see TsGAOR, f. 102, 1912 g., op. 104, d. 130, ch. 62 (Saratov province), l. 22; for other examples of peasants' views of deputyships purely as sources of income, see ibid., ch. 4, l. 10b; ch. 7, l. 3; and op. 121, d. 274, ll. 75–77. This attitude led to the defeat during the early stages of the electoral process of most of the peasant deputies in the Third Duma. Commenting upon their defeats, a high official reported to the Ministry of the Interior that "they were not re-elected as a matter of principle. They [i.e., the peasant electorate] say: 'he's had his fill [*pokormilsia i dovol'no*].'" See TsGIA, f. 1276, op. 1, ed. 35, ll. 23–30, cited in Doctorow, "The Government and the Fourth Duma."

53. TsGAOR f. 102, 1912 g., op. 121, d. 274, ll. 68–680b.

54. For the estate and party memberships of the deputies elected from Tula, see Vinogradoff, op. cit., p.355; see also pp.106 and 291–92.

55. As noted in the quotation above, the rightist bloc controlled forty-four votes. Sinitsyn was elected on the first ballot by a majority of forty-seven to thirty-seven, which indicates that three oppositionists probably supported him and one did not vote (there were eighty-five electors present, according to the police chief). For Sinitsyn's majority, see TsGIA, f. 1327, 1912 g., op. 1/1430, d. 35, ch. 2, l. 150.

56. Ukazatel' . . . Chetvertyi sozyv, sessiia 1-aia, p.189.

57. TsGIA, loc. cit., d. 33, ch. 3, ll. 108–108ob.

58. Twenty-two peasant electors were elected. They ranged from a non-party rightist to a Social Democrat, and the largest groups consisted of ten nonparty peasants, six or seven revolutionary "leftists" and three or four liberals (the ambiguity in the latter two numbers stems from the fact that F. O. Keinis, a Trudovik deputy in the Third and Fourth Dumas, was reported to be a Lithuanian Nationalist [and was thus grouped with liberals] after his election as an elector.)

None of the reports indicate whether the nonparty electors and the rightists united with the liberal-revolutionary bloc, but it seems likely that they did because all the peasant electors were said to be "sympathetic" to Lithuanian Nationalism. For the report on the electors, see TsGIA, f. 1327, 1912 g., op. 1, d. 26, ll. 2–18; for a summary of this and other reports, see Vinogradoff, op. cit., pp.137–42, 224–27, 235–36, 344.

59. In addition to the peasants, a member of the Belorussian-Lithuanian-Polish group was elected the landowners' deputy and a Kadet was elected the deputy from the city curiae. The peasants were N. O. Ianushkevich, M. M. Ichas, and F. O. Keinis; for reports on them, see Vinogradoff, op. cit., pp.224–27 and 235–36.

60. TsGIA, f. 1327, 1912 g., op. 1/1430, d. 33, ch. 1, ll. 166ob–167; see also Vinogradoff, op. cit., pp.226–27 and 291–92.

61. It has long been known that the peasants of different regions responded very differently to the Stolypin land reform program. The enclosure movement in particular was received much more favorably by the peasants of the Baltic littoral and Kovno province, where it facilitated their production for the market, than by the peasants of the Central Black-Soil region, where market production was less well developed than in any other region of the empire. See P. N. Pershin, Uchastkovoe zemelepol'zovanie v Rossii. Khutora i otruba, ikh rasprostranenie za desiatiletie 1907–1916 gg. i sud'by vo vremia revoliutsii (1917–1920 gg.) (Moscow: "Novaia derevnia," 1922), pp.8–9.

62. For the most complete report on Siberian peasant electors, which illustrates this point, see TsGAOR, f. 102, 1912 g., op. 104, d. 130, ch. 20, ll. 6–60ob. For additional information, including these electors' behavior during the balloting at the Provincial Electoral Assembly, see Vinogradoff, op. cit., pp.124–26.

63. Prior to the first stage of the elections, peasants were reported to be indifferent toward the elections and the Duma in all Siberian provinces from which reports were forthcoming, and the rightist and nonparty electors shared this attitude. During the balloting at electoral assemblies, even nonpeasant Trudovik candidates sometimes approached the peasant electors much as landowners in European Russia did, relying very heavily on personal

appeals (e.g., one met with success by dressing "simply and even sloppily" in order to appear more sympathetic to the peasant electors; see TsGIA, f. 1327, 1912 g., op. 1/1430, d. 33, ch. 3, ll. 252–53) and on attestations of good character from other nonpeasants.

64. For the police chief's report, see TsGAOR, f. 102, 1912 g., op. 104, d. 130, ch. 1, l. 8. For the principal report on the electors of Vologda, see ibid., ch. 12, ll. 9–12. For a summary of reports on Levanidov, see Vinogradoff, op. cit., p.246.

65. The other two Grodno peasant deputies were the Nationalists P. D. Pesliak and T. Ia. Tarasevich; for summaries of reports about them, see Vinogradoff, op. cit., pp.272–73, 298. For information about the Vilno deputy M. E. Tsiunelis, see in addition TsGIA, loc. cit., ch. 1, ll. 300b–31.

66. TsGIA, f. 1327, 1912 g., op. 1/1430, d. 33, ch. 1, ll. 73–730b; see also Vinogradoff, op. cit., pp. 189–90.

67. Vinogradoff, op. cit.

68. For the report on the St. Petersburg representatives and electors, see TsGAOR, f. 102, 1912 g., op. 104, d. 130, ch. 61, lit. B, ll. 2–4 and 10–15; for reports on I. T. Evseev, the peasant deputy from the province who displayed all the characteristics of estate peasants, see Vinogradoff, op. cit., p.215.

69. In 1914, the population of St. Petersburg province was 73.9 percent urban; of Moscow—52.9 percent; of Lifland—39.1 percent; of Kurland—27.0 percent; of Estonia—22.1 percent; and of Kovno—10.5 percent. For these and similar figures for other provinces, see A. G. Rashin, *Naselenie Rossii za sto let (1811–1913 gg.). Statisticheskii ocherk* (Moscow: Gosudarstvennoe statisticheskoe izdatel'stvo, 1956), p. 101.

70. For the most recent general survey of regional variations in peasant marketing activities, see P. N. Pershin, *Agrarnaia revoliutsiia v Rossii*, vol. 1, pp.63–79. The Witte system in particular tended to force the peasants of the central regions of European Russia onto the market while giving the peasants of the peripheral regions more favorable terms of trade.

71. For information on the multifield systems of the Baltic region and Kovno province, see Michael Confino, *Systemes Agraires et Progres Agricole. L'assolement triennal en Russie aux XVIIIe–XIXe siecles. Etude d'economie et de sociologie rurales* (Paris, The Hague: Mouton & Co., 1969), pp.216–18 (Confino here summarizes the researches of H. Strods and N. N. Ulashchik), and A. S. Ermolov, *Organizatsiia polevogo khoziaistva. Sistemy zemledeliia i sevooboroty* (2d rev. ed.; St. Petersburg: Izd. A. F. Devriena, 1891), pp. 25–26. See also Vinogradoff, op. cit., pp.189–91.

72. Confino, op. cit., pp.26–55. For a different analysis of the three-field system, see Eugene D. Vinogradoff, "The 'Invisible Hand' and the Russian Peasant," in *Peasant Studies Newsletter*, vol. 4, no. 3, July 1975, pp.6–19; see also the commentaries of M. P. Moore and Teodor Shanin and Vinogradoff's reply in ibid., vol. 5, no. 2, April 1976, pp.18–25. The specific information about the three-field system presented below is taken from this article.

73. For the present author's thoughts about the possible relationships between the three-field system and the estate mentality of the peasants of most of European Russia, see Eugene D. Vinogradoff, "The Political Con-

sciousness of the Peasantry of Central Russia during the Early Twentieth Century," in *Russian History* (forthcoming).

74. The powers of villages over their constituent households (including the *de jure* powers of communes in Great Russia) constituted these insurance mechanisms, in the opinion of the present author, and so did a number of traditional social practices, such as the partitioning of wealthy households. For an exposition of this view, see Vinogradoff, "Household and Systemic Insurance Mechanisms among the Peasants of Central Russia, 1861–1929," presented to the First Annual Conference of the Social Science History Association, 1976.

Partitions of wealthy households and mergers of poor households produced cyclical socioeconomic mobility patterns among three-field peasants, according to the recent work of Teodor Shanin (*The Awkward Class: Political Sociology of Peasantry in a Developing Country: Russia, 1910–1925* [Oxford: Clarendon Press, 1972]). Such mobility patterns would obviously have tended to prevent the emergence of different programmatic objectives among wealthy and poor peasants.

Conclusion: Observations on the Politics of the Russian Countryside (1905-14)

LEOPOLD H. HAIMSON

I have repeatedly referred in the introduction to this volume to the dual, Janus-like character of the sense of identity that the Russian landowning nobility drew from its historical origins and brought into the twentieth century. The first dimension of this self-image—and of the realities on which it rested—was the often suppressed but never wholly extinguished sense of being a particularistic group in the body politic, which this nobility maintained even as Russia painfully and slowly evolved from a society of *sosloviia* into a society of classes: particularistic in the specificity of its political, social, and economic interests, and in the contradiction between these interests and those of other groups in society; particularistic too—especially in the setting of the countryside—in the relatively hermetic character of its culture, its values, its style of life. The other dimension of this self-image was a broader and even more deep-seated identification with the state power; the sense of being first and foremost a service class, whose *raison d'être* rested in its service in peace, and especially in war, to a state that was itself viewed as a superordinate authority—arching over Russia's deeply divided society—the only spokesman for general, as against particular, interests.

It was by virtue of this sense of identification with the state, and the realities of service on which it rested, even after the emancipation of the nobility in 1762 from compulsory service; it was also by virtue of the special qualities of honor, self-discipline, and self-sacrifice, which this service ostensibly entailed, that the Russian landowning nobility had traditionally justified its special privileges, and especially its claim to rule—in the name of the Tsar, of the State, and of the Fatherland. This identification with the state and with its sovereign had provided an essential element of the landowning nobility's sense of self-worth and self-justification—of its "ideology"—one that it almost invariably had brought, in reflex fashion, to the fore, whenever in the history of post-Petrine Russia its superior and privileged position had been challenged by other groups in society, or even by the Autocrat himself.

This had been the central element not only in the Russian nobility's rhetoric but also in its own sense of moral justification, and therefore in its psychological capacity to resist the attempted encroachments on its privileges by representatives of other estates in the Commission of 1767; the banner around which its spokesmen had rallied against the half-hearted attempts by Alexander I and some of his officials to reform, if not eliminate, the institution of serfdom; the mechanism of defense mobilized by the most obdurate of its spokesmen in the final and decisive debates over Emancipation.

This dual sense of identity of the Russian landowning nobility was never fully eradicated. However, by the beginning of the twentieth century, its constituent elements—its chemistry—had been substantially modified, if not transformed. Reference was already made in the introduction to this volume, and especially in Roberta Manning's essay, to some of the catalytic factors in this significant, if subtle, transformation. On one hand, there was the increasingly important factor of the growth and transformation of the bureaucratic state and of its increasing encroachments on the position of the landowning nobility, as the state regularized its procedures, sought to impose them on the noble or noble-dominated organs of local self-government, and followed economic policies seemingly inimical to the interests of the landowning nobility. By the end of the nineteenth century, as we have seen, this sense of encroachment was all the more deeply felt because the state pursued and implemented these policies through a bureaucracy, which even in its higher reaches was increasingly recruited from members of other estates, or men who, even though they held noble titles, demonstrated in their day-to-day behavior a growing difference of interests, outlook, and life style from those of the provincial landowning nobility. The other major element in this dynamic was the return, under the pressure of economic necessity, of much of the Russian provincial nobility to the land in the 1880s and nineties, at least in the most agricultural regions of the empire (the Central Agricultural Region, the Volga, the Ukraine).

In studying the growing rift between the landowning nobility and the central bureaucracy, which eventuated as a result of these two factors, we should not lay excessive stress on the processes of economic modernization of noble-run agriculture and on their effects on the social and political psychology of the Russian landowning nobility, even if we are prepared to recognize that those who were involved in such processes of economic modernization played a role disproportionate to their numbers in the politics of the landowning nobility, especially after 1905. The essential factor, I believe, was the return to the land per se, for both the few who actually engaged in such a modernization of their estates (let alone were successful in such efforts), and the many who did not. By virtue of their new or renewed engagement in the administration of their estates, of their concomitant absorption or reabsorption in the affairs of their local corporate organizations and organs of local self-government; by virtue of the new or renewed ties that they forged with one another in these local institutions, and in their social contacts on their estates as well as in the salons, the clubs, and the boulevards of their county towns and provincial capitals, these noble landowners established, really for the first time in modern Russian history, a truly provincial society. A relatively closed society, to be sure, but one that, by the same token, was all the more harmonious, integral, and capable of upholding and defending interests and values that it now considered more genuinely its own.

Thus it was, precisely as these new values and style of life crystallized and came into conflict with the growing bureaucratic state and its faceless officials, that the members of this new provincial society also came to feel, in their confrontation of this increasingly impersonal state power, the sense of "we" and "they" that already animated other elements in society—most importantly, of course, the Russian intelligentsia. The psychological change, to be sure, was one of degree—such responses having occasionally been evoked in earlier periods of Russian history—but, however relatively so, it made for a political phenomenon that was novel, at least in its scope and depth, and that was duly exploited after the turn of the century by the leadership of the Liberation Movement, and especially its noble elements.

In accounting for the ultimate fragility of the Liberation Movement, we must, to be sure, recognize that the leaders of this movement, who, so successfully at first, exacerbated and manipulated the disaffection of the landowning nobility—gave it political shape, as well as eventual organization—were, in significant respects, men of a different stamp than their would-be constituents in this provincial noble society. It is true that many of them were themselves noble landowners, indeed originating for the most part from landowning families that were wealthier, as well as socially more prominent and distinguished, than their followers. But the outlook and the adult values of these leaders of the Liberation Movement had been shaped, at least in part, in a quite different environment: that of the universities, the cities, and even more precisely, of the cosmopolitan culture—both Russian and European—in which they travelled so freely and were now so fully absorbed.

In fact, if not in theory, these men were members of the intelligentsia—of an intelligentsia that, as Marc Raeff has reminded us,[1] had itself drawn many of its psychological and social features from its nobiliar origins, but that in the course of its nineteenth-century travails had also substantially transformed them. Of course, even as Russia entered the twentieth century, some of the most militant and liberal, if not radical, spokesmen of this noble intelligentsia—the Dolgorukovs and the Shakhovskois, if not the Petrunkeviches and the Potresovs—continued to draw, however subtly, part of their sense of mission from their nobiliar origins: their desire to serve the people, or more precisely by this time, the nation, if not the state; their implicit claim to lead, if not to rule it; their sense of their own political importance, as well as their willingness to sacrifice. But in the social and psychological melting pot of intelligentsia life, this sense of mission had by now been translated by this noble intelligentsia into an image of themselves as members of a group, which in its own psychological as well as social makeup had effectively bridged the divisions among Russian social classes and estates, and which, precisely by virtue of its unique noncaste and nonclass social characteristics, as well as its equally special, if universalistic, political and moral values, was now entitled to shape and mobilize the new nation it now saw in the making against an obscurantist state.

Still, notwithstanding these psychological as well as social differences between leaders and led, and the admittedly manipulative character of the activities of the Liberation Movement, we should recognize the genuineness of the echoes that the appeals of its intelligentsia leadership were able to evoke by 1905 among the rank and file of the Russian provincial landowning nobility and take due note of the psychological and social sources of this response.

First and foremost, the collective self-affirmation against the state power that the leaders of the Liberation Movement sought to rouse among the landowning nobility found a genuine reflection in the sense of collective autonomy that these nobles had gradually developed, as we have seen, as their own provincial society had coalesced and crystallized. It also found a political base and a locus of political expression in their now vitalized corporate organizations and local organs of self-government. These new social bonds, and the sense of solidarity and rootedness that they fostered, thus provided the grounds for the psychological changes that the provincial nobility underwent in the process of their political liberalization in 1904, and especially in 1905.

This process bore at least some superficial similarities to the political evolution, described so well for us by Namier and others, of the English gentry in the eighteenth century.[2] It was originally marked by the emergence of a sense—genuine if ultimately delusory—among many of these Russian provincial nobles that they were identified with the values and interests of their localities, more precisely with the *general* interest of the population of these localities—nobles and peasants alike—and that by virtue of this identity of interests and values, they were genuinely entitled to represent them. And from this sense of representing their localities, there was but a step, if a long step, to the emergence of the sense of truly representing a nation, a nation entitled to govern itself, rather than being led by the nose by an increasingly "blind," "inept," and above all "alien," bureaucracy.

In her essay, Manning has described the sweeping and genuine character of the psychological leap that the Russian landowning nobility made in 1905—a leap that admittedly occurred against the background of humiliating military defeats borne by the state power, as well as of the growing internal paralysis, if not collapse, of its bureaucracy—in substance, in the face of the seeming inability of the state power and its agents to fulfill their primal, most elementary, functions: to preserve some semblance of domestic order and maintain the integrity of the empire. Be that as it may—against this background of disorder, confusion, and yes, inebriation (characteristic, after all, of all revolutionary situations)—many, if not most, of these Russian provincial noble landowners made an immense psychological jump, especially during the summer months of 1905. They now appeared genuinely to respond to the appeals of liberal leaders not only for representative government but also for universal and equal suffrage, and even in a remarkable number of cases for the voluntary relinquishment of the special privileges of their noble estate.

To be sure, such a willingness to sacrifice had already been evidenced, if only by a relatively small minority of the Russian landowning nobility, in earlier political crises of modern Russian history. Already on these earlier occasions—during the debates preceding and following the issuance of the Edict of Emancipation, and again during the political crisis of the late 1870s and eighties—it had been characteristic of many of those assemblies of nobility and/or zemstvo assemblies that had issued the most sweeping claims for unfettered local self-government, and even for a national constitutional representation, to couple these demands with a proclaimed willingness to abolish all special *soslovie* privileges and discriminations: to recognize that all members of the new body politic, nobles and peasants alike, should be equal before the law.[3]

But in the summer of 1905 such sentiments were voiced, or at least silently accepted, by Russian provincial noble landowners on a much more sweeping scale. Indeed, there was an inherent logic in the giant step that these nobles now took. *Qua* separate, even if ruling, *soslovie*, *qua* particularistic culture—separated from other groups by legal discriminations, as well as sharp differences and conflicts of interests and values—the Russian landowning nobility could not have psychologically and politically afforded to assert itself so sharply against the state power, and above all to claim genuinely to represent, in this confrontation, their own localities, if not a united nation. If they were now to transfer their traditional allegiance from the state power to a newborn nation-state, they could feel capable and entitled to do so only on the basis of the assertion of a community of values and interests with other social groups to which they had to be prepared to give institutional expression.

It may well be argued that this discovery of a community of values was shaky, if not skin-deep, even during this heady summer of 1905, and especially that it was never extended beyond the bounds of *rural* Russia—beyond the vision of an essentially agrarian society. But however flimsy, this vision was truly a precondition for the conversion of so many of this landowning nobility to constitutional government, and especially to a vision of a national representation based on equality before the law. One should concede even more readily that this new bucolic vision of rural Russia never entailed, for those noble landowners who temporarily grasped for it, the abandonment of their continued expectation, if not explicit claim, to rule it. Manning has wisely emphasized the significance of the political fact that even during the tumultuous, disorienting, intoxicating, and ultimately frightening summer of 1905—when so many of them became almost literally unhinged, as they would later woefully recall—most of the noble landowners attending the county and provincial zemstvo assemblies never pronounced themselves in favor of four-tail suffrage. Almost all of them voted, or were prepared to vote, for universal, and even equal and secret, suffrage; but most of them *did not* express themselves in favor of *direct* suffrage.

This pervasive, if often muted, opposition to direct suffrage was variously justified, on those occasions when it was in fact articulated: direct suffrage would open the door to irresponsible party politics, conducted by irresponsible intelligentsia demagogues; in contrast, indirect elections were the only way to insure, especially in the light of the political immaturity of the peasants, that the latter would in fact elect deserving and responsible representatives, whom they personally knew to be experienced in local affairs and sensitive to the real need of their localities. Underlying these formulations, of course, was the expectation on the part of the members of the landowning nobility who voiced them that it was to them that the voters of their localities —peasants and nonpeasants alike—would entrust the safeguard of their interests and the promotion of their aspirations.

The discovery that this was not the case—the brutal realization, in the course of the elections to the first two Dumas, that their peasants would under almost no circumstances select them to represent their interests—however well-intentioned and "enlightened" they might be— was a profoundly traumatic experience for the vast majority of Russian noble provincial landowners. As traumatic as the burning of their manors and poplar trees, the Kadets' sweeping proposals for the partial expropriation of their land, or, even more broadly, the betrayal, so they felt, by the liberal noble intelligentsia of their duties to their sovereign, to the empire, and to their own kind. And the psychological trauma created by this political repudiation—in word and deed—by their local peasantry, contributed greatly to the scope and the depth of the reaction among the Russian landowning nobility, which has been the chief object of our attention in this volume.

But it is also extremely significant, and suggestive of the persistent features of the political psychology of these noble landowners, that the flag under which this reaction began—the first major rallying point for those who emerged as the leaders, at least on the national level, of their confused, if embittered, ranks—was provided not by the various conflicts of interest that had now been so nakedly exposed between them and their peasants, or even between them and urban Russia, but by the principle of the "integrity of the empire," now threatened, so these leaders of the nobility claimed, by the demands for autonomy for the Kingdom of Poland, and the support for this demand among the liberal and radical parties.

There was, admittedly, some discrepancy, even at this stage, between the national leadership of this gentry reaction (which was largely provided by those who soon emerged as the leaders of the Octobrist party) and the rank and file of the provincial nobility, which often rallied around local parties (*partii pravogo poriadka*) more candid in their espousal of the restoration of law and order. Yet the fact remains that this was the original rhetoric—the ideology in a Marxist sense— that the national spokesmen for the landed nobility advanced against the leaders of the Liberation Movement whom they now so sweepingly repudiated. And in this, as in other instances, ideology *was* important: now that they had been compelled by bitter experience to give up their vision of a united nation, and especially of their claim to represent it, it was psychologically important, if not imperative, for these spokesmen for the Russian nobility to do so, at least at first, not on the basis of selfish interests of caste or class, but rather in the name of their traditional allegiance to the empire, to the monarch, to the state.

To be sure, the rediscovery of a sense of loyalty to the state on the part of the Russian landowning nobility remained circumscribed, especially during the Stolypin era. In part, this was because during these early years of reaction, the memory was still too vivid among them of the many instances in which, during the period of revolutionary upheaval, officials of the state bureaucracy—from governors to ministers and even premiers—had become paralyzed, or even evidenced in their panic a willingness to sell them down the river, especially on the land question, if only, so these bureaucrats argued, for the sake of saving the state and the monarchy. During the early years of Stolypin's premiership, as some of the essays in this volume have shown, there was the added irritant of the central bureaucracy's velleities for reforms whose effect would have been to undermine some of the institutional props through which this provincial nobility was now firmly intent— especially after all they had been through—to maintain its ruling position in the Russian land.

Thus it was that, even through the period of reaction, the Russian landowning nobility was by no means averse to using the dominant position in Russia's new representative institutions that the political "constitution" afforded it, especially after June 1907, to defend their interests against the encroachments of the bureaucratic state as well as those of other groups in society. Indeed, these noble landowners were at first willing to do so under a politically more experienced leadership, which included constitutionally minded, if more conservative, spokesmen, and they repudiated these spokesmen only when the latter themselves displayed excessive zeal in collaborating with reforming bureaucrats on schemes that would have undermined the landowning nobility's position in the countryside.

One of the significant contributions of this volume, it seems to me, has been to suggest that the deepening of the gentry reaction between 1907 and 1911—the weakening of the political base of the Left Octobrists, the emergence and consolidation of the bloc of moderate rights and Nationalists, and more importantly the mobilization of much of the provincial landowning gentry around their more conservative provincial marshals, as well as in support of such reactionary organizations as the United Nobility—occurred, not so much over such well-publicized symbolic issues as the Naval General Staff bill as over the much more tangible and basic threat presented to the position of the landowning nobility by the government's Octobrist-supported projects of reform of local government.

Be that as it may, we should not reach the end of this survey of the evolution of attitudes of the Russian landed nobility until the war with the image of a still visibly alarmed, militant, mobilized gentry reaction. By 1914, as this volume has shown, the state bureaucracy's reforming impulses were now strictly contained, if not entirely exhausted; rural Russia was quiet, and social and political unrest still tightly contained in urban and industrial Russia. Under these circumstances, most of the members of the landowning nobility could afford to relax, and did so, most visibly. The available evidence on the elections to the Fourth Duma (just as that on the zemstvo elections in 1912–13, as we have seen) provides many signs of this relaxation among the rank and file of the Russian provincial nobility, which stand in dramatic contrast to the often compulsive efforts of the bureaucrats of the Ministry of Internal Affairs to tighten their control and intensify their manipulation of all phases of the electoral process.

What sentiments typically appeared to animate most of the thirty-thousand Russian nobles who qualified for full census in the landowners' curia in these, the last, Duma elections held before the outbreak of the war?[4] The picture we draw from various reports is that by this time most of these noble landowners still regarded themselves as defenders of the *ordre établi*, upholders of sound, conservative, moral, religious, social, and political values and institutions—for themselves and especially for the peasants over whom they ruled. In this broad sense, most of them viewed themselves as "rightists," *pravye*, but by no means as reactionaries. For now that their hold over their estates, over local life, and over the body politic as a whole appeared to have been fully restored, they no longer felt enraged: indeed, they had lost much of their zeal to purge or to punish those who, on minor issues or in minor ways, appeared occasionally to stray from their ranks. Most of these Russian provincial landowners now felt contemptuous not only of such "low-class," rabble-rousing organizations as the Union of the Russian People, but also of the deputies of the extreme right in the Duma—the Purishkeviches and Markovs II—who made such unseemly scenes during Duma sessions and generally engaged so nakedly in political demagoguery. By and large, they now saw it as their task to elect honorable and responsible gentlemen to the State Duma and the State Council—gentlemen who, whenever they could, would loyally cooperate with the government, but who, when necessary, would also prove capable of holding it and its bureaucracy in check.

Actually, now that their grip on Russia's representative institutions appeared so fully secure, most of these provincial noble landowners were no longer deeply interested in the State Duma and its activities, and under the circumstances, many of them did not even bother to vote. But the most typical and general feature of the political attitudes of these Russian provincial nobles by the eve of the war is that they saw themselves as above the party system, which had now sunk such deep roots in the political culture of urban industrial Russia, and which the government was now seeking to introduce, however haphazardly, into rural Russia itself (largely through the promotion of the Nationalist Union). By and large, the picture we draw is that these men were now indifferent to, if not contemptuous of, party organizations (which by this time had almost entirely disappeared from rural Russia); contemptuous of notions of party discipline; indifferent to, if not ignorant of, most of the details of party platforms; indeed contemptuous, in most cases, of the concept of parties per se, which—like the English country gentlemen in the House of Commons of George III— most of them now regarded as political factions or cabals, pursuing and promoting selfish political ends.

Most Russian provincial noble landowners now appeared content to assert and organize their political values and interests through their corporate organizations of nobility as well as through the county and provincial zemstvos, which they now so securely dominated. And the politics in which they engaged continued to be marked by, or had now reverted back to, a more traditional and personal style: that of the relations maintained within their narrow and coherent political culture between one worthy, self-respecting, autonomous noble landowning family and another; as well as, on occasion, that of the dependence of less wealthy and less socially prominent families on the wealthier and more distinguished, a pattern of relationships that occasionally smacked of those of clients to patrons, superficially reminding us once again of eighteenth-century England, although in the earlier age of the great Whig families.

This last reference is of some importance, for notwithstanding the identification of political parties with cabals to which I have referred, personal ambitions, animus, group loyalties and conflicts, were by no means absent in this traditional noble political culture. Such sentiments and the political behavior to which they gave rise were occasionally displayed in the elections to the Fourth Duma, not so much in the selection of provincial electors, for which the competition was not so keen, as in the eventual selection of Duma deputies by noble electors of the landowners' curia at the provincial electoral assemblies. As often as not, these electors could not readily agree on whom to elect, and under these circumstances one occasionally witnessed at the provincial electoral assemblies infights among veritable cabals of noble landowners, which were sometimes exploited by opposition electors from other curiae (much to the chagrin of government officials) to elect some of their own members to the Duma. In this fashion, not infrequently, the best-laid plans of provincial governors were laid low, in scenes of almost total bedlam at the provincial electoral assemblies, about which these governors eventually had to report woefully to their government superiors.

To be sure, such spectacles tended to be the exception rather than the rule. Judging from official reports, *most* Russian provincial landowners were not drawn even to these more traditional forms of "party" politics. The majority of them appeared content to select, first as electors, and eventually as deputies, the more prominent and active members of their provincial society, those who had displayed over the years the greatest will as well as willingness to serve, whether in the assemblies of nobility or the zemstvos.

By the same token, most of these Russian provincial landowners were reluctant to join in the occasional efforts of especially zealous officials to purge Left Octobrist candidates who had offended the government by their excessive constitutionalist zeal. Indeed, even though, more often than not, they did not themselves espouse such constitutionalist sentiments, these rank-and-file nobles, and even their provincial marshals, often shared the indignation and sense of personal affront felt by those Left Octobrist noblemen who were called upon by lowly officials, on the instructions of their superiors, to withdraw their candidacies. They shared the feeling that such injunctions constituted an infringement on the nobility's corporate rights, and indeed on their collective honor and dignity as the first servants of the tsar and of the state. Most self-respecting noble landowners would not join in the efforts to purge such distinguished and honorable men of their own estate from the body politic, and in their efforts to get rid of Left Octobrist candidates, government officials had to resort to the support of members of the clergy.

This, by and large, appears to have been the general pattern of political sentiment and behavior among the Russian provincial landowning nobility on the eve of the First World War—the picture that we draw both from the Fourth Duma elections and the elections to zemstvo assemblies in 1912–13, which Manning and MacNaughton have discussed in their essay. When we survey the various counties and provinces of European Russia, we find but few exceptions to this general pattern. Robert Edelman has described one significant regional deviation, but it is an exception that confirms the rule. In the southwest, especially in Kiev province, which provided during the prewar period the only substantial grass-roots support for the Nationalist Union, Russian noble landowners had traditionally lacked the institutional framework available to Russian nobles in other areas for the maintenance of their grip on the countryside. They had specifically lacked elected zemstvo institutions, and they had been confronted in their corporative organizations by the formidable presence of generally wealthier Polish noble landowners—for them an essentially alien culture, animated by quite different national, religious, as well as social and political values. As Edelman has described, it is under these conditions—in the absence of the institutional props available to them elsewhere, and in the face of the political threat posed by their simultaneous confrontation with the peasants under their rule and with this alien element in their own ranks—as well as under the stimulus and the challenge of an urban culture, in which they were now much more firmly implanted than the Russian noble landowners of other provinces —that the Russian noble landowners of Kiev province developed, however superficially, a more modern political culture and a more modern sense of party.

But elsewhere, particularly in central European Russia, the gentry provincial culture that we have described at such length appeared still firmly in place, its cohesion unmarred by such divisions of nationality, religion, or political sentiment, and its control over the countryside, through its traditional corporate organizations and organs of self-government, largely unchallenged from any quarter. Under the circumstances, Russian noble landowners did not need to develop even a bare facsimile of a more modern political culture, and one encountered even vague semblances of party sentiments and organization among them only in those rare areas of Great Russia in which nobles still appeared especially scarred by the memory of bitter divisions *within their own ranks* during the great upheavals of 1905–1907. (Kursk *guberniia* is a case in point, the only province in Great Russia in which the Union of the Russian People was still effectively functioning in 1912 with the support of the landowning nobility.) Almost everywhere else, Russian provincial landowners recoiled from such political phenomena and were content to select their representatives through the more traditional forms of politics that we have discussed.

One of the major political consequences of this more traditional and personal style of politics among the Russian provincial nobility was that it worked greatly to the benefit of the loose political association that the Union of 17 October represented in both the Third and Fourth Dumas. As the contributions of Michael Brainerd and Robert Edelman have suggested, the representation of the Octobrists—the number of Duma seats that they won in both the Third and Fourth Duma elections—vastly exceeded the extent of their actual support, or more precisely of the sense of identification with their party, among voters in the landowners' curia. The swollen representation of the Octobrists in the Duma resulted in part from the Octobrists' nominal position at the center of the political spectrum of the electorate (as defined and weighted under the System of the Third of June), a position that enabled Octobrist electors to coalesce at the various provincial electoral assemblies, now with the right, now with the left, depending largely on the basis of political expediency. In and of itself, this flexibility helped swell the numbers of Octobrist deputies well beyond the actual percentage of their political sympathizers among the electors at the various provincial electoral assemblies.[5] But a more basic factor underlay the Octobrists' successes in these elections, and indeed accounted in part precisely for the effectiveness of such political maneuvers: it was the ultimately quite loose sense of political, and especially party, identification, which we already noted among the voters and electors of the landowners' curia who dominated the electoral process. Although we lack the evidence to demonstrate the fact statistically, there is little question in my mind that, by and large, Octobrist, or more precisely "moderate," *vyborshchiki* were themselves elected to the provincial electoral assemblies in both the Third and Fourth Duma elections, as well as in contemporary elections to provincial zemstvo assemblies, in numbers far exceeding the actual proportion of supporters for this party among the voters in the landowners' curia. In part, this was because of the relative lack of competition that generally characterized these elections, given the shrinking number of landowners with full census and the rate of political absenteeism among them (well over 40 percent).[6] But this rate of absenteeism and the lack of political competition that it reflected, just as the number of votes that Octobrist candidates actually garnered, rested on a sense of political equanimity among noble landowners that made them willing to select their representatives on the basis of the more personal and traditional criteria that we have discussed (criteria that, by the eve of the war, stood in such glaring contrast to the more modern forms of political partisanship evident in urban Russia). It was this style of politics, and the serenity that underlay it, that accounted in good measure for the willingness of noble landowners to support Octobrist candidates, if only because they were such distinguished and honorable men.

But lest we be deceived by this bucolic picture, we need to remind ourselves that the political tolerance that the noble landowners of provincial Russia so proudly displayed even as the war approached had very stringent limits—limits that had been clearly set in the wake of Russia's First Revolution. Most of these noble landowners might have recovered from the successive traumas that they had experienced during these years, but they had by no means forgotten them. At no point during these immediate prewar years did these Russian provincial noble landowners display the slightest willingness to vote in support of the few remaining Kadet or Kadet sympathizers in their ranks—this notwithstanding the Kadets' years of good behavior in the Third Duma, and the deliberately moderate and responsible tone of their electoral campaign to the Fourth Duma. It would take the great turmoil of the war years, and the displays of Kadet patriotism during these years, to make a dent finally in these unforgiving attitudes.

Neither had most noble provincial landowners forgiven or forgotten their peasants' behavior during the great upheavals of 1905–1907, and even though their peasants had now relapsed into political quiescence and by and large appeared to heed obediently the orders and injunctions of their superiors, most noble landowners were still prone to discern in their visages, if not in their words, a suppressed but still pervasive yearning for their landed estates.

Fundamentally, these Russian provincial nobles had come out of the nightmares of the Revolution of 1905 and the challenges to their position during the Stolypin era with their traditional, Janus-like, dual visage altered, but also reinforced. More than ever before, they now constituted and sought to maintain a particularistic culture in the countryside, and in the body politic as a whole. It was not merely that the more rooted provincial society that they had sought to establish by the turn of the century had emerged from Russia's First Revolution with a more acute sense of its differences of interests and values from other groups in national life, but also that their consequent sense of social isolation was now becoming ever more profound, and their claim to exclusiveness ever more rigid, as their numbers dwindled and their economic fortunes declined.

By the same token, however, in their efforts to hold on to their tight, hermetic, if steadily contracting, provincial society, to hold the rest of the world at bay, *even while persisting in their claim to rule it*, they were now also more dependent than ever before on the support of the state power. They were economically dependent on the official salaries and emoluments, the subsidies and loads, that they received from the state in order to slow down, if not halt, the process of economic decline, which all but the wealthiest and most enterprising of them continued to experience, given their inability—indeed, their unwillingness—to adapt to the economic requirements of the modern age. They were politically dependent on the continued support of the state and its officials to maintain their grip over the countryside, and over the body politic as a whole. But also, and above all, they were psychologically dependent on their identification with the state, and especially with the monarch, the *Gosudar*, to provide the justification—the only possible justification that they could offer others, but also themselves—for their claim to continued supremacy over the Russian land.

As *pomeshchiki*, seeking to maintain their exclusive grip on rural Russia and to hold urban Russia at bay, they could not possibly view their interests as more than particular interests: in conflict with, or at best complementary to, those of other groups in national life. And by the same token, the only way in which they could deny the charge of *soslovnost'*, of caste egoism and exclusivism, that was now leveled at them, and justify their claim to rule was by reasserting, more than ever before, their historic role as servants of the state.

Indeed, we should note that as Russia continued, however slowly, to evolve into a society of classes, many of these noble landowners and their elected representatives no longer advertised themselves as a *soslovie*, as they sought to defend their particular identity and values, their particular way of life, in this generally moving and evolving society. It was not merely that they knew that in this society (and especially in urban Russia) the mere title of nobleman—no more than any other *soslovie* title—was any longer an index of what an individual did or of the way he lived, let alone of the reliability of his political attitudes and behavior. More importantly, the very term *soslovie* had now undergone, especially in political discourse, a fundamental change in meaning. Once, deep in the historical past, it had signified over and above all the notion of a department or compartment of the state that these nobles had served, from which they had drawn their duties and privileges, and their very sense of identity. By now, however, the term —or more precisely, its derivative, *soslovnost'*—was coming to be widely used by their accusers and indeed by those noble landowners themselves, in the political debates in Russia's representative institutions, but also in these nobles' more private exchanges with officials, to suggest a particular and special interest, in conflict not only with other particular and special interests but also with the *general* interest, represented by the state, if not the nation.

Because of this, to distinguish in public discourse the particular society that they represented, and its particular interests, life style, and values, the spokesmen of the landed nobility now frequently used in preference to *soslovie* the term *kulturno-bytovaia gruppa*. By this term, so close in meaning to the term culture (in the modern anthropological sense), they meant in part to distinguish the values and the way of life of the island of civilization that more than ever they felt they represented in the otherwise still dark, savage, and ever potentially wild countryside. But the term also suggested a more incontrovertible reality. It was that as Russia evolved from a society of *sosloviia* into a class society, the Russian provincial landowning nobility had itself turned into a socioeconomic group distinguished, as we have seen, by a whole series of characteristics, which were becoming even more selective as they became manifold.

The tragedy was that precisely as a result of this ever-narrowing process of selection, the members of this *kulturno-bytovaia gruppa* now were—and saw themselves as—more separate than ever before from other groups, an isolated and self-isolated island in the body politic. Notwithstanding the appeals of their more modern-minded representatives—the Golitsyns, the Shidlovskys, the Meyendorffs—to induce them to develop and manifest politically a broader and more flexible sense of class, a mental gulf continued to separate them from the commercial-industrial class of the cities and towns, and indeed from many of the noble property owners who had been absorbed in urban life, the very groups whom the authors of the June 1907 coup d'état had sought to make the other, if lesser, pillar of the System of the Third of June. And, as some of the essays in this volume have shown, even in the countryside such a mental gulf continued to separate them not only from their peasants but also from the growing number of other landowners of non-nobiliar origin, with whom even some of their more conservative members urged them to combine for the promotion of common economic, if not political, interests.

As we have noted, this persistently rigid particularism of their provincial culture made these noble landowners more dependent than ever for their claim to rule on the support of the state power. As a result, when early in the Stolypin era the dominant position they occupied in the institutional framework of rural Russia was challenged by reforming bureaucrats in the debates over the new projects of local reforms, it was their symbiotic relationship with the state that the provincial marshals of nobility reasserted most powerfully in response to the charge of *soslovnost'*. In no way was their opposition to these projects motivated by *soslovnost'*—by caste egoism and exclusiveness —they asserted time and again as these debates droned on.[7] The provincial landed nobility that they represented did constitute a *kulturno-bytovaia gruppa*, a distinct cultural and socioeconomic group, which it would be folly for the government to undermine, since it also constituted the only island of stability and progress in the countryside. But above all, they and the nobles for whom they spoke remained what they had always been—since the very formation of the Muscovite state—a true service class, animated solely by its sense of honor and fidelity to the interests of the state and of the monarch.

Of course, this term, service, *sluzhba,* on which these formidable provincial marshals elaborated in the debates, in insistent tones more reminiscent of the seventeenth and early eighteenth than of the twentieth century, now hardly corresponded to the provincial landed nobility's actual relationship to the state power. But its reassertion in their political language, with its ancient references and allusions—to the *sluzhilie liudi* of the Muscovite state, if not to the slavelike *slugi pod dvortsem* of an even earlier age—reflected, even more than they knew, the reemergence, in the face of their isolation in the body politic, of an almost archaic sense of dependence on the state and on the monarch.

Indeed, one comes away with the impression that under the stresses of these debates, and of the changes in Russian society that they reflected, the concept of *soslovie,* on which the more conservative members of the Russian landed nobility had once anchored their sense of identity, had at least temporarily been split into two even more distinct, and mutually contradictory, components. To draw on an only partially far-fetched historical analogy, to the late sixteenth century and the time of Ivan the Terrible, it was as if in the visages they alternately assumed in these debates—in their assertions that they represented a *kulturno-bytovaia gruppa,* a particular and distinct culture deeply rooted in the Russian countryside, and yet also a service class, indistinguishable from the *general* interest represented by the state and the monarch—the persona, or at least the language, of these provincial marshals had undergone a deep, schizophrenic, historical regression. As if, under the impact of their collective traumas of 1905 and of the new and psychologically even more difficult challenge issued to them by the state's reforming bureaucrats, they were seeking to enact the ghosts of a *zemshchina* and *oprichnina,* to represent phantom *boiars* and *oprichniki,* at one and the same time.

Even when the pressure that they were under was removed and relative complacency restored in their ranks, neither of the basic psychological features of the Russian landowning nobility that these debates had so glaringly brought out—its particularism in the body politic and the obverse side of this particularism, its dependence on, and identification with, the state and the monarch—was conducive to firm attitudes about representative, let alone constitutional, government.

By 1912 the typical Russian *pomeshchik* could pride himself on being autonomous and nonpartisan, but he could hardly be induced to follow those who called on him, in the name of his ostensible common interests with other groups in the body politic, to engage in a true constitutionalist confrontation with state power: he could not do so, because he could not afford to. And this is what the leaders of the Union of 17 October, or more precisely the constitutionalist Left Octobrists in their midst, ultimately discovered, much to their sorrow. We suggested earlier in this discussion that the diffuse character of the Union of 17 October, and the even more diffuse nature of its political support among Russian provincial noble landowners, enabled the Octobrist party to win far more votes in the elections to the Third and even

the Fourth Duma than was warranted by the degree of actual identification among the landowning nobility with the "principles" that
Octobrist, especially Left Octobrist, leaders espoused within the walls
of the Taurus Palace. As Michael Brainerd has suggested in his contribution to this volume, this diffuseness ultimately proved to be a
fatal source of political weakness for the Octobrist party. During the
Third Duma period, this political weakness was partially contained
by Guchkov's device of keeping the deputies of the Octobrist parliamentary faction as insulated as possible from their constituents. But
when, in the fall and winter of 1913–14, the moment of truth came—
in the face of the political and social crisis boiling up in urban Russia
—and the leaders of the Union of 17 October finally steeled themselves
to assume a posture of "declarative" opposition to the state power, these
party activists proved to be leaders without followers. The party split
at the seams, and only twenty-two out of one hundred Octobrist deputies joined the ranks of the Duma opposition. The vast majority of the
remaining Octobrist deputies, who eventually formed a new parliamentary group of zemstvo Octobrists, as well as the few who were
recruited into the even more conservative center party, probably acted
in accord with their own feelings, but more importantly with those of
their constituents.

Even at this critical moment, most of these constituents undoubtedly
did not feel the gravity of the political crisis from which their representatives had not recoiled. For even by 1914 most Russian provincial
noble landowners continued to be confirmed in their political equanimity by all the dimensions of their immediate experience, and the
bounds of their political culture remained sufficiently hermetic to make
urban Russia seem far away.

A crucial source of this sense of equanimity that these *pomeshchiki*
preserved, even as the roof was about to fall upon them, was, of course,
the political passivity of their peasants. In his analysis of voting patterns in the peasant curia in the elections to the Fourth Duma, Eugene
Vinogradoff has laid great emphasis on the massive political apathy
that Russian peasants displayed during these elections in most provinces of European Russia. The picture he has drawn of those strata
of the Russian peasantry that he has categorized as "estate peasants"
is generally congruent with official reports on the Fourth Duma elections, including the detailed accounts submitted to the Ministry of
Internal Affairs by the various provincial governors and their subordi-
nates about the successive stages of the electoral process in the peasant curia.[8]

These official reports almost invariably stressed the massive indifference that most Russian peasants, especially in Great Russia, were now displaying toward political parties and the very institution of the State Duma. Indeed, they usually noted that the only members of the peasants' district and county assemblies who evidenced the slightest interest in the electoral process were those who wanted to get elected to the Duma—if only because of the big *zhalovanie*, the substantial financial emolument that Duma deputies received. Under the circumstances, most if not all of the peasant electors who attended the provincial electoral assemblies sought to advance their own candidacies to the Duma. And in the ensuing scramble, few of the peasant deputies of the Third Duma were reelected, since—by the standards of peasant justice—these incumbents had already had their chance to feed at the public trough. *"Ony dostatochno zhraly";* it was time to give others a chance.[9]

Finally, official reports generally concur with Vinogradoff's observation that this plethora of peasant candidates was by and large all too willing to assume the conservative (or on occasion, "moderate" Octobrist) political garb most likely to promote their chances for support among the electors of the landowning gentry and of the clergy—in whose hands their individual fortunes usually rested. The only deviation from this pattern allegedly occurred in those instances when peasant electors found it more expedient to promote their personal ambitions by aligning themselves with opposition electors from other curiae (generally when the electors of the landowners' curia split into rival factions, and for this reason lost control of the proceedings of the provincial electoral assemblies).

This is the picture usually drawn in the various official reports of peasant political behavior in the Fourth Duma elections, and it is generally in accord with available statistical data, including the rough correlation that it suggests between the distribution of "rightist" and "moderate" peasant electors in different provinces of Great Russia and the political distribution in these same areas of their actual or potential patrons among the nobles and clergymen of the landowners' curia.

What is far more difficult to establish, it seems to me, is the relative importance we should assign to the variety of factors that may have underlain these patterns of political behavior. Specifically to be weighed in the balance is the relative significance of the *political conditions* under which peasants had to vote by the time of the Fourth

Duma elections, including the various alterations that had been imposed in the electoral system, as against that of some of the *more enduring features of peasant attitudes and political culture*. Obviously,
to draw even the most tentative impression of the relative significance
of these two sets of factors, one has to survey the political behavior
of the Russian peasantry over a much longer time period than Vinogradoff was able to use in his article—a period that ideally should
stretch from the agrarian disorders of Russia's First Revolution and
the elections to the first two Dumas through the elections to the Constituent Assembly in the fall of 1917.

From this much broader time perspective, I feel most comfortable
with the ideal type of political culture of "estate peasants" that Vinogradoff has drawn, as well as with the explanatory scheme that, however tentatively, he has presented to account for it, with respect to one
particular group of the Russian peasantry of the empire, that of the
peasants of the Central Agricultural Region, especially in those areas
of this region most removed from urban centers. It is these areas of
the C.A.R., of course, which, more than any others in the empire,
maintained into the twentieth century the combination of objective
characteristics that Vinogradoff and others have emphasized in their
analyses of the traditional agrarian system of the Russian peasantry:
communal tenure, a three-field agrarian system relatively unmodified
by the influence of a market economy, a growing land pressure aggravated by the deterioration of the land as well as by the absence of
the safety valve of opportunities for urban and industrial employment,
and finally, what is perhaps most important from a social and political
point of view, the almost total isolation of peasant communities from
urban, commercial, industrial centers, and indeed from one other. The
evidence appears to me overwhelming that in these isolated and over-
populated areas of the C.A.R., the members of peasant communes
displayed both in the agrarian disorders of 1905–1907 and in the elections to the first two Dumas the single-minded preoccupation with
the land question, and particularly with the repartition of noble estates, which Vinogradoff has so strongly emphasized as an explanatory
principle for peasant political behavior. The available data clearly
suggest that in these areas the agrarian disorders of 1905–1907 were
almost exclusively against noble estates; and especially at the occupation of the meadow and forest lands of these estates, of which the
peasants of C.A.R., under the pressures of their three-field system, were
by this time so grievously short. And it also appears that in the seizure

of these gentry lands, individual peasant communities in this region often acted not only in isolation from, but even in competition with, one another.[10]

Vinogradoff also seems to me on very firm ground in his insistence that in both the First and Second Duma elections, the peasant electorate of these areas displayed above all the same insistent concern with the land question. In the First Duma elections, they selected a great many provincial electors and eventually peasant deputies who were originally unaffiliated with any political parties. Many of these non-party deputies eventually joined the new *trudovik* parliamentary group, which was formed *after* the First Duma convened; some of them did not. But whether they did or not, almost all of these peasant deputies displayed throughout the deliberations of the First Duma a single-minded preoccupation with the expropriation of gentry lands. In the elections to the Second Duma, this pattern changed only superficially. The peasants of the C.A.R. now elected a far more substantial number of electors and deputies who were formally affiliated with political parties and parliamentary groups: *trudoviki,* but also *narodnye sotsialisty,* and even SR's; but in the *nakazy,* the cahiers that they issued for their guidance, they often gave these peasant deputies the specific instructions that they should not allow themselves to be diverted in the Duma's deliberations by "extraneous" political issues, and that they dare not come back to them without a land settlement in hand.[11]

In these respects, as we shall see, the political behavior of the peasants in the C.A.R. was distinctive from that of other peasants, in degree if not in kind. Yet we should note that even the voters of some of the more remote peasant communities of the C.A.R. also displayed, in the first two Duma elections, certain patterns of political behavior more congruent with those of peasants in less isolated areas. The first of these was a remarkably high degree of political cohesion in at least one fundamental respect: that of seeking to elect to the Duma as many representatives as possible of their own estate, and of rejecting in this process the candidacies of noble landowners, almost irrespective of the latter's political affiliation, or even presumed sympathies for the peasant estate. To be sure, a number of noble Kadet landowners were elected to the First Duma with the support of peasant votes. But it is my impression that, more often than not, they won this peasant support not by their liberal stand, even on the land question, but by engaging in *coalition* politics with peasant electors, which guaranteed the peasants, when they needed this reassurance, a generous quota of Duma seats.[12]

The second pattern of political behavior that the peasants of the C.A.R. displayed in common with those of other areas was often to bring—or more precisely, to allow to come—to the fore the most politically sophisticated members of their own peasant estate; those who, in one fashion or another, had been more exposed to the breezes of a larger political culture and environment: members of their peasant intelligentsia (village teachers, bookkeepers, statisticians, doctors' assistants, and the like); also peasants who had worked in cities, or in industry, or who had been in the army; and above all, peasants who were among the most literate members of their communities, and who were therefore assumed to be best able to cope with the strange outer world that they would now have to face.

To be sure, in the First and even the Second Duma elections, the peasants of the C.A.R. also selected from their ranks, as electors and eventually deputies, a good many representatives who were far more typical of the average "grey" (*serye*) peasants of the area. In part, the election of such "greys" was often motivated by attitudes we already noted in connection with the Third and Fourth Duma elections—the greed and mutual jealousies of peasant electors competing for the salaries attached to Duma seats and ultimately settling, because of their mutual jealousies, ón such lackluster representatives. On occasion, however, this betting on the "greys" apparently derived from the rationale that they were more likely to remain faithful to the basic concerns of the average peasants—less likely to be deflected by the rhetoric of the "gentlemen," the *gospoda*, from the goal of obtaining their lands for the peasant estate.[13]

Yet the fact remains that in both the First and Second Duma elections, peasants of the C.A.R., under the spur of the quite different rationale that I outlined earlier, also selected, in disproportionate numbers, more sophisticated and literate spokesmen, many of them unusually young for such hitherto tradition-bound communities. In some areas of the C.A.R., interestingly enough, this phenomenon was more characteristic of peasant behavior in the initial, rather than the later, phases of these peasant communities' political revolt and mobilization against the *gospoda–pomeshchik* masters and officials alike—but presumably also against the traditional hierarchies of their peasant communities, which these *gospoda* had supported and controlled. (Tambov, one of the most disturbed provinces of the C.A.R., provided a striking example of this phenomenon in the period of agrarian disorders of 1905–1907—in which young peasants played an unusually prominent role—and also in the First Duma elections, only to revert by the time of the Second Duma elections to the leadership of older and more traditional representatives of its peasant communities.)[14]

The pattern of selecting more sophisticated and literate representatives was more sharply characteristic, especially in the Second Duma elections, of peasants in regions of European Russia outside the C.A.R.: the Lake region, certain provinces of the C.I.R. and Little Russia; and especially New Russia, the Central and Lower Volga, and the Urals. As has often been noted, this made for a group of peasant deputies in the Second Duma that on the average was remarkably young, and included an equally remarkable proportion of representatives from the peasant intelligentsia: zemstvo and village clerks, statisticians, veterinarians, occasional journalists, and especially school teachers. (And to the best that one can determine, this pattern appears to have been characteristic, if to a lesser degree, of the earlier, just as of the later, stages of the elections in the peasant curia.)[15]

However, in both the First and Second Duma elections, there were some notable differences between the political behavior of the peasants of these other areas of the empire and those of the C.A.R. In many of these other areas, peasant voters, or at least peasant electors, appeared animated by a concern over a much broader range of political issues than just the land question—even if, admittedly, these other issues remain largely identified in their minds with the specific interests of the peasant estate: a concern for the elimination of all legal discriminations against peasants; for a more equitable tax system; for the democratization of organs of local self-government; and especially for the abolition of the position of the hated Land Captains (*zemskie nachal'niki*), who hovered over these peasants' daily lives and the functioning of their institutions. And in some cases, peasant electors outside the C.A.R. even displayed an interest in such broad national issues as the abolition of the State Council and establishment of a unicameral legislature—elected by four-tail suffrage and endowed with full powers—which would at last give the peasants a voice in the body politic equal to that of other estates (Tver province is a striking case in point, even in the First Duma elections).

In some areas of the country, especially the Volga and the Urals, this broader range of political concerns among Russian peasants was even reflected in a sense (albeit a tenuous one) of identification with such political formations as the Peasant Union and the P.S.R. In others, it created some programmatic grounds for peasants to engage in coalition politics, at their various provincial electoral assemblies, with oppositionally minded electors from other estates (especially from the urban curiae) animated by similar if not identical concerns. (I emphasize this term "coalition politics," rather than a full sense of identification with national parties and their platforms for society as a whole, as generally characteristic of the degree of involvement of Russian peasants in national politics, even during this period.)

Finally, it does not appear to me by any means clear that in those areas of European Russia in which peasants had by this time accumulated especially significant holdings in private tenure, and where, by the same token, landownership and especially management of their estates by nobles had undergone an especially precipitous decline, differences in economic interests among Russian peasants did not in fact surface, at least in some degree, in what Vinogradoff has termed "class" patterns of political behavior. (However sparse and hard to extricate from the electoral returns, the available evidence suggests that certain areas of the C.I.R., especially Kostroma and Tver provinces, deserve further investigation on this point.)

The coup d'état of June 1907—the arbitrary dissolution of the Second Duma; the restoration of order, often achieved by brute force; the substitution for any form of expropriation of gentry lands of the Stolypin land legislation; and last but not least, the imposition of the various changes incorporated by fiat in the new electoral law—did bring, almost immediately, to many, if not most, Russian peasants the realization that the new Duma elections, called for the fall of 1907, would inevitably return a legislature dominated by *pomeshchiki* from whom little attention, and even fewer concessions to the interests of the peasant estate could be expected.

Even so, when one scrutinizes carefully the returns from the peasant curia available on the Third Duma elections, it is notable (especially from the official statistics available about peasant provincial electors) that the traces of the peculiar brand of political activism and radicalism that peasant voters had displayed in the first two Duma elections had, even by this time, by no means been erased.[16]

Admittedly, the opposition political leanings that official statistics still attributed to many peasant electors in Great, Little, and New Russia were not usually reflected in the profiles of the peasant deputies ultimately selected from these areas, except in the Urals, where peasants were still able to combine forces, even in the Third Duma elections, with the subversive electors whom the clergy of the area continued to bring forth in the landowners' curia. But this very qualification suggests that the general absence of opposition deputies from the peasant curia in most provinces of European Russia was mainly dictated by the new balance of forces that the electoral law of June 1907 had created in the various provincial electoral assemblies concerned—a balance that made it practically impossible to mobilize at these assemblies the support from other curiae needed to elect peasant candidates identified with the opposition. Given the new electoral law, the only circumstance under which such opposition peasant deputies could have been elected (at least to the curial seats still reserved for the peasantry) would have been, as Vinogradoff has noted, for *all the peasant electors* in attendance at these assemblies to display *monolithic* unity. Such behavior was admittedly absent among peasant electors (in contrast to the quite extraordinary degree of unity and fidelity that electors of the workers' curia usually displayed to each other and to *their* workers' party). But the fact remains that it was not until the elections to the Fourth Duma that the traces of peasant radicalism in the voting behavior of the curia of the communal peasantry were largely eliminated.

Given these facts, in accounting for the major changes in peasant voting behavior between the First, Second, and even Third Duma elections, and those to the Fourth Duma, I would assign very considerable importance to the various formal and informal restrictions and pressures that the regime inflicted on the Russian peasantry in the intervening years to achieve their political subdual. Vinogradoff has summarized quite adequately the various changes that the electoral law of June 1907 imposed on the character of the peasant electorate and on its role in the electoral process. But let us consider more fully the political implications of these changes in light of the political experience of the first two Duma elections.

We should first take note of the political effect of the restriction of the suffrage among voters in the peasant curia to heads of households, in possession of, and permanently involved in the cultivation of, allotment lands—a provision that had already been officially established on the eve of the Second Duma elections but that was not fully and systematically applied by local officials until the Third and especially the Fourth Duma elections. This restriction of the suffrage virtually eliminated from participation in the electoral process precisely those elements of the peasant estate which, as we have seen, had played the most prominent part in the first two Duma elections in the mobilization and especially the articulation of radical tendencies in the peasant curia: the peasant intelligentsia; peasants whose life experience outside the village had subjected them to the subversive political influence of life and work in urban and industrial centers; and last but not least, the younger and more literate strata of the peasant population.

The new electoral law also eliminated, it will be recalled, the requirement that members of the *volostnye skhody* (the peasant district assemblies) themselves be elected anew in the first stage of Duma elections in the peasant curia. Again, we should note that this requirement had already been dropped on the eve of the Third Duma elections, but it seems altogether likely that the full effect of this change was not felt until the elections to the Fourth Duma. By that time, local authorities (especially the ever watchful Land Captains, whose charge it was to preside over these assemblies at election time) had had ample opportunity, over a five-year period, to seek to eliminate from the membership of these assemblies any peasant representatives whom they considered in the least politically unreliable or suspect. (It is partly for this reason, I think, that the proportion of peasants with official posts selected by these peasants' district assemblies to represent them was even greater in the Fourth than in the Third Duma elections.)

Finally, the most important effect of the new electoral law was undoubtedly the direct, as well as indirect, impact (on the peasants' political morale) of the dramatic reallocation of provincial electors, imposed upon the peasant and landowners' curiae. It will be recalled that this reallocation of political power was especially drastic in precisely those provinces in which the peasants had dominated the transactions of the provincial electoral assemblies in the first two Duma elections and had exercised this domination most fully for the purpose of electing peasant deputies animated by radical sentiments, at least on the land question. Given the almost universally conservative complexion of the provincial electors selected by the landowners' curia in both the Third and Fourth Duma elections (whether nobles or priests), as well as the sprinkling of conservative electors that could still be collected in the urban curiae of most provinces, the possibility for peasant electors to elect opposition deputies by forming coalitions at the provincial electoral assemblies with opposition-minded electors from other curiae was, by this time, drastically reduced if not altogether eliminated. By and large, in the Fourth Duma elections such opportunities arose, at least in Great Russia, only in those relatively rare instances where Russian noble landowners split into bitterly divided rival factions, usually, as we have seen, on the basis of individual and group loyalties rather than broader political grounds. And in these relatively rare instances, peasant electors *did,* more often than not, exploit such opportunities for maneuver, when they arose, at least to elect a larger number of deputies from their own ranks.

As this illustration suggests, for the political controls over peasant political behavior to be *maximally* effective presupposed a number of political conditions. It required, in the first place, that noble land-owners be present in adequate numbers on their estates to maintain a firm hold over peasant life. It also presupposed that this impact not be contained or diluted by differences of nationality or religion among these noble landowners, or between them, local officials, and the local Orthodox church hierarchy. Last but not least, it presupposed the absence of such religious and/or national barriers between these various figures of authority and the peasants whom they sought to control.

To be sure, even in the partial absence of these conditions, in the west and southwest, for example, Russian local officials and noble landowners did succeed—with a major assist of the local Orthodox clergy—in rallying the Russian peasants of their localities against both Polish landowners and the predominantly Jewish opposition voters of local cities and towns, but they managed to do so only on significantly different political terms. Specifically, the peasants of these areas, especially those of the southwest, managed to elect from their own ranks a much greater proportion of the at-large deputies assigned to their provinces than was the case in the rest of European Russia, and in many instances these at-large peasant deputies appear to have had notably different social as well as political profiles from those deputies elected in Great Russia.[17]

This last illustration about the Fourth Duma elections in the peasant curia brings me to the broad and vexing question of the relative weight to be assigned in these changing and varying patterns of peasant voting behavior (when we consider them in the perspective of the elections to *all four* Dumas) to the more basic and enduring features of the attitudes of Russian peasants toward the political process, the party system, and the very concept of political representation.

In his contribution to this volume, Vinogradoff has laid great emphasis on the differences in political culture to be observed between the peasants of the Baltic provinces (especially those of Lifland and Estland) and the Russian peasantry, even in those areas populated by Russian peasants that he had singled out as exceptional (such as Siberia and the north). The available evidence suggests that the contrast is indeed dramatic, and I would even extend this contrast in political attitudes and behavior to non-Russian peasants of other border regions of the empire such as Poles, Lithuanians, Georgians, and the like.

What we witness in most of these border areas after 1905 is the emergence of political parties that, to a considerable degree, appear to transcend the mental barriers between city and country—whether on the basis of a sense of common cultural, if not national, identity between rural and urban voters; of perceived common socioeconomic interests among certain categories of these voters; or more usually, of a subtle and complex combination of the two. And the peasants who vote for these more truly national parties do indeed appear to develop a far firmer sense of identification with them (with their programs and platforms, as well as with their candidates) than is generally characteristic of Russian peasants.[18]

One should, however, be wary of attributing these dramatic contrasts in political behavior solely to differences in the nature of agrarian systems. It appears obvious to me that differences of nationality and religion, exacerbated by the discriminations that the Regime of the Third of June imposed on national minorities, greatly contributed to the differences in political behavior between non-Russian and Russian peasants, as well as to the capacity of the parties that emerged among the national minorities of the empire to transcend at least some of the cultural boundaries between city and country.

This is not entirely to dismiss the political significance of differences in agrarian systems between these border areas of the empire and Great Russia in the development among their peasants of more modern political cultures. To the degree that the agrarian systems in existence in these border areas *did* contribute to the emergence of stable patterns of economic differentiation among the local peasantry, and especially to the development of closer market relations between city and country, they undoubtedly provided a major stimulus to the mutual integration of their urban and rural political cultures and, by the same token, to the emergence among their peasants of more modern forms of political consciousness.

Indeed, there is some evidence to suggest that, at least to a limited degree, the same phenomenon also occurred among Russian peasants. As Vinogradoff has noted in his Ph.D. dissertation, Russian peasants in close proximity to major metropolitan centers such as St. Petersburg and Moscow, who in many cases engaged in more complex forms of multicrop agriculture (or handicrafts) for the large urban markets within their reach, appear to have displayed in both the Third and Fourth Duma elections some sense of connection with the voters, the electors, and even the parties of the urban, oppositionally minded curiae with whom their economic lives brought them into contact.

It was precisely such a sense of identification with national parties, and the prerequisite for it—a sense of community of interests and values with other groups in society—that was so lacking among the vast majority of other Russian peasants. What these peasants expected of political parties, and of the institutions in which these parties sought representation (even in those areas in which peasants had them identified in their minds) was, above all, that these parties should satisfy the interests and aspirations of the peasant estate. And when political parties as well as the national representative institutions in which they competed were unwilling, or unable, to satisfy these peasant concerns, the interest in them on the part of most Russian peasants dramatically waned.

This political particularism, and the sense of—if not the preference for—psychological isolation from other social groups, to which so many aspects of their life continued to contribute even by the eve of the war, would maintain a persistent psychological grip over the political attitudes and behavior of much of the Russian peasantry well beyond the period of Russian history that we are considering in this volume.

The one-day proceedings of the Constituent Assembly in January 1918, themselves the product of the freest elections ever held in the Russian land, offer us a striking example of the persistence of this particularistic mentality. As will be recalled, by the time the Assembly met in January 1918, all the political parties and factions represented in it—including the by then warring factions of the left and right SR's —were maneuvering to find the most suitable grounds on which to join their now irreconcilable conflict. Yet, well into the proceedings of this single if interminable session, well after the leaders of the left SR's, just as the Bolsheviks, had already irrevocably decided to leave the Assembly demonstratively, one witnesses the spectacle of a peasant spokesman of the left SR's (Sorokin) climbing to the rostrum to read the belligerent and adamant official statement of his party, only to conclude "with a few words of [his] own," reminding his fellow peasant deputies that "many millions of peasants have sent us here to gain for them 'land and freedom,'" and calling on them, regardless of faction, not to disperse without having passed legislation on the land question.[19]

This personal statement, which was greeted with dismay by the leaders of Sorokin's own party—and with cheers and applause by their opponents in the center and right rows of the Taurus Palace—is a particularly telling example of the stubborn political particularism that, even at this late date, the Russian peasantry continued to display. And as the example also suggests, this particularism made—even under these most critical and dramatic of circumstances—for a most tenuous sense of identification with the political parties that competed for the support of the Russian peasantry, including those parties which these peasants had favored with their votes.

Even the peasants of northern Russia and Siberia, whom Vinogradoff has singled out for our attention, were not immune to this political particularism. In the elections to the Constituent Assembly, these peasants, like those of so many other regions outside the C.I.R., voted overwhelmingly for the Party of Socialist Revolutionaries—the party that had always idealized them, and to which, in however more modulated a fashion, they now returned the compliment. But after the Assembly was dissolved, and the Bolsheviks, with their decree on the land, stole the SRs' thunder away from them, the peasants of Siberia and northern Russia displayed as little zeal as those of the Urals and the Volga to give any effective support to the PSR, now that they had achieved possession of the land. They failed to do so even in eastern Russia during the period of the SR-dominated Directory, and indeed most of them remained largely bystanders in the civil war that eventually raged over the whole Russian land, except when the warring factions in this bitter and drawn-out conflict interfered *directly* with the pattern of their immediate existence.

To return to our immediate concerns, the psychological isolation of the Russian peasantry from other groups in the body politic unquestionably made them more vulnerable—once political order was restored after the great turmoils of 1905–1907—to the political restrictions, pressures, and alterations in the rules of the political game to which they were subjected by the Regime of the Third of June. Yet, as I have indicated, it would be erroneous to regard these Russian peasants, even during the years of reaction, as relapsing into political apathy *simply* by virtue of the features of their political culture that we have discussed, and *regardless* of the political conditions to which they were immediately subjected, *regardless* of the specific political framework within which they had to operate, and of the opportunities, or lack of opportunities, that this particular framework afforded them to promote their individual and group interests.

For example, Vinogradoff has drawn our attention to the fact that even in the elections to the Fourth Duma, *some* Russian peasants, specifically those of Arkhangel and Siberia, displayed significantly different political behavior from most other Russian peasants, and indeed selected even at this time peasant provincial electors and deputies who eventually lined up with opposition parties. What appears to me most distinctive and politically significant about these areas was the total absence in them of a landowners' curia, as well as the presence in their urban curiae of a significant number of oppositionally minded electors. *By virute of this combination of circumstances,* the Russian peasants of Arkhangel and Siberia, unlike those in other provinces, still had, even in the Fourth Duma elections, a genuine opportunity *to engage successfully in coalition politics with voters and electors of other curiae* to select candidates of their own choosing. Many of these peasant candidates and electors may have been radicalized in the course of the electoral process by their partners in these politics of coalition, but the more basic point, it seems to me, is that they were free to develop these radical tendencies, and still have the opportunity to get elected, under the specific political conditions obtaining at their respective provincial electoral assemblies. Under the new electoral system, Russian peasants in other areas (with the partial exception of the west and southwest) substantially lacked *this objective possibility* to engage successfully in coalition politics[20]—to select representatives who would be free to articulate the interests of their own estate.

This last point brings me back to one of our major emphases at the opening of this discussion: the degree to which the electoral system established after the coup d'état of June 1907 rested on the domination of the body politic by a now overwhelmingly conservative landowners' curia—a political stranglehold that Russian *pomeshchiki* holding full census in this curia were usually able to maintain by their own resources, but when necessary, with a vigorous assist by representatives of the Orthodox clergy.

As I suggested earlier, the centrality of the political role exercised in the System of the Third of June by this remarkably small, if cohesive, group of Russian society becomes even more apparent when we stretch our vision beyond the electoral system governing Duma elections to a view of the functioning of the political system as a whole: when we observe the even tighter grip that this group maintained over the reorganized State Council through their elected representatives as well as many of the Council's appointed members; when we consider the additional pressures that they were able to exercise on the Court and the government through their now much better organized formal and informal corporate organizations, including the United Nobility (pressures that proved especially formidable in such organs as the Council of Local Economy). And our sense of the formidable political clout of these thirty-odd-thousand families is even further reinforced when we shift our gaze from the national scene to the vast stretches of the Russian countryside: to its organs of local self-government, in which, as Manning has reminded us, their domination appeared by the eve of the war, secure and even unchallenged by a now seemingly apathetic peasantry; to the whole structure of local bureaucratic administration, from the county level down to the village, which, now that these nobles had successfully resisted Stolypin's projects of local reforms, they appeared to dominate with equal ease through their county marshals and their various local agents. And our sense of the power of these noble landowners is even further magnified when we consider the variety of informal socioeconomic as well as political pressures and controls that they were still able to apply, individually and collectively, to the peasants who leased or worked their lands, and to the peasant representatives who were elected or appointed to administer peasant affairs.

It bears repeating that the political culture of the noble Russian landowners that we have sought to describe emerged from the travails of 1905 more powerful, as well as more sophisticated, than ever before. Indeed, by the eve of the war, the tsarist regime appeared more dependent on the Russian landed nobility, and the Russian landed nobility, in turn, more dependent on the state—their respective political fates appeared more inextricably joined—than at any time since the Pugachev Rebellion of the late eighteenth century, which had so frightened Catherine and *her* nobles.

Both sides in this union remained true to each other almost to the last. It was not until very late, until the fall and winter of 1916, and only under the pressure of military defeats, pervasive if false rumors of treason, as well as total incompetence in the highest offices of the land, that most of the member organizations of the United Nobility (to cite an admittedly extreme example) finally turned against the government and their own leadership and sided with the Progressive bloc. But while the support among the Russian landed nobility for the Regime of the Third of June still seemed secure and unwavering on the eve of the war, even as discontent and turmoil were surfacing in almost all of urban-commercial-industrial Russia, this base of political support was, of course, extraordinarily narrow and fragile, making it extremely difficult for the regime to adapt to, and ultimately cope with, the pressures for political and social change from that other—new, growing, and more dynamic—Russia.

It was not merely that the political base of the System of the Third of June only consisted of the thirty thousand families of Russian noble landowners on which we have focused attention. Or even that these families were in fact playing in the country's economic, social, and cultural development a role of steadily decreasing importance. Even more glaring was the fact that, quite literally, the socioeconomic and political culture of which these families were members—the culture that now supported the whole existing political and administrative structure of the country—was well on its way to physical extinction.

With every passing month, as more of them sold their estates and moved to the city or to other occupations, there were less and less members of this group available to vote in their county assemblies, in numbers sufficient even to fill the number of electoral seats allocated to their curia; less of them to participate in the affairs of local self-government, supervise local administration, and keep a watchful eye over the peasantry.

Even the government had been aware of this during the premierships of Witte and Stolypin, and this realization on its part had provided one of the major spurs for the efforts to reform local administration, which have repeatedly been referred to in this volume. Indeed, a number of these reforming bureaucrats had come fully to the realization, which they expressed at times with considerable eloquence, that the old society of *sosloviia* was inextricably dying even before their eyes, and that a new and different society of classes was now growing even in the Russian countryside. In their statements to the Duma and eventually to the Council of Local Economy, these bureaucrats had urged that the census requirements for participation in local organs of self-government be modified to allow more room in local affairs for representatives of the commercial-industrial class, or at the very least (when they were forced to retreat under fire) for non-noble land proprietors. They had pleaded, in this connection, that at least some account be taken of economic realities: that census requirements, for example, be calculated on the basis of the profitability—the market value rather than the sheer size—of landed estates. They had pressed simultaneously for the extension, at long last in Russian history, of the facsimile of a modern bureaucratic system to the localities—to the county if not the district level—and had called, in this connection, for the replacement, as the administrative heads of the counties, of the county marshals of nobility by appointed officials (*uezdnye nachal'niki*), directly accountable to the Ministry of Internal Affairs. But at every step along the way, during both the Witte and Stolypin eras, these reforming bureaucrats had run into the ultimately immovable resistance of the corporate organizations of the Russian landed nobility, headed by their formidable provincial marshals.

In these confrontations, especially in the Council of Local Economy, the spokesmen of the landed nobility had unleashed, usually with considerable skill and eloquence, a veritable torrent of rhetoric—appealing alternatively to sentiment, to fear, and even to sweet reason:[21] the reforms for which the government was calling were unnecessary, ill-conceived, or at least premature—given the period of turmoil from which the country had now barely emerged. The government was proposing to impose the likes of French prefects upon the aged heads of its faithful nobility, and generally to treat them like Frenchmen. If only in the light of the Russian nobility's long tradition of honorable service to their sovereign and to the state, they did not deserve this humiliation. Besides, even if reform was indicated, the government should not seek to impose it from above, in the way that the French had periodically done, with political and social consequences that had been demonstrated all too dramatically in the course of France's strife-torn historical experience. Rather, Russia should follow the historical example of Britain, where local government had evolved as a result of an organic process: slowly, peacefully, harmoniously. Finally, what is most important, as we have noted, is that these spokesmen of the landed nobility had vehemently rejected the charge that in their administration of the Russian countryside, and in their objections to the changes now being proposed, they were animated by any narrow and selfish caste considerations.

As they found themselves increasingly pressed against the wall, the government's spokesmen feebly responded to these harangues that all that the marshals of nobility were arguing might well be true, but that already at this moment there were too few noble landowners available to discharge their various responsibilities—too few of them even to provide suitable candidates for the positions of county marshals, which they so zealously sought to guard—and that with every passing year, the scarcity of their numbers was leaving at the base of Russia's administrative system a greater and greater vacuum.

It was at this point in these interminable and repetitive colloquies (in the committee discussions of the Council on Local Economy, as well as at the plenary sessions devoted to this issue) that the speeches of some of these provincial marshals clearly sounded their most sincere, if not most eloquent, notes. It was unfortunately true, some of them acknowledged, that with the passage of time there were indeed less and less of them to fill their charge, and possibly even true that the days of the culture that they represented were now numbered. But even if this were so, the government owed it to them, because of their past services to the monarch and to the state, to allow their culture to die a natural death, and not to bury it, as it was now seeking to do, by administrative fiat.

As we have seen, the provincial marshals largely got their way. Almost all the vast projects of local reform were allowed to die. And indeed, after the death of Stolypin, no more challenges to the power that they insisted on maintaining to the very last would effectively be mobilized until the Revolution. Their grip and that of their constituents over the administration and politics of the countryside now appeared secure and unchallenged, and through it their stranglehold over the body politic as a whole. But precisely because of this fact, the basic contradictions that were now all too apparent between city and country—between the increasingly restless, if divided, constituent groups of the new and growing political cultures of urban, commercial, industrial Russia and those of the still largely tranquil countryside— were allowed to build up to an explosive point, with no outlet really available for their peaceful resolution.

And by the same token, it was this fundamental cleavage in political cultures between rural and urban Russia—along with the growing social and political conflicts within urban Russia itself—that made for the torturously slow and halting character of the second Russian prerevolution, for the full dimensions of the crisis that Russian liberalism experienced as this prerevolution painfully unfolded, and ultimately for the acuteness of the convulsions that would afflict the Russian body politic in 1917 and its Civil War aftermath.

NOTES

1. See particularly Marc Raeff, *The Origins of the Russian Intelligentsia: The Eighteenth Century Nobility,* New York, 1966.

2. See "Country Gentlemen in Parliament, 1756–84," in Sir Lewis Namier, *Crossroads of Power,* New York, 1962.

3. For a most recent and authoritative treatment of this problem, focusing particularly on the Tver nobility, see Terence Emmons, *The Russian Landed Gentry and the Peasant Emancipation of 1861,* Cambridge, England, 1968.

4. Particularly the reports submitted by, and under the direction of, the various provincial governors to the Ministry of Internal Affairs, deposited in TsGIA, fond 1327, opis 2.

5. On the eve of the convocation of the Third Duma, 110 of the elected Duma deputies described themselves as Octobrists (24.9 percent of the total), and 29 as "moderates" (6.6 percent); altogether, 31.5 percent of the Duma's membership. After the Duma was convoked, 155 (35.1 percent)

joined the parliamentary fraction of the *Gruppa Soiuza 17 Oktiabria i primykaiushchikh.* By comparison, the number of *provincial electors* categorized as "moderates" by the Electoral Commission (the label usually applied to Octobrists and Octobrist sympathizers) was 1,046, or 20 percent of the total of 5,150 provincial electors in the 51 provinces of European Russia. In the landowners' curia, as we have seen, the number of electors classified as "moderates" was 585, or 23 percent of the total of 2,542 electors allocated to this curia in these 51 provinces. See M. V. D. (Ministerstvo vnutrennykh del), *Vybory v Gosudarstvennuiu Dumu Tret'ego Sozyva. Statisticheskii otchet Osobogo Deloproizvodstva,* St. Petersburg, 1911.

6. See note 13 to the introduction of this volume.

7. The records of the discussions of the various commissions and plenary sessions of the Council of Local Economy of the Ministry of Internal Affairs are deposited in TsGIA, fond 1288. The most revealing and eloquent debates about the position of the landed nobility, and the general issue of *soslovie* organization, are those that unfolded in 1908–1909 over the government's project for reform of county administration (*uezdnoe upravlenie*), and in particular, over the proposal to replace, as heads of the administrative apparatus of the counties, the county marshals of nobility by *uezdnye nachal'niki,* bureaucratic officials appointed by the Ministry of Internal Affairs.

8. These detailed reports, for each province of the empire, are in TsGIA, fond 1327, opis 2.

9. We should note parenthetically that this massive peasant indifference was not reflected in the contemporary percentage of voter absenteeism in the peasant curia. The district assemblies (*volostnye skhodi*) to which the electorate of the peasant curia had been confined since the Third Duma elections, and which by the time of the elections of the Fourth Duma, consisted even more overwhelmingly than ever before of peasant-elected officials (village and especially district elders, chairmen of peasant district courts, peasant members of Land Consolidation Commissions, and the like) duly met in most cases, if only in response to the injunctions of their members' bureaucratic superiors. (In the Third Duma elections, the rate of attendance at these district assemblies in the 51 provinces of European Russia was officially reported as 65 percent, 972,639 out of 1,494,751. In the Fourth Duma elections, for which we lack adequate figures, it was probably even higher.) For the Third Duma election figures, see M. V. D., op. cit., p.100.

10. The best survey of the agrarian disorders of 1905–1906 is still the study conducted by the Free Economic Society, on the basis of questionnaires sent out in 1907 to various local institutions and individual correspondents. See III Otdelenie Imperatorskogo Vol'nogo Ekonomicheskogo Obshchestva, *Agrarnoe dvizhenie v Rossii 1905–1906 gg., Ottisk iz trudov I. V. E. Obshchestva,* St. Petersburg, 1908.

11. The more recent Soviet publications that scrutinize the mood of voters and elected representatives of the peasantry during the period of the First and Second Dumas include N. P. Pershin, *Agrarnaia Revoliutsiia v Rossii,* Moscow, 1966, vol. 1, annd two interesting articles by D. A. Kolesnichenko, "Vozniknovenie i deiatel'nost' Trudovoi gruppy," *Istoriia SSSR,* vol. 11, no. 4, and "Agrarnye proekty Trudovoi gruppy v I Gosudarstvennoi Dume,"

in *Istoricheskie Zapiski*, vol. 82 (1968). Maslov's article, "Narodnicheskie partii," in Martov et al. (eds.), *Obshchestvennoe dvizhenie v Rossii v nachale XX veka*, vol. 3, St. Petersburg, 1909–12, is still useful. Information on the peasant deputies elected to the various Dumas may be found in a variety of sources. On the First Duma deputies, see, *inter alia, Pervaia Gosudarstvennaia Duma. Literaturno-khudozhestvennoe izdanie*, pod red. N. Pruzhanskogo, St. Petersburg, 1906; *Predstaviteli Gosudarstvennoi Dumy 27 aprelia– 8 iiulia, 1906 g.* Red. G. V. Malakhovskii, St. Petersburg, n.d.; and *Gosudarstvennaia Duma v portretakh, 27/IV–8/VII, 1906*, Izdanie K. A. Fisher, Moscow, n.d.; and *Trudovaia gruppa v Gosudarstvennoi Dume*, sostavil V. Sh., St. Petersburg, n.d. On the deputies to the Second Duma, see *Chleny 2-oi Gosudarstvennoi Dumy. Biografii. Sravnitel'naia kharakteristika chlenov 1-oi i 2-oi Dumy*, St. Petersburg, 1907. On the deputies to the Third and Fourth Dumas, see the various *lichnye ukazateli* to the *Stenograficheskie otchety* of the Third and Fourth Duma sessions. See also *3-yi sozyv Gosudarstvennoi Dumy. Portrety. Biografii, Aftografii*, red. N. Olchanskii, St. Petersburg, 1910, and *4-yi sozyv Gosudarstvennoi Dumy. Khudozhestvennyi fotokopicheskii al'bom s portretami i biografiiami*. Izdanie N. Olchanskago, St. Petersburg, 1913. The articles "Gosudarstvennaia Duma" and "Osoboe prilozhenie: Chleny Gosudarstvennoi Dumy" in F. A. Brokgauz and I. A. Efron, eds., *Novyi entsiklopedicheskii slovar'*, St. Petersburg, n.d., vol. 14, pp.405–12 and II–LXXI, also contain useful information.

12. A recent case study of the First Duma elections, with special attention to the electoral process in the peasant curia, is Daniel S. Vanderheide, "The Elections to the First Duma" (M.A. Essay, Columbia University, 1977).

13. I am indebted to Professor Terence Emmons for this valuable observation.

14. On First Duma elections, see Daniel Vanderheide, op. cit. For Second Duma election returns, see volumes listed in note 15.

15. The most detailed study of the elections to the Second Duma is still Aleksei Smirnov (ed.), *Kak proshli vybory vo 2-iu Gosudarstvennuiu Dumu*, St. Petersburg, 1907. For an analysis of the biographical information about the members of the Second Duma, flawed by methodological errors, see *Chleny 2-oi Gosudarstvennoi Dumy*, op. cit. Both works have a Kadet bias, but contain useful information.

16. We find in these statistics indications of substantial political opposition among voters of the peasant curia, not only in the north and in Siberia, but also in the Lake region (especially Novgorod and St. Petersburg provinces, the C.I.R. (Moscow and Tver), Little Russia (particularly the historically strife-prone province of Poltava); and especially New Russia (Don oblast, Ekaterinoslav, Kherson, and Taurus provinces), the Middle and Lower Volga (Kazan, Saratov, Samara), and the Urals (Viatka, Orenburg, Perm), where the roots of peasant radicalism proved especially hardy. See M. V. D., *Vybory v Gosudarstvennuiu Dumu tret'iago sozyva*.

17. As Vinogradoff has noted in his Ph.D. dissertation, the peasant deputies from Volynia, in particular, were notably younger than other peasant deputies, and were considered by local officials to be totally unreliable on the land question, notwithstanding their ostensibly conservative affiliations.

18. One dramatic illustration of this point will suffice. In Vilno province,

which Vinogradoff has used to illustrate the differences in political culture that he emphasized, the peasant curia in both the Third and Fourth Duma elections was divided into two subcuriae: one reserved for the Russian Orthodox peasant minority of this province; the other, for the majority of non-Russian, Catholic peasants. In the Third Duma elections, for which I have detailed breakdowns, the Russian peasants of this province, spurred by their local Orthodox clergy against the Polish landowners of the area, se-lected exclusively "rightist" electors to represent them at the provincial electoral assembly; the Catholic peasants of Vilno province elected none. See M. V. D., *Vybory v Gosudarstvennuiu Dumu tret'iago sozyva.*

19. The relevant section of Sorokin's speech reads:

> I will say a few words of my own. Many millions of peasants have sent us here. We are under the obligation to work for this peasantry without laying down our hands. We must give this deprived, forgotten, hungry, cold peasantry land and freedom. All of us came here with the order and instructions not to return to the countryside without this.
>
> Therefore, comrade peasants, I am appealing to all of you without exception, whatever faction you belong to: we will obtain this land and freedom and only then, freely, with a clear conscience, return to our countryside [Applause]. And then the peasantry will greet us with open arms. If we fail to do so, the peasantry will be entitled to hold us in contempt and to hate us. [Voices: "Correct!" Applause in center and right of the hall, i.e. among the *opponents* of the Left SR's in the Taurus Palace.] I hope, comrade peasants, that we shall fulfill our mission to the end. [Noise from the left: "Sabotage!"]
>
> In this respect, there are no differences among us peasants [Ex-tended applause in center and right]. We are all alike here, rights and lefts. ["Correct!" Prolonged applause on center and right]. My last request to you, peasants, is that we fulfill precisely these commands and requests. [Applause.]

Uchreditel'noe sobranie. Stenograficheskii otchet, Petrograd, 1918, pp.56–57.

20. Even the contrast that Vinogradoff has drawn for us between the voting behavior of peasants in two neighboring provinces of northern Russia, Arkhangel and Vologda, appears to me to dramatize the point in the most glaring manner. It is of course true that noble landowners were scarce in Vologda. But they were still present in sufficient number (in contrast to Arkhangel) to justify (if only by the government's political standards) the creation in this province of a landowners' curia.

This curia was arbitrarily assigned thirty out of the total of seventy electors allocated to Vologda province. In fact, in the elections to the Third Duma, because of the scarcity of noble landowners in this province, only six of these thirty electors turned out to be noble landowners, while twenty-one were representatives of the clergy, mobilized by their hierarchy to elect appropriately conservative candidates. The point remains that none of the thirty electors selected from the landowners' curia in Vologda province, in the Third Duma elections, were listed as supporters of opposition parties. To be sure, these thirty electors did not constitute, by themselves, an abso-lute majority at the provincial electoral assembly. But they did constitute such a majority in combination with the electors of the first urban curia, who in this particularly backward province were all "rightists." Thus, the peasants of Vologda, whose curia was assigned but nineteen electors, could under no circumstances have contributed to the formation of an opposition majority at their provincial electoral assembly. By contrast, in Arkhangel province (as in Siberia), where there was no landowners' curia and where both urban curiae elected a substantial number of opposition electors, peasant voters and electors, in combination with electors from other curiae, *could* form such opposition majorities at their provincial electoral assemblies, *and they did so*. See M. V. D., *Vybory v Gosudarstvennuiu Dumu tret'iago sozyva*.

21. As I have noted earlier, the records of these confrontations have been preserved in TsGIA, fond 1288. Especially striking are the various dela of this fond in which are recorded the debates that unfolded over the projects of reform of uezd administration, both in commission and plenary sessions. Some of these discussions are summarized in V. S. Diakin's article, "Stolypin i dvorianstvo (Proval mestnoi reformy)," in Institut istorii ANSSSR (Leningrad), *Problemy krest'ianskogo zemlevladeniia i vnutrennei politiki Rossii*, Leningrad, 1972.

The Contributors

Michael C. Brainerd is a Visiting Scholar at the Russian Institute, Columbia University. He was Assistant Professor of Russian History at Middlebury College from 1974 to 1978.

Robert S. Edelman is Assistant Professor of History at the University of California, San Diego. He has recently completed work on a book dealing with the rise and fall of the Russian Nationalist Party, 1907–17.

Leopold H. Haimson is Professor of History at Columbia University. He is the author of *Decision-Making and Communications in Soviet Industry*, Vol. II of *Studies in Soviet Communications* (M.I.T. Press, 1952), and *The Russian Marxists and the Origins of Bolshevism* (Harvard University Press, 1955). He edited *The Mensheviks: From the Revolution of 1917 to the Second World War* (The University of Chicago Press, 1975) and is Director and General Editor of other studies of the Project on the History of the Menshevik Movement. His articles have appeared in numerous books and periodicals. At present he is preparing a four-volume work entitled *Russian Society and Politics on the Eve of the First World War* (to be published by W. W. Norton & Co., Inc.)

Geoffrey A. Hosking is Chairman of the Department of History at the University of Essex, England. He is the author of *The Russian Constitutional Experiment: Government and Duma, 1907–14* (Cambridge University Press, 1973). He has recently completed a book on the search for an image of man in contemporary Soviet fiction.

Alexandra Shecket Korros is a former staff researcher at the Ben-Gurion Research Institute and Archives of the Ben-Gurion University of the Negev, Israel. She is currently Assistant Executive Director of the Miami University–Hamilton Campus.

Ruth Delia MacNaughton is an associate at Cahill, Gordon and Reindel, a New York City law firm. She is a member of the New York State Bar Association.

Roberta Thompson Manning is Assistant Professor of History at Boston College and Managing Editor of *Russian History*. She is presently at work on a book concerning the crisis of the Russian nobility during the last years of the old regime.

Eugene Vinogradoff is a Research Associate and Assistant Professor of History at the University of Pittsburgh. Currently he has two works in progress: one dealing with rural Russia during the 1905–1907 Revolution and another with contemporary education in the USSR (with Janice T. Gibson).

Index